palgrave macmillan law masters

sports law

mark james

Reader in Law, University of Salford

Series Editor: Marise Cremona

Professor of European Law
European University Institute
Florence
Italy

palgrave
macmillan

First published 2010 by
PALGRAVE MACMILLAN

Palgrave Macmillan in the UK is an imprint of Macmillan Publishers Limited,
registered in England, company number 785998, of Houndmills, Basingstoke,
Hampshire RG21 6XS.

Palgrave Macmillan in the US is a division of St Martin's Press LLC,
175 Fifth Avenue, New York, NY 10010.

Palgrave Macmillan is the global academic imprint of the above companies
and has companies and representatives throughout the world.

Palgrave® and Macmillan® are registered trademarks in the United States,
the United Kingdom, Europe and other countries

ISBN 978–0–230–22341–7 paperback

This book is printed on paper suitable for recycling and made from fully
managed and sustained forest sources. Logging, pulping and manufacturing
processes are expected to conform to the environmental regulations of the
country of origin.

A catalogue record for this book is available from the British Library.

10   9   8   7   6   5   4   3
19   18   17   16   15   14   13   12

Printed and bound in Great Britain by
CPI Antony Rowe, Chippenham and Eastbourne

Contents

Preface

One of the most common questions asked of anyone working in this area is, 'What is sports law?' To answer this question requires an analysis of how and why the law has become involved in sports disputes and an examination of whether there are any underlying themes or theories that link the disparate legal interventions under discussion into a coherent subject. In an emergent and fast moving subject such as this it is easy to compartmentalise disputes into more traditional legal categories such as sports torts, sports crimes, commercial and competition law cases. The challenge for the sports lawyer is to explain what is so special about sport and why it is important that it is on many occasions treated differently by the law.

The aim of this book is to introduce readers to the challenges and controversies facing sport and the law when they interact with each other. It will explain how sport has evolved to take account of the requirements imposed on it by the law and how the law has provided sport with the legal tools necessary to govern itself effectively and resolve the many and varied disputes to which it can give rise. By its very nature sports law requires an examination of the operation of the law in a specific context and as a result draws on issues and disputes from across a range of legal disciplines. These disparate strands are brought together here to provide a coherent insight into sports law and its location within the undergraduate curriculum. *Sports Law* is divided into four parts. Each of these parts contains groups of issues that can be studied together either because the applicable legal principles or the sporting subject matter are of a similar nature.

Part 1 provides an explanation of what sports law is and why it has become such an important and popular field of legal study in recent years. It traces the origins of sports law as a discrete subject and its legislative, judicial, political and sporting sources. It explains how and why the law becomes involved with sport and the ways by which the rules, decisions and procedures of the governing bodies of sport are most frequently challenged. Instead of joining the *Sports Law* v. *Sport and the Law* debate, it draws out the common threads of the jurisprudence of the various sources of sports law and their interactions with each other.

Chapter 1 analyses the juridification of sport and of the decision-making procedures followed by sports governing bodies. It highlights how, as a result of various challenges, sports tribunals and their procedures have become more legalistic in their approach and have come to usurp some of the functions of the courts. Chapter 2 builds on this by analysing the specific relationship between national law and the decision-making procedures followed by the governing bodies of sport. It explains how and why challenges are made to the rules and decisions of sports governing bodies and the impact that these decisions and those of the courts have had on each other. In particular it analyses the growing importance of the decisions of sports tribunals in the light of the procedural developments that many of them have recently undergone. Chapter 3 provides an analysis of how European and international law and the jurisprudence of the

Court of Arbitration for Sport have had a corresponding impact on the operations of international sports federations, enabling an understanding of how and why sport and the law interact in the ways that they do and of why sports law has developed in the ways that it has.

Part 2 examines the application of the law to disputes involving sports injuries and the legality of inherently dangerous sports. Cases involving sports injuries are some of the most commonly occurring applications of sports law as they can be based on incidents arising from any sport and at any level of participation, from the international elite to the recreational amateur player. It explains how athletes who have suffered injuries whilst playing sport can be compensated and the circumstances in which it is considered to be appropriate to punish those who have caused harm to them. The reporting of these cases has helped to bring sports law to the attention of the wider public, if only because of the media's frequent predictions (inaccurate so far) of the end of sport as we know it each time that a high profile player, coach, club or governing body is forced to change their behaviour when they have caused or contributed to the death or serious injury of an athlete.

Chapter 4 traces the development of the law of negligence and its application to sports injury cases. It focuses on actions between players and, where professionals are concerned, the vicarious liability of the defendant-player's club. Chapter 5 examines the extension of the law of negligence to a wider range of defendants including coaches and instructors, match officials, governing bodies, international federations and medical professionals. This recent growth in personal injury litigation is contrasted with the courts' reluctance to impose criminal liability for assaults that occur during the course of play, discussed in Chapter 6. Here the long involvement of the criminal law with sports participation is examined in the context of the challenges posed by the prosecution of sports participants to a governing body's ability to self-regulate on matters of discipline. Chapter 7 concludes this part by examining the legal status of boxing and other combat sports from a variety of jurisprudential, social and moral perspectives. Despite their being acknowledged as lawful activities by the courts the legality of these sports continues to be debated each time that a participant is killed or seriously injured during the course of a bout.

In Part 3 the legal issues that arise from the organisation and hosting of a sports event are discussed. It explains how the owners and operators of sports venues can be held liable for the injuries caused to users of their facilities and the duty of care owed by sports participants to spectators. In particular the major sporting disasters of the twentieth century are examined to enable an analysis of the comparative importance of spectator safety and crowd disorder to be undertaken. By examining the stadium disasters that have occurred in football separately from issues of violence and disorder it is possible to see how the focus of both the government and the football authorities was turned away from spectator safety to crowd control during the 1970s and 1980s. The analysis of the historical and political contexts in which these responses took place demonstrates a disregard for sports' fans and their safety that to a certain extent continues to this day.

Chapter 8 focuses on the causes of action that can be used by a person who has been injured as a result of an incident that has occurred from the staging of a sports event. This includes actions brought against an event's organisers, the occupiers of the stadium where the event is taking place and the athletes competing in it by claimants including participants in the event, the spectators present at it and those living in the vicinity of the premises hosting the event. These claims include actions in negligence, private nuisance and under the Occupiers' Liability Acts 1957 and 1984. Chapters 9 and 10 unpick the problems associated with discussions surrounding spectator safety and crowd disorder. These two topics are usually examined together, often leaving issues of spectator safety viewed through a 'hooligan lens' and being seen as secondary in importance to the apparently more pressing socio-political problem of how to control a disorderly crowd. Chapter 9 examines the political, legal and sporting build up to the Hillsborough disaster of 1989. It analyses the opportunities presented to, and wasted by, various governments to impose minimum standards of safety on sports grounds following official enquiries into the disasters at Burnden Park in 1946, Ibrox Park in 1971 and Valley Parade in 1985. Chapter 10 examines governmental responses to sports-related disorder and in particular what is popularly referred to as football hooliganism. It analyses the piecemeal approach taken by Parliament in response to various high profile outbreaks of disorder that took place throughout the 1960s–1990s and the legality of the cornerstone of the current regulatory framework, the Football Banning Order.

Part 4 analyses the law's key role in the commercialisation of modern sport. It examines how the law has been used to challenge common practices that have become entrenched in sport and the role of the law in regulating the ways in which sport is administered, played and consumed. As governing bodies, clubs and event organisers have sought to exploit new income streams with ever increasing efficiency, they have resorted to the law to protect their commercial rights from unauthorised use by others. At the same time players have used the law to secure for themselves a greater share of this new income whilst fans have tried to find ways of limiting the near constant demands on their financial resources. These various strands of law and policy are brought together in an examination of the legal regulation of the London Olympics and how the protections afforded to them are likely to extend to other major events in the future.

Chapter 11 examines a variety of relationships and the ways that the law has been used to regulate some of the more unusual practices that have over time become commonplace in sport. It examines how restrictive terms can be incorporated into contracts of employment and membership agreements and how their legality can be challenged. In particular it examines how contractual terms and sporting rules that are in restraint of trade or discriminatory have been accepted as normal elements of a sporting relationship. Chapter 12 expands the analysis of these issues by examining how challenges to their legality can be made under the free movement and competition provisions of EU law. In this way the law is able to ensure a level of good governance is imposed on both governing bodies and clubs by subjecting them to a variety of checks on the quality of their administrative rules and procedures. In Chapter 13 the ways in which the commercialisation and commodification of sport have had an impact on fan culture is examined. As fans are treated increasingly like loyal consumers by clubs and event organisers seeking ever more creative ways to grow their income streams, the law has been used to test the extent of the protections that can be afforded to the exploitation of these commercial rights. The regulation of secondary and grey markets in tickets, merchandise and broadcasting has been the main focus of the challenges by fans and consumer groups to the increasing cost of following sport, all of which are examined here. In Chapter 14 this analysis is developed further in respect of the specific ways in which the commercial rights in the Olympic Games are protected. In particular it examines the protections afforded to the Olympic symbols and the restrictions on advertising that will be imposed in and around Olympic venues to curb ambush marketing.

Throughout the book the appropriateness of the law as a mechanism for sports dispute resolution is examined. This provides a deeper understanding not only of what the law currently is but why it has evolved in the ways that it has and how sports law may develop further in the future. Each chapter contains a summary of the main points discussed in it, a detailed list of further reading and a discussion of a key legal issue in the Hot topics section. These should provide the reader with both an understanding of the subject under discussion in each chapter and with the tools to follow it up in greater detail should they need or want to.

To aid clarity 'claimant' is used to describe the person bringing the claim even where in the original judgment they would have been identified as the 'plaintiff'. For ease of cross-referencing where EU legislation is referred to, the Article numbers cited here are those currently used in the consolidated version of the Treaty on the Functioning of the European Union following the ratification of the Treaty of Lisbon, even if when the case was heard the corresponding provision had a different reference number at the time. A table of equivalence can be found at p.xiii.

The companion website for *Sports Law* can be found at:

http://www.palgrave.com/law/james.

Here you will find links to relevant websites and additional documents on a chapter by chapter basis. Updates on the latest sports law developments will be posted here on a regular basis.

Many thanks to Rob Gibson at Palgrave Macmillan for his advice and support throughout the preparation of this book and for the helpful comments of the anonymous reviewers. I would also like to thank in particular Ken Foster, Guy Osborn, Richard Parrish and David McArdle for their encouragement and advice throughout the writing up period, Samuli Miettinen and Parveen Tamadon-Nejad at Salford Law School for their comments on EU and IP law and my wife Fiona for her endless supply of patience and support.

This book is based on material available to me on 13 November 2009.

Table of equivalences for the Treaty establishing the European Community and the Treaty on the functioning of the European Union

New numbering of the Treaty on the functioning of the European Union	Old numbering of the Treaty establishing the European Community	Original numbering of the Treaty establishing the European Economic Community
Article 18	Article 12	Article 6
Article 45	Article 39	Article 48
Article 49	Article 43	Article 52
Article 56	Article 49	Article 59
Article 101	Article 81	Article 85
Article 102	Article 82	Article 86
Article 106	Article 86	Article 90
Article 165	Article 149	Article 126
Article 263	Article 230	Article 173
Article 267	Article 234	Article 177

In this book, Treaty Articles will be referenced in the following way: Art.45 TFEU (ex Art.39 ECT) or Art.45 TFEU (ex Art.48 TEEC), providing both the new and original citations for the sake of clarity.

Table of cases

Table of statutes

Part 1

Origins and sources of sports law

Chapter 1

What is sports law?

Key words

▶ **Juridification** – the process by which a privately regulated sphere of activity becomes colonised by law and lawyers.
▶ **Domestic sports law** – the body of internally applicable legal norms created and adhered to by national governing bodies of sport.
▶ **Global sports law** – the autonomous transnational legal order through which the body of law and jurisprudence applied by international sports federations is created; in particular it includes the jurisprudence of the Court of Arbitration for Sport and its creation and harmonisation of sporting-legal norms.
▶ **National sports law** – the law created by national parliaments, courts and enforcement agencies that directly affects the regulation or governance of sport or which has been developed to resolve sports disputes.
▶ **European sports law** – the law created by the institutions of the European Union, in particular the European Court of Justice, that affects the regulation or governance of sport or which has been developed to resolve sports disputes.
▶ **International sports law** – the general or universal principles of law which are part of international customary law, or the *jus commune*, that are applied to sports disputes.
▶ **National governing body** – the body responsible for the governance and administration of a sport, or a group of related sports, at national or state level.
▶ **International sports federation** – the body responsible for the governance and administration of a sport, or a group of related sports, at the continental or world level.

1.1 What is sports law and where do we find it?

UK law has no formal definition of sport and consequently no formal definition of sports law. Although we know what sport is when we see it and when we play it, we struggle to define it in a way that is not either so wide as to include all forms of physical exercise or so narrow as to exclude specific activities that are normally considered to be sports. The same can be said of sports law; we know what it is but we struggle to define it when called upon to do so.

1.1.1 The governance of sport in the UK

In the UK, the state has a more non-interventionist approach to sports governance than is seen in many other countries. Sport in the UK is administered almost exclusively by private entities, the national governing bodies of sports, whose rules bind other private entities, whether these are individual clubs or individual athletes. As a result, there has not been a need for the state to define sport as it has often been regarded as being one of Parliament's less important spheres of competence; the Minister for Sport is a junior minister in the Department for Culture, Media and Sport (DCMS) rather than a Secretary of State with cabinet level responsibilities. Even the Minister for the Olympics, who is based in the Cabinet Office, is only a junior minister detailed to provide specific advice to the Prime Minister and the Cabinet on matters relating to the London 2012 Olympic Games.

The role of DCMS is to provide access to and encourage participation in all levels of sport. In doing this, its twin aims are to promote health and a more active lifestyle amongst UK citizens whilst at the same time producing world class performers. To achieve these aims, DCMS distributes funding, particularly that raised by the National Lottery, to UK Sport and to the home country sports councils: Sport England, sportscotland, the Sports Council for Wales and the Sports Council for Northern Ireland. This funding is used, amongst other things, for building or improving sports facilities, widening participation schemes and supporting elite performers.

Of particular note has been DCMS' role in the development of policies and procedures that have increased safety and improved specific spheres of sports governance. For example DCMS, together with the National Society for the Prevention of Cruelty to Children, helped to establish the Child Protection in Sport Unit in 2001 (see further, chapter 6.7). It oversees the work of the Football Licensing Authority (see further, chapter 9.6.2.4) and assists governing bodies in bidding to host major events such as the Olympic Games and the football World Cup.

The implementation of DCMS' policies is carried out on a day-to-day basis by UK Sport and the four home country sports councils. UK Sport distributes public and National Lottery funding for the development of sporting infrastructures and the support of elite level athletes. The four sports councils' complementary aim is to encourage participation in sport through partnerships with clubs, local authorities and national and regional governing bodies. As of 14 December 2009, UK Sport's anti-doping functions were taken over by a newly created specialist agency, UK Anti-Doping (UKAD). UKAD will fulfil the role of national anti-doping organisation, as required by Art.20.5 World Anti-Doping Agency Code, and will administer drug testing programmes throughout the UK. It will also work more closely with law enforcement agencies than has previously been the case in an attempt to control more effectively the importation and supply of banned performance enhancing substances.

Thus sport in the UK is not seen as being a public service that is the responsibility of the state. Instead, the day-to-day running of sport is left almost entirely to the private sector: athletes are members of clubs who provide them with training and the opportunity to participate; the clubs are members of local and/or national governing bodies who administer fixture lists, training for coaches and match officials, disciplinary tribunals and representative teams; the national governing bodies of sports are members of continental and/or world bodies that ensure harmonisation of their rules and procedures and which organise international club and representative tournaments. Although a simplistic outline of the governance structures of most sports, what should be clear from this brief description is that the role of the state in the everyday administration and governance of sport in the UK is minimal. Consequently there is little legislation in place to govern sport, making the identification of what constitutes sports law more difficult.

1.1.2   Sources of sports law

Which still leaves the all important question: what is sports law? The most effective way to answer this question is to begin by identifying the various sources of sports law and the jurisprudence that each is developing. Building on the nomenclature developed by

Foster in 'Is there a Global Sports Law?' (2003) 2(1) *Entertainment and Sports Law Journal*, online, two main groups of sports law sources can be identified. The first group reflects the application of legal principles by the tribunals granted jurisdiction to hear disputes by the national governing bodies of sport and by international sports federations; these are referred to here as domestic sports law and global sports law. These two sources highlight the desire of these bodies to self-regulate disputes that affect their sports and their claims that they are developing a completely new branch of law that is often referred to as *lex sportiva*.

The second group consists of the sources of sports law that evidence the application of national, European and international law, together with generally or universally applicable legal principles, before specific courts; these sources are referred to here as national sports law, European sports law and international sports law. This group of sources explains how the law of a nation state, or a group of nation states, applies to a sports dispute. The key distinction between the two groups of sources is that the former is underpinned by a series of contractual agreements entered into by, for example, the athlete, his or her club, their club's national governing body and the appropriate international sports federation; it is a private contractual order that claims to be making and applying its own set of rules. The latter is the law imposed by a nation state on its citizens or which is constituted by the treaties entered into by communities of nation states, for example, the members of the EU being bound by the law enshrined in the Treaty on the Functioning of the European Union.

1.1.3　The increasing importance of domestic and global sports law

One of the most important recent developments in sports law has been the growing sophistication and technicality of the jurisprudence of specialist sports tribunals and appeals panels. Where once these bodies acted almost exclusively as disciplinary tribunals, they are now often hearing cases that require a detailed knowledge of the law and a determination of how specific legal issues should apply in the context of a sports dispute.

The impact of this development can be seen in three specific ways. First it has required the further juridification and formalisation of how sports tribunals operate: their procedures have become more court-like in appearance as they are required to adhere to the rules of natural justice; legal representation is now commonplace where professional sport is concerned; lay panel members have been replaced by lawyers and judges; the applicable rules are more tightly drafted in order to minimise the scope for challenge; the decisions are handed down in the same style as court judgments and the punishments imposed are justified in a similarly judicial style (see further, chapter 2.4). The juridification of these tribunals has ensured a greater degree of acceptance of their decisions by the parties appearing before them which in turn has led to fewer challenges to their authority coming before the courts.

Secondly these specialist tribunals are able to utilise more easily a sports-sympathetic approach to the disputes coming before them. They are more readily prepared to accept the importance of protecting the 'specificity of sport' from the application of the law (see further, chapter 3.2.2) and are more likely to accept without question that certain aspects of sports governance are acceptable, unless they are the focus of the challenge before them. For example, the regulations concerning the transfer of players in professional team sports could eventually be the subject of a legal challenge under EU law. However they are currently accepted as lawful and valid by all sports tribunals up to and including the Court of Arbitration for Sport (*FC Shaktar Donetsk* v. *Matuzalem Francelino da Silva, Real Zaragoza SAD and FIFA* CAS 2008/A/1519 and 1520) (see further, chapters 3.3.2.1 and 12.2.2.2). The benefits of using alternative dispute resolution mechanisms such as these are well known: the panel has sport specific and/or sports law knowledge; the rules are less formal and less restrictive of the evidence that they can hear and the disputes are usually settled much more quickly than they would be before the courts leading to significant savings on costs. A further advantage is that by keeping a dispute within the sporting community, the authority and stability of the international sports federation in question is maintained. The main disadvantage is that it can allow restrictive and potentially unlawful rules and practices to become entrenched in sporting culture.

Thirdly the increased use of specialist tribunals is preventing many sports disputes from coming before national courts and the European Court of Justice. This can create a problem with legal certainty; the paucity of cases reaching the courts means that the judiciary is deprived of the opportunity to develop national and EU law in a way that is appropriate to both its general application and the development of any derogations or exemptions that may be necessary for the proper administration of sport. This in turn gives rise to the possibility that different interpretations of the law and applicable legal norms will be developed by the courts and the specialist sports panels leading to the potential for much more serious disputes in the future. Thus the evolution of the relationship between the various sources of sports law will have a significant impact on its future development.

1.2 Domestic sports law

Domestic sports law is the creation of an autonomous legal order by a sport's national governing body (NGB) to regulate the conduct of its members and those playing its sport; it is the body of internally applicable law and procedure that has been developed by each sport's NGB. Every NGB has its own constitution that has been created by its members, or their representatives, which defines the extent of its powers and its jurisdiction over disputes affecting its members and players. This constitution is administered, along with the body's other main organisational powers, by an executive or management committee. The power to administer the NGB's disciplinary powers in respect of the breach of its playing, financial or administrative rules is delegated to a specialist committee or tribunal. Thus NGBs have in place an entire system to create and administer their own rules that replicates the machinery of justice of a nation state corresponding to its legislature, executive and courts.

Following challenges to the legitimacy of their rules, their decision-making procedures and their findings, the system of governance operated by many NGBs has become more formalised, often taking on a form that is quasi-judicial in both appearance and operation (see further, chapter 2). Some NGBs require their tribunal chairs to be legally qualified whilst at the elite levels of many sports, players and clubs will be legally represented as a matter of course. This process of juridification has also seen disciplinary tribunals publishing the charges laid against those who have transgressed the NGB's rules and the publication of both the determination of the hearing and a detailed explanation of how and why that decision was reached; in other words the tribunal is operating as a 'court' which is applying the 'laws' of its 'Parliament' and which is publishing its 'judgments' which can then be used as precedents in future cases.

The jurisprudence of sports disciplinary tribunals and associated arbitrations is becoming increasingly important as these panels become more court-like in their procedures and as they deal with ever more complex legal issues, as was seen in the various actions brought by Sheffield United FC in respect of their relegation from the Premier League at the end of the 2006–07 football season. These included challenging the decision of the Premier League's Disciplinary Commission to fine and not deduct points from West Ham United FC when it had fielded an ineligible player (*Sheffield United Football Club Ltd* v. *Football Association Premier League Ltd* [2007] 3 ISLR SLR 77), claiming compensation from West Ham for its breaching the rules of the Premier League by knowingly fielding an ineligible player (*Sheffield United Football Club Ltd* v. *West Ham United Football Club Plc* [2009] 1 ISLR SLR 25) and obtaining an injunction preventing West Ham from appealing the decision of the arbitrators to award compensation to the Court of Arbitration for Sport (*Sheffield United Football Club Ltd* v. *West Ham United Football Club Plc* [2008] EWHC 2855 (Comm)) (see further, chapter 2.4.3 and chapter 11 Hot Topic).

Moreover the decisions of Sports Resolutions UK, particularly when it sits as the National Anti-Doping Panel, are becoming of increasing importance as more NGBs now make references to it. However in reality these tribunals are applying national legal norms to sports disputes rather than creating entirely new law or legal principles; they are explaining how the law applies in the specific context of sport or using standard techniques of statutory and contractual interpretation when determining the meaning of an NGB's rules. Thus although domestic sports law is not a new legal specialism, because these tribunals are making and enforcing decisions on legal matters they are becoming an increasingly important source of sports law as the cases coming before them would otherwise end up being heard before the national courts.

1.3 Global sports law

In the same way that the basic structure of an NGB is mirrored on the world stage by that of an international sports federation (ISF), so is the development of domestic sports law mirrored in the transnational arena by the emergence of a global sports law. Global sports law aspires to be an autonomous transnational legal order created by the private bodies that govern sport at the world level. Each ISF regulates the conduct of its members, usually continental and national governing bodies, and through them the participants who play its sport. As with domestic sports law, global sports law is the body of internally applicable law and procedure that has been developed by each ISF through the operation of the tribunals to which they allow disputes affecting their sports to be submitted.

As most major ISFs now allow appeals from their own disciplinary tribunals or dispute resolution chambers to the Court of Arbitration for Sport (CAS), global sports law could be said to reach its apotheosis in what is frequently referred to as the *lex sportiva* created by CAS (see further, chapter 3.3). This distinctive body operates in parallel to existing national and transnational court structures to provide interpretations on the legality and applicability of the rules and decision-making procedures of many ISFs. Its aim is to create new legal and interpretative norms within sport that enable disputes to avoid having to be brought before national courts and, in particular, the European Court of Justice. Applications for arbitration and adjudication before CAS reinforce the desire for the self-regulation of all sports disputes by ISFs. This private system of justice, resort to which is enforced by contracts between the various parties, often forces NGBs, clubs and individual participants to submit to the jurisdiction of CAS rather than to the courts.

As with domestic tribunals, CAS regularly hears applications that contain complex legal issues concerning for example the interpretation of the terms of a professional footballer's employment contract and whether they enabled him to move to another employer as in *FC Shaktar Donetsk* v. *Matuzalem Francelino da Silva, Real Zaragoza SAD and FIFA* CAS 2008/A/1519 and 1520 (see further, chapters 3.3.2.1 and 12.2.2.2), and the legality of potentially discriminatory bans on the use of performance enhancing equipment by a disabled athlete (*Pistorius* v. *IAAF* CAS 2008/A/1480) (see further, chapters 3.3.2.2 and 11.5.4). Again many of these applications would be heard by national courts if they were not brought before CAS. Thus when the parties agree that the decision and its reasoning can be published, it can provide an important source of sports law that can be applied in other similar cases. However as a private arbitral body, where the parties do not agree to have the decision published, or the rules of the relevant ISF do not allow for publication, it can occasionally be limited in its ability to provide guidance.

It can be argued that the decisions of an ISF's disciplinary tribunal or dispute resolution chamber, and of independent appeals and arbitration tribunals like CAS, are not creating a unique category of law or new legal norms, a true *lex sportiva*, but are instead simply applying national or EU law, or the general principles of international law, to transnational sports disputes. Global sports law sees the adjudicative or arbitral body approach sports disputes through a well-developed sports-specific lens. However its importance as a source of sports law is often from its application of more traditional legal norms and principles rather than from its development of a distinct or unique jurisprudence.

1.4   National sports law

In contrast to domestic sports law, national sports law is the development of a body of law and legal principles that is applied directly to sport by Parliament and the judiciary. In other words national sports law is the Acts of Parliament and the decisions of the courts that affect the governance, administration, consumption and participation in sport in the UK; it is the application of 'real law' to sport.

There are no specific Acts of Parliament whose aim is to define 'sport' and the ways that sport should be governed in UK law. This is in stark contrast to France, for example, where the Loi du Sport (Loi No. 84-610 du 16–07–1984) provides a framework within which many aspects of sport are regulated. Without such a rigid public law framework being in place, the decisions of the UK courts are much more numerous than are the piecemeal and often reactive responses of the legislature. A further source of national sports law can be found in the decisions of the Office of Fair Trading (OFT), which investigates potential abuses of competition law and can demand changes in the activities of sports bodies that are found to have been acting anti-competitively.

1.4.1   Decisions of the domestic courts

Whatever the reasons behind the increased use of the law as a means of resolving sports disputes, as those involved with sport have become more litigious an ever-wider variety of legal problems have been brought before the UK courts. As a result, decisions of the national courts have had a profound impact on the way that sport is administered, played and consumed in the UK.

For example cases have challenged the rules and accepted practices that govern the way that sports are administered. Eighty-four years before possibly the most well-known sports law case, *Union Royal Belge des Societe de Football Association ASBL* v. *Jean-Marc Bosman* (C-415/93) [1995] ECR I-4921 (see further, chapter 12.2.1), the legality of the transfer system in English football was challenged in *Kingaby* v. *Aston Villa Football Club* [1912] The Times, 28 March. Although this action failed, it should have alerted football's governing bodies to there being something strange, legally, about being able to 'buy' and 'sell' an employee (see further, chapter 11.4).

Further cases challenged the procedures used by NGBs when applying these rules to specific cases brought before them. The finding of the High Court in *Jones* v. *Welsh Rugby Union* [1998] The Times, 6 January (see further, chapter 2.4.4), which highlighted that many NGBs were failing to operate the rules of natural justice in their disciplinary tribunals and were therefore not acting fairly when conducting their hearings, led to many sports completely rewriting their decision-making procedures. This in turn can be said to have increased the process of juridification of the decision-making process of NGBs by making them more legalistic in their operations. This ability to challenge a governing body's internal rules and procedures in English law led to the International Amateur Athletics Federation moving its headquarters from London to Monaco in an attempt to protect itself from further legal actions (*Gasser* v. *Stinson* (unreported) High Court (QBD), 15 June 1998) (see further, chapter 11.4.2.3).

In other cases participants have sued each other for injuries that until then had been accepted as an unfortunate but almost inevitable risk of participation in contact sports (*Condon* v. *Basi* [1985] 1 WLR 866) (see further, chapter 4.4.1.1) and the match officials for failing to apply the safety rules applicable to a specific aspect of a game (*Smoldon* v. *Whitworth and Nolan* [1997] ELR 249) (see further, chapter 5.3). Meanwhile those living in the vicinity of sports venues have challenged, with varying degrees of success, the right of clubs to host events in the locality; whereas compensation was awarded to a householder whose land was regularly damaged by cricket balls in *Miller* v. *Jackson* [1977] QB 966 but the club was allowed to continue playing at the same venue (see further, chapter 8.3.1.1), the Romford Bombers Speedway Team were completely banned from racing at the Brooklands Stadium in Romford because of the noise generated during race meetings (*Stretch* v. *Romford Football Club* (1971) 115 Sol J 741) (see further, chapter 8.3.1.2).

The decisions of the UK courts are currently the most important source of national sports law because of the wide variety of legal principles that have been debated before them. Although the decisions of the European Court of Justice are more authoritative in terms of precedent, they cover a much narrower range of legal issues, focusing in particular on those concerning the freedom of movement guaranteed to workers and service providers and competition law (see further, chapter 3). What is somewhat strange, given the massive growth in sports-related litigation since the beginning of the 1980s, is how few sports cases have reached the House of Lords (now the Supreme Court). This leaves sports lawyers with the problems of trying to determine when and why the law will engage with a sports dispute, trying to establish whether there is a pattern to the law's engagement with sport and trying to establish whether or not there is any underlying theory that unites the cases into a coherent body of sports law jurisprudence.

Legislation from the national Parliament

Direct state intervention by Parliament on issues relating to sport has generally been poor, rushed and reactive and as a result could often be described as panic law. Without a coherent policy for sport and its administration and with no clearly defined role for the state in this field of activity, this is unlikely to change in the immediate future.

There is little doubt that some Parliamentary intervention has been both necessary for and beneficial to encouraging participation in sport. For example the Public Health Act 1875 allowed urban authorities to purchase land to be able to provide places for public recreation. The Act's aim was to ensure that the people living in the new urban centres had open spaces where they could exercise and hopefully maintain a basic level of fitness. Further, the establishment of the Football Licensing Authority by the Football Spectators Act 1989 (see further, chapter 9.6.2.4) and the licensing regime imposed on adventure centres by the Activity Centres (Young Persons' Safety) Act 1995 (see further, chapter 8.5) have undoubtedly made watching football and engaging in outdoor pursuits safer activities than was previously the case.

However this can be contrasted with the legislation passed to control the behaviour of disorderly football spectators and that which enables the London Olympic and Paralymic Games to take place in 2012, some of which appears to be ill thought through and overly restrictive. The many and varied Acts that have been passed in an attempt to control crowd disorder at football matches have led to the development of invasive surveillance techniques by the police and the imposition of quasi-criminal restraining orders, Football Banning Orders, by the courts (see further, chapter 10.6). These legal responses have been justified by the courts as being for the protection of the general public from football-related disorder, even where those subjected to them have never been proved to have acted criminally at or in connection with a football match (*Gough* v. *Chief Constable of Derbyshire* [2002] EWCA Civ 351) and despite their appearing to be contrary to the provisions of the Human Rights Act 1998 (see further, chapter 10.6.2).

Although not suffering from the same claims of illegality, some sections of the London Olympic and Paralympic Games Act 2006 appear to have been inserted at the behest of a purely private body, the International Olympic Committee, rather than on the basis of a rational legal justification. Why the Olympic and Paralympic Games are so special that the use of their symbols and sales of tickets to their events need legislative protection – protections not previously extended to other national or international sporting or cultural events held in the UK – has never been fully debated either in Parliament or before the courts (see further, chapter 14).

Thus although Acts of Parliament can and do have a dramatic impact on sport, and are an important source of national sports law, there is little coherence to the justifications behind these interventions. Reasons as varied as the promotion of public health, the prevention of public disorder and the protection of commercial rights are behind some of the more recent legislative interventions; what is unclear, because of the lack of a clearly defined role for the state in respect of sport, is when and why the government will choose to intervene from one Parliamentary term to the next. The reality appears to be that the national sports law created by Parliament is driven more by political pragmatism than for the intrinsic benefit of sport.

1.4.3   Investigations by the Office of Fair Trading

The role and powers of the Office of Fair Trading (OFT) were consolidated in the Enterprise Act 2002 enabling it to act with the aim of promoting and protecting consumer interests and preventing anti-competitive behaviour. It has the power to enforce a wide range of consumer protection legislation, investigate and punish businesses for infringements of the Competition Act 1998 and refer conduct that distorts a particular market to the Competition Commission. Although relatively narrow in its overall remit, the investigations that have been undertaken by the OFT into sport have had a significant impact on the way that sport is administered and consumed.

In *Re Televising Premier League Football Matches* [2000] EMLR 78, the OFT referred the agreement between the FA Premier League and the broadcaster BSkyB to the Restrictive Practices Court to determine whether the collective selling of its media rights was anti-competitive. The Court's decision that it was in the public interest for a sports league to sell the rights to the entire competition, rather than allowing the individual clubs the right to sell their own home games, was based in part on the benefits to the consumer of only having to purchase one 'product' and the redistribution of income that was included in the collective agreement in an attempt to maintain a competitive balance between the teams in the league (see further, chapter 13.4). Further investigations have led to reductions in the price of replica kits after it was found that various retailers were guilty of fixing the prices at an artificially high level (*JJB Sports plc* v. *OFT; Allsports Ltd* v. *OFT* [2004] CAT 17) (see further, chapter 13.3.1).

Following complaints from fans of Tottenham Hotspur FC and Manchester United FC, the OFT investigated whether a number of terms in the season tickets of these two clubs and the information supplied by them concerning refunds and the purchasing of additional tickets were in breach of consumer protection legislation. As a result of the investigations, both clubs agreed to amend their terms and to provide clearer information to purchasers in order to avoid potential litigation. Thus the OFT plays an important role in ensuring that businesses connected with sport are complying with competition law and consumer protection legislation. In its clarification of the applicable law in these fields, it is an important source of national sports law.

1.5   European sports law

The link between domestic and national sports law is replicated at the transnational level by the relationships between global sports law and European and international sports law. European sports law is the law generated by the institutions of the European Union (EU) and the explanations of how and why that law has been applied to sport in the decisions of the European Court of Justice (ECJ). International sports law, of which European sports law is by far the most important sub-category, is discussed separately (below, 1.6).

Following the ratification and entry into force of the Treaty on the Functioning of the European Union (TFEU), Art.6 provides the EU with the competence to act in support of, to coordinate and to supplement the actions of member states in the field of sport. This specific reference to sport in the TFEU should enable a more coordinated approach to the development of European sports law to evolve in the future. The failure to mention sport in previous treaties has meant that the application of EU law and policy fell under the jurisdiction of several of the European Commission's Directorates General, including in particular the Directorate General for Education and Culture and the Directorate General for Competition. The Sport Unit, which is located within the Directorate General for Education and Culture, currently acts as an umbrella for the disparate sources of EU sports law and policy and is likely to play an increasingly important role in the future development of European sports law as a result of the implementation of Art.165 (below, 1.5.3).

The EU's involvement with sport to date has mainly occurred where specific sports practices have engaged EU law, in particular the provisions that protect the operation of the internal market and competition law. The EU's sports policy that has emerged from these interactions is derived from consultation with stakeholders in sport, particularly ISFs, social dialogue and through cooperation with the member states. The result has often been a piecemeal approach similar to that seen in the UK but with one significant difference: the UK Parliament chooses its non-interventionist approach to sport whereas the EU did not have a mandate to intervene directly on matters relating to sport prior to the ratification of the TFEU. This lack of coherence in approach to sport has been only partially remedied by the various decisions of the ECJ and the non-binding pronouncements of the European Commission and the Council of Ministers. Thus to date the most authoritative source of European sports law has been the rulings of the ECJ. However the TFEU has provided the EU with the opportunity to take a more proactive and distinctive role in its future development.

1.5.1   Decisions of the European Court of Justice

As sport has become more commercialised and more internationalised, it has developed a cross-border aspect that has engaged EU law. The European Commission's *White Paper on Sport* (COM (2007) 39 Final) provides an estimate of the economic importance of sport, showing it to have a value-added impact of €407bn, representing 3.7 per cent of EU Gross Domestic Product (GDP), and that around 15 million people, or 5.4 per cent of the total EU workforce, are employed in jobs connected with sport. Although the decisions of the ECJ have had the greatest impact on professional sports participants, there is no prohibition on the application of EU law to a purely amateur sportsperson. In the *Staff Working Document* (SEC (2007) 935) that accompanied the publication of the *White Paper on Sport*, it was stated that amateur sport was not outside the scope of the fundamental principles of free movement because access to sport is a social advantage that can affect a worker's ability to take up employment in another member state. Thus all sporting relationships can, in certain circumstances, be regulated by EU law.

In the early 1970s the ECJ declared in *Walrave and Koch* v. *Association Union Cycliste Internationale* (36/74) [1974] ECR 1405 that sporting relationships, particularly those involving professional sportspersons, were subject to EU law where the conduct in question constituted an economic activity (see further, chapter 3.2.2). From this point onwards it became clear that sport did not have the immunity from EU law that it appeared to have assumed was the case. Since *Walrave*, the test for when sport will be subject to EU law has developed considerably with a detailed jurisprudence emerging that explains how and why it will become engaged with a sports dispute. These developments have occurred particularly in respect of the provisions relating to the free movement of workers and are doing so to an increasing extent in the field of competition law (see further, chapters 3.2.6 and 12.4).

The next major landmark was *Union Royal Belge des Societe de Football Association ASBL v. Jean-Marc Bosman* (C-415/93) [1995] ECR I-4921 (see further, chapters 3.2.3 and 12.2.1), which involved an application of Art.45 TFEU (ex Art.48 TEEC) and determined the legality of the transfer system as it operated in Belgian football in particular and European football in general. Where many media commentators, and many football fans, still consider 'doing a *Bosman*' to be something not quite right in sporting terms, in EU law terms it simply enabled an employee whose fixed-term employment contract had come to a natural end to seek work with another employer elsewhere in the EU without any restriction; something that all non-athletes would consider to be a normal part of their working life. *Bosman* and its progeny still have a significant impact on how sport is organised in the EU and beyond; to the Union of European Football Associations (UEFA) and the Federation of International Football Associations (FIFA) in particular, the decision has become something of a bête-noire as they seek ever-more elaborate rules that are capable of avoiding its application. Thus it is likely that the legality of the 'home-grown player' rule introduced by UEFA at the start of the 2006–07 season and the even more restrictive '6+5' rule proposed by FIFA, will have their legality tested before the ECJ in due course (see further, chapter 12 Hot Topic).

As applicants have become more creative in presenting their cases before national courts, so has the complexity of the references made to the ECJ on questions of EU law increased. When the compatibility of the IOC's anti-doping regime with EU law was challenged in *Meca-Medina and Majcen* v. *Commision of the European Communities* (C-519/04 P) [2006] ECR I-6991 (see further, chapters 3.2.2 and 12.3), the eventual appeal to the ECJ was made in terms of breaching both competition law, contrary to Arts.101 and 102 TFEU (ex Arts.81 and 82 ECT), and the provisions on the freedom to provide services under Art.56 (ex Art.49 ECT). For procedural reasons the decision was handed down in terms of the anti-doping penalties being compatible with Arts.101 and 102 with no further comment being made on the applicability of Art.56 in these circumstances. The ECJ held that the rules had as their legitimate objective the proper conduct of competitive sport by ensuring healthy rivalry between the competitors. Further the length of the penalties imposed, a two-year ban on competing in swimming events, was considered to be proportionate for the purposes of achieving the legitimate objective of organising sport in an appropriate manner. Although judgment was not given on the possibility of the anti-doping regime infringing Art.56 TFEU, it is likely that this claim would also have failed on the grounds of the ban being a proportionate response for the purposes of achieving a legitimate sporting objective. Following *Motosykletistiki Omospondia Ellados NPID (MOTOE)* v. *Greece* (C-49/07) [2008] ECR I-4863, the possibility of claims that NGBs and ISFs are abusing their position through the application of rules that protect their own commercial interests, rather than acting for the benefit of their sport as a whole, is one that is likely to result in further litigation in the future (see further, chapters 3.2.6 and 12.4).

Until these and other cases were heard by the ECJ, transfer systems, anti-doping regulations and other monopolistic and restrictive practices had long been considered to be integral parts of the way that many sports operated. However their impact on the relatively short careers of professional sports participants had not previously been interrogated from a legal perspective. The impact of the ECJ's decisions in these and other cases has had a dramatic impact on the way that sport is administered, ensuring that any new rules, such as those proposed by FIFA and UEFA concerning the constitution of professional football teams, must be designed and applied so that they conform with EU law.

Despite the best efforts of some ISFs, and some intensive lobbying by FIFA and UEFA in particular, sport is subject to EU law. Their attempts to argue for a specific exemption for sport from the operation of EU law have so far failed. The ECJ will now examine any sporting rule that comes before it to determine whether, because of the 'specificity of sport', EU law should apply to the rule's operation in a particular sporting context or whether the rule should be specifically exempted (see further, chapter 3.2.2). This development, whilst still in its infancy, may go some way to appeasing some ISFs. However others continue to miss the point being made implicitly by the ECJ; where rich and successful ISFs appear to be acting for their own commercial benefit and to protect the earnings of their star performers, the ECJ is attempting to act for the benefit of all levels of all sports. Until the ISFs can construct an argument that justifies the exemption of their rules from EU law, their views will continue to conflict with those of the ECJ and the decisions of the highest court in the EU will continue to provide a rich source of European sports law.

1.5.2　Decisions of the European Commission on competition issues

Where an undertaking is suspected of engaging in anti-competitive conduct capable of interfering with the operation of the single market (see further, chapter 12.4), the European Commission has been granted special powers of investigation and sanction under Council Regulation (EC) 1/2003. The outcomes of the Commission's investigations are published as 'Decisions' and provide important guidance on how Arts.101 and 102 TFEU should be interpreted. The legality of these Decisions can be challenged before the ECJ following the Art.263 TFEU procedure (ex Art.230 ECT). The Commission can launch an investigation either on its own initiative, where it has reason to suspect an undertaking of anti-competitive behaviour, or following a complaint from a natural or legal person with a legitimate interest in curtailing the anti-competitive conduct, or at the instigation of a member state under Art.7 Regulation 1/2003.

Art.20 Regulation 1/2003 grants to the Commission the power to inspect the books, records and premises of an undertaking in order to determine whether a breach of the competition provisions has occurred. Under Art.23(1) Regulation 1/2003, failure to cooperate with the investigation process can result in an undertaking being fined up to one per cent of its turnover from the previous business year. Where an infringement of Arts.101 or 102 TFEU is established, a Decision taken in accordance with Art.7 Regulation 1/2003 can force changes to an undertaking's behaviour, or in extreme cases to its structure, in order to curtail the anti-competitive conduct. Alternatively where the undertaking's anti-competitive conduct is considered to be sufficiently serious, a fine of up to ten per cent of its turnover in the preceding business year can be imposed under Art.23(2) Regulation 1/2003.

The Commission has investigated the conduct of ISFs and major event organisers on a number of occasions. For example in *Royal Excelsior Mouscron* IP/99/965 9 December 1999 (see further, chapters 3.2.5 and 12.4.3.3), the Commission held that the 'home-and-away' rule operated by UEFA in its football competitions affected only the proper organisation of sport, not sport as an economic activity, and therefore was not subject to Arts.101 and

102 TFEU, thus preventing the need for further litigation on the issue. Further, in *FIFA 2006 World Cup Ticketing Arrangements* IP/05/519 2 May 2005, an increased range of payment options was offered to purchasers of tickets to the World Cup Finals Tournament following a complaint made to the Commission by the consumer organisation *Which?*. Although not having the status of judgments of the ECJ, Decisions of the Commission on competition law issues have a great deal of authority because of the expertise of the body involved and its interest in creating consistency of interpretation across all member states of the EU.

<table>
<tr><td>1.5.3</td><td></td></tr>
</table>

1.5.3   Sport and the European Treaties

The need to protect the special status of sport was recognised during the negotiations that led to the Treaty of Amsterdam in 1997. Although the Declaration that was appended to the Treaty was not legally binding, it enabled the EU to take into account the importance of sport to the citizens of the EU and to the EU's cultural makeup when developing its own law and policies. The most visible development that came out of the Declaration was the creation of the Directorate General for Education and Culture's Sport Unit.

> ▶ **Treaty of Amsterdam 1997 Declaration 29**
>
> 'The Conference emphasises the social significance of sport, in particular its role in forging identity and bringing people together. The Conference therefore calls on the bodies of the European Union to listen to sports associations when important questions affecting sport are at issue. In this connection, special consideration should be given to the particular characteristics of amateur sport.'

At the end of the French Presidency of the EU in 2000, the Nice Declaration was annexed to the Presidency Conclusions. Like the Amsterdam Declaration it was not legally binding, however once again it reiterated the importance of sport by requiring the EU to take into consideration its social, educational and cultural functions when creating new laws and policies. The task of organising sport was left to the various NGBs and ISFs, although it was noted in the Declaration that these bodies must operate within national and EU law if they are to avoid censure.

Since these two Declarations were made, a group of the leading ISFs, spearheaded by FIFA and UEFA, has campaigned vigorously for sport to be specifically exempted from the operation of EU. This has not found favour with the European Council, Commission or Parliament and instead the EU has reserved for itself the competence to act on matters relating to sport within the limits provided by Arts.6 and 165 TFEU. This in turn could lead to a more proactive and coherent development of European sports law in the future, though it is unlikely that this will result in the exemption sought by the ISFs materialising.

> ▶ **Treaty on the Functioning of the European Union Art.165**
>
> '1. [The] Union shall contribute to the promotion of European sporting issues, while taking account of the specific nature of sport, its structures based on voluntary activity and its social and educational function.

2. Union action shall be aimed at:

[– developing] the European dimension in sport, by promoting fairness and openness in sporting competitions and cooperation between bodies responsible for sports, and by protecting the physical and moral integrity of sportsmen and sportswomen, especially the youngest sportsmen and sportswomen.

3. The Union and the member states shall foster cooperation with third countries and the competent international organisations in the field of education and sport, in particular the Council of Europe.'

This amendment to the sphere of competence of the EU will enable it to support, coordinate and most importantly supplement the actions of the member states in respect of sport. The EU will be able to promote European sporting issues, ensure that the specific nature of sport is protected and develop its social and educational functions. In particular it aims at promoting transparency in sporting competitions, cooperation between sporting bodies and protecting the physical and moral integrity of sports participants. However despite the potential for an increased role for the EU in the regulation of sport provided for in Art.165, its potential impact remains vague.

Importantly it is implicit in the wording of Art.165 that the 'specificity of sport' will continue to be a decisive factor in determining whether or not EU law applies to a particular situation and that current administrative structures are to be protected. Thus both the conditional autonomy currently enjoyed by governing bodies and the pyramidal structure according to which most European sport is organised are likely to be unaffected by the implementation of Art.165. The more likely areas of development will be in the creation of a more coherent sports policy aimed at protecting grassroots and youth sport rather than the creation of legal measures specifically aimed at the greater regulation of the commercial aspects of professional sport.

1.5.4 The development of European sports law

The further expansion of European sports law is dependent on the evolution of the relationship between the ECJ and CAS and on the interpretation of the scope of Art.165. The resolution of the tension that exists between the jurisprudence of CAS and the degree of influence that the EU is able to exert over sports disputes will be key to the harmonious development of both global and European sports law. As the scope of CAS's influence continues to grow and as it hands down an increasing number of decisions requiring it to interpret and apply EU law, the opportunity for differences of opinion between the decisions of CAS and the ECJ becomes more likely. Even though CAS is bound by the interpretations of EU law delivered by the ECJ, the much more rapid development of its jurisprudence creates at least the possibility of divergence between its decisions and those of the ECJ. With the language of CAS often replicating that of the ECJ, particularly where discussions of the 'specificity of sport' are concerned, a greater degree of consultation, or perhaps even collaboration, between these two bodies may eventually become necessary to ensure that the law develops in a way that is of benefit to sport.

Following the ratification of the TFEU, perhaps the clearest indication of how EU sports law and policy will develop can be found in the European Commission's *White Paper on Sport* (COM (2007) 39 Final). The *White Paper* provides a strategic orientation of the current societal role, economic dimension and organisational framework of sport and identifies how the Commission may see its own role in respect of these issues evolving in the future. The potential for the development of European sports law can be seen most explicitly in the chapters covering the societal role of sport and the organisation of sport. Regarding the former, the Commission appears to see a role for itself in developing policies and ultimately law, covering amongst other things anti-racism, crowd disorder and doping control. However it is in respect of the organisation of sport that the Commission could develop a more interventionist role in the creation of European sports law. It identifies freedom of movement, the transfer of players between clubs, the regulation of sports agents and the protection of minors as potential areas for regulatory development, albeit set against the emerging ECJ principle that requires the specificity of sport to be taken into consideration if the Commission does eventually decide to act. Thus the Commission has made it clear how and why it sees a more active role for the EU developing in respect of sport.

1.6 International sports law

International sports law is the general or universal principles of law, particularly of international law, that are applicable to sport. According to Foster, these general principles are those which are a part of international customary law, or the *jus commune*, and include but are not limited to: the principle that agreements are binding; the prohibition on unjust enrichment; the guarantee of procedural fairness and the doctrines of proportionality and personal liability. As these general principles of law are universally applicable, they cannot be avoided or reinterpreted by ISFs as they see fit. Moreover as legal principles they can be enforced before an appropriate national or transnational court; in other words, their existence limits an ISF's opportunity for complete self-regulation by imposing upon it basic standards of good governance. From a practical perspective, most of these universally applicable principles have been incorporated into sports law through national courts, as occurred in *Jones* v. *Welsh Rugby Union* [1998] The Times, 6 January (see further, chapter 2.4.4).

This kind of universally pervasive international law is further reflected in the mission of the Council of Europe, which seeks as one of its core aims to create a common legal area that ensures respect for human rights and the rule of law and is epitomised by its Conventions that seek to promote the harmonisation of legal principles and procedures rather than creating specific laws, as occurs in EU law. The Council of Europe is a supra-national organisation based in Strasbourg, France. It is separate from, and much larger than, the EU counting 47 states amongst its members, including all current member states of the EU. Apart from the European sports law developed by the EU institutions and the principles of law that constitute the *jus commune*, the only significant current source of international sports law is that which can be found in the Conventions of the Council of Europe.

The Council has created two specific Conventions that apply to sport. The first, following the tragedy at the Heysel Stadium, Brussels in 1985, focuses on developing closer cooperation between members on issues relating to crowd disorder at football matches (see further, chapter 10.3.6). The second responds to the need for a more coordinated approach to the control of doping in sport (see further, chapter 3.3.2.3). Despite both Conventions being signed by the UK, they do not have legal effect in UK law, though both have played a significant part in developing UK policy in both of these areas. Thus these Conventions are only weak sources of international sports law.

1.6.1 European Convention on Spectator Violence and Misbehaviour at Sports Events and in Particular at Football Matches 1985

The aim of the Convention on Spectator Violence is to create common and cooperative action amongst the signatories in their attempts to prevent and control spectator disorder. At the national level it encourages greater cooperation between government, NGBs and the police to provide adequate resources to control public disorder and the development of an effective regime to punish those involved with acts of hooliganism, including banning them from attending matches. All of the recommendations made by the Convention reflect the findings of the various reports commissioned by the UK government into crowd control and spectator safety throughout the twentieth century.

The Convention also recommends greater cooperation at the transnational level between signatories. In particular it envisages the sharing of information on risk spectators between law enforcement and border control agencies and the prevention of known troublemakers from travelling abroad to watch football matches and potentially take part in disorder.

Although the Convention has no legal force in the UK, most of the policy initiatives raised within it have, in the aftermath of the disasters at Heysel Stadium, Brussels in 1985 and Hillsborough Stadium, Sheffield in 1989, been introduced. In particular the exchange of information between police forces both within the UK and with their counterparts abroad and the imposition of Football Banning Orders on those convicted or suspected of being involved with football-related disorder have been cornerstones of the fight against football hooliganism (see further, chapter 10). Therefore the regulatory framework provided by the Convention has been created but the real source of the relevant law is national sports law rather than international sports law.

1.6.2 The Anti-Doping Convention 1989

The Council of Europe's Anti-Doping Convention was the culmination of over twenty years of discussions on the importance of producing a coordinated international response to doping in sport. Its importance can be seen from the fact that non-European nations including Australia, Canada and Tunisia have also considered it worthwhile to become signatories of the Convention and to ratify it. The Convention begins with the premise that doping is cheating and that it is important to reduce and ultimately eliminate it from all sporting competitions.

The Convention requires signatories to begin by coordinating the agencies responsible for their domestic response to anti-doping and to restrict the availability of banned substances and methods by legislation where appropriate. Alongside these measures the Convention also encourages signatories to establish high quality testing facilities and schemes to educate athletes about the moral and physical dangers associated with taking performance enhancing drugs. Finally, as with the Convention on Spectator Violence, it encourages cooperation between signatories in eradicating doping in sport by, amongst other things, the exchange of information on testing procedures and on athletes who have tested positive for banned substances.

To a great extent the purpose behind the Anti-Doping Convention has now been superseded by the activities of the World Anti-Doping Agency (WADA), its Code and the hearing of most major doping disputes before the Court of Arbitration for Sport. This global level of coordination and cooperation is the driving force behind WADA and its harmonisation of anti-doping procedures across sports and nations. However recognition of the pioneering work of the Council of Europe can be seen in its position as a Foundation Board Member of WADA's Board and Executive Committee. Thus although a weak source of international sports law, the Convention has been a key driver in the development of global anti-doping policies and has established the platform upon which CAS's anti-doping jurisprudence has been built.

1.7 Conclusion

When answering the question, 'What is sports law?' the answer is that it is a combination of the law and legal theory found in all of these different sources. It is the interaction of sport and the law, it is the law, legal principles and legal procedures that resolve sports disputes and it can be seen in action by the impact that it has had on how sport is currently administered, participated in and consumed. Whether it is referred to as 'sport and the law' as is preferred by many legal practitioners, or 'sports law' as here, there is no doubt about its growing importance as a field of academic enquiry. Sports law cases such as *Bosman* have changed the core features of sport as it had developed since the late 1800s. Others have led the way in developing entirely new areas of the law applicable not only to sport but to all contexts, such as the discussion of how to protect a person's image rights in *Irvine* v. *Talksport Ltd* [2002] EWHC 367 (Ch).

'Sport and the law' is more properly the simple application of national and EU law to a sports dispute. It does not specifically consider in any detail the special nature of sport, just whether or not the law is an appropriate forum for resolving the particular dispute that has arisen.

'Sports law' attempts to provide an underlying explanation of why sports as a group of related activities are, and should continue to be, treated differently by the law; it is the development of an underlying theory that draws together cases using disparate legal principles into a single coherent subject. This is at its clearest in the ECJ's development of what constitutes the 'specificity of sport' and that Court's provision of a more detailed explanation of the reasons why sport should be treated differently in certain circumstances. It is the 'specificity of sport' that allows monopolistic private bodies to control the conduct of huge sections of society without significant interference from the law; that enables participants to inflict injuries on each other with a degree of immunity from the law; that justifies the criminalisation of breach of contract when a tout resells a ticket to a football match or an Olympic event; that enables a governing body to prevent a player from earning a living from their chosen profession because they have boosted their performance by using particular substances or equipment; that prevents men and women from working together and competing against one another; that enables discriminatory nationality quotas to be imposed on employers and that forces employers to release their employees to another profit-making organisation without recompense. Sports law is the jurisprudence that has evolved to justify that sport is different and which enables a justification of how and why the law applies in the way that it does to be provided.

Hot topic . . .

WHY HAS THE LAW BECOME INVOLVED IN SPORT?

The law's intervention in matters relating to sport prior to the 1980s was erratic and piecemeal. Until this time there had been a disproportionately large number of prosecutions where the legality of boxing and prize fighting was explored and a few notable examinations of contractual and financial issues. This latter group of cases, including the clarification of the tax status of benefit events that were held for professional cricketers (*Seymour* v. *Reed* [1927] AC 554) and a challenge to the transfer system in football (*Eastham* v. *Newcastle United Football Club* [1964] Ch 413) paved the way for the recent explosion in sports-related litigation. As a result, almost every field of law has infiltrated almost every aspect of sport, from the obvious freedom movement claim in *Bosman* to the obscure regulations concerning advertising in the London Olympic and Paralympic Games Act 2006, and from the politically motivated restrictions imposed on the movement of football fans in the Football Spectators Act 1989 to the faintly ridiculous trial to determine whether a father and his five-year-old son kicking a ball to each other in a park constituted a game of football (*Lawton* v. *Fleming-Brown* [2006] EWHC 3146 (Admin)). There is now no doubt that sport is subject to the law and that this subjection has not resulted in the end of sport as we know it; a claim that is made by administrators and commentators almost every time that a high profile sporting case reaches the courts.

What is much more difficult however is trying to provide an explanation for why this process of juridification has occurred, both in terms of the increased use of the law to regulate activities related to sport in general and the legalising effect that the law has had on the ways that sport is administered. The simple answer is that nobody really knows why so many cases have come before the courts and why Parliament has been more open to passing legislation on sporting issues; there is no single clearly identifiable explanation for this phenomenon.

The more complex response is that it is the product of a series of unrelated developments that were occurring in both sport and society from the late 1970s onwards and which combined to create the perfect conditions from which sports law could emerge. The commercialisation and commodification of sport during this period attracted law and lawyers like no previous period in sports history. As sport became more commercial, more money was invested into it and increased profits were created, which in turn led to disputes that required law and lawyers to resolve them (*Greig* v. *Insole* [1978] 1 WLR 302). Alongside this commercialisation the marketing, branding and repackaging of sport became more sophisticated; games and events became products or commodities that could be sold to the highest bidder, with the best example in British sport being the creation of the Premier League in 1992. A by-product of these commercial developments was the great strain that they caused to the antiquated governance structures of many NGBs. Systems that had been designed to organise amateur sport in the latter part of the nineteenth century could no longer cope with the demands imposed on them by the newly professional players who challenged their procedures in court and forced them to modernise (*Jones* v. *Welsh Rugby Union*).

Developments in the political sphere occurred at both the national and European levels. The stadium disasters of the 1980s finally forced the government to take legislative action and create regulatory frameworks that ensured that football stadiums became safer places for spectators to watch matches and football hooligans could be monitored and punished more effectively. At the same time the European Commission had been warning UEFA that the transfer system did not comply with EU law; UEFA's failure to act on these warnings eventually resulted in the *Bosman* decision and the many cases that have followed it.

Finally easier access to legal advice and a greater awareness of legal rights provided an impetus to sports-related litigation from within society. The advent of contingency fees removed the financial risk of litigation for many claimants as they could be charged by their solicitors on a no-win-no-fee basis, whilst the adverts of many claims agents actively encouraged injured sports participants to pursue compensation from their opponents. Although Parliament has moved to limit the impact of such litigation on sport through s.1 Compensation Act 2006, the perception persists that the UK is currently in the grip of a blame-focused claims culture, particularly where personal injury is concerned.

The only aspects of sport that are effectively immune from legal intervention are the rules and codes of ethics that regulate the actual playing of games. National and European courts as well as the Court of Arbitration for Sport have regularly stated that they will not review the decisions of match officials that are taken during the course of a game. The aim of such an exemption is to uphold as far as is possible the authority of the match officials and to preserve the finality of the end of game result. The only time that the courts may consider such a claim to be justiciable is where their application of the rules of the game promotes illegality in some way (*Pallante* v. *Stadiums Pty Ltd* No.1 [1976] VR 331). It is also possible that where an aspect of a sport has become too dangerous to be allowed to continue the courts may require the NGB and/or ISF to change its rules. Apart from these two very limited situations the playing rules and practices of sport cannot be reviewed before the courts.

Thus the law has engaged with sport for a variety of reasons. A combination of changing circumstances in sport and society, together with the pursuit of specific political aims at national and EU levels, has been responsible for the emergence of sports law as such an important field of legal study and practice. This knowledge of the impact of the law on sport has fuelled further litigation as lawyers apply the lessons that they have learned in one area of sports law to others that have not previously been attempted. In response NGBs and ISFs have amended their rules and procedures as a result of risk assessment strategies and in order to comply with the rules of natural justice in an attempt to avoid further litigation. The most important question now is not, 'Why has the law become involved with sport?' but 'Where is sports law going next?'

Summary

1.1 There is no formal definition of sport in English law. This can be explained in part by the non-interventionist approach of the UK Parliament to matters connected with sport. This in turn leaves the day-to-day governance of British sport to the NGBs; these bodies are in general answerable to the appropriate ISF rather than directly to Parliament or a government department. Thus there is no single identifiable authoritative source of sports law. Instead the ability to identify the law, legal norms and legal procedures that constitute sports law requires an understanding of its various national and international sources.

1.2 As sports disputes have become increasingly juridified, so have the internal tribunals operated by NGBs taken on a more obviously quasi-judicial role in their resolution. Following a series of challenges to their authority and decision-making processes, these tribunals and independent bodies such as Sports Disputes UK are now capable of hearing and resolving sports disputes involving complex legal issues. They have become an important source of domestic sports law because although they rarely create new law and legal norms they are hearing cases that would otherwise be heard before the national courts.

1.3 Global sports law is evolving from the autonomous legal order created by ISFs for resolving transnational sporting disputes. In particular the jurisprudence of the Court of Arbitration for Sport (CAS) provides leadership and guidance to affected parties by harmonising approaches across sports to the interpretation and application of legal norms to sporting disputes. The decisions of CAS and of the dispute resolution chambers of many ISFs provide an important source of global sports law by hearing complex legal issues that would otherwise be heard before national courts and the European Court of Justice.

1.4 National sports law is that which is created by Parliament or found in the judgments and decisions of national courts and enforcement agencies. The non-interventionist approach to the governance of sport by the state in the UK means that there are few Acts of Parliament that apply specifically to sporting activities. Instead the decisions of the courts and of bodies like the Office of Fair Trading have had the greatest impact on the administration of, participation in and consumption of sport and are the richest source of national sports law.

1.5 In the absence of any specific mention of sport in the earlier treaties, the application of EU law to sport has largely been seen in the decisions of the ECJ when it has been called upon to interpret whether various provisions apply to the conduct of ISFs and NGBs. However the EU has been active in the development of its own sports policy and the 2007 *White Paper on Sport* gives a clear indication of how European sports law could develop following the ratification of the Treaty on the Functioning of the European Union and the powers granted to the EU in respect of sport in Arts.6 and 165.

1.6 The universally applicable principles of international customary law ensure that the parties to legal disputes are treated fairly and proportionately. They have been incorporated into international sports law by actions before national courts and CAS that have forced NGBs and ISFs to adopt quasi-judicial procedures and norms when acting quasi-judicially. It is perhaps

Summary cont'd

the most difficult source of sports law to identify because of sport being administered by a series of private relationships rather than through a network of international treaties ratified by nation states. Where such transnational agreements are in place, for example the sports-specific Conventions of the Council of Europe, they are more likely to be indicators of how national sports law will develop rather than being specific sources of international sports law.

1.7 There continues to be discussion about whether 'sport and the law' or 'sports law' is the correct title of this field of legal enquiry. 'Sport and the law' accurately reflects how sports disputes are litigated before the courts; it is the application of discrete fields of law to a dispute that happens to be between parties connected with the administration of, participation in or consumption of sport. However 'sports law' suggests that there is an underpinning theory that justifies how and why sports disputes are treated differently by the courts and why CAS considers that it is creating a new series of legal norms that it refers to as *lex sportiva*. This unifying theory has been identified by the ECJ as the 'specificity of sport' and goes a long way to explaining when it is appropriate for sport to be subjected to the law and when it should be left to regulate itself.

Further reading

Lewis and Taylor (eds), *Sport: Law and Practice* (2nd edn, 2008, Tottel) ch A1
Parrish and Miettinen, *The sporting exception in European Union Law* (2008, TMC Asser Press)

Beloff, 'Is there a *lex sportiva*?' [2008] 3 *International Sports Law Review* 49
Foster, 'Is there a Global Sports Law?' (2003) 2(1) *Entertainment and Sports Law Journal*, online
Humphrey, 'The politics of sport: the why, when and how of sports law development and implementation' [2008] 2/3 *International Sports Law Review* 30
Taylor and O'Sullivan, 'How should national governing bodies of sport be governed in the UK? An exploratory study of board structure' (2009) 17(6) *Corporate Governance* 681

Links to relevant websites can be found at www.palgrave.com/law/james

Chapter 2

Domestic and national sports law

Key words

- **Judicial review** – the power granted to the courts to review the decision-making procedures of public bodies.
- **Declaration** – a court order that states whether the procedure operated by an NGB is lawful or not.
- **Injunction** – a court order that requires its subject either to take specific action (mandatory injunction) or to stop doing something that is unlawful (prohibitory injunction).

2.1 The relationship between domestic and national sports law

Most national governing bodies of sport (NGBs) operate their own internal quasi-legal system. The NGB itself is the rule-making body (Parliament or legislature) whose rules (laws) are interpreted and enforced by a disciplinary tribunal, panel or committee (court). When originally created, these internal justice systems operated in an informal manner with, in public law terms, no true separation of powers and very few procedural safeguards. Their main purpose was to enforce playing bans for on-field foul play and off-field financial misconduct. This ideal of self-regulation went largely unchallenged for most of the twentieth century as NGBs dealt with all aspects of sporting misconduct, or matters that brought their game into disrepute, in-house. When the occasional case did appear before the judiciary, the judges showed little enthusiasm to interfere in matters that they considered could be better dealt with elsewhere, with Lord Denning MR stating in *Enderby Town FC* v. *The Football Association* [1971] Ch 591 at 605, that:

> 'In many cases it may be a good thing for the proceedings of a domestic tribunal to be conducted informally without legal representation. Justice can often be done in them better by a good layman than by a bad lawyer. This is especially so in activities like football and other sports, where no points of law are likely to arise, and it is all part of the proper regulation of the game.'

This hands-off approach to the conduct of disciplinary hearings changed dramatically as sport in the UK became more openly professional and the participants became much more substantially rewarded. As bans began to affect not only an athlete's ability to take part in a sport but also their income, sports participants began to expect a more formal approach from their internal justice systems and the ability to refer to the national courts to rectify any perceived inadequacies (*Jones* v. *Welsh Rugby Union* [1998] The Times, 6 January) (below, 2.4.4). Further, with the financial rewards now available through increased commercial streams, particularly television money, clubs also expect not only a fair hearing but a robust and legally defensible explanation of how and why the tribunal has reached its decision (*Sheffield United Football Club Ltd* v. *Football Association Premier League Ltd* [2007] 3 ISLR SLR 77) (below, 2.4.3 and chapter 11 Hot Topic).

The tension that has arisen between the NGBs' desire for self-regulation of all disputes that affect the governance and administration of their sports and the expectations of players and clubs that they will receive a standard of justice equivalent to that which is available in actions before the national courts has been key to the development of the procedural norms applied in sports disciplinary tribunals. Instead of simply tracing the various challenges that have been made to the authority of and procedures followed by NGBs, this chapter explains how the decisions of the courts, the national sports law, have affected the operations of sports disciplinary tribunals and consequently domestic sports law. It begins by explaining the legal status of an NGB in English law before analysing how challenges to an NGB's rules, procedures and decisions can be brought before the national courts. Finally it examines how and why sports disciplinary tribunals operate in the way that they now do.

2.2 The role of governing bodies and their legal status in English law

Sport in the UK is organised on a private basis, meaning that there is very little direct state intervention in the day-to-day administration of sporting activities (see further, chapter 1.1). A governing body is comprised of its members, who will usually be the individual players as is the case with male professional tennis players being members of the ATP Tour, or a group of clubs as is the case for the vast majority of team sports in the UK. In either case the clubs or the athletes will have agreed together, for the time being, to be bound by the rules and procedures of the NGB that they have created or of which they are constituent members.

2.2.1 The jurisdiction of governing bodies over their members

NGBs have no specific or inalienable legal right to govern the sport over which they have jurisdiction; their power derives only from the agreement of their current members to be bound by the NGB's rules. Thus there must be in place a contract, or a relationship equivalent to that created by a contract, capable of binding all relevant parties to the rules and regulations of the NGB for it to be able to operate effectively. Such an agreement can be expressly entered into by the relevant parties or implied from their conduct, as can be seen in the litigation arising out of the suspension of professional tennis player Petr Korda for a doping offence.

> ▶ **The Petr Korda litigation**
>
> On 7 May 1998 Petr Korda completed and signed the application form to compete in the All England Lawn Tennis and Croquet Club's Championships at Wimbledon. The application form stated that the event was to be played under the Rules of Tennis as approved by the International Tennis Federation (ITF), including its anti-doping and drug testing programme. Following his defeat in the Round of 16, Korda provided a urine sample for testing, which was later found to contain two metabolites of the banned substance nandrolone.
>
> At a hearing before the Independent Anti-Doping Review Board (IADRB) it was concluded that Korda was guilty of a first violation of the ITF's Anti-Doping Programme and that he should be subject to the mandatory penalty of suspension from all ITF sanctioned events for one year and the forfeiture of all ranking points and prize money awarded at Wimbledon. Korda appealed to the ITF's Appeals Committee (AC) against the imposition of the suspension on the grounds that there were 'exceptional circumstances' for the presence of nandrolone in his urine sample. The AC accepted Korda's claim that he had not knowingly taken, or had administered to him, a prohibited substance and overturned the playing ban that had been imposed upon him. The ITF lodged an appeal with the Court of Arbitration for Sport (CAS) against this decision on the basis that the AC had incorrectly found there to be

'exceptional circumstances' that warranted a reduction in the penalty imposed. Korda applied to the High Court for an injunction preventing the ITF from pursuing its appeal to CAS on the basis he was not contractually bound by the ITF's rules and that even if he was, the rules did not provide for such an appeal in these circumstances.

▶ *Korda* v. *ITF Ltd* (unreported) High Court (Ch), 29 January 1999

Contrary to Korda's claims, the High Court found there to be a contractual relationship in place between the player and the ITF. Although there had been neither a written nor an oral agreement between the two parties, the existence of a contract could be inferred from their conduct. Of particular importance was Korda's submission to the drug testing programme by his providing a urine sample, the exercise of his right to appeal from the original decision of the IADRB to the AC and his assertion that if the appeal to the AC went against him then he would exercise his right to appeal to CAS. The Court held that Korda's submission to the jurisdiction of the AC was evidence of his acceptance of a contractual relationship between himself and the ITF whose terms required that the procedures provided for in the ITF's Anti-Doping Programme be followed.

▶ *Korda* v. *ITF Ltd* (unreported) Court of Appeal (Civ), 25 March 1999

Having established the existence of a contractual relationship between the parties in the High Court, the dispute then focused on the circumstances in which the contract allowed an appeal to be made from a decision of the AC to CAS. The Court of Appeal interpreted s.(V)3 ITF Anti-Doping Programme to mean that either party could appeal to CAS for a full re-hearing of the case where there was any dispute arising from any decision made by the AC. As there was a clear dispute concerning whether the AC had correctly interpreted the meaning of 'exceptional circumstances' and whether it had imposed an appropriate punishment on Korda, s.(V)3 entitled the ITF to appeal to CAS for final resolution of the matter.

▶ *ITF Ltd* v. *K* CAS 99/A/223

CAS began by agreeing with both of the findings of the English courts: first that a contractual relationship existed between Korda and the ITF and second, that s.(V)3 ITF Anti-Doping Programme allowed either party the right of appeal to CAS in the case of any dispute arising from any decision of the AC. Having established its jurisdiction to hear the appeal, the panel then went on to determine whether Korda was able to prove on the balance of probabilities that there were 'exceptional circumstances' present that could justify the imposition of a penalty lower than that required in the ordinary course of events by the Anti-Doping Programme. Their finding was that a claim by the athlete that he had no idea how a prohibited substance had come to be present in his urine sample, in the absence of any evidence that he was not at fault for the positive test, was not sufficient to establish the presence of 'exceptional circumstances' that could justify the imposition of a reduced penalty. Thus CAS reinstated the original penalties imposed by the IADRB of a one year suspension from competition and the forfeiture of the ranking points and prize money earned at Wimbledon.

This series of hearings demonstrates how the governance of sport in English law is based firmly in contract. Without the existence of either an express or implied contract between the governing body and the clubs and/or athletes playing its sport, there is no legal basis for it being able to exercise regulatory powers over them. If a contract can be identified then its terms need to be scrutinised to determine whether or not the governing body has the power to act in the way that it has. Further, as the relationship is based in contract it should be possible to determine the circumstances in which the members of an NGB can decide not to submit to its jurisdiction any longer.

2.2.2   Establishing a rival organisation

Provided that the members follow the procedures by which they are currently bound, there is nothing to stop them from resigning their membership and establishing their own rival organisation when they no longer want to be bound by the rules or administrative structures of the existing NGB. For example in 1992 a group of the leading professional darts players broke away from the British Darts Organisation (BDO) to establish the World Darts Council, now known as the Professional Darts Corporation (PDC). The PDC sees itself as being more professionally and commercially minded than the BDO and has established a series of lucrative professional competitions for its members. Meanwhile the BDO has continued to organise darts at all levels of play including professional competitions and to develop the game amongst young players and women. As a result in 2005 it obtained the recognition of the four home country sports councils as the official NGB for darts in the UK. The two bodies provide administrative and organisational frameworks for the same sport, played according to the same rules, though with different missions and differing memberships.

In the most extreme case this can result in a completely new sport being created as the breakaway organisation seeks to establish its own separate identity and ethos, as occurred in rugby. In 1895 a group of clubs from the north of England resigned their membership of the Rugby Football Union in order to establish the Northern Rugby Football Union following a dispute over paying players who had taken time off work to play for their club. Although Northern Union was originally played by the same rules that had been established by the Rugby Football Union, these quickly changed with the abolition of line-outs in 1897 and a reduction to 13 players per side in 1907. From a dispute over whether a club should reimburse its players for the pay they lost whilst playing, the new sport of rugby league evolved. Thus provided that those breaking away do so in accordance with the rules of membership of their original NGB, there is little that can be done to prevent them from leaving and establishing a new governing body and, eventually, a new sport.

2.2.3   The legal status of governing bodies

When originally created, the NGBs of English sport had a wide variety of legal forms. Some, like the Marylebone Cricket Club (MCC), are private members clubs that have over the years divested themselves of their powers of governance to more recently established limited companies, in this case the England and Wales Cricket Board. Others were even more informal groupings of clubs that constituted unincorporated associations. These are bodies with no separate or distinct legal personality from that of its members; thus if sued, each individual member is liable for a share of the damages payable to the successful claimant.

To avoid the members being placed in the position of being individually liable for any claim made against the governing body, most NGBs have incorporated to become companies limited by guarantee. Where this has occurred, the NGB now has a separate legal personality that insulates its members from liability leaving the NGB to be sued in its own right. Not only are the members protected by their NGB incorporating, but so is the sport. Following the debts accrued by the British Athletics Federation during its protracted litigation with Diane Modhal (below, 2.3.3.1), the Federation was forced into bankruptcy and British athletics was left without a fully functioning NGB for a period of time. However because the Federation was incorporated and had few assets, the sport itself was relatively unaffected. After a review of the needs of the sport was conducted by an independent steering group in 1997–98, a new NGB, UK Athletics Ltd, was formed in 1999 again as a company limited by guarantee.

The one high profile exception to these more standard legal forms was the Jockey Club. Originally a private members club, the Jockey Club had over time taken on responsibility for the regulation of horseracing in the UK, in much the same way as the MCC had for cricket. In 1970 its powers over British horseracing were consolidated when it was re-established by Royal Charter. As its powers were now an exercise of the Royal Prerogative, the Jockey Club had the appearance of being an organ of the state, clearly differentiating its legal status from all other British NGBs. Despite this unusual position, in *R v. Disciplinary Committee of the Jockey Club ex parte Aga Khan* [1993] 1 WLR 909, it was eventually established that even the Jockey Club was a private body whose framework of consensual relationships was not governed by public law (below, 2.3.1). What the various challenges to its authority did highlight however, was that there was a potential conflict of interest between the Jockey Club's regulatory and commercial roles. In 2007 the British Horseracing Authority was established as the NGB for horseracing in the UK, taking over the regulatory work of the Jockey Club and leaving it free to pursue its commercial and charitable enterprises. The new Authority, like the vast majority of NGBs based in the UK, is a company limited by guarantee.

2.3 Challenging governing bodies' decisions in the English courts

Almost anyone connected with a sport, whether a player, coach, agent, club or owner, may have reason to challenge the decisions of an NGB. Most challenges are made because the individual or club involved has been punished in some way by the NGB, for example by being banned from playing or working in a particular sport, having points docked, or being prevented from using a particular type of equipment. Most of the developments that have resulted in the juridification of sports authorities' decision-making processes have been imposed on NGBs following a successful challenge to a rule, decision or procedure that was brought before the national courts because of its negative financial impact on the applicant. Although many NGBs, and the ISFs of which they are members, usually discourage recourse to national courts for the purposes of dispute resolution, dissatisfied parties can, and do, still bring legal actions in an attempt to reach a more favourable outcome for themselves.

2.3.1 The unavailability of judicial review in England and Wales

Before discussing the causes of action by which a claimant can challenge the actions of a NGB, it is important to mention briefly one that cannot. Because the internal disciplinary framework of an NGB bears more than a passing resemblance to a fully operational justice system, it has long been argued by claimants that these decision-making procedures should be amenable to judicial review. Under Part 54 Civil Procedure Rules, judicial review enables a person who has been adversely affected by an enactment or a decision of a public body such as a local authority to challenge its lawfulness before the High Court. The purpose of the review is to establish whether the decision-making process followed by the relevant public body was lawful; the Court does not interfere with the substance of the decision. Thus if the Court finds that the decision was taken in excess of the powers granted to the body and was therefore *ultra vires*, or that no reasonable body acting in that capacity would have come to the same decision according to the test established in *Associated Provincial Picture Houses Ltd* v. *Wednesbury Corporation* [1948] 1 KB 223, or that it had failed to follow its own procedures in coming to its decision, or that the rules of natural justice were not complied with, or the rule against bias was breached, then the decision can be set aside. In such circumstances the decision-making body must either retake the decision whilst following its own procedures correctly or, if the procedures themselves are defective, amend them before rehearing the complaint as though for the first time.

Judicial review is a quick and efficient means of remedying defective public law procedures and on the face of it would appear to be ideally suited to ensuring that any party coming before a sports disciplinary tribunal received a fair hearing. As each of the developments mentioned in chapter 2.4 are in reality public law concepts that have been incorporated into private relationships, judicial review would appear to be the most appropriate means of ensuring that the disciplinary mechanisms used by NGBs are in fact fair. However despite the number of occasions that such an argument has been raised before the English courts, the judiciary has taken a narrow view of the 'public' nature of NGBs and repeatedly declared that as they are private bodies that are not exercising any recognisable public function their actions cannot be subjected to judicial review.

▶ *R v. Disciplinary Committee of the Jockey Club (ex parte Aga Khan)* **[1993] 1 WLR 909**

The Aga Khan was the owner of a racehorse, Aliysa, which had won the 1989 Oaks at Epsom. Following a routine examination after the race a metabolite of camphor, a prohibited substance, was found in Aliysa's urine sample and the horse was disqualified by the Disciplinary Committee of the Jockey Club. The Aga Khan sought judicial review of the Committee's decision on the grounds of unfairness.

It was argued on behalf of the applicant that judicial review was the appropriate means of challenging the Committee's decision as the Jockey Club was acting as a public body in respect of its role as the regulator of horseracing in the UK. This was evidenced by the Jockey Club being the sole controller of a significant national activity, by its powers being of a nature and scope that affected a significant section of the public, by its establishment by means of a Royal Charter and because if the Jockey Club had not been granted these powers to act in this way then the government would have been obliged to establish a body capable of carrying out its functions. It was further argued that the relationship between the Jockey Club and those who were involved with racing was not strictly consensual as they had no option but to submit to its jurisdiction if they wished to work in the racing industry in the UK. Therefore it was argued that although the Jockey Club was not exercising governmental or statutory powers, by virtue of its monopolistic control of an activity of national significance that could have an impact on people's rights and ability to earn a living, it was acting as a public body that should be susceptible to judicial review.

The Court rejected these arguments and held that despite the grant of a Royal Charter to the Jockey Club in 1970, it remained a private body because its powers were in no sense governmental and it could not in any way be described as being an emanation of the state. The power accorded to the Jockey Club over all persons associated with racing derived from the agreement of those persons to be bound by the Rules of Racing as administered by the Club. This was a private relationship, the lawfulness of which could be reviewed in the law of contract, or where no contract existed through the supervisory jurisdiction of the courts; it was not a public law relationship that was susceptible to judicial review.

The best chance of the actions of any NGB being found capable of being subjected to judicial review was if the Jockey Club had been declared to be exercising a public function. Since even a body that had been established by Royal Prerogative was found to be acting only as a private entity then, despite their monopolistic attributes and their decisions having an impact on wide sections of society, no NGB can have its decisions judicially reviewed in England and Wales. Despite the ongoing debate that NGBs should be subject to the judicial review procedure, all potential lines of argument now appear to have been closed. This outcome does not leave aggrieved parties without the ability to challenge the decision-making procedures of an NGB before the courts; this can be achieved by invoking the supervisory jurisdiction of the court (*Nagle* v. *Feilden* [1966] 2 QB 633) (below, 2.4.6) by claiming that the decision was in breach of contract (*Aberavon and Port Talbot Rugby Football Club* v. *Welsh Rugby Union Ltd* [2003] EWCA Civ 584) (below, 2.3.3.1), or that the NGB has acted in restraint of trade (*Eastham* v. *Newcastle United FC and the Football Association* [1964] Ch 413) (below, 2.3.4).

In reality the protections sought by applicants through judicial review have been imposed on NGBs through these alternative causes of action. Although it has been argued in some quarters that the procedural protections contained in the Human Rights Act 1998 should be imposed on NGBs post-*Bradley* (below, 2.3.2), it is unlikely that such a claim will be sustained as they are not public authorities; where necessary and appropriate, such protections would be likely to be imposed through the supervisory jurisdiction of the courts as being in the public interest.

2.3.2 Supervisory jurisdiction of the courts

It has long been accepted by the courts that although the decision-making procedures of NGBs and their tribunals cannot be subjected to judicial review under Part 54 Civil Procedure Rules, they can be reviewed under the courts' inherent supervisory jurisdiction at common law (*Nagle* v. *Feilden* [1966] 2 QB 633). There is no need to establish the existence of a contractual relationship to engage this jurisdiction, although where such a contract is in place an additional cause of action may be raised by a claimant (below, 2.3.3). To enable a decision to be reviewed by the courts, the claimant must establish that the NGB exercised a significant degree of control over a significant part of a sport and that its decision had a significant impact on the claimant, particularly where it affects the claimant's ability to earn a living from the sport, by the exercise of its regulatory functions. The NGB is under an obligation to act fairly and within its own rules and the law; it is not obliged to get the decision correct. Complaints about the correctness of a decision should be cured by an appeal to the appropriate appeals or arbitration tribunal, not the courts.

▶ *Bradley* v. *Jockey Club* [2005] EWCA Civ 1056

The applicant, a former jockey and now bloodstock agent, had been a witness in the trial of another jockey on charges of drug smuggling. In the course of cross-examination at the trial, the applicant admitted that he had received gifts from a third party in exchange for information relating to races. He was charged by the Jockey Club with breaching the prohibitions on providing information to prospective gamblers contained in the Rules of Racing. The Disciplinary Committee of the Jockey Club disqualified the applicant for eight years, which was later reduced by an independent Appeals Board to five years. The applicant challenged the length of the disqualification on the basis that it was disproportionate and would have the effect of preventing him from conducting his business as a bloodstock agent.

As there was no contract in place between the applicant and the Appeals Board, it was accepted that the Jockey Club should stand as defendant to the application as it would be the body that implemented the Appeals Board's decision. The Court was unequivocal in its finding that, even in the absence of a contract, the court had jurisdiction to grant declarations and injunctions in respect of the decisions of private tribunals that affect a person's right to work. However such jurisdiction was supervisory only, not appellate in function; the function of the court was not to take the primary decision on the merits of the case but to ensure that the primary decision-maker had operated within lawful limits.

In exercising this supervisory jurisdiction, the court will follow a very similar procedure to that used during a judicial review under Part 54 Civil Procedure Rules, even though it was determining questions of private law. Thus the court would need to determine whether the decision-making procedure followed was fair, whether there had been any errors of law in making the decision and whether any exercise of discretion or judgment, including the penalty imposed, fell within the range of available options open to the tribunal.

Provided that the decision of the NGB, or its designated tribunal, has sufficient impact on the person or organisation that is its subject, the process followed by the sports body is capable of being reviewed by the courts under its common law supervisory jurisdiction. The grounds for review will be the same as those used by the Administrative Court when challenges are made to the decision-making procedures of a public body and include claims that the NGB, or its disciplinary bodies, have acted: outside the scope of their powers as defined in their own rules or regulations; contrary to the general law; contrary to the rules of natural justice; contrary to the rule against bias; unreasonably, irrationally, arbitrarily, capriciously or disproportionately or on the basis of irrelevant considerations or where it has failed to take account of relevant considerations.

A similar approach to the review of a decision-making process was taken in a Football Association Premier League Rule S Arbitration, *Sheffield United Football Club Ltd* v. *Football Association Premier League Ltd* [2007] 3 ISLR SLR 77. The Panel held that the League was the appropriate respondent even though the decision being challenged had been made by an independent tribunal to which disciplinary powers had been delegated. Further, the same grounds of review as had been identified in *Bradley* were accepted as being appropriate in cases falling under the Panel's jurisdiction. Thus the same approach to the review has emerged in both domestic and national sports law.

2.3.3   Actions of the NGB amounting to a breach of contract

In many cases the relationship between the person or body affected by a decision and the NGB making it will have been created by a contract, making it much easier for the aggrieved party to seek clarification of the legality of the NGB's conduct before the courts. Where a contractual nexus between the parties can be established, the party disputing the lawfulness of the decision or the decision-making process of the NGB can therefore bring an action for breach of either the express or implied terms of any contract existing between them. The contractual nexus can be either direct or indirect; it is direct if a contract has been specifically entered into by the parties and indirect where a chain of relationships needs to be established to create the necessary link. Once the existence of a contract can be proved, the claimant can bring an action for either a declaration or injunction that will force the NGB to amend its procedures, or for compensation for any losses caused.

2.3.3.1 Direct contractual relationship

Where a claim is made by a member of a sport's governing body against the NGB itself, proving the existence of a contract between them will be a relatively straightforward exercise.

> ▶ *Aberavon and Port Talbot Rugby Football Club* v. *Welsh Rugby Union Ltd* [2003] EWCA Civ 584
>
> The claimant was a club member of the defendant NGB, the Welsh Rugby Union (WRU). At the end of the 2000–01 season the claimant finished first in the First Division of the WRU National League and sought to be promoted to the Premier League. As a result of changes to the structure of the leagues in Wales before the start of the 2000–01 season, the Premier League was to be reduced in size, the consequence of which was that Aberavon, although the winners of their league, were not promoted.
>
> Aberavon claimed that it was contractually entitled to be promoted on the basis of a promise made by the defendants at a Special General Meeting in 1997 that it would give at least 12 months' notice before implementing any changes to the league structures, particularly if such changes affected promotion and relegation. It was further claimed that the club had expended large amounts of money on securing promotion, which it otherwise would not have done, on the basis that no changes could take place before the start of the 2001–02 season.
>
> The Court found that there was in existence an 'umbrella contract' between the club and the NGB that consisted of the Constitution and bye-laws of the WRU, resolutions passed by it and the membership agreement entered into by the parties. However a fetter on the ability of the WRU to make changes to the way that it ran its business in the way claimed by the claimant could only have been made by means of change to its Constitution. Such a change would have required a formal resolution to have been passed by two-thirds of the voting members present at the SGM in 1997 and as there was no evidence that this had occurred, the claimant failed to establish that the contract in place between the parties had been amended in the way claimed.

Where athletes are concerned, a completed registration form which contains an undertaking that they will observe the bye-laws, resolutions and regulations of the NGB provides evidence of binding contractual relationship between them. On the one hand the athlete agrees to be bound by the relevant rules of the NGB whilst on the other the NGB agrees to operate its decision-making processes fairly (*Jones* v. *Welsh Rugby Union* (unreported) Court of Appeal (Civ), 19 December 1997) (below, 2.4.4).

Where the claim is made by a non-member, for example where an athlete, coach, trainer or owner seeks to challenge the lawfulness of the NGB's actions, then it is still possible to infer the existence of a direct contractual relationship between the parties. In *Korda* (above, 2.2.1) both the Court of Appeal and CAS were prepared to infer a contractual relationship between the parties on the basis of the player's submission to the ITF's drug testing procedures and to the jurisdiction of its Review Board and Appeals Committee. More recently in *Bradley* (above, 2.3.2) a contract between a bloodstock agent and the Jockey Club was implied on the basis of the claimant's choice to submit to the jurisdiction of the Club as though he had been licensed by it.

▶ *Modahl* v. *British Athletic Federation Ltd* **[2001] EWCA Civ 1447**

The claimant was a professional athlete of international standing. Following her participation in an event in Portugal she submitted herself to the anti-doping programme that was being administered according to the rules of the International Amateur Athletics Federation, where her urine sample tested positive for the banned steroid testosterone. She was subsequently found to have committed a doping offence by BAF's Disciplinary Committee and banned from competition for four years. On appeal to the Independent Appeal Panel Modahl was acquitted on the basis that there was scientific evidence that demonstrated a possibility that the samples provided by her had been degraded by bacterial contamination which could have affected the reliability of the results.

The claimant sought compensation from the defendant as she had not been able to earn money from competing for the period of time between the initial finding of guilt and her ultimate acquittal. She claimed that BAF had breached its contract with her by failing to act fairly during the disciplinary process as members of the panel at the first instance hearing were biased against her.

As no written or oral contract had been entered into between the claimant and the defendant, the Court of Appeal had to determine whether there were any grounds for implying the necessary contractual relationship. The Court found that there were three ways that the existence of contract could be justified: the 'club basis' (below, 2.3.3.2), the 'participation basis' and the 'submission basis'. The 'participation basis' provides evidence of the existence of a contractual relationship because of the athlete's repeated participation in events organised or sanctioned by the NGB. As the claimant was an elite level athlete taking part in such events, and in some representative events participating at the invitation of the defendant, both parties were aware of the existence of the applicable anti-doping and disciplinary regimes and that these must be operated fairly. The 'submission basis' is where an athlete submits themselves to the anti-doping testing procedures and makes use of the appeals procedures provided by the NGB. Latham LJ stated that a contract arose on the participation basis whilst Mance LJ thought that a combination of the three bases would provide sufficient evidence of the existence of a contractual relationship. Thus a contract was implied to be in place that contained a term that BAF must operate a fair disciplinary process.

2.3.3.2 Indirect contractual relationship

In some cases, although there is a clear relationship between the person affected by the decision and the NGB making it, it is difficult to identify immediately the existence of a contract. This will usually be because there is at least one other body standing between for example the athlete and the NGB. Traditionally the courts had shown a high degree of reluctance to invent what they saw as fictitious contracts simply for the purposes of legal expediency (*Enderby Town FC* v. *The Football Association* [1971] Ch 591). In these circumstances the affected party would not be left without any possibility of resorting to the law as they would still be able to engage the supervisory jurisdiction of the courts.

However where a claimant is seeking compensation for harm caused by the unlawful conduct of their NGB, the action must be brought in contract as only a declaration or injunction can be applied for under the court's supervisory jurisdiction. This has led claimants to seek to establish a sufficiently strong contractual nexus between themselves and the NGB so that a contract can be implied to be in place to govern their relationship. This can be proved where a series of contracts link an athlete to their club and then to its governing body and ultimately to the relevant ISF.

In *Modahl*, this was referred to as the 'club basis' for implying the existence of a contract between an athlete and the relevant decision-making body and which is established through a chain of mutually interdependent contracts. The first is the contract of membership or employment entered into between the athlete and their club, which will usually contain a term that requires the athlete to submit to the rules and disciplinary procedures of the relevant NGB and/or ISF. The second is the contract of membership between the club and the NGB, which will require the club and all those associated with it to abide by the NGB's rules and disciplinary procedures and those of the relevant ISF. The final contract, again one of membership, is between the NGB and ISF, which will also contain a term requiring the NGB to enforce the rules and disciplinary procedures operated by the ISF. Variations in this chain can occur, as was seen in *Jones* v. *WRU* (above, 2.3.3.1) where the player's registration documents created a direct link with the NGB. However the contractual link between athlete, club, NGB and ISF can be established on the production of comparatively basic documentation.

2.3.3.3 Breach of the contract

Once a contractual relationship has been established, the claimant must then prove that there has been a breach of that contract by the conduct of the NGB. The breach could be of a specific term of the contract, for example where the NGB has not followed its own rules or procedures, or more likely where the NGB has breached an implied term of the contract that the court has found it necessary to include in it for the proper functioning of the relationship. In all cases it has been found that the contract either expressly or impliedly contains terms that mirror the grounds for review found under the court's supervisory jurisdiction (above, 2.3.2). In other words the court will review whether the NGB's procedures were fair, whether there had been any errors of law in making the decision and whether any exercise of discretion or judgment fell within the range of available options open to the tribunal (see below, chapter 2.4 for examples of the impact of challenges to the lawfulness of NGB's procedures before in the courts). Thus even though the decision-making procedures of an NGB cannot be challenged in public law by judicial review, the same outcome can be arrived at by a claimant engaging the supervisory jurisdiction of the court or by bringing an action for breach of contract.

2.3.4 Restraint of trade

The doctrine of restraint of trade aims at ensuring that a person is not restricted from their ability to earn a living (see further, chapter 11). The doctrine has three aspects to it: firstly the claimant must be able to show that they have in fact been restrained from earning a living; secondly the defendant must show that any restraint affecting the claimant is reasonable and proportionate as between them; thirdly the claimant must then show that the restraint is not in the public interest (*Nordenfelt* v. *Maxim Nordenfelt Guns* [1894] AC 535).

The rules and decisions of an NGB, as well as the contracts that it enters into with members and competitors, are all capable of restraining trade. However the mere fact that a restriction exists does not mean that the NGB is acting in restraint of trade. Where the rules are necessary and proportionate for the proper administration of a sport and they are in the public interest, as has been held to be the case in respect of properly administered anti-doping regimes, then the restraint can be justified.

For example the four year ban imposed on Sandra Gasser after she had been found guilty of committing a doping offence was clearly a restraint of trade as it would prevent her from competing as a professional athlete for a considerable period of time. However the ban was considered at the time to be a necessary and proportionate means of protecting the interests of the athletes by deterring drug-taking, and the public by protecting the integrity of the sport (*Gasser* v. *Stinson* (unreported) High Court (QBD), 15 June 1988) (see further, 11.4.2.3).

Furthermore the application of the FA's transfer regulations such that they prevented an out-of-contract player moving to a new employing club without payment of a fee was also a clear restraint of trade. In this case however, as there was no evidence provided to the court to justify why a player should be prevented from taking up new employment in this way, the regulations were struck down (*Eastham* v. *Newcastle United FC and the Football Association* [1964] Ch 413) (see further, 11.4.2.4).

Finally when the Football Association of Wales (FAW) tried to force all Welsh professional clubs to join the newly created League of Wales in 1992, it introduced a rule that prevented any team choosing to remain playing in the English league structure from playing their home games in Wales. This would have impacted significantly on the clubs' ability to attract spectators to their matches and was therefore a restraint of trade. However as the FAW was unable to provide a satisfactory explanation for the necessity of its rule, it was struck out for being unreasonable and disproportionate (*Newport County FC* v. *Football Association of Wales Ltd* (unreported) High Court (QBD), 12 April 1995) (see further, 11.4.1).

Any challenge to a rule on the grounds of restraint of trade must be timely; it must be made at the start of the competition or as soon as the restraint is identified. The affected party cannot play by the rules and then challenge them at a later date when they are adversely affected by them. In *Stevenage Borough FC* v. *Football League Ltd* (unreported) High Court (QBD), 23 July 1996 (see further, 11.4.1) the club argued that the Football League's rules governing promotion were acting as a restraint by preventing it from being promoted from the Football Conference. The Court held that even if there was a restraint, the fact that the club had waited until the end of the season to challenge the rules instead of complaining about their lawfulness from the start caused their action to fail. The Court would not allow the rules of the game to be changed at the end of the competition because of the impact that such a decision would have on the sport as a whole; if everyone has played by the same rules all season, they cannot be changed at the end of the competition for the benefit of one club. Similar reasoning was used by the High Court to refuse Dwain Chambers' application for an injunction that would have enabled him to compete in the 2008 Olympic Games in Beijing (*Chambers* v. *British Olympic Association* [2008] EWHC 2028 (QBD)) (below, Hot Topic).

The extension of the supervisory jurisdiction of the courts (above, 2.3.2) and developments in UK and EU competition law (see further, chapters 3.2 and 12) mean that this cause of action is only infrequently relied upon when challenging the decisions of an NGB. However significant challenges have been made to the restrictive practices of many NGBs using the doctrine of restraint of trade over the years and it remains a powerful means of reviewing the lawfulness of such restraints.

2.4 The impact of national sports law on disciplinary and appeals tribunals

The structure of most NGBs' disciplinary mechanisms used to follow the same basic pattern. The executive committee, comprising representatives of the NGB's members, would appoint the members of the disciplinary tribunal and, where necessary, the members of any second tier appeals tribunal. Often, though not always, the disciplinary tribunal members would be a sub-committee of the national executive committee. In some cases the members of the appeals tribunal would be drawn from the same sub-committee as the members of the first instance disciplinary tribunal. It was possible therefore for a member of the rule-making body to sit on the panel which had the task of interpreting and enforcing those rules. It was also possible for that same person to sit on the appeals tribunal when they had already been a member of the panel that heard the initial complaint.

In public law terms there was no effective separation of powers between the various roles being carried out by the legislative, executive and judicial branches of the governing body and no ability for one part of the system to provide the necessary checks and balances to the decision-making processes of the other parts because they were all too closely interlinked. Further, questions began to be raised about whether the defendant in a disciplinary system that operated in this way was receiving a fair hearing. Despite Lord Denning MR's faith in NGBs being capable of regulating themselves more effectively without the intervention of lawyers (above, 2.1), as sports participants began to have more at stake on the outcome of a disciplinary hearing, it became apparent that changes to NGBs' procedures were required to ensure that a fair hearing was given to all who appeared before them. Thus as a body of national sports law began to develop following the legal challenges made to NGBs' decision-making procedures, the norms adhered to by these tribunals and committees began to be juridified, taking on a more openly legalistic approach to sporting justice. The following examples, which have resulted from a variety of challenges brought under the supervisory jurisdiction of the courts, or for breaches of contract, or because of restraints of trade, demonstrate how this process of juridification has occurred over time.

2.4.1 The NGB must act within its own rules and in accordance with the law

In *Aberavon v. WRU* (above, 2.3.3.1) the claimant argued that the WRU was contractually obliged to follow a rule that, it was claimed, had been amended at a Special General Meeting of the Union. The amended rule would have required the WRU to give 12 months' notice to its members, including Aberavon, before implementing changes to the league structures in Wales. If the amended rule was followed Aberavon would have been promoted to the Premier League. The Court held that the WRU could only amend its own rules by following the procedures laid down in them. The change claimed by Aberavon would have required two-thirds of the members present at the SGM to vote in favour of the rule change. As there was no evidence that this procedure had been followed, the rule stood in its original form, enabling the WRU to alter the league structures and to deny promotion to Aberavon.

As well as following their own rules and the decision-making procedures laid down in them, NGBs must also act within the general law. Each of the following sections provides specific instances of where breaches or misinterpretations of the law, or of general principles of the law, have been raised by claimants who have been affected by the conduct of NGBs.

2.4.2 The NGB must not base its decision on errors of fact

When hearing the appeal against the decision of the Disciplinary Committee in *Modahl* v. *BAF* (above, 2.3.3.1) the Appeal Panel held that the original finding of guilt had been based on an error of fact. New scientific evidence that had not been available at the first instance hearing provided evidence of a possibility that the samples provided by Modahl had been degraded by bacterial contamination; this in turn could have affected the reliability of the results. Thus as the factual basis on which the Disciplinary Committee based its decision was wrong, the Appeal Panel overturned its decision and acquitted Modahl of any wrongdoing.

2.4.3 The NGB must not take into account irrelevant considerations

This ground of challenge to an NGB's conduct has two bases; firstly that the NGB must take into consideration all relevant factors and secondly that it must not take into account any irrelevant considerations. Challenges to a decision on these grounds often form an integral aspect of a claim that the NGB has acted unreasonably in coming to its decision (below, 2.4.6).

> ▶ *Sheffield United Football Club Ltd* v. *Football Association Premier League Ltd* [2007] 3 **ISLR SLR 77**
>
> As a result of the Premier League's Disciplinary Commission failing to deduct points from West Ham United FC for fielding an ineligible player, Sheffield United FC challenged the Commission's decision before an arbitration panel constituted under s.S Football Association Premier League Rules. The basis of Sheffield United's claim was that in coming to its decision on the penalty to be imposed on West Ham, the Disciplinary Commission had taken into account irrelevant considerations whilst failing to take proper account of other relevant considerations. Firstly Sheffield United challenged the Disciplinary Commission's decision to give weight to West Ham being under new ownership at the time that the penalty was imposed as this did not prevent the breach of the rules from having taken place nor its impact on the Premier League in general and Sheffield United in particular. Secondly, by taking into account that a deduction in points after the completion of the season would guarantee West Ham's relegation, the Disciplinary Commission failed to consider that by imposing only a fine, Sheffield United was condemned to be relegated when it should not have been. Finally, when taking account of the adverse impact that relegation would have on the players and fans of West Ham, no account had been taken of the impact that relegation would have on Sheffield United, its players and fans. Furthermore Sheffield United claimed that the Commission had failed to take into account the need to restore competitive balance to the league and that it had given insufficient weight to the deliberateness of the deceit practised by West Ham in concealing the true nature of Tevez's contractual position.
>
> The panel held that although on the basis of these claims it would have made a points deduction, the Disciplinary Commission's decision to impose only a fine on West Ham was within the reasonable range of conclusions that it could have reached. Thus despite the admitted and deliberate breach of the rules practised by West Ham and the negative impact that the decision had on the finances of Sheffield United and the morale of its players and fans, the original penalty was upheld.

2.4.4 The NGB must act in accordance with the rules of natural justice

The rules of natural justice guarantee that certain minimum standards of procedural fairness are conformed to by NGBs and their disciplinary panels. There is no definitive list of rules with which an NGB's procedures must always comply; instead it is under an obligation to act fairly in its dealings with those who are affected by its decisions and those of its associated tribunals. The fluid definition given by the courts to 'fairness' means that different safeguards can be required depending on whether the affected person is applying to join a body, or where they have an expectation that they will be treated in a particular way, or where they have been brought before a disciplinary tribunal that has the power to suspend them from participation in the sport (*McInnes* v. *Onslow-Fane* [1978] 1 WLR 1520). Moreover the need for procedural safeguards can change over time, for example where the informal procedures established to hear cases involving amateur players no longer meet the requirements of hearings involving highly paid professionals (*Jones* v. *WRU*) (below).

From the cases where challenges have been made to the procedures followed by NGBs, or the panels to which they have delegated jurisdiction to hear specific cases, a series of procedural requirements can be identified. Firstly the NGB is under a general duty to act fairly when coming to its decisions, though consideration is always given to NGBs being private domestic bodies and not courts or tribunals that are accountable to public law (*Enderby Town FC* v. *The Football Association* [1971] Ch 591).

Secondly the NGB must allow the person subject to its jurisdiction a proper opportunity to be heard. This requires that the NGB provide the person who will be affected by its decision with details of the case against them, with the opportunity to respond to and cross-examine the case against them and the ability to adduce evidence in support of their own case.

▶ *Jones* v. *Welsh Rugby Union* **(unreported) High Court (QBD), 27 February 1997**

Jones was a professional rugby union player who had been sent off for fighting during a league game. At his disciplinary hearing before the WRU's Disciplinary Committee, Jones was not permitted to question the evidence put forward by the referee nor to put forward his own version of events, nor was he allowed to be formally represented, although a club representative was allowed to speak on his behalf as he suffered from a stammer. Furthermore the Disciplinary Committee retired to consider video evidence of the incident in private and did not allow Jones to provide his own interpretation or explanation of the events as they unfolded. As a result the Disciplinary Committee found Jones guilty of punching an opponent and banned him from playing for four weeks.

Jones applied to the High Court for a declaration that the WRU had acted in breach of contract by failing to provide him with a fair hearing. The Court held that the Disciplinary Committee's failure to examine the video in public, which was an important part of the evidence against Jones, its failure to allow him to challenge the evidence laid against him and the failure to allow him to adduce evidence in his own defence constituted procedural defects that resulted in a failure to provide him with a fair hearing.

The original decision of the Disciplinary Committee was set aside and the WRU were required to amend their disciplinary procedures before rehearing the case. Despite the new procedural safeguards being in place, Jones failed to attend the new hearing and was again banned for four weeks (*Jones* v. *WRU* (unreported) Court of Appeal (Civ), 19 December 1997).

The conclusion of the Court was less clear in respect of the right of the player to be represented. An outright ban on representation will be held to be unfair, though an NGB can retain the discretion to allow a legal or other representative to be present at a hearing. In reality most NGBs do now allow those appearing before them to be represented and it is good practice to do so.

Thirdly the NGB must require an appropriate burden of proof in order for a case to be both proved and defended. Where the NGB is seeking to suspend a player or club, it must be prepared to prove its case to a high standard, generally so that the tribunal is satisfied that the ban should be imposed. Where the burden falls on the player or club, it will be to prove their version of events or to disprove the case against them on the balance of probabilities. In doping cases the NGB is permitted to presume the liability of a participant whose A and B samples have tested positive for a prohibited substance. However the participant must be given the opportunity to rebut any such presumption on the balance of probabilities (*Wilander* v. *Tobin (No.1)* (unreported) Court of Appeal (Civ), 26 March 1996).

Fourthly, when determining whether or not the procedures followed by an NGB are defective, it is important that the court examines the entire decision-making process not just individual aspects of it. Thus where there are defects at the stage of the initial hearing, there is no unfairness to the respondent where they have been able to make recourse to an appropriate appeals tribunal that rectifies the problem encountered at first instance (*Modahl* v. *British Athletic Federation (No.2)* [2001] EWCA Civ 1447) (above, 2.3.3.1).

It is worth noting that the rules of natural justice are supplemented by the protections contained in the European Convention on Human Rights and Fundamental Freedoms as enacted by the Human Rights Act 1998, where the hearing is before a tribunal that is subject to public law. Although the decisions of the national courts will be informed by these rights when hearing sports law cases, it must be remembered that NGBs are not public bodies and so, at present, are not directly affected by the Convention (*Bradley* v. *Jockey Club* [2005] EWCA Civ 1056) (above, 2.3.2).

2.4.5 The NGB must not reach its decision under the influence of bias

The person or body responsible for making a decision must neither show bias towards one outcome or another, nor must there be a perception of bias in the decision-making process; justice must not only be done, it must be seen to be done. Actual bias is where the decision-maker demonstrates a predisposition against a party's case for reasons unconnected with its merits. The test for establishing a perception of bias is objective and requires that a fair-minded person would conclude on the facts that there was a real possibility that the decision-maker was biased. Furthermore the decision-maker must not have any financial interest in the outcome of the decision.

One of the claims put forward in the *Modhal* litigation was that certain members of the Disciplinary Committee were biased against the athlete and had prejudged the case against her. The Court of Appeal found that there was no evidence of actual bias and could find no perception that the decision-making body had been tainted by bias. The Court also held that even if members of the Disciplinary Committee had reached a biased conclusion, this would have been rendered irrelevant as the unbiased decision of the Appeal Panel would have cured any defects in the first instance hearing.

In *Flaherty* v. *National Greyhound Racing Club* [2005] EWCA Civ 1117, actual bias and a perception of bias was alleged against a witness and procedural impropriety was alleged on the basis that the chief executive of the defendants retired with the panel members whilst they discussed the merits of the case in private. The Court of Appeal rejected any allegations of bias concerning the witness before turning to the issue concerning the presence of the chief executive at the deliberations. Although this was an irregularity that had the potential to undermine the separation of power between the executive and judicial braches of the defendant, the chief executive's explanation that he was acting as a clerk who was advising the panel only on how previous cases had been determined and on interpretations of the rules of the Club was accepted by the court. As this was a minor defect in the procedure it did not so taint the proceedings as to render them either biased or unfair.

2.4.6   The NGB must not act unreasonably, arbitrarily or capriciously

A claim of unreasonable, arbitrary or capricious conduct by the NGB in arriving at its decision can only be established where the person challenging its findings can prove that no similarly constituted body that had properly instructed itself according to the rules by which it was governed could have reached the same conclusion. In *Nagle* v. *Feilden* [1966] 2 QB 633, the Jockey Club had repeatedly refused to grant the applicant a trainer's licence on the sole ground that she was a woman. The Court or Appeal held that in doing so, the Club was acting arbitrarily and capriciously and that it should consider her application on its merits not on her gender.

The boundaries of unreasonableness have been extended to include the ability of the court to analyse the proportionality of the punishments handed down by an NGB or its disciplinary panel. In *Bradley* (above, 2.3.2) the claimant argued that a suspension from all activities associated with racing for five years would effectively prevent him from being able to act as a bloodstock agent. The Court of Appeal found that the decision of the Appeals Board was within range of acceptable responses available to it and therefore a reasonable and proportionate punishment.

2.4.7   The development of the current structural framework

As a result of these developments, all NGBs now ensure that the rules of natural justice are adhered to in their tribunals. This has in turn led to an increased juridification of the procedures that are followed in many sports hearings and the ways in which the panels' decisions are formulated. Further, many now also ensure that there is complete separation of powers between the rule-making body and the members of the disciplinary panels, particularly at the appeals level. Where, usually for reasons of cost, it is not reasonably practicable for an NGB to operate such a system, it will often allow an appeal to a specialist independent tribunal such as Sports Disputes UK, which operates in much the same way as CAS does but at a national level (see further, 3.3), ensuring that the standard of justice now available from NGBs is approaching that which is available before the courts.

Hot topic . . .

DWAIN CHAMBERS AND THE LEGALITY OF THE OLYMPIC BAN FOR DOPING

On 12 July 2008 Dwain Chambers won the 100m at the Olympic Trials. Under normal circumstances he would have been invited by the British Olympic Association (BOA) to represent Team GB in this event at the Olympic Games in Beijing. However as a person who had previously been found guilty of a serious doping offence, Chambers was not considered to be eligible for selection under the BOA's Bye-law 25. The following week Chambers applied to the High Court for an interlocutory injunction that would prevent the BOA from enforcing Bye-law 25 and in effect force them to select him for the 100m at the Olympics.

The grounds of his claim were that the bye-law operated as a restraint of trade at common law, that it was in conflict with Arts.101 and 102 Treaty on the Functioning of the European Union (ex Arts.81 and 82 ECT) and that it was irrational and should be set aside under the court's supervisory jurisdiction; the EU law challenges were not pursued at the hearing. As this was an application for an injunction and not a full trial of the legality of Bye-law 25, the judge would normally only have to be satisfied that the applicant had proved that he had a serious issue to be tried. However in this case if the injunction was granted the final trial would never take place as Chambers would have already competed in Beijing and would see no point in arguing further about its lawfulness. In such circumstances the judge is permitted to take into account the underlying merits of the case and will only grant an injunction where satisfied with a high degree of assurance that the applicant will succeed at trial.

To establish that the bye-law was a restraint of trade, Chambers had to prove that it prevented him from earning his living as a professional athlete. The Court held that it would be difficult for Chambers to establish that his ability to earn money as an athlete had been restrained because he was only prevented from competing in one championship, the Olympics, where in any event no prize money is awarded. Further it was held unlikely that he would have been placed highly enough in his event to earn significant sums through sponsorships and endorsements as a result of his participation in the Games. The judge also stated that even if this reasoning was wrong, he considered the bye-law to be necessary and proportionate for pursuing a legitimate aim of the BOA, namely to protect the Olympic ideal of fair play. Therefore the judge was not sufficiently satisfied that there was an actionable restraint of trade to grant the injunction.

The judge also refused to exercise the court's supervisory discretion on the grounds of delay, as occurred in the *Stevenage Borough FC* case. Chambers was well aware of Bye-law 25 at the time that he resumed his athletic career in 2008 and that the BOA would be unlikely to select him because of his previous doping infringement. He could therefore have made his challenge at any time from when he restarted his training programme with the intent of competing in Beijing. Instead he left making his application so late that the hearing took place less than 72 hours before the BOA had to send its final team selection to the International Olympic Committee (IOC) and no full trial of the issues was possible. As a result the judge refused to grant an injunction and Chambers did not go to Beijing.

The most straightforward ground for denying the injunction was delay; if Chambers wanted to challenge the BOA's eligibility rules, of which all athletes were aware, he should have done so at the earliest opportunity not at the last minute when a proper trial of the issues could not be undertaken. Unfortunately the hurried nature of the litigation means that the discussions on restraint of trade leave many issues inadequately resolved. Bye-law 25 does appear to be a restraint on an athlete's ability to earn money from their event, even if such earnings are difficult to quantify because they will take the form of appearance money and winnings at competitions after the Olympics or sponsorship agreements entered into as a result of participation in the Games. Whether such a restraint has a sufficient impact on an athlete's earning power to be unlawful however was never fully examined.

Moreover the discussions on proportionality were unconvincing. Although the protection of the ethos and ideals of the Olympics is undoubtedly a legitimate goal of the BOA, its automatic refusal to consider in any capacity a person who has been found guilty of a serious doping offence for life does not take into account that all ISFs anticipate the possibility of an athlete's rehabilitation after serving a period of suspension. The assumption of Bye-law 25 appears to be that such a person can never be rehabilitated and can never set a good example to young athletes.

In response to the furore generated by the Chambers litigation, the IOC introduced Rule 45 Olympic Charter which prevents a person who has committed a doping offence that has resulted in the imposition of a ban of six months or more from entering the next edition of the Games after the end of their ban (see further, chapter 14.1.2). Despite the impact that this Rule could have on the relatively short career of a professional sportsperson, it is much more likely to be found to be proportionate than the complete refusal of the BOA to consider such a person as eligible to compete in or attend the Olympic Games in any capacity whatsoever. Therefore as the lawfulness of the BOA's bye-law was not fully examined at trial, further challenges are likely in the future particularly if its rules are not brought into line with those of the IOC, and in the light of the European Court of Justice's decisions in *Meca-Medina and Majcen* v. *Commision of the European Communities* (C-519/04 P) [2006] ECR I-6991 and *Motosykletistiki Omospondia Ellados NPID (MOTOE)* v. *Greece* (C-49/07) [2008] ECR I-4863 (see further, chapter 3.2.2).

Summary

2.1 A symbiotic relationship has developed between domestic and national sports law in respect of challenges to the decision-making procedures operated by NGBs. Where those affected by the decisions of NGBs have successfully challenged their unlawful practices before the courts, NGBs have changed their procedures and developed new procedural norms. As NGBs' procedures have become increasingly juridified, the decisions of sporting and legal tribunals are able to inform each other on the most effective means of resolving sports disputes.

2.2 NGBs have no special legal status in English law. Their existence is based on consensus with their power deriving from the agreement of their members to be subject to their rules. As a result many sporting relationships are based on either express or implied contracts. Most NGBs are now companies limited by guarantee so that the body itself has a separate legal identity that can be sued, rather than its members being exposed to the prospect of individual liability if it remains as an unincorporated association.

2.3 There are three main causes of action by which the decision of an NGB can be challenged. Firstly where there is no contract in place between the parties the challenger can invoke the supervisory jurisdiction of the court to review the lawfulness of the decision-making process. Secondly where a contract is in place between the parties the challenger can allege that the NGB is in breach of contract by acting unlawfully. Where there is no contract expressly entered into by the parties a contractual relationship can be implied on one of three bases: the club basis, the participation basis and the submission basis. Thirdly the challenger can claim that the decision on the NGB operates in restraint of trade. A challenger will be successful against an NGB where it has acted unfairly, outside of the jurisdiction granted to it by its own rules or unlawfully. NGBs cannot be subjected to the judicial review process under Part 54 Civil Procedure Rules as they are not public bodies.

2.4 As a result of the challenges made to the conduct of NGBs and their disciplinary tribunals the procedures followed by them have become increasingly juridified. NGBs must act within their own rules and within the law, they must only take into account relevant considerations and not irrelevant factors and they must act in accordance with the rules of natural justice and procedural fairness by allowing persons appearing before them a proper opportunity to be heard, to defend themselves and to be adequately represented. Further, NGBs must make their decisions fairly and without bias and impose reasonable and proportionate sanctions on those who are found to be in breach of their rules.

Further reading

Lewis and Taylor (eds), *Sport: Law and Practice* (2nd edn, 2008, Tottel) ch A4

Bradley and Ewing, *Constitutional and Administrative Law* (14th edn, 2007, Longman) chs 5, 30 and 31

Anderson, 'An accident of history: why the decisions of sports governing bodies are not amenable to judicial review' (2006) 35(3) *Common Law World Review* 173

Further reading cont'd

Beloff, 'Judicial review in England and Wales: the state of the art revisited' (2009) 13(2) *Jersey and Guernsey Law Review* 143

Beloff, 'Watching out for the googly: judicial review in the world of sport' (2009) 14(2) *Judicial Review* 136

Ellson and Lohn, 'Whose rules are we playing by?' (2005) 3(2) *Entertainment and Sports Law Journal*, online

Taylor and O'Sullivan, 'How should national governing bodies of sport be governed in the UK? An exploratory study of board structure' (2009) 17(6) *Corporate Governance* 681

Links to relevant websites can be found at www.palgrave.com/law/james

Chapter 3
Global and European sports law

Key words

> **Lex sportiva** – the body of sports-specific jurisprudence and redefined legal norms created mainly by the Court of Arbitration for Sport for application in sports law cases.
> **Member state** – one of the 27 nation states that are full members of the European Union.
> **Undertaking** – an entity that is, for the purposes of European Union law, engaged in economic activity, irrespective of its legal form or the way that it is financed.

3.1 The relationship between global and European sports law

In the same way that national governing bodies (NGBs) operate their own internal quasi-legal system, so too do the international sports federations (ISFs). The role of the ISFs in this framework usually takes one or more of four forms. Firstly the ISF will be responsible for defining the rules of the sport that it governs and for ensuring harmonisation in the implementation of those rules throughout the world. Secondly it can ratify the decisions of NGBs and ensure that they are enforced worldwide. This ensures that, for example, a person banned from playing or coaching a sport in the UK does not simply move to France to ply their trade. Thirdly the ISF may provide an appellate body to which appeals against the decisions of an NGB can be made. Fourthly the ISF itself may provide the necessary disciplinary structures to be used at international representative fixtures, at other events that it organises or where a dispute contains a cross-border element. Where a dispute still remains after the exhaustion of any available internal remedies, most major ISFs now allow an appeal to be made to the Court of Arbitration for Sport (CAS) for final determination of the matter.

As was the case with the relationship between domestic and national sports law, the interactions between and overlap of global, international and European sports law only came to light with the increased internationalisation and commercialisation of sport. When the rules, decisions and common practices of ISFs began to affect sports participants' earnings, or spectators' safety when travelling abroad, or the ability of clubs to maximise their earnings, sports law began to develop a transnational perspective.

This chapter will focus on global and European sports law. As far as the creation of law and legal norms is concerned, international sports law is of much less significance than its two much more developed relations. The most important source of international sports law is that created by the Council of Europe (see further, chapter 1.6). However as the Conventions and Resolutions passed by the Council are not automatically binding on the UK Parliament, its role is much more relevant to the development of international sports policy and cooperation rather than sports law. This is evidenced most recently by the Council of Ministers of the Council of Europe adopting Resolution CM/Res (2007)/8 which created the Enlarged Partial Agreement on Sport. This sub-Convention level cooperation agreement focuses the work of the Council on sports ethics and the protection of the autonomy of sport from political interference rather than creating specific legal frameworks within which sport can function more effectively.

European sports law is created by the institutions of the European Union (EU) and is currently found almost entirely in the decisions of the European Court of Justice (ECJ) (below, 3.2 and further, chapter 12). However following the ratification of the Treaty on the Functioning of the European Union (TFEU), there is now scope for a more direct and proactive approach to its creation under Arts.6 and 165 (see further, chapter 1.5.3). EU law is engaged when the rules, decisions or actions of a person, undertaking or member state breach the provisions of the TFEU. Thus although not mentioned in previous Treaties, EU law has always applied to sport even though the ISFs and NGBs have often refused to acknowledge that this is the case. Where sports disputes are concerned, this engagement occurs most commonly when there is an interference with the freedom of movement of workers contrary to Art.45 (ex Art.39 ECT), the freedom of establishment under Art.49 (ex Art.43 ECT), the freedom to provide services contrary to Art.56 (ex Art.49 ECT) and/or an infringement of competition law, which is governed by Arts.101 and 102 (ex Arts.81 and 82 ECT) (below, 3.2.3–6).

Global sports law is the jurisprudence created by the tribunals operated by ISFs, such as FIFA's Dispute Resolution Chamber, and CAS. It is only ever engaged by the agreement of the parties. This can be by means of a contractual obligation imposed on a participant through their standard form employment contract (see further, chapters 2.2.1 and 2.3.3) or by a specific agreement between the parties to submit to arbitration before CAS. The sport-specific tribunals ensure that the rules of an ISF are imposed uniformly on all those connected with its sport with the aim of creating harmonisation of interpretation and punishment wherever in the world the sport is played. On top of this ideal, CAS also aims at developing a harmonised approach across all sports through the creation of a *lex sportiva* (below, 3.3).

Much of the time these panels are applying national and/or EU law or the underlying generic legal principles that are common to all modern legal systems, the *jus commune*, rather than creating completely new legal norms. However it is their development of the meaning of the 'specificity of sport', based loosely on the reasoning of the ECJ in *Meca-Medina and Majcen* v. *Commission* (C-519/04 P) [2006] ECR I-6991, and their ability to hear cases that might otherwise cause significant problems to both sport and the law if heard by national courts, as was the case in *FC Shaktar Donetsk* v. *Matazulem and Real Zaragoza SAD and FIFA* CAS 2008/A/1519 and 1520 (below, 3.3.2.1 and chapter 12.2.2.2), that demonstrate the real importance of global sports law. As ISFs' final appeals tribunals in general and CAS in particular appear to be more prepared than the courts to examine the sporting context from which these disputes arise rather than mechanically applying the letter of the law, global sports law has developed a more sports-sympathetic approach to their resolution.

The relationship between global and European sports law is an uneasy one with both CAS and the ECJ able to claim jurisdiction over the same disputes. There is no doubt that their decisions can influence each other. However although CAS will apply EU law where necessary and appropriate to a dispute before it and the implementation of its decisions will be subject to EU law, the ECJ is not similarly bound to take account of the decisions of CAS. Therefore it is imperative that any athlete challenging the conduct of an ISF begins their action in the correct forum as there is at least a possibility of the two bodies reaching different answers to the case before them.

As all cases examine the conduct complained of in the context of the needs of the sport and as the principles underpinning the *lex sportiva* being developed by CAS are common to EU law and the laws of all EU member states, they will usually arrive at the same result. This is of particular importance because of the number of applications heard by CAS and the final appeals tribunals of many ISFs that contain a significant EU law element, especially in the fields of anti-doping regulation and transnational player transfers. It would defeat the purpose of these panels if they got the law wrong and the affected party was able to assert their rights before the ECJ at a later date, as occurred in *Union Royale Belge des Societes de Football Association ASBL v. Bosman* (Case C-415/93) [1995] ECR I-4921. However a tension will remain whilst the ISFs continue to try to find ways around the decisions of the ECJ that they do not like and the ECJ continues to champion the supremacy of EU law. This is where the real difference between global sports law and European sports law is likely to emerge.

3.2 The applicability of EU law to sport

The development of European sports law has been relatively slow, piecemeal and reactive. Until the implementation of Art.165 TFEU, no EU institution had the specific competence to act on issues relating to sport. Thus the evolution of European sports law has to be traced through the jurisprudence of the ECJ and its interpretations of how EU law applies to sports disputes in the references and appeals that have come before it and in the decisions of the European Commission on the applicability of competition law to sport. This meant that it could take many years for a sports-specific test to develop as only relatively few references whose subject is a sports dispute are made to the ECJ. This problem is further compounded by many of those affected by the conduct of an ISF challenging its practices only before the sport's internal tribunals. Thus it has taken nearly 40 years for the ECJ to produce a working definition of when and why EU law is engaged by a sports dispute.

This slow pace of development has been affected by the attitudes of all concerned with sport towards what is often seen as the intrusion of EU law into their relationships with each other. In the same way that NGBs appeared to assume that national law either should not apply to them, or if it did then it should apply differently or on their terms, it also appeared that the ISFs, and many of the players over whom they exercised control, assumed that EU law did not apply to them either. As a result, practices that are clearly contrary to EU law became entrenched in sport instead of being challenged before the appropriate courts. This problem appeared to be further compounded by an entirely erroneous belief that because some major ISFs were based outside of the EU, for example in Switzerland, then EU law was not applicable to their conduct. Provided that the conduct of an undertaking has an impact on the rights protected by the Treaty on the Functioning of the European Union (TFEU) then EU law is engaged whenever it affects events on EU territory.

Any sports dispute can engage EU law if a provision of the TFEU is contravened by the conduct or practices of a club, NGB or ISF. This occurs most frequently where an unlawful restriction is placed on the freedom granted to workers to move to another member state in order to take up an offer of work under Art.45 (ex Art.39 ECT), or on their freedom to establish in another member state under Art.49 (ex Art.43 ECT), or on their freedom to provide services in another member state under Art.56 (ex Art.49 ECT), or where there has been a breach of the competition provisions in Arts.101 and 102 (ex Arts.81 and 82 ECT) by either the use of a restrictive practice or the abuse of a dominant position in a specific market. Following *Deutscher Handballbund eV* v. *Kolpak* (Case C-438/00) [2003] ECR I-4135 and *Simutenkov* v. *Ministerio de Educacion y Cultura* (Case C-265/03) [2005] ECR I-2579, rights similar to those protected by the TFEU can in certain circumstances be relied on by citizens of countries with which the EU has Association Agreements and Agreements on Partnership and Cooperation. This enabled Kolpak, a Slovakian national and professional handball player (prior to Slovakia's accession to the EU in 2004), and Simutenkov, a Russian national and professional footballer, to rely on the employment and non-discrimination protections contained in their home countries' Agreements with the EU and not be treated as a 'foreign' players under their ISFs' nationality rules.

3.2.1 The European Court of Justice's jurisdiction to hear disputes – making a reference under Art.267 TFEU (ex Art.234 ECT)

Where sports disputes are concerned, the usual procedure for seeking a preliminary ruling on the interpretation of the TFEU will be by invoking the jurisdiction of the ECJ under Art.267 TFEU. Where a national court considers that such an interpretation is necessary for it to be able to pass judgment on the case before it, the national court may submit specific questions to the ECJ requesting it to clarify the meaning of the appropriate issue of EU law; if this situation arises before the final court of appeal in a member state, for example the Supreme Court in the UK, then the court must refer the issue to the ECJ.

Three important procedural issues must be noted at this point. Firstly it is the national court, not one or more of the parties to the dispute, which makes the reference to the ECJ under Art.267. Secondly the national court must provide the full legal and factual context to the ECJ so that the Court is in a position to give the appropriate general guidance on how the TFEU should be interpreted. If insufficient information is provided to the ECJ, it may not be in a position to show that it was in fact necessary to make the interpretations requested of it. Thirdly the ECJ does not act as an appellate court when references are made to it under Art.267; its purpose is to provide authoritative interpretations of the TFEU that can then be applied in all courts throughout the EU, not just in the case currently before it. Thus, having answered the questions put to it in its preliminary ruling, the ECJ will return the case to the national court for a final ruling according to the law of the member state from which the reference originated (*Van Gend en Loos* v. *Nederlandse Administratie der Belastingen* (Case 26/62) [1963] ECR 1).

3.2.2 The European Court of Justice's jurisdiction to hear sports disputes

Once it is established that EU law is at least in principle engaged by the dispute, it is then necessary to determine whether sport is an appropriate context in which EU law should be enforced.

▶ *Walrave and Koch v. Association Union Cycliste Internationale* (Case 36/74) [1974] ECR 1405

The two claimants were employed as pacemakers for cyclists in competitions organised by the defendant ISF, the UCI. Each cyclist had their own individual pacemaker with whom they worked as a team and even at world championship events it was not unusual for each team member to be of a different nationality; for example the claimants were Dutch yet they usually worked with Belgian or German cyclists. In 1970 the UCI announced that from 1973 all pacemakers must be of the same nationality as the cyclists with whom they were working. As this rule change would have a significant impact on the claimants' ability to earn a living from their chosen profession, they challenged its compatibility with Arts.18, 45 and 56 TFEU (ex Arts.6, 48 and 59 TEEC) by claiming that they were being discriminated against on the grounds of their nationality.

In response to the questions posed by the Utrecht District Court, the ECJ made a number of important rulings concerning the applicability of EU law to sporting relationships. Firstly it held that Arts.18, 45 and 56 apply to the rules of collective regulatory bodies such as ISFs, where they regulate participants' employment rights and their ability to provide their services to others. As this rule restricted the claimants' ability to earn a living, it constituted a regulation affecting their right to work for, or provide services to, elite cyclists. Secondly it held that sporting relationships will be subject to EU law only where they constitute an 'economic activity'. As the two claimants were both professional pacemakers who were paid for their work, the rule change clearly affected an 'economic activity' with which they were engaged. Thirdly the ECJ held that where the rules of an ISF were concerned only with matters of a 'purely sporting interest' then EU law did not apply, even where the rules affected a person's economic interests. The ECJ explained that as the rule concerned the composition of a national representative team competing in the World Championships and was therefore nothing to do with economic activity, the rule was not subject to EU law provided that it was limited to achieving only its proper object. In the case, the proper objective was the organisation of international representative competitive cycling events and the rule was therefore lawful.

The difficulty inherent in *Walrave* is that it required a trial court to distinguish between rules that have economic effects and those that are for purely sporting purposes, when in reality most rules will fall into both categories. In the intervening years sport has changed dramatically so that it is unlikely that the ECJ would today hold that international representative sport is 'nothing to do with economic activity' and therefore outside of the scope of EU law. The increased commercialisation and internationalisation of much elite sport will mean that almost every dispute involving a professional athlete will be an 'economic activity' that will, at least on the face of it, engage EU law. Thus although a similar outcome to that produced by the ECJ in *Walrave* would be reached today, it would be on modified grounds; instead of examining only whether or not the rule affects an economic activity, the ECJ has begun to develop a test that requires the courts to determine whether the rule was inherent in the proper organisation of the sporting competition in question.

▶ *Meca-Medina and Majcen* v. *Commission* (C-519/04 P) [2006] ECR I-6991

The applicants were professional swimmers who had been banned for two years by their ISF, FINA, after having tested positive for the banned substance nandrolone. In the first instance they complained to the European Commission that the anti-doping regime operated by FINA and the IOC was anti-competitive contrary to Arts.101 and 102 TFEU (ex Arts.81 and 82 ECT). Following the Commission's rejection of their complaint they applied to the European Court of First Instance (CFI) for an annulment of its decision under Art.263 TFEU (ex Art.230 ECT); this was also rejected. Finally the applicants appealed to the ECJ to determine the legality of the anti-doping procedures operated by FINA and the IOC and of the punishments imposed upon them.

The ECJ began by stating, in accordance with *Walrave* and the decisions following it, that sport is subject to EU law when it constitutes an economic activity and that EU law is not engaged by rules that are of a purely sporting interest. It made the further point that where the participants are either employed or paid for their services, they are engaged in an economic activity. However as it is often not easy to distinguish clearly between rules impacting on an economic activity and those that are of a purely sporting interest, trying to create such a distinction can be somewhat artificial and unhelpful. In reality many rules and procedures of ISFs, including those establishing anti-doping regimes, fall into both categories.

Therefore in circumstances where what appears to be a purely sporting purpose has at least an incidental economic impact, the relationship between the athletes and FINA can be subject to the provisions of the TFEU. To be lawful, FINA and the IOC would have to be able to demonstrate that their anti-doping procedures complied with Arts.101 and 102 TFEU. In order to do this the ECJ held that it must take account of the overall context in which the rules were adopted, whether their objectives were legitimate and whether any restrictive consequences of the rules were inherent in the pursuit of those legitimate objectives and proportionate to their achievement. In this case the overall objectives of the rules were to combat doping in order to ensure that the sport was conducted fairly, that equality of chance was safeguarded for the athletes, that their health was protected and that the integrity and objectivity of competitive sport and its ethical values were upheld.

To be lawful, both the definition of the offence of doping and the imposition of the penalties following any infringement of the rules had to comply with the provisions of the TFEU. The ECJ held that both the anti-doping regime operated by the IOC and FINA and the restrictions imposed on the applicants by means of a participation ban were inherent in the organisation and proper conduct of competitive sport and no more than was necessary to ensure a healthy rivalry between athletes. Further, as the claimants had not pursued the issue of proportionality, it was held that the IOC and FINA had acted lawfully in their pursuit of a legitimate objective.

Meca-Medina has proved to be a controversial decision with many ISFs seeing it as a direct attack on their autonomy. In making this complaint however, it must be borne in mind that many of the leading ISFs have been lobbying for some time for a complete exemption from EU law, so any decision that did not specifically serve their purposes was likely to come in for attack from this interest group. In reality the decision is more of a warning shot than a direct attack. The ECJ is requiring the ISFs to explain why certain rules and procedures are necessary and proportionate for the proper functioning of their sports and is making them produce cogent evidence to back up the claims being made in support of their legality. For example FINA provided scientific evidence to justify the level at which a positive test for nandrolone would be recorded in an athlete's urine sample, whilst the athletes could provide no evidence for why this level should be raised. FINA could therefore explain why this was not an arbitrarily defined offence whereas the claimants could not provide a robust explanation for why the rule needed to be changed.

There are three main criticisms that can be levelled at *Meca-Medina*. Firstly the ECJ failed to examine in detail whether the IOC and FINA were undertakings for the purposes of competition law. In particular the Court did not examine whether it was possible for bodies of this nature to be undertakings for some purposes but not for others and therefore whether EU competition law was the appropriate means of challenging FINA's rules in these circumstances. This issue was later clarified in *Motosykletistiki Omospondia Ellados NPID (MOTOE)* v. *Eilliniko Dimosio* (Case C-49/07) [2008] ECR I-4863 (below, 3.2.6). Secondly the ECJ failed to interrogate rigorously the proportionality of FINA's anti-doping regime. Instead of requiring FINA to establish that its restrictive though inherently necessary rule was proportionate, the Court refused to engage with this aspect of the analysis because the claimants had not challenged the anti-doping rules on this basis. In general the party seeking to rely on a restrictive rule has to prove not only that it is inherent but also that it is proportionate in order for it to be found to be lawful; this central issue was therefore left unexamined by the Court. Thirdly the judgment does not explain whether taking account of the 'specificity of sport' requires consideration of different issues in competition law cases from those which are relevant for challenges brought under the free movement provisions, leaving the possibility of some degree of divergence in the application of this concept in these two different situations.

This last point could not be examined further in *Meca-Medina* because the ECJ did not have jurisdiction to hear the challenges made to the anti-doping rules under Arts.45 and 56 TFEU (ex Arts.39 and 49 ECT). Although there is a possibility of convergence in how the law will be applied in the future, there are at present two similar though distinct approaches for determining the legality of an ISF's rules and procedures under EU law. The correct choice of approach is dependent on whether the challenge is made under the competition law or free movement provisions of the TFEU.

Following *Meca-Medina* and *MOTOE*, and in line with the discussions in para.2.1.2 of Annex 1 *Staff Working Document* (SEC (2007) 935) published alongside the Commission's *White Paper on Sport* (COM (2007) 39 Final), whether or not a rule conforms with EU competition law can be determined by asking four questions. Firstly is the collective regulatory body that is seeking to rely on the potentially restrictive rule an undertaking or an association of undertakings? Secondly is the rule a restriction of competition contrary to Art.101(1) TFEU or an abuse of a dominant position under Art.102 TFEU? In answering this question the Court will examine the overall context in which the rule was adopted or produces its effects, the objectives behind the adoption and operation of the rule, whether the restrictions caused by the rule are inherent in the pursuit of those objectives and whether the rule is proportionate in light of the objectives being pursued. If the rule is inherent in the organisation and proper conduct of the sport, for example because it protects the integrity of the competition, or protects athletes' health, or encourages the training and education of young athletes, or ensures the financial stability of the participating teams, then there is no restriction and it falls outside of the scope of the Treaty. Thirdly if the rule is a restriction, does it affect trade between member states? Fourthly if it does affect trade within the internal market, can it be justified under Art.101(3) TFEU (see further 12.4.) on the basis that its beneficial effects outweigh the restrictions that it imposes? For example, by Commission Decision of 23 July 2003, Comp/C-2/37.398 Joint Selling of the Commercial Rights to the UEFA Champions League, UEFA's proposal for selling the rights to its Champions League tournament was found to be a restriction under Art.101(1) TFEU (ex Art.81(1) ECT). However this restriction was justified and therefore lawful, on the basis that it promoted economic efficiency and was of benefit to consumers (see further, chapter 13.4.1).

However a slightly different four stage approach is used where the rule is challenged under the free movement provisions of the TFEU. Following *Bosman* (see further, 12.2.1) and *Deliège* v. *ASBL Ligue Francophone de Judo and others* (Cases C-51/96 and C-191/97) [2000] ECR I-2549 (see further, chapter 12.3.1), the Court must begin by determining whether the rule in question is a restriction on a worker's freedom of movement under Art.45 TFEU, or a person's freedom of establishment under Art.49 TFEU, or on their freedom to provide services under Art.56 TFEU. Again, if the rule is inherent in the organisation and proper conduct of the sport or, following *Walrave*, it is a purely sporting rule, then there is no restriction and the rule falls outside of the scope of the Treaty. Secondly if the rule is a restriction, is its use capable of being justified objectively? Where a rule is directly discriminatory, it can only be justified on the grounds of public policy, public security or public health (Art.45(3) TFEU) which are rarely likely to apply to most sporting rules. Where a rule is indirectly discriminatory, or non-discriminatory, it can be objectively justified if its purpose is, for example, to protect the integrity of the competition and competitive balance, to protect athletes' health, or to encourage the training and education of young athletes. Thirdly is the rule effective in promoting the objectives pursued? Fourthly is the rule a proportionate means of achieving the objectives? These last two questions are to ensure that the restriction is capable of achieving a legitimate objective and is an appropriate means of doing so.

Thus where a rule is inherent in the organisation and proper conduct of a sport, it will fall outside of the scope of the Treaty altogether. If the rule is a restriction according to EU competition law and affects trade in the internal market, then it can only be lawful if it can be justified under Art.101(3) TFEU. Alternatively if the rule is a restriction of the free movement provisions it will be lawful only if it can be objectively justified.

What *Meca-Medina* does confirm is that ISFs have only what Weatherill refers to as a 'conditional autonomy' to self-regulate; they are free to govern their own sports in the way that they see fit provided that where they engage in or have an impact on an economic activity they comply with EU law or can prove that their conduct falls outside of its scope. The development of the concept of what has come to be referred to as the 'specificity of sport' means that it is now not only rules that are of a purely sporting interest that fall outside of the scope of the TFEU, as was the case after *Walrave*; those rules which are necessary for the proper functioning of sport are also not subject to the Treaty's provisions.

If Dwain Chambers had focused his challenge to the British Olympic Association's refusal to invite him to the Beijing Olympics on Arts.101 and 102 TFEU (*Chambers* v. *British Olympic Association* [2008] EWHC 2028 (QBD)) the court would have been forced to assess the legality of Bye-law 25 in the light of *Meca-Medina*. Unless evidence could be provided to explain why the Olympics is so different to all other athletic championships and why the Association's Rules should be so different to those of the vast majority of other National Olympic Committees, the decision to refuse to invite him to compete at the Olympics for the remainder of his career might be unable to satisfy the requirements of the 'specificity of sport' test (see further, chapter 2 Hot Topic).

Although EU law will generally be applicable to professional sport, or at least sporting relationships that involve some form of payment, the Staff Working Document that was published alongside of the European Commission's *White Paper on Sport* (COM (2007) 391) states unequivocally that amateur sport is not to be considered exempt from the operation of EU law. In particular the Commission expressed concern that discriminatory practices in sport could discourage workers from working in other member states if they were not allowed the same access to sport as the nationals of the country to which they were moving. In making these statements the Commission acknowledges that sport is a social advantage and recognises its importance as a tool of social integration that should be protected by the principles of free movement where necessary and appropriate.

3.2.3   Free movement of workers – Art.45 TFEU (ex Art.39 ECT)

The right of workers to move freely throughout the EU for employment purposes is secured by Art.45 TFEU (see further, chapter 12.2). This enables workers to accept and take up offers of employment in any member state of the EU and to remain there for the purpose of working. It also makes it unlawful to discriminate against a worker on the grounds of their nationality, ensuring equal access to employment and social advantages, equal pay for equal work and equality of treatment for all workers.

The free movement of workers was at issue in *Bosman*, perhaps the most famous of all sports law cases, when a Belgian professional footballer was prevented from taking up an offer of employment in France by the conduct of his previous club (see further, chapter 12.2.1). In circumstances bearing more than a little resemblance to *Eastham v. Newcastle United FC and the Football Association* [1964] Ch 413, the English restraint of trade case (see further, chapter 11.4.2.4), Bosman claimed that it was unlawful for his previous employer, Belgian club RC Liege, to demand a transfer fee from his prospective employer, French club US Dunkerque; he also claimed that UEFA's rule imposing nationality quotas on the number of foreign players who could play for a club was unlawful. In both cases he said that the rules as operated in Belgium acted as restrictions on his freedom to take up an offer of employment in another member state contrary to Art.45 TFEU. The ECJ reiterated its earlier finding in *Walrave* that the TFEU in general and Art.45 in particular applied to collective regulatory bodies such as ISFs and NGBs. It then went on to hold that demanding a transfer fee for an out of contract player, in other words a player who is no longer legally employed by their previous club, was an unjustified restriction on their freedom of movement as a worker and therefore unlawful, as was the imposition of a nationality quota. Despite claims that the transfer system was not an 'economic activity' and that its abolition would undermine the autonomy and proper governance of football, the ECJ applied a technical and robust interpretation of Art.45, the repercussions of which are still being felt today.

3.2.4   Freedom to provide services – Art. 56 TFEU (ex Art.49 ECT)

Whereas Art.45 protects the rights of workers, or employees, Art.56 TFEU provides similar protection to individuals who are self-employed and who wish to provide their services temporarily in another country within the EU (see further, chapter 12.3). The aim of the provision is once again to outlaw discriminatory practices that prevent a person from earning a living by making it unlawful to place restrictions on their freedom to provide their services to individuals and undertakings in any other member state.

In *Walrave* the claimants had based their challenge to the UCI's rule change on the grounds that there had been a breach of either Art.45 or Art.56. Although the ECJ could not pass judgment on whether the pacemakers were employees or self-employed persons providing their professional services to others as this was a matter for the trial court, it did hold that Art.56 could apply to sporting relationships. In *Deliège* (see further, chapter 12.3.1), Art.56 (ex Art.49 ECT) was the central issue of the case brought by a Belgian judoka against the NGB that had failed to pick her for several major tournaments. She argued that these decisions had breached Art.56 by denying her the opportunity to further her career and increase her earnings capacity as a result of the exposure that she would have received at these competitions. Although the ECJ left the question of whether or not

Deliège's activities constituted an economic activity to the Belgian courts, it held that the selection criteria used by the defendant were not in breach of Art.56 because they derived from a need inherent in the organisation of international sporting competitions.

3.2.5 Freedom of establishment – Art.49 TFEU (ex Art.43 ECT)

The third of the freedoms protected by the TFEU that is relevant to sport is the freedom of establishment under Art.49. The effect of Art.49 is twofold: it guarantees self-employed persons the right to take up and pursue activities in other member states and it provides undertakings with the right to set up businesses in any country in the EU. In both cases establishment should be capable of being effected under the same conditions as would be imposed on nationals of the country where they seek to operate. Thus it is unlawful to prevent or restrict the ability of either a person or a business that originated in one member state from operating from a base in another member state on the grounds of nationality.

There is no sports-related litigation on this point, although the possibility has arisen on several occasions. In the late 1990s Wimbledon FC, which was established in England, and Clydebank FC, which was established in Scotland, both attempted to relocate to Dublin but remain playing in the English and Scottish league structures respectively. The Football Association of Ireland (FAI) refused to sanction the moves and its decisions were enforced by the English and Scottish Football Associations. The two clubs could have argued that Art.49 TFEU enabled them to establish their business in another member state, in this case Ireland, and that to prevent them from doing so on the sole basis of where they were currently established was unlawful.

By analogy to the reasoning of the European Commission in *Royal Excelsior Mouscron/UEFA* IP/99/965 9 December 1999, it is unlikely that an action under Art.49 would have succeeded in justifying the attempts by these two clubs to play their home games in another member state (see further, chapter 12.4.3.3). Mouscron, a Belgian football team with a small home ground, sought to play a UEFA Cup match in the nearest large stadium to where it was based in order to maximise its profits and increase spectator safety; the ideal candidate happened to be based in France. One of reasons ascribed to the Commission's decision to uphold UEFA's decision to refuse Mouscron permission to play a home game outside of Belgium was that the rule was necessary for the organisation of sporting competitions of this kind and was therefore outside of the scope of the competition law rules. It is likely that the decisions of both the FAI and UEFA would be found to be necessary and proportionate means of protecting the integrity of these sporting competitions and for their proper organisation in accordance with the European model of sport.

3.2.6 Competition law – Arts.101 and 102 TFEU (ex Arts.81 and 82 ECT)

The main provisions defining EU competition law are found in Arts.101 and 102 TFEU. Article 101 prohibits agreements between undertakings and decisions made by associations of undertakings which have as their object or effect the prevention, restriction or distortion of competition within the EU. Article 102 prohibits a monopoly or market-dominating undertaking from taking unfair advantage of its position by abusing its dominant position. If either of these kinds of anti-competitive conduct affect trade between member states then the undertaking is acting unlawfully (see further, chapter 12.4).

In sport most NGBs and ISFs are undertakings for at least part of the time. By their constitution it is also possible for them to be associations of undertakings. An NGB or ISF is an undertaking when it is engaged in economic activity, irrespective of its legal form or the way that it is financed (*Hofner and Elser* (Case C-41/90) [1991] ECR I-1979). Either body can also be an association of undertakings where it is comprised of members who are themselves undertakings; NGBs are usually associations of clubs, whilst ISFs are usually associations of NGBs. Not only can they be undertakings for the purposes of EU competition law, they can also act as monopolies in their fields of governance. As most sports have one NGB per country and one global ISF per sport, the circumstances by which sport is governed are inherently monopolistic in form. However the mere existence of undertakings acting in concert and of monopolies does not automatically mean that there are breaches of the competition provisions. Only where there is an abuse of that position that affects trade between member states will an NGB or ISF be acting anti-competitively and therefore unlawfully.

The failure of the ECJ to examine whether FINA and the IOC were undertakings is one of the main criticisms that has been aimed at the decision in *Meca-Medina*, as only undertakings are subject to Arts.101 and 102 (above, 3.2.2). The variety of functions undertaken by NGBs and ISFs means that they are not always engaged in economic activity when governing their sport. On the one hand they can be acting as a quasi-public regulatory body that grants the authority to compete in or host an event. On the other, they can be acting as private commercial organisations whose aim is to generate income by, for example, selling broadcasting rights or organising competitions. As sports authorities can have such disparate functions, it is important to be able to determine whether they could be undertakings in respect of some of their activities but not in others, or whether once it has been established that they are engaged in some economic activity they should be considered to be an undertaking in respect of all of their activities.

▶ *Motosykletistiki Omospondia Ellados NPID (MOTOE)* v. *Eilliniko Dimosio* (Case C-49/07) [2008] ECR I-4863

Under Greek law, any body seeking to organise a motorcycling competition in Greece first had to secure authorisation from the Minister for Public Order. Part of this authorisation process required the consent of the national motor racing organisation, Elliniki Leskhi Aftokinitou kai Periigiseon (ELPA), which is the official representative in Greece of the ISF for motorcycling, the Federation Internationale de Motocyclisme (FIM). ELPA had two main roles: it acted as both the official regulator of motorcycling by authorising events and competitions run by other bodies and as a commercial entity that organised competitions in its own name.

MOTOE applied for authorisation from the government to run a motorcycle competition but failed to secure the necessary consent from ELPA, suffering financial losses of GDr5m as a result. MOTOE sued Greece under Arts.102 and 106 TFEU, arguing that the body to which the Greek state had granted these powers, ELPA, was abusing its monopoly position as the sole authorising body for motorcycling events by refusing to give its consent to a competition organised by a commercial rival.

In order to engage EU competition law, it first needed to be established whether ELPA was an undertaking. MOTOE argued that ELPA was an undertaking on the basis that when it organised its own events and competitions it was engaging in commercially orientated economic activity. ELPA countered that as it was a non-profit-making regulatory body it was not engaged in any economic activity and therefore could not be an undertaking.

To a limited extent, the ECJ agreed with both points of view; ELPA was a commercial entity engaging in economic activity when it organised its own events by reason of its entering into sponsorship and advertising agreements and insurance contracts; however when acting purely as a regulator it was not acting as an undertaking. This led the ECJ to identify a third alternative where ELPA was acting in a 'dual role' where its regulatory decisions, such as whether to grant consent to MOTOE's application, could be influenced by its own commercial imperatives, such as the need to limit the number of competitions that could act as direct competitors to its own events. Where an entity operated with this dual role, it was an undertaking for the purposes of EU competition law.

The next step was to determine whether ELPA was in a dominant market position. As MOTOE had no opportunity to apply to a body other than ELPA for permission to organise such an event, there was no substitutable or sufficiently interchangeable service provider for it to make use of and therefore the relevant market was defined as being the organisation of motorcycling competitions in Greece. Dominance is established where an undertaking is in such a position of strength in the relevant market that it is able to prevent effective competition and act to an appreciable extent independently of its competitors and consumers (*United Brands and United Brands Continentaal v. Commission* (Case 27/76) [1978] ECR 207). By virtue of its structure and its control over the relevant market as the sole and state-sanctioned authorising body of such events, ELPA was found to be in a dominant position in the market for organising motorcycling competitions in Greece.

The final stage for determining a breach of Art.102 is to establish whether the undertaking is abusing its dominant position. If ELPA had been acting in bad faith when refusing to give its consent to MOTOE's application, a clear case of abuse of its dominant position would be established. However the ECJ went considerably further by holding that a breach of Art.102 could also be established where the rights granted to an undertaking by the state gave rise to a *risk* of an abuse of its dominant position. Therefore it was possible that ELPA might deny other operators access to the market or distort competition by favouring events that it organised or those in whose organisation it participates. Thus there was something approaching an assumption of anti-competitive behaviour that was based on the conflict of interest between ELPA's regulatory and commercial roles. As neither Greece nor ELPA could provide a justification for operating a decision-making process with no appropriate safeguards to minimise the opportunity for abuse, it was held to be anti-competitive.

This decision appears to cause particular problems for NGBs and ISFs which are inherently monopolistic in their governance of sports. As many will also fulfil the 'dual role' referred to by the ECJ, there is a real possibility of their actions engaging EU competition law. However just because EU competition law is engaged does not automatically mean that it is also breached. The ECJ only found that the way in which ELPA fulfilled its dual role was anti-competitive, not that the concept of the dual role was always anti-competitive. Therefore there is no immediate need for a sports body that fulfils a dual role to divest itself of its commercial activities; as was the case in *Meca-Medina*, where the conduct of an NGB can be justified objectively, it can still be found to be lawful.

The power granted to ELPA to give or refuse its consent to MOTOE to organise a motorcycle competition was not subject to any restrictions or obligations to review. Furthermore the Greek government had not laid down any procedures that needed to be followed or any means of challenging ELPA's decisions. Thus the power granted to ELPA was open to abuse, even if it had not actually been abused. In effect the ECJ appears to be acting in a similar to way to the High Court when it exercises its supervisory jurisdiction over sports disputes (see further, chapter 2.3.2). To ensure the legality of the decision-making process, all decisions should be taken in accordance with objectively justifiable criteria, following a fair hearing where the applicant is able to present their own case, where reasons for the eventual decision are given and where there is an opportunity to appeal against it or to apply for some other form of review. If such a procedure is followed, then the opportunity for abuse is significantly reduced, if not entirely negated.

The ECJ in *MOTOE* accepted that sport should be treated as a special case because its organisation has inherent features that are different from any other sector that are worthy of protection. However it is not so special that it should be granted an automatic exemption from the operation of EU law in general and competition law in particular. Provided that ISFs and NGBs can justify objectively conduct that would in other circumstances be considered to be anti-competitive, or can provide sufficient safeguards against the abuse of its inherently monopolistic position, then although subject to EU law they will not be in breach of it.

It is likely that further clarification will be required on the future interpretation of *MOTOE* and its application of EU competition law because of the potential impact that it could have on the administration of sport in the EU. If the 'dual role' is justified as being necessary for the proper administration of sport, then few infrastructural changes will be required other than the procedural amendments already mentioned. However if a stricter interpretation of Arts.101 and 102 ECT is applied to the dual role performed by most ISFs and NGBs, then these bodies could be required to divest themselves of one or other of the regulatory or commercial roles which would in turn completely change the way that sport is organised in Europe.

3.3 The Court of Arbitration for Sport

The Court of Arbitration for Sport (CAS) was established in 1984 under the auspices of the International Olympic Committee (IOC). There was some initial concern that CAS was merely an emanation of the IOC, that there was no real separation of powers between the two organisations and that its decisions could not therefore be impartial and independent. This came to a head following CAS's decision in *Gundel v. FEI* CAS 1992/A/63, where the applicant who had been banned for one month following a partially successful appeal to CAS challenged the legality of its finding before the Swiss courts. The Swiss Federal Tribunal declared CAS to be a true court under Swiss law and that it was sufficiently independent of the FEI that its decision was legally valid (*Gundel v. FEI and CAS* Recueil Officiel des Arêtes du Tribunal Fédéral 119 II 271, 15 March 1993). However it also stated that because of the links that existed at the time between CAS and the IOC, CAS could not be considered to be truly independent where the IOC was a party to the proceedings before it and that any decision that it made in these circumstances would be invalid.

In order to address the issues raised by the Swiss Federal Court and to secure for itself the position as the world's most important sports tribunal, CAS was re-established as a completely independent body in 1994 to ensure that there could be no undue influence exerted on it by either the IOC or any ISF. CAS is based in Lausanne, Switzerland and is regulated by Swiss law; it has two further permanent offices in Sydney, Australia and New York, USA. It also sits at many finals tournaments and major championships, including the UEFA European Football Championships, the Commonwealth Games and the Olympics, as the CAS Ad Hoc Division, where it provides rapid responses to disputes that arise during the course of these intensive short-term events (below, 3.3.2).

Although most major ISFs operate their own independent dispute resolution chambers and arbitral panels to hear disputes arising out of their own sports, almost all now allow an appeal to CAS for a final and binding decision. These decisions are binding arbitration agreements that are legally enforceable by each of the parties to the dispute. As well as acting as a tribunal of final appeal, CAS provides a number of services that are aimed at keeping sports disputes out of the courts, including arbitration and mediation facilities. It also has the power to provide advisory opinions to sporting authorities seeking clarification on a point of law or on the interpretation of a particular rule. This more proactive role can ensure that a sport is able to revise its rules or procedures before the dispute escalates into litigation.

The decisions and opinions of CAS are becoming increasingly important as a source of sports law, or *lex sportiva* as CAS refers to it, because of the number of applications that it hears that would otherwise end up in national and/or European courts. In particular its decisions on the interpretation and application of FIFA's Regulations for the Status and Transfer of Players have undoubtedly prevented highly complex litigation from reaching the ECJ. More important however is its ability to impose a degree of harmonisation on the decision-making procedures of ISFs; regardless of the sport from which the dispute arose, CAS will impose the same standards of procedural fairness and due process on all governing bodies and adhere to the same interpretative norms when establishing the true meaning of their rules.

Hearings are generally before a panel of three arbitrators. Each party selects an arbitrator from CAS's list and an independent chair is then chosen by either the parties' arbitrators or by the President of the Ordinary Arbitration Division or the Appeals Arbitration Division depending on the nature of the procedure followed. The outcomes of ordinary arbitrations and mediations are private and usually confidential, however the decisions of the Appeals Arbitration Division and Advisory Opinions are generally published on the CAS website.

CAS has been a key driver in the modernisation and standardisation of the rules and procedures of many sporting authorities. Its sports-sympathetic approach has ensured its acceptance amongst the sporting community and its development of the meaning of the 'specificity of sport' has helped it to justify how and why it interprets legal norms in the way that it does. Whether it is truly developing a completely new *lex sportiva* is however still a matter of debate.

3.3.1   The jurisdiction of the Court of Arbitration for Sport

CAS has the general jurisdiction to hear any dispute that is either directly or indirectly linked to sport. More specifically it will hear applications where the rules of an ISF allow the parties to make a reference to it or where they have agreed to submit to CAS's jurisdiction. For the most part it hears commercial and disciplinary disputes although its jurisdiction is not specifically limited to these issues. As with the other sources of sports law, the cases coming before it can usually be further sub-divided according to two underlying themes: good governance and procedural fairness (see further, chapter 1.6). In many ways it could be said to operate a supervisory jurisdiction over sports disputes similar to that of the High Court (see further, 2.3.2), however one that allows it to review the substance of a sporting authority's decisions when acting in its appellate capacity. Thus CAS will examine whether the rules of an ISF are reasonable and being applied and interpreted lawfully and that any penalties imposed are necessary, reasonable and proportionate.

CAS has made it clear on a number of occasions however that it will not review the in-game decisions of the match officials unless bad faith or illegality can be proved against them. In refusing jurisdiction over such disputes, its aim is to preserve the autonomy of the match officials in coming to their decisions in the heat of competition and to uphold the finality of the outcome. It is also an acknowledgment that whereas the match officials are trained to take decisions in relation to their sport, the CAS panel is not.

> ▶ *Mendy* v. *Association Internationale de Boxing Amateur (AIBA)* CAS 1996/H/OG Atlanta
> 1996/006
>
> The claimant had been disqualified from the boxing tournament at the Atlanta Olympics for landing a punch below the belt of his opponent. He applied to have the disqualification overturned on the grounds that the point of impact was clearly above the belt and therefore lawful. CAS refused to review the decision of the AIBA on the basis that the application of the purely technical rules of the sport was the responsibility of the ISF concerned. The justification for this stance was because the CAS panel was less well-placed to decide an in-game issue after the event than was a qualified referee who was in the ring or the team of judges who were based ringside.

This refusal of jurisdiction was taken to its extreme in *Yang Tae Young and Korean Olympic Committee* v. *International Gymnastics Federation (FIG)* CAS 2004/A/704, where the panel refused to intervene in a dispute where the judging panel in the men's all-around final failed to follow the correct procedures in scoring Young's performance. Although a simple recalculation of the marks awarded could have been applied, and which would have resulted in Young finishing in the gold medal position, CAS refused to intervene on the basis that he should have followed the correct procedures as laid down by FIG and appealed within one round of the mistake occurring. Thus even though it was acknowledged that the officials had made a mistake that could be rectified with comparative ease, the panel remained resolute in its position that the in-game decisions of match officials are non-justiciable before CAS just as they are before the national courts; the officials' decisions are final.

3.3.2   Arbitrations and appeals

CAS has jurisdiction to hear two specific kinds of arbitration: ordinary arbitrations and appeals arbitrations. Ordinary arbitration can only take place where both parties agree to submit to a private dispute resolution procedure. Their consent to submit to arbitration can be by formal agreement to have an individual dispute resolved by an arbitrator or panel of arbitrators, or can be in accordance with the rules of the governing body concerned. The decision of the arbitrators is binding on both parties and avoids the need for the dispute to be heard in court. Ordinary arbitrations usually involve preliminary clarifications of the meaning of a rule before a more formal Appeal is made against the final decision on an ISF (*Boxing Australia* v. *Association Internationale de Boxing Amateur* CAS 2008/O/1455).

Appeals arbitrations are appeals from the decisions of ISFs to CAS which then acts as a tribunal of last instance following a rehearing of the dispute. The level of legal complexity and the breadth of law involved in the appeals applications that are made to CAS are evidence of its growing importance as a source of sports law.

3.3.2.1 Commercial disputes

Many of the commercial disputes that have been brought before CAS have arisen out of the complexity of the FIFA Regulations for the Status and Transfer of Players and appeals brought by either players or clubs against the decisions of FIFA's Dispute Resolution Chamber (DRC). These Regulations, which have been developed post-*Bosman* in an attempt to maintain a transfer system of some kind in professional football, have given rise to a number of disputes that would almost undoubtedly have ended up being heard before the courts were it not for the existence of CAS.

> ▶ *FC Shaktar Donetsk v. Matuzalem Francelino da Silva, Real Zaragoza SAD and FIFA* **CAS 2008/A/1519 and 1520**
>
> Three years into a five-year playing contract, Matuzalem, a Brazilian national, unilaterally and without any due cause terminated his contractual relationship with the Ukrainian football club FC Shaktar Donetsk, claiming to have done so in accordance with Art.17 FIFA Regulations. Two days later he signed a three-year contract with the Spanish club Real Zaragoza. Shaktar initiated proceedings against both the player and Zaragoza before FIFA's DRC claiming €25m, the minimum fee payable under the contract's release clause. Shaktar was awarded €6.8m in compensation and appealed to CAS in the hope of securing a much higher sum for the loss of its top scorer and captain.
>
> CAS began by stating that Art.17 did not give players the right to unilaterally breach their playing contracts and move to a new club. As its purpose was to reinforce contractual stability not create greater uncertainty, it should instead be read as defining the consequences of either a player or club choosing to breach their agreement. Thus as Matuzalem had breached his contract by failing to report for training at Shaktar and signing for Zaragoza, compensation was due to Shaktar.
>
> Having established the breach of contract, it was held the amount of compensation payable should be calculated in accordance with Art.17 FIFA Regulations, not the release clause, as the circumstances in which Matuzalem had left Shaktar were not those anticipated by the contract. The release clause could only be activated where a club seeking to secure Matuzalem's services directly approached Shaktar with an offer of €25m or greater; it did not cover the situation where Matuzalem unilaterally breached his contract. CAS held that the value of the player's services to Shaktar, his status and standing at the club, his behaviour and the timing of his departure should all be taken into account when calculating the amount of compensation payable. This amount should then be reduced by the sum of money that Shaktar would not have to pay Matuzalem in terms of his salary. Thus the total amount payable was €11.9m.

The comparative simplicity of this decision, that one party to a contract does not have the unfettered right to refuse to perform their obligations with impunity, hides the extraordinarily wide range of legal issues that are raised by this case. The first question was to determine the law applicable to the dispute. Although a contract to work in the Ukraine was at issue, CAS held that as it contained no choice of law clause the applicable law was, according to the FIFA Regulations, Swiss law, not Ukrainian or Spanish law.

Secondly it had to determine whether the release clause was a properly constructed liquidated damages clause or a genuine buy-out clause. The former would explain how the amount of compensation payable on breach should be calculated, whilst the latter would identify the amount payable by a club seeking to secure the transfer of Matuzalem. CAS held that the release clause was a buy-out clause that would be triggered automatically where another club paid Shaktar at least €25m; in such circumstances Shaktar would have to release Matuzalem, whether it wanted to or not. A liquidated damages clause would have set out the factors to be taken into account when calculating the amount of compensation payable, not simply state a fixed sum to be paid on breach.

Thirdly CAS identified how the sum to be paid should be calculated following a breach of contract of this kind. This needed to take into account not only the specific requirements of Art.17 but also the domestic law of the country where the employment relationship took place. Although no submissions were made on this point in *Matuzalem*, local law could be a significant complicating factor in the light of the various ways in which compensation for breach of contract is calculated in different jurisdictions.

Matazulem is a clear example of a dispute that would normally be expected to be heard before the national courts of the country where the work is taking place and potentially even the ECJ where an EU national is involved (see further, chapter 12.2.2.2). Instead it was resolved (in legal terms) quickly by two expert sports tribunals with all the attendant costs savings to both parties. By keeping disputes such as this away from the national courts, there is the added advantage to FIFA that there was no detailed investigation of the legality of its Regulations and the transfer system as it currently operates. Before CAS it was assumed without question that the Regulations were lawful and the case turned instead on the interpretation of the disputed contractual term and Art.17, leaving scope for further disputes in future cases.

3.3.2.2 Eligibility disputes

Eligibility to compete is usually determined by reference to the rules of the particular competition. Although challenges to these rules are rare, when disputes about the right to compete do arise they can engage complex and unusual areas of the law. In *Pistorius v. International Association of Athletics Federations (IAAF)* CAS 2008/A/1480 (see further, chapter 11.5.4), CAS was asked to determine whether the IAAF's refusal to allow 400m runner Oscar Pistorius to use 'Cheetah Flex-Foot' prosthetic legs was unlawful on the grounds of disability discrimination. On finding for the IAAF, CAS held that as the decision to classify the prosthetics as capable of unfairly enhancing an athlete's performance was based on scientific evidence, it was objectively justifiable and therefore not discriminatory. This leaves open the possibility that the next generation of prosthetics may be found to be lawful, thereby enabling some disabled athletes to compete alongside able-bodied athletes.

A more politically sensitive issue has been raised in respect of whether Gibraltar is eligible to compete in international tournaments in its own right. In *Gibraltar Badminton Association (GBA) v. International Badminton Federation (IBF)* CAS 2001/A/309, the GBA asked CAS to set aside the conditions imposed on it by the IBF (now the Badminton World Federation) that would enable Gibraltar to compete in the 2001 World Team Championships in Seville, Spain. The IBF had stated that players from Gibraltar could only take part in the opening ceremony as members of an IBF team competing under the IBF flag with no mention of their representing Gibraltar and that the players would not be able to wear tracksuits or competition shirts that had the name Gibraltar printed on the back. The GBA claimed that as a full member of the IBF it should be able to compete under the same conditions as any other member association and that the IBF was acting in a discriminatory manner by imposing these additional conditions on its players.

CAS dismissed the application on two grounds. Firstly that the IBF had not acted discriminatorily against Gibraltar as discrimination was defined in its Rules and by the Olympic Charter as being where there was differential treatment against a country or an individual on the grounds of a person's race, religion, politics or sex. As Gibraltar was, according to international law, an overseas territory of the UK and not an independent nation state, it was not a 'country' and therefore could not be the subject of discrimination. Furthermore CAS noted that any conditions imposed on the GBA were for the benefit of the sport as a whole as they were necessary and proportionate in order for the competition to take place in Spain and for the Gibraltar team to participate in it; therefore the conditions imposed on the GBA were lawful.

3.3.2.3 Doping disputes

One of the most common reasons for appealing to CAS is to challenge the legality of bans imposed for anti-doping infringements. Since 2003, Art.13 World Anti-Doping Code has included a provision nominating CAS as the final tribunal of appeal for all doping disputes arising from participation in an International Event or which involve an International-Level Athlete. An International Event is defined as one that is organised by the IOC, an ISF, the International Paralympic Committee or a major event organiser such as the Commonwealth Games Committee. An International-Level Athlete is one who is on the registered testing list for at least one ISF. All national-level disputes would be heard by the National Anti-Doping Panel in the UK (see further, chapter 1.2).

The Word Anti-Doping Code has evolved significantly in response to sporting, pharmaceutical and legal developments. Of particular importance from a legal perspective, and as a means of avoiding the litigation and uncertainty previously experienced in countries like the UK (see further, chapter 2.4), is that the preamble of the Code states unequivocally that it applies to all athletes and their support personnel on the basis of their participation in the sport. This is reinforced by a requirement that ISFs bring to the attention of all participants the relevant anti-doping rules and procedures, effectively ensuring that athletes are also subject to the Code on the submission basis (see further, chapter 2.3.3.1). Art.3 of the Code imposes the burden of proof on the body seeking to prove the anti-doping violation and requires it to establish its case to the comfortable satisfaction of the panel; this standard lies somewhere between the balance of probabilities required in a civil action and proof beyond reasonable doubt as needed for a criminal conviction. Further, the Code defines and enshrines the right to a fair hearing in Art.8.

The result of these developments is that most doping appeals now focus on challenges to the length of the ban imposed on an athlete or procedural impropriety, on the basis that the correct rules and procedures have not been followed, rather than challenging the existence of the anti-doping regime itself. After the decision of the ECJ in *Meca-Medina* (above, 3.2.2), it is unlikely that the anti-doping regime as a whole could now be challenged as being unlawful. As all ISFs that are members of the IOC, as well as many National Olympic Committees, national governments and transnational bodies such as the Council of Europe have ratified the World Anti-Doping Code, the position of CAS as the tribunal responsible for its interpretation has enabled its panels to play a significant role in harmonising procedures and establishing legal norms in doping disputes.

3.3.3   Advisory Opinions

Much less used but no less important is the ability of CAS to provide Advisory Opinions to the IOC, ISFs, the World Anti-Doping Agency, National Olympic Committees and the organising committees of an Olympic Games. This pre-emptive procedure enables each of these bodies to request CAS to provide advice on the legality of an existing or proposed rule or procedure. CAS will provide an Opinion only where to do so does not involve an investigation of the underlying merits of a case or where the request for an Opinion does not subvert the normal appeals procedure. For example in *Australian Olympic Committee (AOC)* CAS 2000/C/267, CAS was asked by the AOC to investigate the legality of the then recently introduced 'sharkskin' half-body swimming suits. It declined to do so on the basis that as FINA had followed the correct procedures when coming to its decision, it was not within the jurisdiction of CAS to comment on the technical merits of whether or not these swimming suits were buoyancy aids.

CAS will provide an Opinion where there is a genuine concern about the legality of a rule or the way that it is being interpreted, or a clear loophole that was not considered by the rule's drafters. In *International Baseball Association* CAS 1998/C/215, CAS was asked whether it was possible for a player with dual nationality to change their sporting nationality. By drawing an analogy with a person who changed their sporting and/or legal nationality from one country to another, it advised that there was no reason why a player with dual nationality could not change their sporting nationality between the countries of which they were legal nationals. In such a situation the player would have to wait three years from either their last appearance for one country before being able to play for another, or from the time of informing the relevant ISF that they wished to change their sporting nationality.

3.3.4   Mediations

Mediation is similar to arbitration except that the outcome is non-binding. It requires that both parties agree to submit to the mediation process during which a neutral third party mediator attempts to achieve a settlement of the dispute that is acceptable to both parties. If successful it obviates the need for further litigation as the aim of mediation is to achieve agreement between the parties. As a private mechanism, as with ordinary arbitrations, the outcome cannot be published without the agreement of both parties.

3.3.5   The role of the Ad Hoc Division

The Ad Hoc Division provides an instant hearing and appeals framework at many major international events, including the Olympics and the Commonwealth Games. Its aim is to provide rapid and authoritative responses to emerging disputes thereby enabling decisions to be made that minimise delays to the competitions in progress. The Ad Hoc Division follows the same basic rules and procedures that CAS would normally follow but in a shorter timescale. Although the majority of its work is the same as that usually undertaken by CAS, in the heat of competition some more unusual disputes have come before the Ad Hoc Division. For example in *A, W and L v. NOC Cape Verde* CAS 1996/H/OG Atlanta 96/002 and 005, a dispute had arisen over who should carry the Cape Verde flag at the opening ceremony of the Atlanta Olympics. The sole athlete representing Cape Verde had snatched the flag from the Chef de Mission and carried it into the stadium and as a result had had his accreditation revoked. Without expressing a view on the underlying merits of the case, the Ad Hoc Division required that due process was followed in punishing the athlete in this manner and reminded all involved about the need to uphold the Olympic spirit.

Hot topic . . .

THE LEGALITY OF COMPULSORY PLAYER RELEASE CLAUSES FOR INTERNATIONAL REPRESENTATIVE MATCHES

Since the introduction of competitive international matches into the sporting calendar, it has become the convention in almost all team sports that the pinnacle of a player's career is to be picked to play for their country in a continental or world championships tournament. This almost universal assumption has led to a practice that would be considered to be untenable in any other industry: the requirement that an employer (the club) lend its employee (the player) to another commercial body (an NGB) for it to use the employee's services for free.

In the past there were few serious complaints about this system as the assumption of the primacy of international sport went unquestioned. However the leading football clubs no longer appear to be so ready to accept that the release of their players for international matches is in their own best interests. In particular they are concerned that their star players are returned tired and/or injured, that they receive no contribution to their pay during their absence and no compensation if the player is unable to play because of injuries sustained whilst on international duty. These complaints are made against the backdrop of FIFA and UEFA making huge profits out of the tournaments that they organise and in which the clubs' employees are playing. Furthermore there is a growing conflict of commercial interests as the clubs, FIFA and UEFA all seek to maximise their profits from merchandising and broadcast income from the same audiences: the fans and the media companies.

The current rules on player release are found in Annexe 1 FIFA Regulations on the Status and Transfer of Players. Art.1 requires clubs to release their registered players for international fixtures when called on to do so by the relevant national team for a period of 48 hours before a friendly match and four days before a competitive fixture that is included on the coordinated international match calendar. They must also be released for the duration of any approved tournament. Art.2 FIFA Regulations states that it is the responsibility of the clubs to insure their players against illness and injury whilst they are on international duty and that the clubs are not entitled to any financial compensation should any of their players suffer injury during one of these fixtures. Should any litigation on this rule reach the ECJ, it will be necessary to determine whether it is compatible with Arts.101 and 102 TFEU in the light of the reasoning developed in *Meca-Medina* and *MOTOE*.

Firstly FIFA is operating as either an undertaking in its own right or as an association of undertakings made up of the individual national and continental football associations that constitute its membership. Following *MOTOE*, FIFA is likely to be found to be acting in a dual role when it organises international representative fixtures; it is acting as a regulatory body by formulating the applicable rules and regulations for football on a worldwide basis but it is also acting as a commercial entity by organising the World Cup and other officially sanctioned championships. Despite the ECJ stating in *Walrave* that

international sport is not an economic activity, the player release rules appear to have an impact on an economic activity as they have the potential to impede a player's ability to perform their contractual obligations and are for the purpose of enabling tournaments in respect of which FIFA will have entered into sponsorship, advertising, broadcasting and insurance contracts to take place.

Secondly the rule has the potential to restrict competition under Art.101(1) TFEU as being a decision of a group of undertakings (the NGBs) or a concerted practice that forces the clubs to release their players for international competitions to their own competitive detriment. Further, it could be argued that FIFA is abusing its dominant position contrary to Art.102 TFEU by forcing clubs to release their players for use in competitions that it has sanctioned and by reserving to itself the power to punish those clubs who refuse to comply. The response to any such claim would be that the player release rules are inherent in the organisation and proper conduct of international competitive football and are no more than is necessary to achieve the legitimate objective of running a major championship. FIFA and most other ISFs would argue that international tournaments are at the top of the sporting pyramid according to the European model of sport and that therefore players must be released in order to participate in these competitions. Moreover as the money generated by these competitions is distributed throughout all levels of the sport, it would undermine grassroots funding if the professional clubs were able to secure for themselves a much larger share of this income in order to be compensated for the loss of one of their players. On the other hand the clubs argue that the success of these tournaments is predicated on the release of their star players who often return from international duty unable to perform to the best of their abilities for their full-time employers. They would argue that the current system of compulsory player release should be either abolished on the basis of its being an unlawful restriction or radically reformed because it is a disproportionate means of achieving its objective.

This second part of the test is central to the determination of the legality of the compulsory player release rules. If the rules are held to be a restriction then there is little doubt that they affect trade within the internal market and it will be difficult to justify them under Art.101(3) TFEU unless it can be argued that there is some benefit to consumers in watching international fixtures. The compulsory player release rules are undoubtedly necessary for the proper functioning of international competitive sport in the way that it is currently conducted. However FIFA and the other ISFs have so far been unable to provide an explanation of why they consider country-based international competitions to be such an important part of the proper organisation of their sports that inherently anti-competitive rules should be allowed to support their continuation. It has instead always been assumed that the organisation of international sport is a legitimate objective of an ISF; it has never been proved that it is. As was seen in *Bosman*, arguments based on sentiment and history rather than objective evidence are unlikely to succeed before the ECJ. Even if a sufficiently robust justification can be advanced, it must then be shown that the compulsory and uncompensated release of players for international duty is proportionate for the organisation of these tournaments. In the light of the revenue generated by FIFA from its international competitions, it is likely that a less restrictive alternative could be found by, for example, providing insurance and some form of compensation to those who are injured whilst representing their country.

If the legality of compulsory player release clauses was ever challenged, it is likely that both the ECJ and European Commission would provide limited support to the ISFs' position. EU law protects the autonomy of sport and its governing bodies, if only conditionally, and the preservation of international competition would appear to be one of the 'specificities of sport' that requires different treatment. However the unfettered right of an ISF to demand that a player represent his country is unlikely to be lawful without a more robust justification for why international sport is so much more special than that which is played between the leading professional clubs.

Summary

3.1 The relationship between global and European sports law is becoming increasingly important in the light of both the CAS and the ECJ claiming jurisdiction over many of the same disputes. As the caseload of CAS continues to grow and as it is asked to resolve disputes of increasing legal complexity which often require an interpretation of EU law, this relationship could become symbiotic where each tribunal takes into consideration the jurisprudence of the other, or one of extreme tension where each tries to gain precedence over the other. As the goals of each tribunal are not necessarily the same, with the ECJ seeking to promote European integration whilst CAS seeks to protect the best interests of sport, the possibility for conflict and disagreement in the future will need to be addressed. Although both bodies take into account the 'specificity of sport' when reaching their decisions, CAS has been more sympathetic to the needs of sport than has the ECJ in the development of its own *lex sportiva*.

3.2 EU law, particularly the provisions of the TFEU, apply to sports disputes where the conduct or relationship concerned can be said to be, or have an impact on, an economic activity. Only rules that are inherent and necessary for the proper playing and administration of the sport in question will fall outside of the scope of EU law. Further, the ECJ will not review the rules of a game or the decisions of the match officials. However this means that almost all conduct of a club, NGB and ISF that involves professional and semi-professional sport will affect an economic activity and has the potential to engage EU law. Where a rule is inherent in the organisation and proper conduct of a sport, it will be lawful. If the rule is a restriction according to EU competition law and affects trade within the internal market, then it can only be lawful if it can be justified under Art.101(3) TFEU. Alternatively if the rule is a restriction of the free movement provisions, it will be lawful if it can be objectively justified. Thus the ECJ will take into account the 'specificity of sport' but it will not grant a blanket exemption from the operation of EU law to sport.

Summary cont'd

3.3 The jurisprudence of CAS is becoming an increasingly important source of sports law in the light of the number and complexity of the cases that it hears. As one of its aims is to standardise the legal norms applied by all sports bodies, its proactive approach to the development of legally robust rules and procedures has played a significant role in the development of sporting justice. Its sports-sympathetic approach attempts to improve standards of good governance and fairness whilst minimising the negative impact of its decisions on ISFs. However the development by CAS of a *lex sportiva* may at some point in the future come into conflict with the jurisprudence of the ECJ in disputes requiring an interpretation of EU law.

Further reading

Craig and De Burca, *EU Law* (4th edn, 2008, Oxford University Press) ch 13

Lewis and Taylor (eds), *Sport: Law and Practice* (2nd edn, 2008, Tottel) chs B2 and 3

Parrish and Miettinen, *The sporting exception in European Union Law* (2008, TMC Asser Press)

Weatherill, *Cases and Materials on EU Law* (8th edn, 2007, Oxford University Press) chs 7, 13, 14 and 16

Beloff, 'The Court of Arbitration for Sport at the Beijing Olympics' [2009] 1 *International Sports Law Review* 3

Foster, 'Lex sportiva and lex ludica: the Court of Arbitration for Sport's jurisprudence' (2004) 3(2) *Entertainment and Sports Law Journal*, online

Miettinen, 'Policing the boundaries between regulation and commercial exploitation: lessons from the MOTOE case' [2008] 3/4 *International Sports Law Journal* 13

Rincon, 'EC competition and internal market law: on the existence of a sporting exemption and its withdrawal' (2007) 3(3) *Journal of Contemporary European Research* 224

Subiotto, 'How a lack of analytical rigour has resulted in an overbroad application of EC competition law in the sports sector' [2009] 2 *International Sports Law Review* 21

Szyszczak, 'Competition and sport' (2007) 32(1) *European Law Review* 95

Wathelet, 'Sport governance and EU legal order' in Gardiner, Parrish and Siekmann (eds), *EU, Sport, Law and Policy* (2009, TMC Asser Press) ch 4

Weatherill, 'The influence of EU law on sports governance' in Gardiner, Parrish and Siekmann (eds), *EU, Sport, Law and Policy* (2009, TMC Asser Press) ch 5

Weatherill, 'The *White Paper on Sport* as an exercise in "Better Regulation"' in Gardiner, Parrish and Siekmann (eds), *EU, Sport, Law and Policy* (2009, TMC Asser Press) ch 6

Weatherill, 'Anti-doping revisited – the demise of the rule of 'purely sporting interest'? (2006) 27(12) *European Competition Law Review* 645

Weatherill, 'Article 82 EC and sporting 'conflict of interest': the judgment in MOTOE' [2009] 1/2 *International Sports Law Journal* 3

Links to relevant websites can be found at www.palgrave.com/law/james

Part 2

Sports injuries and dangerous sports

Chapter 4

Liability for injuries caused by other participants

Key words

- **Damages** – the compensation awarded to a claimant following a successful claim.
- **Man of straw** – a defendant, or potential defendant, who has insufficient funds to meet any award of damages made against him.
- **Negligence** – the defendant owes a duty of care not to cause harm to the claimant and has breached that duty by falling below the standard of conduct expected in the circumstances and has caused reasonably foreseeable harm.
- **Tort** – unlawful conduct actionable in the civil courts, usually to recover damages.
- **Trespass to the person (battery)** – the direct and intentional application of force to the person of the claimant by the defendant where the touching was made without the claimant's consent.
- **Vicarious liability** – the employer is responsible for the tortious acts of its employee where the tort committed has sufficient connection to the employee's employment.

4.1 The growth of sports torts

The use of the law of tort to secure compensation for injury is the most commonly occurring example of sports law in action. Although only attracting mainstream media attention where there has been a catastrophic injury or where the injured person is a high profile athlete, many thousands of claims are made each year at all levels of participation and across many different sporting disciplines. The growth in litigation in this area has been rapid: the first reported case involving one sportsperson suing another came before the Court of Appeal as recently as 1985 in *Condon* v. *Basi* [1985] 1 WLR 866 (below, 4.4.1.1). Perhaps the only surprising point to be made about this rapid expansion of the law is the lack of a definitive ruling from the House of Lords or Supreme Court on the application of the law of tort to cases involving sports injuries.

This area of sports law, as with all tortious claims for personal injury, is dominated by issues of public policy and insurance. Whether or not the defendant is adequately insured will often determine whether or not a claim should be brought against them; if the defendant is an uninsured 'man of straw' then any judgment entered against them will be at best a hollow victory for the claimant. The ability or otherwise of the defendant to meet any damages award may trigger a search for other potential defendants against whom a claim is not only likely to be successful but who can also afford to pay the compensation awarded (see further, chapter 5).

There is no specific identifiable reason for the growth in the use of the law to resolve sports disputes of this kind. The existence of a so-called compensation culture may help to explain why people have a greater knowledge of their legal rights when they are injured, or it may be that potential claimants are less likely to accept that accidents happen rather than there being someone to blame for their misfortune. Section 1 Compensation Act 2006 was introduced to limit specifically the deterrent effect that excessive litigation may have on participation in, and the organisation of, risky activities such as sports. Whether or not s.1 has any impact on the ongoing juridification of this area is as yet uncertain.

4.1.1 Choice of tort – negligence or trespass to the person?

The first important decision that an injured sportsperson will have to make is whether to pursue their claim in trespass to the person or negligence. Until *Gravil v. Carroll and Redruth Rugby Football Club* [2008] EWCA Civ 689 (below, 4.5.3), where the claimant received compensation for injuries caused by a punch thrown by an opponent, it was assumed that only very rarely would a claimant rely on trespass to the person as the appropriate cause of action as most insurance policies exclude liability for deliberately caused injury. In *Elliott v. Saunders and Liverpool FC* (unreported) High Court (QBD) 10 June 1994, the initial claim for trespass, arising from a challenge in a professional football match, was dropped and only the claim in negligence pursued after it was brought to the attention of the claimant that Liverpool FC's employer's liability insurance would not meet a claim for deliberately inflicted injury. Thus in the vast majority of cases the claimant will bring their claim in negligence.

4.2 Trespass to the person

Trespass to the person comprises three distinct torts: assault, battery and false imprisonment. In the sports context only battery will be considered as the other two torts are unlikely ever to be actionable. This is because they rarely result in physical injury to the claimant and are generally used to protect rights rather than secure compensation for harm caused. The tort of assault is committed where the defendant threatens the claimant with immediate unlawful force. The tort of false imprisonment is where the defendant imposes a total restraint on the claimant's freedom of movement from a particular place. Where sports participants are involved, battery, which requires that the defendant applies physical force to the claimant, will be the most appropriate cause of action.

4.2.1 Battery

In order to establish a successful claim in battery, the claimant must prove that there has been a direct and intentional application of force to their person by the defendant and that the touching was made without their consent. There is no need to establish that any injury has been caused; the tort is completed by the defendant interfering with the claimant's right not to have their bodily integrity interfered with as every person's body is considered inviolate (*Collins v. Wilcock* [1984] 1 WLR 1172). The degree of injury caused will only affect the quantum of damages awarded as compensation, not whether the tort has been committed in the first place.

4.2.1.1 Direct contact

The contact made with the claimant must be direct. In essence this means that there must be actual physical contact between the defendant and the claimant. Direct contacts include those where the defendant causes an object such as a hockey stick, or a missile such as a ball, to come into contact with the claimant (*Scott v. Shepherd* (1773) 96 ER 525). The unlawful contact can also include what is referred to as a 'continuing battery'. This is where a contact which was originally lawful, for example because it was consented to, becomes unlawful because it continues to be performed by the defendant for a length of time or with a degree of force to which the claimant does not consent (*Fagan* v. *Metropolitan Police Commissioner* [1969] 1 QB 439). For example if a defendant wrestler is awarded a bout on the basis of a submission but refuses to let go of the claimant after the referee has counted his opponent out, the continuing nature of the battery will mean that what was originally a legitimate touching becomes an unlawful and actionable battery.

4.2.1.2 Intentional contact

The contact with the claimant must be made intentionally by the defendant. Where the contact is made carelessly, any legal action should be brought in negligence (*Letang* v. *Cooper* [1965] QB 232). There is no specific definition of intention in the case law, however it can be described as a requirement that the defendant acts deliberately and that contact with the claimant is the desired outcome of the deliberately performed act. There is no need for the defendant to intend any harm to be caused to the claimant. The difficulties associated with proving not only that the defendant intended to act in the way that he did, but also that he intended to make contact with the claimant, mean that battery will only rarely be pleaded.

It has recently been accepted by the courts that intention is wide enough to include what is referred to as 'transferred intent'. This occurs where for example the defendant aims a punch at a person who ducks out of the way and is unharmed, but the claimant is unexpectedly struck by the blow instead. In such a situation the intent to hit the original target of the punch is transferred to the claimant and the tort is completed (*Bici* v. *Ministry of Defence* [2004] EWHC 786).

4.2.1.3 Contact without the claimant's consent

Finally the contact must be made without, or in excess of, the consent of the claimant (below, 4.6.1.1). Consent can either be express or implied. Express consent is where the claimant agrees in advance that certain contacts may be made with him or her in certain circumstances. Implied consent is where the claimant's agreement to the contact can be inferred from the situation in which they have placed themselves. For example a rugby player may not specifically explain to each of his opponents before kick-off that they can tackle him when he has the ball, however it can be inferred by his taking to the field to take part in the game that he has agreed to be tackled in ways allowed by the rules. Thus a tackle around the legs when the player is carrying the ball will be consented to but a punch thrown at him at any time will not.

4.3   Negligence

The tort of negligence has developed over the years to provide compensation to those who have been caused harm by the careless actions of others. It judges a defendant objectively against the standard of behaviour expected of the reasonable person performing the injury-causing activity with a reasonable degree of care and skill. If the defendant has acted in accordance with those standards, then the duty is discharged and no liability will be imposed, however if the relevant standard of behaviour has not been reached then liability is likely to follow.

To establish negligence against a defendant, the claimant must prove that a duty of care was owed to them in the circumstances in which the activity was taking place (*Caparo Industries plc v. Dickman* [1990] 2 AC 605). If a duty was owed then it must be established that when injuring the claimant, the defendant had breached the duty by dropping below the expected standard of behaviour in the circumstances (*Nettleship v. Weston* [1971] 2 QB 691). If breach of duty can also be established then the claimant must next prove that there was a causal link between the breach and any harm caused by asking whether, but for the actions of the defendant, the claimant would still have suffered the same harm (*Barnett v. Chelsea and Kensington Hospital Management Committee* [1969] 1 QB 428). Finally the claimant must establish that the injuries suffered were a reasonably foreseeable consequence of the defendant's actions (*The Wagon Mound (No1)* [1961] AC 388). Where each of these elements of the tort are established on the balance of probabilities by the claimant and the defendant is unable to raise any appropriate defence, then the action in negligence will be successful.

An action in negligence is the most common means of securing compensation for injuries caused during sporting competition. In this section, actions against other participants, and where appropriate their employers, will be considered, whilst actions against others who may have caused the harm to the athlete, for example the coach, referee, event organiser or stadium owner, are considered in Chapter 5. Regardless of the category of defendant against whom an action is brought, liability is determined according to the same basic test: whether the defendant has breached the duty of care that they owed to the claimant and whether the breach of that duty caused the claimant's injuries. Only the content of the specific duty owed and the reasonable person against whom the defendant's conduct is judged change from case to case.

4.4 Negligence in sports cases

To date there has not been a negligence claim involving sports injuries that has reached the House of Lords or Supreme Court. Despite this, the law in this area has over the years become relatively settled. As will be seen, there are still some areas where vagueness and inconsistency would benefit from clarification from the Supreme Court, however the cases that have been reported provide sufficient guidance to cover the vast majority of incidents that occur.

4.4.1 Duty of care

4.4.1.1 The emergence of a sport-specific duty of care

The first step towards establishing a claim of negligence is to define the duty of care owed by the defendant to the claimant.

▶ *Condon v. Basi* [1985] 1 WLR 866

The defendant challenged the claimant in an attempt to tackle him whilst playing in an amateur football match. The tackle was performed by means of a slide from about three metres away and contact was made with the back of the claimant's leg about 30 cm off the ground with the studs pointing forwards. The tackle, for which the defendant was sent off, was described as reckless and dangerous and broke the claimant's right leg. The Court of

Appeal held that despite the lack of previous authority on the point, a duty of care was owed by those taking part in competitive sport to their co-participants and which was objectively defined according to all the relevant circumstances. If a player fell below the standard of care reasonably to be expected of those taking part in the game, then he would be liable to anyone injured as a consequence of his actions.

At trial Judge Wootton saw no need to define the duty of care as there was, in his opinion, such a clear breach of the expected standards of play by the defendant as he had injured the claimant by an act of serious and dangerous foul play. In the Court of Appeal, Donaldson MR accepted the conclusions of the trial judge and put forward two alternative definitions of the duty of care as had been formulated in the Australian case of *Rootes* v. *Shelton* [1968] ALR 33. On the one hand the duty was to take reasonable care not to cause harm to those reasonably foreseeably at risk from the conduct but that injuries caused by inherent risks of participation in the activity would be considered to have been consented to and therefore not actionable. On the other hand the duty was to take all reasonable care not to cause harm to those reasonably foreseeably at risk from the conduct but that the circumstances in which the activity was taking place must always be taken into account. According to either formulation, the defendant's conduct was so far below that which would have been expected in the circumstances that negligence was established.

Donaldson MR preferred the latter construction of the duty, which is also more in line with the way that the generalised duty of care was originally defined by Lord Aitken in *Donoghue* v. *Stevenson* [1932] AC 502. By leaving it open for subsequent courts to choose which version of the duty to impose however, the Court of Appeal introduced an unnecessary degree of uncertainty and confusion.

Since the judgment of the Court of Appeal in *Condon*, it has been accepted that a duty of care is owed by a sports participant to each and every other participant in the contest. What remained at issue was the precise definition of this duty. The cases which were reported over the following 16 years added to this confusion by mixing issues of consent into the definition of duty as required by the first alternative definition above, and by introducing elements of the standard of care into the definition of the duty owed. This leaves many of the cases decided between 1985 and 2001 as being of factual interest but little legal value.

4.4.1.2 Defining sports negligence

In 2001 the Court of Appeal handed down one of its most important sports judgments in *Caldwell* v. *Maguire and Fitzgerald* [2001] EWCA Civ 1054. In approving Holland J's propositions concerning the definition of the duty of care owed by sports participants, the Court of Appeal also clarified how the duty could be breached.

▶ *Caldwell* v. *Maguire and Fitzgerald* [2001] EWCA Civ 1054

The parties were professional jockeys competing in a race. As they entered the final straight, the defendants, who were placed first and second, moved towards the inside barrier causing the third placed horse to move in front of and trip up the fourth placed horse, ridden by the claimant. The claimant was seriously injured as a result of being unseated from his horse. The defendants were found guilty of careless riding by the stewards and banned for three days. The Court of Appeal held that,

1 Each Contestant in a lawful sporting contest … owes a duty of care to each and all other contestants.

2 That duty is to exercise in the course of the contest all care that is objectively reasonable in the prevailing circumstances for the avoidance of infliction of injury to such fellow contestants.

3 The prevailing circumstances are all such properly attendant upon the contest and include its object, the demands inevitably made upon its contestants, its inherent dangers (if any), its rules, conventions and customs, and the standards, skills and judgment reasonably to be expected of a contestant. (For a discussion of the appropriate standard of care see below, 4.4.2.3.1.)

The claim failed on the basis that the interference that had occurred was a commonly occurring inherent risk of professional horse racing.

The first of these propositions merely confirms the basic finding of the Court in *Condon*: that a duty of care is owed. The second proposition is a modern restatement of the law as originally defined in *Donoghue* v. *Stevenson*, with its focus on the need to take account of the prevailing circumstances in which the incident took place. It is the third proposition that provides the detail necessary to enable a court to determine the scope of the specific duty owed by a sports participant in any given situation. By highlighting the various circumstances that may be relevant to a case of sports negligence, the Court enables the same basic test to be used regardless of the sport actually being played at the time that the injury occurred.

In *Caldwell* the Court stated that in the particular case of a horse race the prevailing circumstances include the jockey's obligation to ride their horse over a given course whilst competing with the remaining contestants for the best possible placing, if not for a win. The circumstances must also include the rules or laws of the sport in question, in this case the Rules of Racing, and the standards, skills and judgement of a professional jockey, all as expected by their co-participants. Thus a very specific duty of care can be defined in respect of professional jockeys when competing in a race that takes into consideration their knowledge and training. Further, by making reference to the inherent dangers associated with participating in sport, the test also takes into account that injuries can and do happen to sports participants.

4.4.1.3 The playing culture of a sport

The only part of the judgment that is neither fully explained nor immediately obvious is the reference to the 'conventions and customs' of the game. Assuming that both the trial court and the Court of Appeal did not simply add in this phrase gratuitously, some meaning must be attached to it. It appears to be something beyond the rules of the game as these are specifically mentioned immediately before this phrase, but it has not been explained further by later courts.

Perhaps the most appropriate interpretation of the 'conventions and customs' of a game is if this phrase extends acceptable play to include the unofficial rules or interpretations of how a game is actually played, in contrast to how the letter of the rules of the sport states that it ought to be played. By extending the circumstances which must be taken into account by a court to include the playing culture of a sport, a duty of care that is most appropriate to the actual level of the particular sport can be imposed. This will ensure that commonly occurring acts that are technically foul play, or foul play that is generally not injury-causing, will be considered to be acceptable either because it is a relevant circumstance of the playing of the particular game or because it is an inherent risk associated with it.

For example pushing an opponent is against the rules of both football and basketball. It is entirely possible that someone may fall and be injured by such a push, however this kind of foul play occurs with such regularity in these sports that it would be considered to be an acceptable means of playing the game because it is within the playing culture of the sport, even though a foul would be awarded against the pusher. Where such low-level foul play is known to occur, players can guard against it or take evasive action. Only those fouls more likely to result in serious injury would then be legally actionable as those playing the game would be taken to appreciate that such conduct is unacceptable and unconnected with the proper playing of the game. Although such a view is contrary to the opinions of writers such as Grayson, who considered that all foul play that resulted in injury should be actionable, the introduction of the playing culture of a sport as a relevant circumstance reflects more accurately the way that sport is in fact played.

> ▶ *Leatherland* v. *Edwards*, (unreported) **High Court (QBD), 28 October 1998**
>
> The claimant and defendant were engaged in a game of uni-hockey, a fast-moving, non-contact, short-form version of hockey. It was understood by all participants that the ball was not supposed to rise above the surface of the pitch and that the plastic sticks should not be raised above waist height. The defendant took a shot at goal and continued his follow-through into the face of the claimant causing his eye to implode. It was held that by raising his stick above shoulder height, the defendant had breached a core safety rule of the game that was central to its purpose and spirit. Such dangerous conduct, when players were moving at speed and in close proximity to each other, was a clear breach of the duty of care owed by one sports participant to another and the defendant was found liable for the injuries caused to the claimant.

In contrast, the defendant in *Pitcher* v. *Huddersfield Town Football Club* [2001] All ER (D) 223 was found not liable for a mistimed challenge which broke the claimant's leg. Although both injuries resulted from the foul play of the defendant, only the challenge in *Leatherland* was considered negligent as it was a breach of a safety rule of the game and was therefore totally prohibited; the challenge in *Pitcher* was considered to be an error of judgement that any reasonable First Division footballer could have made.

4.4.1.4 Codes of conduct

In some cases the parties have relied on a code of conduct drawn up by a sport's governing body or international federation that explains specifically the kind of behaviour expected of those participating in that sport. Many sporting codes of conduct are of little use in this context as their phrasing is too vague or because they are nothing more than entreaties to play fair and play by the rules. Others are of such detail that they can almost be elevated to the status of rules of the game.

> ▶ *Lyon* v. *Maidment* [2002] EWHC 1227
>
> The parties were involved in a collision whilst on a skiing holiday together. The defendant had set off down the hill first followed shortly afterwards by the claimant. When defining the scope of the duty of care owed by one skier to another, both the claimant's expert witness and the trial judge made specific reference to the International Ski Federation's '10 FIS Rules for Conduct.' These Rules are applicable to all skiers and snowboarders skiing anywhere in the

world and according to FIS must be considered an ideal pattern of conduct for a responsible and careful skier or snowboarder and their purpose is to avoid accidents on the piste. The preamble to the Rules also gives a clear warning that a failure to adhere to them could expose a skier or snowboarder to civil and/or criminal liability in the event of a collision.

This document and the accompanying explanatory notes make it clear that a duty is imposed on a skier higher up the mountain to look out for, take care to avoid and leave sufficient room when overtaking a skier who is lower down the mountain. Dismissing the claim, the court held that as the claimant had come from higher up the mountain he, not the defendant, should have taken care to ensure that the collision did not take place.

Although an unusual example of an ISF taking such a proactive stance on safety issues, to the extent of informing those who read the Rules of their potential legal liability if they breach them, this is the kind of document that is likely to become more common in the future. Not only does it make the sport safer by explaining how a participant should act in certain circumstances and why, it also helps to insulate FIS from any potential legal action (see further, chapter 5.4).

4.4.2 Breach of duty and the expected standard of behaviour

As with the definition of the duty of care owed, a detailed explanation of how the duty could be breached by a sports participant has been, and to some extent still is, lacking. The basic tortious test for breach of duty is to determine objectively whether or not the conduct of the defendant dropped below the standard of a reasonable and competent person acting in those circumstances. On the face of it, that appears to mean that the test to be applied should be for example, that of the reasonable and competent rugby player, swimmer, basketball player or jockey. Such a broadly defined test gives rise to a number of what appear to be sport-specific problems: who is the relevant comparator, or the reasonable and competent player? Is there a variable standard of care within and between sports and if so how and why does it vary? Does the defendant merely have to drop below the expected standard of care or does he or she have to act with a reckless disregard for the health and safety of the claimant? As with the definition of the duty of care, most of these problems originate from the judgment in *Condon* and its lack of specific detail.

4.4.2.1 The reasonable and competent player

Identifying against whom the defendant's conduct ought to be judged has been a constant source of debate and confusion since *Condon*. To speak of the 'reasonable footballer' is a gross over-simplification of the court's task. Firstly this does not take into account that the duty element of the tort requires an examination of all the relevant circumstances, which will include the level at which the game was being played. Secondly it does not take into account the hierarchical structure by which most sport in this country is organised, where participants, including teams, of similar ability play against each other for a season. Promotion and relegation, whether moving between leagues or up and down ranking tables, is the norm with the aim being to keep mismatches to a minimum.

Unlike driving on the road for example, sport is not a closed system but a series of closed systems. When using the highway, everyone needs to be judged by the same basic standard of care to ensure that a minimum degree of skill is attained and maintained by all road users. This is a closed system where one standard is both necessary and appropriate for all actors (*Nettleship*). Where sport is concerned each league, or perhaps each competition is itself a closed system; as the circumstances change, such as the league or ranking status of the participants, the standard of care changes.

This issue has caused much debate and controversy over the years. The confusion began in *Condon* when Donaldson MR stated that there would be a higher degree of care required of a player in a First Division football match than of a player in a local league football match. Drake J distanced himself from this comment in *Elliott* and returned to the one-size-fits-all test, a test that has attracted much approval. The difficulty with both of these formulations is that they approach the issue from the wrong perspective. Both confuse the duty owed with the standard of care against which the defendant should be judged and both assume that the key to liability lies in the degree of care owed by the defendant to the claimant.

In reality these never change; the defendant owes a duty to act with reasonable care to avoid causing injury to other participants in the contest, taking into account all relevant circumstances, one of which is the level of competition at which the incident occurs. The standard of care owed is that of the reasonable player in the circumstances in which the incident took place; this requires the defendant to be judged against the standard of the reasonable player who is playing at the same level of the sporting pyramid as they are.

4.4.2.2 A variable standard of care?

There is nothing in the law of tort that would consider such an approach to be inappropriate. This is not introducing a variable standard of care that allows a less skilled player to cause more injury than could a more skilled player. It is instead analogous to the tests which are applicable in professional negligence cases. Following *Bolam* v. *Friern Hospital Management Committee* [1957] 1 WLR 582, the court can enquire what the reasonable person of the same level of skill or training or qualification would have done in those circumstances. It also allows the court to ask the defendant to justify the option that they took that led to the injury being caused, as per *Bolitho* v. *City and Hackney Health Authority* [1998] AC 232.

This means that far from allowing less skilled players to cause more injury or to take less care than those who are more skilled, the test asks whether or not the defendant was competent to perform the particular move that led to the claimant's injury. In determining the defendant's level of competence, the court will look at their level of training, the degree of skill expected at that level of the sporting pyramid and the expectations of others playing at the same level. Thus more skilled players may be able to take greater risks as they are more highly trained in performing the particular action safely and their opponents will be more highly skilled in taking the necessary evasive action.

More recent cases have started to define the standard of care in this more specific manner almost as a matter of course. In *Caldwell*, the High Court and Court of Appeal referred to the standard of the professional jockey. In *Pitcher* the High Court referred to the standard of the reasonable First Division footballer and in *Richardson* v. *Davies* [2006] 1 CL 405, the County Court applied the standard of care and skill to be expected of a player in an amateur Sunday league football match.

The civil courts have long been able to apply different standards of care based on a defendant's training, qualifications and expected skill levels. The sports negligence cases are finally coming round to defining the test for breach of duty in line with the way that the law is applied in analogous situations. This is not so much introducing a variable standard of care but ensuring that all the relevant circumstances of the case are properly taken into account when determining the liability of the defendant.

4.4.2.3 Negligence v. reckless disregard

The standard of conduct sufficient to breach the duty of care owed by a sports participant has generated a disproportionate amount of comment and confusion. There are three distinct strands to this confusion. Firstly most of the early reported cases described the defendants' behaviour as being in reckless disregard of the claimants' health and safety. Secondly there has been a misguided reliance on the *dicta* of Diplock LJ in *Wooldridge* v. *Sumner* [1963] 2 QB 43 (see chapter 8.4.3), where he refers to a sports participant being liable in negligence to a spectator at the event only where he has acted with a reckless disregard for the spectator's safety. Thirdly the adversarial nature of English civil litigation means that each side will try to define the parties' conduct in the most extreme terms.

Before addressing each of these issues in turn, it is important to state from the outset that the correct standard to be applied is negligence in all the circumstances. This test is fluid enough to take account of the fact that sports can range from the non-contact, such as tennis, to the full-contact, such as ice hockey. This test is applied throughout the law of negligence and to date there is no authority that requires the application of the less stringent reckless disregard test. If the court identifies the relevant circumstances with sufficient precision, the standard negligence test is more than adequate for determining liability. Reckless disregard can best be described as being a sufficient but not a necessary standard of conduct to establish liability in negligence against a defendant.

4.4.2.3.1 Judicial use of reckless disregard

From *Condon* onwards many of the reported cases have recorded that the defendant acted with a reckless disregard for the claimant's safety. More confusingly, as in *Elliott*, the duty is defined in terms of negligence in all the circumstances yet the defendant was found not liable on the basis that he was not guilty of dangerous or reckless play. Again it was the Court of Appeal in *Caldwell* that clarified the situation in its final two propositions.

▶ *Caldwell* v. *Maguire and Fitzgerald* [2001] EWCA Civ 1054

'4 Given the nature of such prevailing circumstances [above, 4.4.1.2] the threshold for liability is in practice inevitably high; the proof of a breach of duty will not flow from proof of no more than an error of judgement or from mere proof of a momentary lapse in skill (and thus care) respectively when subject to the stresses of [competition]. Such are no more than incidents inherent in the nature of the sport.

5 In practice it may therefore be difficult to prove any such breach of duty absent proof of conduct that in point of fact amounts to reckless disregard for the fellow contestant's safety. I emphasise the distinction between the expression of legal principle and the practicalities of the evidential burden.'

Proposition 4 reinforces that an examination of the circumstances in which the incident took place is of paramount importance. Further, it specifically takes into account that the playing of sport is rarely an exercise in perfection; mistakes are made, errors of judgement occur and injuries do unfortunately happen. Thus before imposing liability for an act of sporting negligence, the court needs to convince itself that the injury-causing act is something more than poor play and is something that no reasonable participant would have done; a clear application of negligence in the circumstances.

Proposition 5 attempts to explain the very fine distinction between the correct legal test and the evidence required to prove breach of duty. The legal test remains that of negligence in all the circumstances but, depending on the act committed or the sport being played, more cogent evidence may be required in order to prove the breach. This simply ensures that the court carries out a full analysis of the acceptability or otherwise of the particular conduct of the defendant. Where dangerous contacts are an inherent part of a sport, then more evidence will be required to prove that the injury-causing act was more than an error of judgement or a mistake. Alternatively, where interpersonal contact is not usually part of the normal playing of the sport, it may be much easier to prove that the injuries caused by such a contact were negligently inflicted. As the level of interference committed by the defendants was of a kind to be expected in a fast-moving sport such as national hunt racing, the claimant was unable to establish that the duty of care owed to him had been breached.

Despite this clear statement of the law and how it should apply to sport, some judges persist in handing down judgments couched in terms of reckless disregard. This may be a simple description of the finding of fact; that in the opinion of the judge the challenge was carried out with a reckless disregard for the safety of the claimant. Or it may be an attempt to discourage an appeal against the judgment by stating that the act was not just negligent but carried out with a reckless disregard for the claimant's safety. If this is the case, then the application of the law is correct even though the use of the specific phrase may cause confusion. What must always be remembered is that reckless disregard is not a standard recognised in the English law of negligence.

4.4.2.3.2 *Wooldridge v. Sumner* [1963] 2 QB 43

A further justification put forward for using the reckless disregard standard comes from a purported reliance on the dictum of Diplock LJ in *Wooldridge* (see further, chapter 8.4.3). Although not referred to by either court in *Condon*, *Wooldridge* is first cited, though not relied on, in *Elliott*. The confusing reference to the defendant in *Elliott* not having acted dangerously or recklessly may have inadvertently left open the door to later parties to rebut a claim of negligence on the basis that reckless disregard should instead be relied on. Thus by sheer force of repetition the reckless disregard standard has been elevated beyond its original status and meaning.

The first criticism that can be made of any specific reliance on *Wooldridge* is that it involves an incident that takes place between a participant in an event and a spectator at it, not two sports participants. It is therefore neither a direct nor a particularly good authority on which to rely. If the correct test of negligence in all the circumstances is applied, then the main distinguishing circumstance here is the status of the claimants. The dynamic interaction between two participants with each other and a participant with a spectator are so different as to negate any possible claim that the cases are analogous. Cases that purport to rely on *Wooldridge* in situations where both claimant and defendant are sports participants therefore could be considered *per incuriam*.

The second criticism is that the passages from *Wooldridge* relied on by those who wish to develop the reckless disregard standard have been taken out of their proper context. There is no doubt that Sellers LJ stated that if the conduct is reckless and in disregard of all safety of others then liability might attach and that later in the judgment Diplock LJ felt that a person attending a sporting event voluntarily runs the risk of injury unless the participant's conduct is such as to evince a reckless disregard of the spectator's safety.

However a closer reading of the surrounding passages makes clear that these statements are a description of the evidence potentially needed to prove a claim in negligence, as per Holland J and Tuckey LJ in *Caldwell*, not an attempt to create a completely new tort of reckless disregard; it is sufficient, though not necessary, to prove that a person acted with reckless disregard in order to establish a claim of negligence against them.

4.4.2.3.3 Civil procedure

That this discussion continues despite the recent pronouncements of the Court of Appeal is most likely explained by the adversarial nature of English civil litigation. All claimants will plead their case in terms of the defendant having dropped below the standard of the reasonable and competent participant at that level of that sport. All defendants will argue that they should only be found liable in negligence if it can be proved that they acted with a reckless disregard for the health and safety of the claimant, a much more difficult standard for the claimant to prove.

Although a defendant's attempted reliance on the reckless disregard standard is wrong in law, by defending their case in this way counsel will be hoping to sow seeds of doubt in the mind of the court. By claiming that he or she should only be liable on a finding of reckless disregard, the defendant will be attempting to demonstrate that the incident was less serious, or more acceptable, than it might otherwise have seemed. This tactical use of reckless disregard is entirely understandable from the defendant's perspective. As long as the judge applies the correct test, no harm is done to the law.

4.4.3　The causal link between the breach of duty and the harm caused

Causation in negligence is examined from two perspectives: causation in fact and causation in law. The former identifies which parties have the relevant proximity to the incident to be potential defendants. The latter limits the ramifications of the negligent act to only those consequences which are reasonably foreseeable.

4.4.3.1 Causation in fact – the 'but for' test

Establishing causation in fact is often referred to as a need to satisfy the 'but for' test (*Barnett*). This simply requires the court to ask itself, 'but for the actions of the defendant, would the claimant have been caused this harm?' If the answer is no, then the actions of the defendant are a factually relevant cause of the claimant's injuries. Where one participant is accused of injuring another during a sporting contest, establishing this element of the causal link between the breach of the duty and the harm caused should not pose any difficulties as there will usually have been direct contact between the parties.

4.4.3.2 Causation in law – the foreseeability of the injuries caused

The general rule for establishing causation in law is that the defendant is liable for all reasonably foreseeable harm flowing from their negligent injury-causing act (*The Wagon Mound No 1*). Thus if the type of harm, for example personal injury by interpersonal contact, is reasonably foreseeable from the point of view of the reasonable person in the position of the defendant at the time that the duty of care is breached, then liability in negligence will be established. In the vast majority of sports negligence cases, this element of the tort will not be problematic; even where the reasonable person would only anticipate a minor injury, such as a bruise, but a more serious injury such as a fracture was caused, the broad type of harm is reasonably foreseeable and liability will be imposed.

Following *Watson and Bradford City AFC (1983) Ltd* v. *Gray and Huddersfield Town AFC Ltd* (1998) The Times 26 November, several cases have applied a variation of this test for which there is neither explanation nor authority. In *Watson* v. *Gray*, Hooper J held that, 'such a forceful, high challenge ... was one that a reasonable professional player would have known carried with it a significant risk of serious injury.' More recently in *Richardson* it was held that, 'a reasonable amateur player in the defendant's position would have known that there was a significant risk that his actions would result in serious injury to [the claimant].'

These variations contain an important error: it is the type of harm caused, such as personal injury, not the degree of harm caused, for example serious injury, that must be foreseen by the reasonable person (*Smith* v. *Leech Brain and Co Ltd* [1962] 2 QB 405). Although the courts may be attempting to filter out claims for minor injuries and ensure that the floodgates are not opened to such actions, foreseeability must be defined as per the *Wagon Mound No 1*.

4.5 Vicarious liability

Vicarious liability is when an employer is held responsible for the tortious acts of one of its employees. It is imposed on an employer where the tort committed has a sufficiently close connection to the employee's employment or job (*Lister* v. *Hesley Hall Ltd* [2001] UKHL 22). The employer does not have to be found liable in negligence for anything that it has done; it is simply liable for the negligent conduct of its employee.

The purpose of vicarious liability is to give the claimant a better opportunity to receive their damages in full as the employer is likely to be better able to meet the award either because it has more available money or better insurance cover than the employee. The justification for imposing liability on the employer despite it not having done anything wrong is twofold. Firstly because the employer reaps the benefit of the acts of the employee, it should pay for the consequences of wrongdoing by that employee. Secondly the threat of vicarious liability being imposed on the employer should ensure that it imposes certain levels of conduct on, and provides sufficient training to, its employees. Taken together, the employer is provided with an incentive to deter its employees from behaving unlawfully whilst acting in the course of their employment.

4.5.1 Bringing a claim based on vicarious liability

To bring a claim based on vicarious liability, the claimant must first establish that there is a contract of employment in place between the defendant and the club. This includes part-time or semi-professional contracts not just full-time contracts, but is not available where the defendant is an amateur or unpaid player (*Gravil*).

Once the existence of an employment contract has been proved, the employer must be added as a defendant to the claim. For example in *McCord* v. *Cornforth and Swansea City AFC* (1997) The Times 11 February, the defendant player, Cornforth, was a professional footballer employed full-time by Swansea City FC. Here Cornforth was accused of having acted negligently by causing injury through foul play whilst Swansea City FC were claimed to be vicariously liable for his negligent conduct. In some more recent cases, for example *Pitcher* v. *Huddersfield Town FC* and *Gaynor* v. *Blackpool FC* [2002] CLY 3280, the player who caused the claimant's injuries is not listed as a defendant because it was accepted from the outset that if a tort can be established against the player the club will be liable to pay the damages awarded on the basis of vicarious liability. The club is not seeking to deny that what occurred did so in the course of the player's employment, only that the injury-causing act was not tortious.

4.5.2 Vicarious liability for negligent acts

Vicarious liability can only be imposed on an employer if it can be established that the employee has committed a tort, in this case negligence, and that the tort has a sufficiently close connection with the purpose of the employment. The existence of a close connection between the negligent act of the employee and the terms of their employment with their employer is usually established by proving that the act was a wrongful and unauthorised mode of carrying out an act otherwise authorised by the employer.

This approach is wide enough to include most negligent acts, including acts of foul play, which occur in the course of playing sport. For example tackling an opponent is authorised by employers of football and rugby players. However, as occurred in *McCord*, where the tackle is high and late and causes injury, the poor quality of the challenge will be held to be an unauthorised mode of carrying out an authorised act for which the employer will be vicariously liable.

> ▶ *Thomas* v. *Thornton and Bramley Rugby League Club* (unreported) County Court (Leeds), 15 January 1999
>
> During the course of a professional rugby league match the defendant, who was in possession of the ball, ran at the claimant, who was about to attempt to tackle him. As the players drew close together, the defendant raised his arm to hand off the claimant in an attempt to avoid being tackled. Instead of using his hand however, the defendant used his forearm and struck the claimant in the face, fracturing his jaw. In holding the defendant liable, the court held that despite players clattering into each other with great force and that it is not always possible for them to time or execute their manoeuvres as they may wish, this was such dangerous play that a reasonable professional player would have known carried with it a significant risk of serious injury to the claimant; this was an unauthorised manner of carrying out an otherwise acceptable move. Having established the negligence of the participant-employee and that they were acting in the course of their employment, liability was imposed on the employing club without the need for proof of any wrongdoing on its part.

4.5.3 Vicarious liability for deliberate acts

Although the following extension of the meaning of 'in the course of the employee's employment' was developed in respect of claims based in negligence (*Mattis* v. *Pollock* [2003] EWCA Civ 887), in reality it is used to cover situations where the defendant employee has acted deliberately when causing harm to the claimant. Thus where the unauthorised act was so closely connected with the employee's employment that it would be fair and just to hold the employer vicariously liable, or where the risk of wrongdoing can fairly be said to be reasonably incidental to the employer's business, the act will be held to have been committed in the course of the employee's employment, regardless of whether the employee was acting deliberately or negligently (*Lister*).

> ▶ *Gravil v. Carroll and Redruth Rugby Football Club* **[2008] EWCA Civ 689**
>
> Following a scrum in a semi-professional rugby union game, and after the referee had blown his whistle to stop play, a fight broke out during which the first defendant hit the claimant causing him serious facial injuries. Having established that the first defendant had committed an actionable battery against the claimant, the question on appeal was whether the second defendant should be vicariously liable for the actions of its employee.
>
> In the Court of Appeal, Clarke MR held that melees of the kind that preceded the punch were frequent occurrences in rugby union matches and that punching was not uncommon. He further described the incident as being an 'ordinary though undesirable' part of modern rugby. Thus the deliberate infliction of injury in circumstances amounting to an actionable battery could be considered to be in the course of the first defendant's employment as a rugby union player because the risk of such wrongdoing can fairly be said to be reasonably incidental to the employer's business of running a rugby club. In other words, a sufficiently close connection between the employee's terms of employment and the injury-causing incident could be established. Further, despite a contractual term specifically prohibiting fighting, it was fair and just to impose vicarious liability on the defendant club because it was better placed to influence and punish the conduct of its players and to purchase adequate insurance to cover their transgressions. Thus the club was found vicariously liable for the acts of its player.

Gravil, though perhaps surprising to non-lawyers, is a simple extension of the law of vicarious liability that was developed in *Lister* and *Mattis* to a sporting context. A specific prohibition on fighting is not of itself sufficient to exonerate the employer from liability (*Rose* v. *Plenty* [1976] 1 WLR 141). Only where the employing club has a strict and well-used internal disciplinary procedure might it be possible for it to avoid liability in a situation like this. Otherwise for injury-causing acts that occur on the field of play, whether they are deliberate or negligent, the club should expect to be found vicariously liable for the acts of its employee players.

4.5.4   Dual employment

Where a sportsperson has two or more employments, the sports employer can be vicariously liable for the acts that occur during the course of the sporting employment. In many professional team sports, the opportunity for dual employment of this kind is usually limited to playing representative fixtures on top of the contractual obligation to play for the main employing club. Being picked to play in a representative match might take two legal forms; a lending of the player by the club to the international team, as in football, or a separate contract of employment, often referred to as a central contract, between the governing body and the player, as occurs in English cricket.

In both cases the international team, not the club, will be vicariously liable for the tortious actions of the player. Where the player is lent to the representative team, the governing body will be entitled to exercise control over their actions as the player will be integrated into their business for the period of the lending (*Mersey Docks and Harbour Board* v. *Coggins and Griffith (Liverpool) Ltd* [1947] AC 1). In cases where players are released by their main employer to fulfil international representative fixtures, the governing body will be liable for any tortious acts committed during that period.

Where the player is concurrently employed by both a club and the governing body, the situation is even more straightforward. In the same way that Redruth RFC was only responsible for the tortious acts of its employees when they were playing rugby for the club (*Gravil*), vicarious liability will only be imposed on the employer for whom the player was playing at the time that they committed the tort. Thus if the tort takes place during an international representative fixture the governing body will be liable but if it occurs whilst the player is playing a club fixture then the employing club will be vicariously liable.

4.6   Defences

Defendants have two options when defending a claim. Firstly they can deny or adduce evidence to prove that they did not commit the tort of which they are accused. Secondly, where the claimant has succeeded in proving on the balance of probabilities that a tort has been committed by the defendant, the latter may be able to raise a defence to the claim made. Different defences can be raised depending on which cause of action is pursued by the claimant.

4.6.1   Defences to trespass to the person

There are two defences open to a defendant to plead when accused of having committed a battery: consent and self-defence. Consent will generally apply to specific contacts that have been inflicted as a necessary or inherent part of the game, such as rugby tackles, but not to acts unconnected with ongoing play, such as punching an opponent (*Gravil*). Self-defence can generally only be raised where the defendant was being, or was about to be, attacked by another person. Both defences if successful are complete defences to a claim.

4.6.1.1 Consent

Where the claimant has given full, free and informed consent to the actions of the defendant, the latter will have a complete defence to any claim made against him (*Re F* [1990] 2 AC 1). The consent given can be either express or implied. Express consent is where the claimant grants permission in advance of participation to the defendant to perform certain specific acts on them in the course of the game. Implied consent is where the claimant is deemed to have consented to all reasonable contacts being made with them on the basis that they are participating in the particular sporting contest. As the vast majority of sports participants do not discuss with their opponents in advance what is and is not an acceptable level of interpersonal contact, a claimant's consent will usually be implied from their participation in the game.

Full, free and informed consent means that, either expressly or impliedly, the claimant was aware of and agreed to the risks of participating in the sport under consideration. In sporting contests, consent will be an objectively defined standard applicable to all participants in the contest; a game would become impossible to manage if each individual player could define which contacts could or could not be applied to them during the game. For example rugby players expect and consent to being tackled even if they would rather not be, whereas tennis players would neither expect nor consent to any interpersonal contact with an opponent during the playing of the game.

The scope of the consent given by a sports participant is defined by reference to the relevant circumstances and playing culture of the game (above, 4.4.1.3–4). Sports participants consent to all interpersonal contact that is an integral part of the game such as a challenge for the ball, to all contacts accepted as occurring as a normal part of playing the game such as collisions, and commonly occurring acts of foul play such as pushing. All contacts unconnected with playing the game such as those occurring when the action has moved to a different part of the arena or after play has stopped, or fighting of any kind, are not consented to (*Gravil*).

4.6.1.2 Self-defence

This defence will only rarely be raised in sports cases as it is only available where the defendant is actually being attacked by another person or on the basis of an honest belief that an attack by another person is about to occur. The defendant must honestly believe that there is a need for the use of some force to defend themselves and this belief must be based on reasonable grounds, for example where the defendant is already being hit or is being threatened. The force actually used in defence must be reasonable and proportionate in the circumstances in which it was used (*Ashley* v. *Chief Constable of Sussex* [2008] 1 AC 962). For example a defendant could punch a person whom he honestly believed was punching him but he could not chase after and punch someone who was running away from him as there is no longer an imminent threat of being attacked; the defendant is not given a license to use an unlimited degree of force. The burden of proof is on the defendant to establish on the balance of probabilities that all elements of the defence were present at the time he hit the claimant.

4.6.2　Defences to negligence

There are two defences available to a defendant accused of negligently causing injury. *Volenti non fit injuria*, or voluntary assumption of risk, acts as a complete defence to negligence claims where the defendant can prove that the claimant agreed in advance to the defendant acting negligently. Contributory negligence is a partial defence that enables the defendant to reduce the amount of damages payable on the basis that the claimant has in some way contributed to their own harm.

4.6.2.1 Volenti non fit injuria or the voluntary assumption of risk

Volenti is a defence that is often pleaded but whose application is rarely fully understood. For *volenti* to apply the claimant must have consented to the defendant acting negligently, not just to the risk of injury inherent in the sporting activity (*Smoldon* v. *Whitworth and Nolan* [1997] ELR 249) (see further, chapter 5.3). It will be an unusual case indeed where the claimant agrees, whether expressly or impliedly, to allow the defendant to act with anything other than reasonable care.

The practical effect of the sports negligence cases decided in recent years is to render this defence functionally otiose. By requiring an explicit and detailed analysis of the relevant circumstances in which an incident took place and the playing culture of the particular sport, *volenti* is left with little and perhaps no role to play. If the injury-causing conduct of the defendant is an acceptable means of playing the sport in question or is within its playing culture, then there is no breach of duty and therefore no liability (*Elliott*). If liability cannot be established then an analysis of *volenti* is unnecessary.

Alternatively if the injury-causing conduct of the defendant is an unacceptable means of playing the sport in question because it is too dangerous, unconnected with the playing of the game or outside of its playing culture, then negligence is established. No question of *volenti* arises as participants do not agree to allow players to act in a manner that is incompatible with the playing culture of the sport. Sports participants agree to the inherent risks associated with playing the game, such as mistakes and errors of judgement, but they do not permit the defendant to act negligently.

▶ *Rollason* v. *Matthews*, (unreported) County Court (Bristol), 31 January 2006

The defendant, in attempting to regain possession of a football of which he had lost control, slid towards the ball and tried to knock it out of the way of the claimant. The claimant got to the ball first and in following through with his challenge, the defendant made contact with and broke the claimant's left leg just below the knee. The court held that in carrying out this initially legitimate attempt to recover possession of the ball, the defendant had fallen below the standard of care expected of him by performing the challenge with both feet raised and with his studs pointing at and making contact with the claimant's leg.

Thus it will now be extremely difficult to raise the defence of *volenti* because of the requirement for a very detailed examination of the applicable duty and its breach. Although defence counsel will often plead *volenti* alongside any appropriate denial of liability, to all intents and purposes the denial is likely to be the more effective approach.

4.6.2.2 Contributory negligence

Contributory negligence is a statutory defence that reduces the amount of compensation payable by a defendant to a claimant.

▶ Law Reform (Contributory Negligence) Act 1945 s.1(1) – apportionment of liability in case of contributory negligence

'Where any person suffers damage as the result partly of his own fault and partly of the fault of any other person or persons, a claim in respect of that damage shall not be defeated by reason of the fault of the person suffering the damage, but the damages recoverable in respect thereof shall be reduced to such extent as the court thinks just and equitable having regard to the claimant's share in the responsibility for the damage.'

Thus where the defendant can prove on the balance of probabilities that the claimant has failed to take reasonable care for their own safety and has contributed to the extent of the harm caused, the damages payable will be reduced accordingly (though never to zero). To date no case involving two participants has seen a successful defence of contributory negligence raised, though damages have been reduced in claims against instructors (*Anderson* v. *Lyotier, Lyotier and Portejoie* [2008] EWHC 2790) (see further, chapter 5.2.2). However a claim of contributory negligence may succeed where the claimant has knowingly put themselves at risk of injury by the defendant by, for example, playing whilst injured, attempting a challenge in the knowledge that contact would be made with the defendant or playing in a game or in a position for which they had not received adequate pre-participation training.

Hot topic . . .

VICARIOUS LIABILITY AND THE FUTURE OF THE HARD MEN OF SPORT

The 'hard man' of a team has been elevated to an almost mythical status amongst British sports fans. Despite the fact that such players will often have hassled and hustled, kicked and punched their way through a significant portion of their careers, they are remembered fondly by fans and commentators alike as players who gave their all for club and country and who never failed to put their bodies on the line for the sake of the team. They were picked both to protect their own team's star players and to intimidate those of the opposition in the hope that they would be put off their game. Although most of these players were in their prime before the law's more regular involvement in sport since *Condon*, their like still exists even if there is now less scope for overt foul play when every move of the professional player can be replayed and analysed in television studios and in online discussions.

The case of *Gravil* v. *Carroll and Redruth RFC* has created a new challenge to the existence of the hard man. Previously only negligent challenges in some way connected to the actual playing of the sport, such as bad tackles, had been the subject of successful claims. *Gravil* not only saw liability imposed for trespass to the person by means of a battery, but also brought sports cases into line with the rest of the law of vicarious liability by holding Reduth RFC liable for the punch thrown by their employee Carroll.

In handing down the judgment in *Gravil*, Clarke MR relied on *Mattis* v. *Pollock*, a case where the defendant had employed a doorman at his nightclub for the specific purpose of intimidating the customers in an attempt to reduce violence inside the establishment. The defendant had encouraged rather than curbed the aggressive tendencies of the doorman, so when an ongoing dispute between him and one of the customers ended in the doorman stabbing the claimant, the defendant was held vicariously liable for the injuries caused as his employee had behaved in the violent and aggressive manner expected of him even though the actual act of stabbing the claimant was unforeseeable. Although an extreme case, it highlights quite dramatically how far the courts are prepared to extend the meaning of actions in the course of one's employment.

The leading cases on vicarious liability have held that where an employer knows of the violent tendencies of an employee, or seeks to exploit them for their own benefit, then the employer will be liable for any harm caused by the employee exhibiting those tendencies. Furthermore where the employer is aware of such a tendency but ignores it, or otherwise fails to control, discipline or retrain the employee, then again the employer will be vicariously liable for any harm caused by the employee that is connected to his employment.

This has the potential to cause significant problems for clubs that employ a player with a known reputation for foul play, or one who over a period of time develops such a reputation whilst playing for a club. Whereas in the past it could have been argued that deliberately violent conduct was outside their course of employment as a sportsperson, or that this was a revenge attack in some way unconnected with the playing of the game, *Gravil* demonstrates that this is no longer the case. A club can now be vicariously liable for one of their players who causes deliberate injury to an opponent.

Redruth RFC were held vicariously liable for the acts of Carroll despite including in the contract of employment specific terms prohibiting physical assaults on opponents and requiring all employees to abide by the rules of the Rugby Football Union and the International Rugby Football Board. It would seem that to be able to insulate themselves from liability, sports clubs will have to take much more specific and proactive steps to control the behaviour of their errant players. This could include taking disciplinary action against them such as fining or suspending them, or dropping and retraining them before considering them again for future selection. A simple prohibition on acting violently without any effective or appropriate reaction is not sufficient.

Regardless of how the law eventually evolves in this area, as Clarke MR acknowledges in *Gravil*, this is an extremely important case for professional sports teams especially where they employ players with a known tendency to violent conduct. It could also lead to the end of the hard man as we once knew him.

Summary

4.1 There has been a rapid development in the law as it applies to sports injuries since *Condon* v. *Basi* in 1985. As a result the most important issues for anyone suffering an injury whilst playing sport are to identify the potential defendants to a claim and to determine whether the appropriate cause of action lies in trespass to the person or negligence.

4.2 A battery is the direct and intentional application of force by the defendant to the claimant without their consent. Claimants rarely pursue an action in battery as most insurance policies exclude claims for deliberately inflicted injury. However after *Gravil* v. *Carroll and Redruth RFC*, an employing club may now be vicariously liable for any conduct of its employee-players that is sufficiently connected to its business, including batteries.

4.3 The generally applicable definition of negligence requires claimants to establish that they were owed a duty of care by the defendant, that the defendant has breached this duty by dropping below the standard of conduct generally expected of a person in their position and that this breach has caused reasonably foreseeable harm to the claimant. This definition has been refined by cases from *Condon* v. *Basi* onwards in respect of its application to sports cases.

4.4 *Caldwell* v. *Maguire and Fitzgerald* provided further clarification of the standard of care required of a sportsperson to discharge the duty of care owed by them and of the standard of proof required to prove a negligence claim. The examination of the reasonableness of a sportsperson's conduct will take into account the specific sporting circumstances in which the injury occurred. Further, because of the dangers inherent in many sports, it was also acknowledged that something more than an error of judgement would be required to establish a claim in negligence.

4.5 An employer-club is responsible for the negligent actions of its employee-players who cause injury to another person whilst they are acting in the course of their employment. Following *Gravil* v. *Carroll and Redruth RFC*, this vicarious liability of the employer-club has been extended to include batteries that are so closely connected to the playing of the game that they can be considered to have occurred in the course of the player's employment. This would appear to include fighting that occurs during the game but, without further legal examination, will not extend beyond to fights after the game has ended.

4.6 Where the claimant has consented to the injury-causing conduct happening to them, the defendant has a complete defence to a claim of battery. Where the claimant consciously ran the risk of the defendant acting negligently, the defendant will be able to raise the defence of *volenti non fit injuria*. After *Caldwell* v. *Maguire and Fitzgerald* both of these defences will be examined alongside the issue of whether or not the defendant has breached their duty of care towards the claimant. The possibility that the defendant could raise the defence of contributory negligence has not yet been fully explored before the courts. Such a claim has a good chance of success given the court's apparent reluctance to allow the defences of consent and *volenti*.

Further reading

Grayson, *Sport and the Law* (3rd edn, 2000, Butterworths) chs 1 and 15

Lewis and Taylor (eds), *Sport: Law and Practice* (2nd edn, 2008, Tottel) ch D5

Steele, *Tort Law: text, cases and materials* (2007, Oxford University Press) chs 3 and 5

Further reading cont'd

Anderson, 'Personal injury liability in sport: emerging trends' (2008) 16 *Tort Law Review* 95

Cox, 'Civil liability for foul play in sport' (2003) 54 *Northern Ireland Law Quarterly* 351

Goodhart, 'The sportsman's charter' (1962) 78 *Law Quarterly Review* 490

Grayson, 'Drake's drumbeat for sporting remedies/injuries' (1994) 144 *New Law Journal* 1094

James and McArdle, 'Player violence or violent players? Vicarious liability for sports participants' (2004) 12 *Tort Law Review* 131

McArdle, 'The enduring legacy of reckless disregard' (2005) 34 (4) *Common Law World Review* 316

McArdle and James, 'Are you experienced? Playing cultures, sporting rules and personal injury litigation after Caldwell v Maguire' (2005) 13 (3) *Tort Law Review* 193

Yeo, 'Determining consent in body contact sports' (1998) 6 *Tort Law Review* 199

Links to relevant websites can be found at www.palgrave.com/law/james

Chapter 5

Liability for injuries caused by non-participants

Key words

▶ **Man of straw** – a defendant, or potential defendant, who has insufficient funds to meet any award of damages made against him.

▶ **Vicarious liability** – the employer is responsible for the tortious acts of an employee, where the tort committed has sufficient connection to the employee's employment.

5.1 Extending sports negligence to new defendants

Although there is evidence of some cases being brought against the defendants discussed in this chapter prior to *Condon* v. *Basi* [1985] 1 WLR 866 (see further, chapter 4.1.1), these were usually restricted to actions against PE teachers and the owners of sports venues. Since 1985 the range of potential defendants has increased dramatically and where authority did previously exist to at least a limited extent, this has been clarified and often extended. Successful personal injury claims have been brought against coaches, instructors and supervisors, match officials, governing bodies and medical staff, all of which are discussed in this chapter. The liability of facility owners and event organisers is explored in Chapter 8 as it brings in the additional causes of action found in the Occupiers' Liability Acts 1957 and 1984 and the law of nuisance. Despite this seemingly massive extension in the number of people who can be sued, the law has not yet fully tested the scope of what these potential defendants might be liable for.

5.1.1 Possible explanations for the expansion of negligence liability

There is no definitive explanation for why there has been this explosion in sports negligence cases, though several theories may help to explain the increase in litigation. Firstly where the injuries were caused by an opponent, the person who actually caused the harm may be a 'man of straw,' in other words a defendant who is unable to meet any claim brought against him. This then leads to a search for others who may have been at fault for facilitating, encouraging or in some other way contributing to the harm caused to the claimant. This could explain the willingness to sue coaches, match officials and governing bodies.

Secondly claimants may now be more aware of their legal rights on being injured. Whether this is because of claims handlers specifically aiming adverts at injured sports participants or because people are now less likely to accept that blameless injury can occur during play, sports negligence litigation continues to grow, whether or not there is any proof of a 'compensation culture.'

Thirdly, since the introduction of conditional fee arrangements in s.58 Courts and Legal Services Act 1990, some of the financial risk of commencing litigation has been removed from claimants. Where such an arrangement is in place, claimants no longer have to pay for their legal advice up front or on an ongoing basis during the course of negotiations. Instead their lawyers only receive their fees if they win, when they are paid directly by the defendants. Thus, where previously the threat of having to meet your own costs up front and, in the case of losing, the costs of both sides was enough to discourage many good claims from being initiated, that gamble can now be avoided by using a conditional fee arrangement.

Regardless of how or why these claims are being made, this area of the law is one that has developed rapidly in recent years. Not only that, it continues to do so and continues to extend legal liability to new contexts and new defendants who sometimes had not previously been thought to be at risk from litigation. In the following sections those defendants against whom successful actions have already been brought will be discussed, as will those who are potentially at risk from claims in the future.

5.1.2   Recent restrictions on liability

This growth in litigation has not gone completely unchecked; many cases fail because the injury has been caused by the obvious or inherent risks associated with the activity. Furthermore Parliament has specifically legislated to protect risky but socially beneficial activities.

> ▶ **Compensation Act 2006 s.1 – deterrent effect of potential liability**
>
> A court considering a claim in negligence or breach of statutory duty may, in determining whether the defendant should have taken particular steps to meet a standard of care (whether by taking precautions against a risk or otherwise), have regard to whether a requirement to take those steps might –
>
> (a) prevent a desirable activity from being undertaken at all, to a particular extent or in a particular way, or
> (b) discourage persons from undertaking functions in connection with a desirable activity.

Although judges rarely refer to the Act as a reason for their decisions, there has been a clear indication that by the use of phrases like 'responsibility for their own personal autonomy' and 'personal responsibility for the risks that they have run,' the judiciary does not want to see sport litigated out of existence. Instead the judges seem only to be ensuring that those deserving of compensation receive what is due to them. The tension between a claimant being responsible for running acceptable risks and a defendant's unacceptable negligence is a constant theme of this chapter.

5.1.3   Relationship with cases involving co-participants

The simple explanation behind the relationship of the cases discussed in this chapter and those in Chapter 4 is that the basic applicable law, the law of negligence, is the same in all of these situations. In each case it must be established that a duty of care is owed by the defendant to the claimant, that the defendant has breached the duty by dropping below the standard of care expected of them in the circumstances and that the breach must have caused the harm suffered by the claimant. What changes in each situation discussed below is the definition of the specific duty owed and how a breach of that duty is determined.

5.2 Coaches, instructors and supervisors

Liability for injuries caused by a failure to train or supervise a sports participant has grown out of a series of cases from the early twentieth century where successful negligence claims were brought against PE teachers and instructors. Although the duty of care owed to children is always higher than that owed to adults (*Jolley* v. *Sutton LBC* [2000] 1 WLR 1082) the teacher cases are illustrative of how and why the law has developed to encompass sports coaches and instructors. For example in *Gibbs* v. *Barking Corporation* [1936] 1 All ER 115, a PE teacher was held to be liable in negligence for the injuries caused to one of his pupils when he failed to assist the boy to land safely on the mats following his vaulting over a horse during a gym session. As the pupils were not yet proficient in completing a vault unaided the duty imposed on the teacher was to ensure that a procedure was in place to enable them to land safely. The system in place did not provide a sufficient level of assistance to the vaulters and therefore the Corporation was vicariously liable for the negligence of the teacher.

In most of the cases involving a coach's potential liability, the argument focuses on whether or not the defendant has followed appropriate procedures, used appropriate techniques, supervised the performances of those under their tuition and generally acted within their sphere of competence. Where coaches have kept their training and qualifications up to date and are working with groups of athletes that they have been trained to coach, it is almost impossible for a claimant to establish liability.

5.2.1 Establishing a claim

5.2.1.1 Duty of care

The duty that is imposed on every coach is to take reasonable care to ensure that they are training the players under their control in a manner that does not cause them reasonably foreseeable harm. This duty, subject to additional detail relevant to the particular activity, will always be imposed on every coach and instructor. It must be noted from the outset that this duty is not absolute; it does not require perfection on the part of the coach. It requires only that the coach take reasonable care to ensure that those under their tuition are taught how to perform moves relevant to the sport in question and appropriate to their level of skill and experience. It does not require that the activity take place in a completely risk free environment, only that the risks are appropriately managed. As was seen in *Gibbs*, participants are allowed to be taught new skills that carry with them a risk of injury provided that the coach has in place and operates a system that ensures that they are reasonably safe when performing the task.

5.2.1.2 Breach of duty and the appropriate standard of care

The more difficult question for the court will usually be determining whether or not the duty has been breached by the coach's conduct. The general test for determining a breach of duty is to measure the conduct of the defendant against the standard of the reasonable and competent person performing that task. As with the liability of sports participants, this is not an abstract concept or a one size fits all test: all of the relevant circumstances in which the incident took place will need to be taken into account, including the particular sport, the level of experience and perhaps the age of the participants, their skill levels and the inherent risks of performing the particular move that leads to the injury, as well as the level of qualification, training and experience of the coach.

The specialist nature of sports coaching means that the professional negligence tests developed from *Bolam* v. *Friern Hospital Management Committee* [1957] 1 WLR 582 and *Bolitho* v. *City and Hackney Health Authority* [1998] AC 232, will be used when a defendant coach's competence is called into question. Following *Bolam* the court can enquire what the reasonable person of the same level of skill or training or qualification would have done in those circumstances. If a body of similarly qualified coaches would have acted in the same way then it is likely that the defendant will be able to establish that they have not breached the duty of care owed to the claimant.

To ensure that negligent practices do not become entrenched through repetition however, *Bolitho* allows the court to ask the defendant to justify the option that they took that led to the injury being caused. Thus a defendant must not only prove that other coaches would have acted in the same way, but that there was good reason for their having acted in that way. Where a claimant cannot prove on the balance of probabilities that the coaching team did anything other than act in accordance with standard safe practice, the injuries caused will be considered to be nothing more than an unfortunate accident.

> ▶ *Hopkins* v. *Pullen and Taylor (trading as Ippon Judo Club)* (unreported) **Crown Court (Preston), 8 December 2005**
>
> During his first judo training session, the claimant was injured whilst performing the Kesa Gatame move. Instruction in how to perform the move was given by an experienced judo coach who was being further supervised by the second defendant. The claimant alleged that he was not taught how to fall or roll away from his training partner. Further, he alleged that his partner was significantly larger than he was and that as a result, when his partner fell on top of him whilst performing the move, he fractured his right clavicle. The court held that although the club owed a duty to ensure that adequate training and supervision were given to the novices by reasonable and competent coaches, this duty had not been breached in these circumstances. All reasonable steps had been taken to ensure the safety of the claimant: he was adequately supervised at all times and the move being performed by him was one that was appropriate to his status as a complete beginner.

In *Gannon* v. *Rotherham Metropolitan Borough Council* (unreported) Crown Court (Nottingham) 6 February 1991, the claimant and others were being taught how to perform racing dives from starting blocks in preparation for a school swimming gala. Having shown them the basic technique, the coach allowed the swimmers to continue to practise diving from the blocks at the shallow end of the pool. The claimant hit his head on the bottom of the pool and broke his neck. Negligence was established on the basis that no reasonable or competent swimming coach would allow anyone, and particularly not those lacking sufficient skill and experience, to dive off racing blocks into the shallow end of the pool. Therefore the Council were vicariously liable for the negligence of the swimming coach.

As a further example a rugby player cannot complain of being injured by a legitimate tackle performed either during training or as a part of the game. However where the tackle is performed on a schoolboy by an older and much larger player and the disparity in size leads to the claimant being injured, then negligence will be established against those picking and coaching the larger player's team.

> ▶ *Mountford* v. *Newlands School* [2007] EWCA Civ 21
>
> The claimant was playing in an under-15 age group rugby union match for his school against the defendant school. The defendant's rugby coach had picked an overage player in its team who was considerably taller and heavier than the claimant who, when lawfully tackled by this larger player, suffered a broken elbow. According to the Junior Rugby Guidelines of the England Rugby Football Schools' Union, players should not normally play in age groupings other than their own as this could compromise the safety of younger and smaller players. The court held that having regard to the older player's size and age, the defendant's rugby coach should not have picked him to play in this fixture. As the rule had been devised to prevent this specific type of harm from eventuating, the defendant was vicariously liable for the negligent selection of the older boy by the coach.

Being tackled in such a way by someone substantially larger is not a risk inherent in age-restricted games. Further, where the injury is caused by a tackle performed by an adult coach on a child participant, this will also be considered to be beyond the normal, inherent risks of the sport and liability will be established against the defendant (*Affuto-Nartoy* v. *Clarke and Inner London Education Authority* (1984) The Times, 9 February).

5.2.2 Defences

The defences that can be raised by a coach accused of negligence are the same as those that can be raised by a player: *volenti non fit injuria*, or voluntary assumption of risk, and contributory negligence (see further, chapter 4.6.2). For a successful claim of *volenti*, the claimant must have consented to the defendant acting negligently, not just to the risk of injury inherent in the sporting activity. Unless the player has specifically agreed in advance to run the risk of injury from, for example, the use of a novel training technique not sanctioned or taught as a part of a normal coaching course, then this defence is unlikely to succeed.

Practically it is more likely and more advisable that a defendant raise the partial defence of contributory negligence (s.1(1) Law Reform (Contributory Negligence) Act 1945) (see further, chapter 4.6.2.2). Contributory negligence can be established where it can be proved on the balance of probabilities that the claimant has failed to take reasonable care for their own safety and has contributed to the extent of the harm caused. The damages payable will be reduced proportionately to the degree of fault exhibited by the claimant. As will be seen in relation to the other defendants discussed in this chapter, there is an inherent tension in many of the cases between the need for care to be taken by the defendant and the risks inherent in many sports. On the one hand the courts do not want to be seen to be allowing or encouraging negligent conduct in the name of sport. On the other hand they do not want sports participants to be absolved of all responsibility for their own safety nor to litigate risky activities out of existence.

> ▶ *Anderson* v. *Lyotier, Lyotier and Portejoie* [2008] EWHC 2790
>
> The claimant had been a member of a mixed ability skiing group that had been under the instruction of the third defendant. They had descended a number of slopes of varying difficulty and had skied off-piste on two occasions during the week's holiday. On the second

occasion the claimant had found the trail particularly challenging and had fallen a number of times. On the final day the third defendant took the group down a particularly steep off-piste trail that descended through some trees. The claimant lost control and skied into a tree, suffering catastrophic injuries as a result. The High Court was asked directly to determine whether this was a case of negligent training, instruction and supervision or a situation where the claimant should have taken personal responsibility for their voluntary participation in a high-risk activity.

It was held that the instructor had acted negligently by failing to assess the competence of each member of the group before making the off-piste descent and that he had failed to appreciate the claimant's lack of ability and confidence when skiing off the main trails. By failing to take account of the individual circumstances of each member of the group and failing to determine prospectively and objectively whether the terrain was reasonably safe for each of them, the instructor had breached his duty. However as the claimant had been contributorily negligent by failing to draw the instructor's attention to his own lack of competence to descend this particular trail, his damages were reduced by one third.

Balancing these contrasting approaches is a difficult task. It is obvious to all skiers, whether they are novices or highly experienced, that there is a risk of falling and being injured at almost any time. It is also obvious that there are additional dangers when skiing off-piste, particularly if the trail runs through trees. This risk of injury through falling and/or crashing is increased where the skier is lacking the necessary skill and experience to ski off-piste. By failing to voice his fears and voluntarily descending this particular off-piste section in the knowledge that he lacked the necessary skill and confidence, the claimant appears implicitly to be running the risk not only of the inherent risks of skiing but also the risks associated with the defendant's misplaced belief that he could ski this specific trail.

After instructing him every day for the past six days however, it should also have been obvious to the defendant that the claimant lacked these skills and either should not have been allowed to ski this section or should have been more closely supervised during the descent. Thus this is also a case where the instructor had failed to teach the necessary skills and provide an appropriate safe system of learning (*Gibbs*) or had failed to provide a reasonably safe system of supervision (*Gannon*). A further reading of this scenario could be that this was a case of the instructor incrementally building up a novice's skills by testing them towards the upper limits of their ability. Liability would be established where instructors had pushed their trainee beyond the limits of their competence but not if they were teaching skills and techniques that were appropriate to their skill level, as was the case in *Hopkins*.

The court eventually held that the instructor's suggestion was not a reasonable one of undertaking something more challenging but an unreasonable one of undertaking an activity that was dangerous and beyond the claimant's capabilities and therefore negligent. However the decision whether or not to make the descent was a collaborative one and the claimant could not abdicate all responsibility for his safety to the instructor. Therefore the claimant was contributorily negligent and had his damages reduced significantly. Although the balance was struck in favour of the claimant the implications of this decision are potentially wide ranging for both sides. How the relationship between a coach and those under his instruction is defined in other sporting activities is the next challenge for the courts.

5.3 Referees and match officials

In 1996 it was widely reported that the UK was about to witness the end of sport as we then knew it. The cause of this hysteria was the decision in *Smoldon* v. *Whitworth and Nolan* [1997] ELR 249, the first reported case of an injured athlete successfully suing a match official in negligence. As has so often been the case where sport and the law collide, sport has been able to adapt to the new challenges laid down by the law and continues in much the same way as it always has. What *Smoldon* did highlight specifically was that injury, in this case catastrophic injury, can be caused by those who have no direct involvement in the contest itself but who are present to ensure the smooth running of the game.

> ▶ *Smoldon* v. *Whitworth and Nolan* [1997] ELR 249
>
> The claimant was playing in the front row of a rugby union scrum when it collapsed causing him serious spinal injuries that paralysed him from the neck down. He alleged that the cause of the collapse was the second defendant referee's mismanagement of the engagement of the scrum and his failure to adhere to specific safety rules that were in place for the protection of front row forwards. The court held that referees and other match officials owe a duty to ensure that those playing the game under their control are reasonably safe and that by failing to impose a variety of safety rules specifically designed to prevent scrums from collapsing, the referee was in breach of that duty of care. Further, the claimant could not be considered to have voluntarily run the risk of injury from the second defendant's failure to uphold the safety rules; although he did agree to run the inherent risks involved with playing in the front row he did not agree to the referee failing to ensure that the game was being played safely.

Liability will only rarely be imposed on match officials. Evidence to support a claim of negligence will usually have to focus on their failure to impose or uphold the safety rules of a sport or on their having acted outside of their sphere of competence, for example by refereeing a level or type of match for which they were not fully qualified. In reality, although most actions will be brought against the referee the aim will be to secure a payout from the referee's own insurers or, if vicarious liability can be proved, against the insurers of the sport's governing body.

5.3.1 Establishing a claim

5.3.1.1 Duty of care

The extension of liability in negligence to match officials was a natural incremental step for the law to take. There are no logical, legal or policy reasons why match officials should be immune from the operation of the law if they behave with such a degree of incompetence that they cause injury to those who are playing sport under their control. After reviewing the previous authorities on sports negligence, both the trial judge and the Court of Appeal in *Smoldon* came to the conclusion that a match official did owe a duty of care to the players and that full account must be taken of the factual context in which the incident occurred. This involved a simple application of negligence in all the circumstances applied to a novel situation: referees officiating a fast-moving contact sport.

In defining the applicable duty the Court took into consideration that referees provide a 'protective mantle' for the players under their control and that they must ensure that the game is played with the players' safety in mind. Thus the referee (and other match officials) owes all of the players in the game a duty to take reasonable care to enforce the rules of the particular sport, to apply them fairly, to control the match in a manner that does not expose the players to an unnecessary risk of injury and, in this particular case, to have especial regard to the age of the players as this was an under-19s match.

Referees will not be liable for injuries caused by the inherent risks of participation in an activity. They will however be liable for their failure to ensure that the players are able to play the game in a reasonably safe environment. *Smoldon* ensures that this includes upholding the safety rules of the sport in question but there is no reason why this could not be extended to the various pre-match inspections that the officials must carry out, including for example whether the playing surface is safe and free from dangerous articles, whether playing equipment like studs meets relevant guidelines and whether goalposts are erected properly and padded where necessary.

Again this is a duty to act reasonably, not to ensure absolutely that no injury can take place. As Bingham LCJ held in *Smoldon* at p.139,

> '[The referee] could not be properly held liable for errors of judgement, oversights or lapses of which any referee might be guilty in the context of a fast-moving and vigorous contest. The threshold of liability is a high one. It will not be easily crossed.'

This last comment explains why so few cases involving the negligence of match officials have been reported. Liability will only be imposed where the number or seriousness of the breaches committed cannot be considered to be an inherent risk of participation in the sport.

5.3.1.2 Breach of duty and the appropriate standard of care

The standard of care against which a match official will be judged is that of the reasonable and competent person officiating at that level of the sport being played. They will be expected to know and to apply the relevant playing and safety rules and to control the players in a way that avoids them being caused or causing each other injury. The three reported cases involving referees, each of them rugby union referees, raise very different issues regarding the establishment of a breach of duty. In each case the claimant suffered a broken neck following the collapse of a scrum.

In *Smoldon* the sheer number of instances of mismanagement of the game ultimately led to the referee being found liable. This was not a case of a referee making the occasional mistake in the heat of the moment but a prolonged period of incompetent refereeing. It was found that the referee:

- Failed to ensure that each scrum consisted of eight players from each side; each team had had a forward sent off, one after 25 minutes play, the other 20 minutes into the second half. Thus for 35 minutes, the scrums were unstable and wheeling, placing additional strain and pressure on the necks and backs of the front row forwards.
- Failed to use the 'crouch-touch-pause-engage' procedure to ensure that the scrums were set correctly without the two packs of forwards charging into each other with undue force.
- Ignored the warnings and advice of the two touch judges, who were also the coaches of the two contesting teams.
- Failed to establish why the scrums were continually collapsing thereby allowing between three and four times the normal number of collapses for a game at this level.

Any one of these mistakes, particularly his allowing at least 25 scrums to collapse, provides potent evidence of negligence. Taken as a whole, this course of conduct was sufficient evidence to prove that the referee had dropped below the standard of conduct expected of him.

In *Vowles* v. *Evans and The Welsh Rugby Union Ltd* [2003] EWCA Civ 318, the seriousness of an incorrect decision formed the basis of the referee's liability. The claimant was the hooker for Llanharan RFC. When one of the prop forwards with whom he was playing had to leave the field with an injury, Llanharan had no trained front row replacement to act as his substitute. The team captain, who had some experience of playing prop, offered to fulfil the role and informed the referee that he was capable of playing in this specialist position.

When a scrum collapsed later in the game, the referee was held liable for the claimant's resulting injuries on the basis that he should not have allowed the Llanharan captain the choice to try himself out in the prop forward position. Either they had a specialist front row replacement who could be used, in which case the game could continue without any necessary changes to the playing rules, or they did not, in which case depowered scrums, where no pushing is allowed, should have been imposed. By allowing the Llanharan captain to determine that he was a specialist, instead of insisting on them using either a specialist front row replacement or moving to depowered scrums, the referee had breached his duty to apply the safety rules of the sport, resulting in the very injury that the rule was designed to prevent.

A further issue, similar to that in *Smoldon*, also arises in the case although it was not fully explored in the judgments because the referee's failure to impose depowered scrums was considered to be so serious as to dispose of the issue of negligence. The scrum that caused the claimant's injuries occurred over 50 minutes after the replacement of the original prop forward by the Llanharan captain. At almost every scrum from that point onwards, there was at least one collapse. The referee should have carried out a constant review of the replacement front row's competence and, when it became apparent that he was not able to scrummage safely, the referee should have moved to depowered scrums. In this way the replacement could have been given the opportunity to prove that he had the necessary skills to play in the position yet the referee would have retained the ability to declare that the player was in fact incompetent to play at prop forward. Using either approach, the seriousness of his oversights was sufficient to justify the imposition of liability.

Finally in *Allport* v. *Wilbraham* [2004] EWCA Civ 1668, the lack of evidence and unreliability of the claimant and his witnesses led to a finding of no negligence on the part of the referee. At issue was whether the referee had called 'engage' or whether he had allowed one side to charge into a scrummage early. The judge held that the referee was the more credible witness and that the weight of evidence supported his version of the facts, leading to the conclusion that he had followed the correct procedure. On top of this, the incident occurred at only the fourth scrummage of the match and after only 20 minutes of play. In contrast to *Smoldon* and *Vowles*, there was no evidence of a sustained course of mismanagement of the safety aspects of the game. As such it becomes significantly more difficult for a claimant to establish negligence on the part of the match officials.

5.3.1.3 Foreseeability of harm

It was argued in *Smoldon* that to be actionable a serious spinal injury should be a highly probable outcome of a collapsed scrum and that as it was not, then such a serious injury could not be considered to be reasonably foreseeable. As was held by the court, this would set the test for causation at too high a level. The outcome of the negligent conduct does not need to be a probable outcome, just one that is not fanciful or far-fetched. In other words, because it is reasonably foreseeable as a possibility that a collapsed scrum may cause a serious spinal injury to a front row forward, causation in law is established.

5.3.2   Defences

The two usual defences of *volenti* and contributory negligence may be available to a defendant match official accused of negligence. Both will however be difficult to raise successfully unless the claimant player has in some way actively contributed to the harm that he has suffered. In *Smoldon* the defendant referee argued that because the claimant was aware of the rules of the game and the dangers associated with collapsed scrums, he had impliedly consented to the risk of injury being caused by the non-application of the various safety rules. In respect of *volenti*, Bingham LCJ stated in *Smoldon* at p.146:

> 'The [claimant] had of course consented to the ordinary incidents of a game of rugby football of the kind in which he was taking part. Given, however, that the rules were framed for the protection of him and other players in the same position, he cannot possibly be said to have consented to a breach of duty on the part of the official whose duty it was to apply the rules and ensure so far as possible that they were observed. If the [claimant] were identified as a prime culprit in causing the collapse of the scrums, then [*volenti* and contributory negligence] might call for consideration.'

Thus if a scrum collapses in the ordinary course of the playing of the game, it will be considered to be a non-actionable inherent risk of the sport, as occurred in *Allport*. Where the match officials have failed to implement the safety rules of the sport and injury is caused as a result of this mismanagement of the game, then negligence will be established and no defence can be raised by the match officials against the claim. Such a conclusion is reinforced by the fact that in most sports in general, and rugby union in particular, there is little or no scope to debate these issues with the match officials without the risk of disciplinary sanctions being imposed. The failure to complain about the risks created by the match officials will not lead to a finding that the claimant has agreed to run them, though following *Anderson* v. *Lyotier* (above, 5.2.2) this may lead to a reduction in damages in certain limited circumstances on the basis of contributory negligence. *Volenti* will fail however because the players do not agree to run the risk of injury from the match officials' failure to enforce the safety rules of the game.

As noted by Bingham LCJ, the possibility of a successful claim of contributory negligence is increased where the claimant has to some degree contributed to the occurrence of the injury-causing incident. His Lordship indentified specifically that where the claimant is the main cause of the collapse, a finding of contributory negligence will be appropriate. Other situations where the defence may succeed could include where the claimant is aware that he or she lacks the appropriate skills to perform a specific task or play in a specific position. For example if the Llanharan captain had been injured whilst playing at prop forward, then as he was aware that he lacked the necessary experience and training to play there, a finding of contributory negligence would have been appropriate. Unless there has been a specific agreement to run a risk or the claimant has voluntarily and knowingly continued to participate in the specific risky environment, then *volenti* and contributory negligence will be extremely difficult for a match official to establish where they are overseeing a game that is being played without adherence to the necessary safety rules and procedures.

5.4 Governing bodies and international federations

This is the least explored area of liability for sports injuries. Although most challenges to the actions of an NGB or ISF occur in respect of their general administrative decisions (see further chapters 2 and 3), the UK courts have accepted that it is fair, just and reasonable to impose a duty of care on them in respect of the safety of sports participants in certain circumstances. The definition and scope of this duty has not yet been fully established or explored before the courts.

Actions based on vicarious liability can be brought against NGBs and ISFs in their roles as employers, just as they can against sports clubs and local education authorities. *Vowles* established that an NGB can be liable for the negligent conduct of its referees. Further, where an NGB employs players, coaches and other support staff for its international teams or uses a system of central contracts for elite performers these will be treated as being analogous to the position of professional clubs (see further, chapter 4.5 and above 5.2.1). As the law relevant to these claims has already been examined, this section will focus on the direct liability of NGBs and ISFs for the harm that they can cause to sports participants.

5.4.1 Establishing a claim

5.4.1.1 Duty of care

The duty of care owed by an NGB derives from the need for the safety of the competitors to be its paramount concern. This can be defined as being the duty to take reasonable care to ensure the safety of the participants taking part in the sporting activity (*Watson v. British Boxing Board of Control* [2001] QB 1134). It can be activated in three main spheres of activity: pre-event administrative checks and the granting of licences to organisers; during event safety provision and associated risk management research; and the playing and safety rules of the game itself.

5.4.1.1.1 Pre-event administration and licensing

Many of the claims brought against NGBs are cases where the organisers of an event have also been sued. The claimant's line of argument is usually that the organiser has dropped below the standard of care expected of them but that this was either because they had been following guidelines prepared negligently by the NGB or that an appropriate permission or licence had been granted negligently to the organiser by the NGB. In either case the accident would not have occurred if the NGB had taken greater care in discharging its own duty to take reasonable care of the safety of the participants.

The first reported instance of an NGB being sued in negligence for harm caused to a competitor was *Stratton v. Hughes and Cumberland Sporting Car Club Ltd and Royal Automobile Club Motor Sports Association Ltd (RAC)* (unreported) Court of Appeal, 17 March 1998. The claimant, the co-driver and navigator of a rally car, sued the driver, event organiser and NGB of the sport. The precise nature of the duty owed is not discussed in great length in the court, however it is assumed that not only is a duty owed but that it is defined in the same terms as that imposed on the organiser; that there is a duty to take reasonable care for the safety of the competitors and that in the context of a specialist activity such as this, conduct should be assessed by reference to the standards of the reasonable and competent organisers of motor rallies.

The role of the RAC as a defendant is because it has responsibility for the production of the competition regulations and the granting of racing permits. One of the conditions of granting such a permit or licence is that the track is appropriate for the particular event being held and that it is reasonably safe for those using it. Although there had been some minor breaches of its regulations, these had not been causative of the accident that occurred. Thus as the regulations themselves were not challenged and the court held that in testing the driving skill of the competitors the layout of this particular track was safe, the granting of the permission to race was not negligent. The liability of NGBs and ISFs has however recently been revisited and extended.

> ▶ *Wattleworth* v. *Goodwood Road Racing Company Ltd and Royal Automobile Club Motor Sports Association Ltd and Federation Internationale de l'Automobile* **[2004] EWHC 140**
>
> Whilst taking part in an informal, non-competitive 'track day' at a motor racing circuit owned and operated by the first defendant, the claimant lost control of his car and crashed into a tyre wall with fatal consequences. The action, brought on behalf of his estate, claimed that the first defendant had acted negligently in its design of the racing track by relying on the advice given to it by the second defendant. Furthermore it was alleged that the RAC, as NGB and the body responsible for inspecting and licensing motor sports circuits in the UK, and Federation Internationale de l'Automobile (FIA) as ISF and originator of the relevant safety guidelines, owed a duty to take reasonable care to ensure that competent and accurate advice on track design and safety was given to the track owners. It was claimed that this duty should be owed to the deceased as he would have expected that the track would be designed and constructed in a manner that ensured that it was safe enough to be used by drivers such as him.
>
> After a comprehensive review of the relevant sporting and non-sporting authorities, the court came to the conclusion that the NGB owed a duty of care to both the race track owner and those driving on it but that it had not been breached in this case because the appropriate advice had been given by reasonable and competent experts in race track safety. The design of the track and attendant safety features such as the tyre wall were sufficient to ensure that it was reasonably safe for the kind of racing with which the claimant was involved and that the inspections carried out by the second defendant prior to granting the relevant licence had been carried out with appropriate care and skill. No duty was owed to the claimant by the FIA as it had legitimately delegated track safety inspections to the appropriate NGB, the RAC.

The duty to the race track owner is easily justified here. The NGB was the sole body able to inspect and license both racing tracks and motor sport events in the UK. Its inspectors worked closely with the track owners and provided expert technical advice over a prolonged period of time, enabling the owners to construct a track that was in accordance with the then current safety guidelines issued by the ISF.

The duty owed to the users of the track was justified on the basis that where advice is given by one person to another that has a direct and foreseeable effect on the safety of a third, then the advisor owes a duty to both the advised party and the third party. Although the NGB was only giving advice to enable the track owners to run competitive events, not informal track days, the nature of safety advice given was said to be the 'highest common denominator.' In other words, if the advice was appropriate to enable a competitive event to be run safely, then it would also enable a track day to be run safely.

The FIA owed no duty to either the track owners or the drivers because of the structure of governance in place between it, as the ISF, and the RAC as the NGB. Regarding track safety and inspections, the FIA delegated all responsibility for domestic arrangements to the RAC. It was therefore sufficiently removed from the advising and inspection process to be absolved of responsibility for the safety advice given. The court did note that the FIA maintained responsibility for safety arrangements at all international level meetings. Although no further comment was made on this, presumably if a similar incident arose at an international competitive fixture, for example the Formula One British Grand Prix, then a duty commensurate to that owed by the NGB in *Wattleworth* would be imposed.

Thus an NGB owes a duty to take reasonable care to ensure that the advice it provides to event organisers, whether through inspections or guidelines, is sufficient to enable the organisers to provide facilities that are reasonably safe for the participants in the sport. This duty is also owed to the participants; the advice given must be sufficient to enable them to compete reasonably safely in the circumstances of the particular sport.

Further, whether or not a duty is owed by an ISF will depend on the relationship between the parties to the action. In *Wattleworth* the ISF had delegated responsibility for safety to the NGB. In cases where such delegation does not take place, then there is no reason why the ISF should not owe exactly the same duty to both organisers and participants that is owed by the NGB: a duty to take reasonable care to ensure that the advice it provides to event organisers, whether through inspections or guidelines, is sufficient to enable the organisers to provide facilities that are reasonably safe for the participants in the sport and that this advice must be sufficient to enable participants to compete reasonably safely in the circumstances of the sport.

5.4.1.1.2 Safety provision and risk management

Pre-dating *Wattleworth* by several years, *Watson v. British Boxing Board of Control* [2001] QB 1134 concerns such an unusual aspect of a governing body's liability in negligence that it requires separate attention. The claimant suffered a catastrophic brain injury from a punch, or series of punches, inflicted on him during the course of a world championship professional boxing bout. His claim was not that boxing was dangerous but that the governing body of professional boxing in the UK, the BBBC, had failed to provide adequate guidelines to those organising boxing contests regarding the quality of ringside medical provision.

▶ *Watson v. British Boxing Board of Control* [2001] QB 1134

The claimant had been knocked out towards the end of a professional boxing bout, causing him to suffer intra-cranial bleeding. Current best practice guidelines provided that treatment of the bleeding and subsequent clotting should take place as soon as possible and preferably within one hour of the injury occurring. The emergency medical provision required of the event organisers by the defendant did not enable pre-operative procedures and emergency first aid to be carried out within this time frame. Furthermore the nearest hospital to where the event took place did not have the necessary neurosurgical arrangements in place. The claimant was eventually operated on over 90 minutes after he had lost consciousness in the ring, the delay causing him lasting brain injury. The court held that the defendant had, through its position as the sole governing body for the sport in the UK, assumed responsibility for determining the nature of the medical facilities and personnel that should be present at a bout and that it should keep itself informed of current best practice relating to all reasonably foreseeable injuries likely to occur during a fight. It was also reasonable for a boxer to rely on the defendant to take reasonable care for his safety during and after a bout. Therefore the defendant had breached the duty it owed the claimant to take reasonable care of his safety.

Almost the entire discussion in the case focuses on whether or not a duty should be imposed on the BBBC in respect of the medical guidelines that it produced for and required to be implemented by the organisers of boxing bouts. The Court of Appeal, in upholding the decision of the trial court, came to a series of important conclusions. Firstly, that because of the degree of control that the BBBC had over every aspect of boxing, it was in the best position to determine what safety protocols ought to be in place. Everyone involved in boxing can only fulfil their role if they have been licensed by the BBBC, leaving it as the sole authority on issues related to participation and safety.

Secondly, that as it considered the safety of boxers to be of paramount importance, the BBBC was under a duty to minimise the risks inherent in this dangerous sport. This included providing guidelines on adequate ringside medical treatment. Thirdly, that this was a body that had, or more rightly ought to have had, special knowledge about the risks involved in the sport that it was overseeing and how those risks could and should be addressed by the drafting of adequate safety protocols. Fourthly, that those advising it on medical and safety issues should have been cognisant of current best practice in the treatment of injuries that were reasonably likely to occur during the course of a bout; this included the initial emergency treatment of serious traumatic brain injuries such as those sustained by the claimant.

In coming to the conclusion that a duty of care was owed to the boxers by the Board, the Court held that the duty was not to take reasonable care to avoid causing personal injury but to take reasonable care to ensure that reasonably foreseeable personal injuries sustained were treated properly. It was fair, just and reasonable to impose a duty on the BBBC because of the degree of control it possessed over the sport and because it was best placed to keep itself informed on developments in relevant fields of medicine. Finally, as in *Wattleworth*, the governing body owed to the participant a duty to ensure that the advice that it gave to event organisers was sufficiently well-prepared to enable the organisers to run a contest safely.

This duty could only be discharged if the BBBC had formulated sufficiently detailed and accurate regulations imposing duties on others to act reasonably and competently. By failing to require suitably qualified medical staff to be present ringside during the bout, with suitable equipment and supplies available to them, the BBBC had failed to act as a reasonable and competent governing body and was therefore in breach of its duty towards the boxers fighting under its rules.

Although not explored in other cases, the liability imposed on the BBBC could be imposed on other governing bodies should they fail to take adequate steps to ensure the safety of participants in their sports. Governing bodies need to ensure that not only is their game safe to play but that there are protocols in place to ensure that an injured player's position is, as a minimum requirement, not made any worse by the actions of those who treat him.

5.4.1.1.3 The rules of the game

To date there have been no reported cases in the UK of a sports participant suing a rule-making body such as an NGB or ISF for the rules of the game being unsafe. On the face of it there would appear to be no reason why the law could not be developed incrementally to impose a duty of care on such a body in these circumstances. Indeed the imposition of a duty, although likely to be fiercely resisted by those who run sport, would not be that much of a step for the law to take in the light of both *Watson* and *Wattleworth*. The difficulty would be in proving that there had been a breach of the duty. This would undoubtedly lead to a rehearsal of the many theoretical and public policy arguments on the meaning and function of sport in our society and to debates on whether it can ever be justifiable to encourage the causing of serious injury in the name of sport and games.

The International Rugby Board was one of the defendants in the Australian case of *Agar* v. *Hyde* [2000] HCA 41, where it was claimed that the known risk of serious neck or spinal injuries being caused by a collapsed scrum was such that it was negligent to allow scrums to continue to be a part of the game (below, Hot Topic). Although the action failed on procedural grounds, there is still a possibility that a similar claim may succeed in the future where the risk of serious injury from the inherent dangers of a sport is high.

This does not mean that ISFs will automatically be found liable for the injuries caused by the dangerous elements of a sport, such as rugby scrums or bouncers in cricket. However it does mean that they may be required to prove that these elements of their sports are integral to their proper functioning and are as safe as is reasonably practicable. This will mean that risk management strategies and patterns of injury will need to be reviewed in order to determine whether a sport needs to be made safer and if so, how. It is unlikely that the potential liability of sports' rule makers will continue to be ignored in the way that it has to date.

Any development in this area of the law will have to be made alongside the further clarification of the role and scope of voluntary assumption of risk and contributory negligence. The vast majority of sports participants are well aware of the degree of risk that they are running when they take part in dangerous sporting activities. As was held in *Anderson* v. *Lyotier, Lyotier and Portejoie* [2008] EWHC 2790 (above, 5.2.2), the decision to run a risk is a collaborative one that is taken by the athlete and, depending on the specific circumstances of the accident, their coach, the match official, and the rule making body. Thus the potential liability of NGBs and ISFs for maintaining the riskier aspects of their sports will be ameliorated by the need to impose a degree of responsibility on the participants for their own actions. This could ensure that the unique characteristics of a sport do not need to be significantly changed whilst requiring sports bodies to make their sports as safe as is reasonably practicable.

5.4.1.2 Breach of duty and the appropriate standard of care

As is the case with coaching and refereeing, the standard of care imposed on an NGB or ISF will be based on the tests from *Bolam* v. *Friern Hospital Management Committee* [1957] 1 WLR 582 and *Bolitho* v. *City and Hackney Health Authority* [1998] AC 232. Therefore the NGB or ISF will be judged by the standard of the reasonable and competent body in the context in which it is acting, whether as an advisor, licensor or rule maker. It will be expected to make decisions and draft guidance and rules in a competent manner and to ensure that what it produces is defensible; something achieved by the RAC in *Wattleworth* but not by the BBBC in *Watson*.

The main difficulty for a claimant bringing an action against either an NGB or ISF is from a practical perspective. It will not be the definition of the test itself that is difficult, which is as above, but providing the necessary evidence to prove that the standard has been breached. In each of these cases many technical experts have given evidence, both from within and outside of sport, in an attempt to establish whether or not the NGB and ISF have acted in a reasonable and competent manner. The difficulty in proving that such a body has acted in breach of this standard of care means that it is likely that only in cases where the governing bodies of sport have failed to keep their technical and safety knowledge up to date, along with training on these matters for their relevant members, that negligence will be established.

5.4.2 Defences

In *Wattleworth*, although not necessary for the disposal of the case and therefore technically *obiter dicta*, the judge addressed claims of both *volenti non fit injura* and contributory negligence. *Volenti* was considered to be an unsustainable defence for the same reasons that were given in *Smoldon* and *Vowles*; although the participant clearly ran the risks inherently involved with motor racing, such as losing control of his car and crashing, he did not voluntarily run the risk that the body with overall responsibility for the safety of the sport would fail to ensure that the track was safe to use.

More interestingly Davis J held that had there been a breach of the relevant duties by the defendants, then the claimant would have been held 20 per cent contributorily negligent. This finding was on the basis of the claimant having taken the wrong racing line when driving into a corner, allowing his wheels to go on to the grass verge on the outside of the bend and losing control of his vehicle. This demonstrates quite clearly that although establishing a defence is difficult it is not impossible, particularly where the claimant's lack of skill in performing a manoeuvre has contributed to the extent of the injuries that they have suffered.

5.5 Medical professionals

In recent years one further group of potential defendants has been added to what is a rapidly expanding list: medical professionals. To some extent this is a fairly obvious fusion of the well-established field of medical law with the growing field of sports law. However the duties imposed on medical practitioners do not always fit well with the way that sports clubs, particularly professional clubs, operate on a day-to-day basis. In the light of the recent (non-medical) case of *Collett* v. *Smith and Middlesbrough Football and Athletics Company (1986) Ltd* [2008] EWHC 1962 (QBD), where a young professional footballer who suffered a career-ending injury before having made his competitive first team debut was awarded £4.5million in compensation, it is important that all those responsible for the health of sports participants are aware of the legal duties imposed on them. This section will briefly examine some of those issues as they apply in professional sports.

The cases of *Bolam* and *Bolitho* already referred to on several occasions were both medical negligence cases. Both highlight that a duty of care is owed by a medical practitioner to their patients and require that the medic reaches the standard of the reasonable and competent person acting in their field of medicine. This is judged by whether the medical professional's conduct would be considered to have been appropriate according to a competent body of similarly qualified medical practitioners. Where more than one alternative course of conduct is open, then the choice must be capable of being justified logically. The cases discussed here do not doubt or alter this basic approach. Instead certain specific problems that sports medicine professionals might come across during their practice are highlighted.

5.5.1   First aid and the initial injury

How any initial injury is treated will depend on the sport in question, the level at which it is being played and the medical protocols in place. Following *Watson* the BBBC overhauled its medical protocols to ensure that emergency treatment and preparation for major surgery can be performed ringside by appropriately qualified experts at professional boxing bouts. Very few sports provide such extensive information, though most will require at least basic first aid to be carried out on injured players.

The initial treatment carried out at the scene of injury will attract as a minimum a duty not to make the injured person's situation any worse. Depending on who else is required to be present during the game, duties appropriate to the level of qualification of the medical personnel present and the equipment and medical supplies to which they have access will be imposed. Thus the duty to act as a reasonable provider of first aid at most amateur sports fixtures or the duty to act as a reasonable and competent anaesthetist at a professional boxing bout could be imposed depending on the circumstances in which the injury occurs.

5.5.2   The design and implementation of return to fitness programmes

Where a physiotherapist for example is part of the team designing a rehabilitation or return to fitness programme, they must also ensure that they discharge their duties in a manner that is both reasonable and competent. The programme must be appropriate for the player, the sport and the injury that they have suffered. The medical professional must also ensure that they have properly and accurately advised the player on when he or she is actually fit to return to play. Just because the player wishes to return to play before being fit enough to do so, or the club insists that they return before being physically and mentally ready, does not absolve the club of responsibility.

Where a potential conflict of interest such as this arises, accurate and contemporaneous note-taking is essential. In *Brady v. Sunderland AFC Ltd* (unreported) Court of Appeal, 17 November 1998, although the quality of the notes taken by a member of the medical team was poor, they were sufficient to demonstrate that appropriate action had been taken in trying to determine the nature of the condition suffered by the claimant.

5.5.3   Referrals for specialist medical treatment

Where an injury is particularly serious, it may require treatment from a specialist rather than a member of the club's in-house medical team.

> ▶ *West Bromwich Albion Football Club Ltd v. El-Safty* **[2006] EWCA Civ 1299**
>
> The defendant consultant surgeon had operated on a member of the claimant's first team professional football squad. The defendant had admitted acting negligently in treating the injury with the result that the player had been forced to retire prematurely from professional football. The claimant brought an action arguing that the defendant owed it a duty to perform the diagnosis and operation competently and that as he had not done so they should be able to claim from him the losses, running into millions of pounds, that they had incurred as a result of needing to recruit a replacement player of similar quality.
>
> The Court of Appeal held that where referrals such as this were concerned, the medical professional owed a duty of care to act reasonably and competently only to their actual patient, not to the patient's employer. This was despite the fact that the referral was made by one of the club's in-house medical team, that the bill was sent to the club and that it was ultimately to be paid for by the club's medical insurance. Even though a negligently performed operation would lead to reasonably foreseeable loss to the club, in that it would have to incur additional expenditure in recruiting a replacement for him, no duty to act with reasonable care and skill was owed to them.

5.5.4 Confidentiality and the disclosure of medical records

The last two points also raise issues relating to doctor–patient confidentiality and the disclosure of medical records. In general a medical professional cannot disclose the medical records of their patient to anyone else without the patient's consent as they are confidential. In practice medical records can be disclosed in certain situations.

Firstly because of the size of many modern medical teams, a number of staff may require access to a patient's records. In this situation the patient's consent to disclose their medical records to enable effective treatment by the team is given implicitly.

Secondly where an examination is required by an employer to determine whether an employee is fit for work, the notes of the examination can be disclosed to the employer. The General Medical Council's guidance on this point recommends that the purpose of the examination and scope of its disclosure be explained to the patient and that a copy of the report be given to them as well as the employer. For good measure the patient's consent to disclose the information should be sought at the outset of the examination. Thus where a member of the in-house medical team examines a player to determine whether they are fit to play, the outcome of such an examination can be disclosed to the team manager or coach to enable a decision to be made regarding the player's fitness, although the player ought to be made aware of this in advance.

However in the *El-Safty* situation above, the consultant owed the duty of confidentiality to the patient alone and was not in a position to disclose the results of his initial negligent examination to the football club. The only situation in which West Bromwich Albion could have legitimately come into possession of the medical records would have been if the player consented to their disclosure.

In many professional sports a clause will be inserted into the employment contract of the player granting explicit consent to the club to have access to all of their medical records and reports. If such a clause exists, even if the external medical professional refused to disclose the medical report to anyone other than the patient, the player would then be contractually obliged to disclose the information to the club.

Hot topic . . .

LIABILITY OF SPORTS ORGANISATIONS FOR THE RULES OF THE GAME – SHOULD SCRUMMAGING BE BANNED?

What has not yet been explored in any reported case in the UK is whether or not an NGB or ISF can be liable for unsafe playing rules of a sport. For example is the risk of spinal injury from a collapsed scrum sufficiently high to mean that all competitive scrummaging should be banned? Can the same be said of the risk of head and facial injuries from bouncers in cricket? Or being unseated by your horse whilst competing in the Grand National at Aintree? Many would see these risks as the very essence of these sports whilst others argue that participants need protecting from themselves and should be forced not to put themselves in such danger. By extending the duty of care by analogy to the developments seen in *Watson* and *Wattleworth*, can an NGB or ISF be found negligent for implementing rules that create unnecessary dangers in the name of sport?

The potential liability of sports' rule makers sees a head-on collision between a strict application of the law of negligence and the policy reasons that inform its practical application to a given situation. There is no reason why a duty of care should not be owed by the rule making body to ensure that a sport is reasonably safe for the participants to play in a way that does not expose them to unnecessary dangers. Thus the key issues here are how to determine what risks can be run by participants in the name of sport and whether those that appear to be the inherent risks of participation in the game are ones that can and should be reasonably run by them.

For example in the Canadian case of *Hamstra* v. *British Columbia Rugby Union* (1989) 1 CCLT (2d) 78, where the claimant, a front row forward, had been rendered quadriplegic by a collapsed scrum, the trial judge examined the availability of scientific and medical evidence concerning the vulnerability of young front row forwards to spinal injury from such collapses. Its conclusion was that in 1986 a regional and amateur body like the BCRU could not be expected to be expert in such matters and that its duty to administer a reasonably safe sport was discharged by following the relevant safety rules and guidelines provided by the NGB, the Canadian Rugby Union. The judge further implies that the more evidence that becomes available, the more it should be taken into account by the relevant rule makers. This statement is very much in line with those given by the Court of Appeal in *Watson*. Thus where dangers are known or ought to be known, they cannot be ignored. Following recent reports in most of the major rugby union playing countries, all domestic Rugby Unions and the International Rugby Board (IRB) are now clearly aware of the risk of catastrophic spinal injury being incurred as a result of a collapsed scrum.

Despite this increased level of knowledge of the dangers associated with collapsed scrums, this does not mean that scrummaging or any other high risk sporting practice should be outlawed; it simply means that they must be made reasonably safe. In some cases it might be found that a practice can no longer be justified as it has become too dangerous to be performed in the name of sport; however no judge has yet decreed that a sport needs to be so radically reformed. This does not mean that they will not do so in the future, but it does mean that NGBs and ISFs need to be aware that their rules need to be constantly reviewed to ensure that safety is not unreasonably compromised.

Some mention needs to be made at this point about the Australian case of *Agar* v. *Hyde* [2000] HCA 41, yet another case of a catastrophic injury being caused by a collapsed scrum in a rugby union game. This decision of the High Court of Australia held that an ISF could not be liable for the rules that it had formulated as there was not a sufficiently close relationship between the player of the game and the body that created and administered the rules of the game. Further, the Court held that allowing the claimant to succeed would leave the rule making body open to claims that it had acted negligently towards an indeterminate class of people; a classic exposition of the floodgates argument.

In the light of *Watson* and *Wattleworth*, this cannot be the case. Where the rule making body is an ISF and it has sole control over the defining of what is and what is not acceptable play in its sport, there is no reason why it should not be subject to a duty to ensure that the players are reasonably safe. Further, the class of potential claimants is not indeterminate; it is large and it is difficult to name them individually but it is not indeterminate. *Wattleworth* demonstrates that a sufficiently close or proximate relationship can be established between the ISF and the class of potential claimants that will be limited to those playing rugby union according to the rules and safety procedures laid down by the IRB.

Proof that the duty has been breached will usually be extremely difficult for the claimant to establish but that does not stop the duty from being imposed. *Watson* determined that the safety of the participants should be of paramount importance to NGBs and ISFs whilst *Wattleworth* demonstrates that where for reasons of consistency the ISF cannot delegate responsibility for safety to the NGBs, it too can be held liable for allowing its sport to become unreasonably dangerous. As with the other potential defendants discussed in this chapter, liability depends on whether those alleged to have caused the harm have been acting reasonably, competently and can justify why they acted in the way that they did. If the rules, practices and protocols of an NGB or ISF are reviewed constantly then it will be extremely difficult for an injured player to establish that the duty to create and run a safe sport has been breached. Where the governing bodies of sport operate only reactively to disasters, then they leave themselves open to claims of having acted negligently.

Summary

5.1 After a comparatively late entry to the field of litigation, sports negligence cases have mushroomed in recent years. Successful claims have been made against defendants who have acted in almost every role connected to the playing, coaching and administering of sport and at all levels of participation.

5.2 Coaches and instructors must ensure that they conduct appropriate risk assessments on all participants and equipment to ensure their suitability for the particular session that they are running. However participants cannot abdicate all responsibility for their personal safety to their coach. Following *Anderson* v. *Lyotier, Lyotier and Portejoie*, they must bring to their coach's attention any concerns that they have over their own competence to participate in a particular activity.

5.3 Referees and match officials must ensure that they enforce the safety rules of the sport under their control as the safety of the players is of paramount importance. Where they fail to do so and an injury that should have been prevented by the application of the rule occurs, the referee will be liable for breaching their duty to ensure that the game has been played in a reasonably safe manner.

5.4 Litigation involving NGBs and ISFs is at present an under-explored field. Although actions against the bodies running sport are likely to increase as claimants search for the defendant most capable of paying their compensation, the creation, implementation and regular revision of effective risk management procedures should ensure that few cases against them can succeed.

5.5 Although the reported cases to date have focussed on injuries caused to professional sports participants, sports-medical litigation is already having an impact on the practice of medicine in this area. The professionalization of sports and exercise medicine, at the expense of the 'man with the cold sponge' is creating an environment where players' health is taken more seriously than in the past. The creation of the Faculty of Sports and Exercise Medicine is clarifying further the standard of conduct required of those working in this specialist field of medical practice.

Further reading

Jackson, *Medical Law: text, cases and materials* (2006, Oxford University Press) ch 6
Lewis and Taylor (eds), *Sport: Law and Practice* (2nd edn, 2008, Tottel) ch D5
Steele, *Tort Law: text, cases and materials* (2007, Oxford University Press) chs 3 and 5

Elvin, 'Liability for negligently refereeing of a rugby match' (2003) 119 *Law Quarterly Review* 560
Gardiner, Liability for sporting injuries' [2008] 1 *Journal of Personal Injury Law* 16
George, 'Negligent rule-making in the Court of Appeal' (2002) 65(1) *Modern Law Review* 106

Further reading cont'd

Kevan, 'Sports personal injury' [2005] 3 *International Sports Law Review* 61

James and Gillett, 'Sports medicine and the law – defining the standard of care' [2009] Apr *Sports Law and Practice* 11

James and Gillett, 'Immediate treatment for on-field injuries' [2009] Jun *Sports Law Administration and Practice* 1

Morgan 'Tort, insurance and incoherence' (2004) 67(3) *Modern Law Review* 384

Opie, 'Negligence liability of rule making bodies in sport' [2002] 2 *International Sports Law Review* 60

Links to relevant websites can be found at www.palgrave.com/law/james

Chapter 6

Violence, injuries and the criminal law

Key words

▶ **Assault** – intentionally or recklessly, the defendant causes another person to apprehend that they will suffer the immediate infliction of unlawful personal force upon themselves.

▶ **Battery** – the intentional or reckless infliction of unlawful force on another person by the defendant.

▶ **Consent** – where, expressly or by implication from the surrounding circumstances, the victim allows the defendant to apply force to their person; in sport, the victim consents to all injury-causing contacts that are part of the acceptable way of playing the particular game.

▶ **Mens rea** – the state of mind required at the time the defendant inflicts force on the victim

6.1 Sports violence and the criminal law

One of the oldest interactions between sport and the law is the prosecution of players for acts of violence towards each other. The first prosecution for violent conduct, *R* v. *Bradshaw* (1878) 14 Cox CC 83 (below, 6.5.1.1), occurred over a hundred years before the corresponding first reported tortious claim in *Condon* v. *Basi* [1985] 1 WLR 866 (see further, chapter 4.4.1.1); many of the cases relating to boxing are even older (see chapter 7). Although the courts and some commentators have long held that during-the-game violence should be treated in exactly the same way as would acts of violence committed anywhere else, this has rarely occurred in practice.

There is no clear reason why this should be the case, though there are a number of possible explanations. Firstly that injury, even where deliberately inflicted, is often considered to be an inherent risk of playing sport and something that players should therefore tolerate. Secondly there appears to be a general feeling amongst athletes that these issues should be sorted out within the sport itself, either by retaliation during the game or by the relevant governing body's disciplinary tribunal after the event. Thirdly that sports violence is not real violence and should not get in the way of the everyday workings of the courts.

The ongoing battle between the proponents of internal self-regulation and external legal regulation has been at the heart of the discussions on sports injuries and the criminal law and is a major theme of this chapter. However where participants attack spectators, or coaches abuse young players or death occurs, there is much less resistance to the use of the criminal law.

6.1.1 Historical context

In 1878 *Bradshaw* set the scene for how it appeared the criminal law would develop in respect of sports assaults. In directing the jury on whether a foul challenge that had led to the death of an opponent was criminal, or simply part of the lawful playing of the game, Bramwell LJ stated at p.85 that:

'No rules or practice of any game whatever can make that lawful which is unlawful by the law of the land … [If] a man is playing according to the rules and practice of the game and not going beyond it, it may be reasonable to infer … that he is not acting in a manner which he knows will be likely to be productive of death or injury. But … if the [defendant] intended to cause serious hurt to the deceased, or … was indifferent or reckless as to whether he would produce serious injury or not, then the act would be unlawful.'

Much like the corresponding tortious cases (see further, chapter 4.4.1.3), the court required an analysis of the player's conduct in the context of it having taken place whilst playing a lawful contact sport, rather than it having been a simple act of violence. Bramwell LJ's direction to the jury states very clearly how the law ought to apply to sports assault cases, including a statement that a finding of foul play will not of itself be sufficient to lead to a conviction. His Lordship directs the jury to consider whether the act was in accordance not just with the rules of the game, but with its 'rules and practice'. Unfortunately 'practice' is not defined in the judgment but presumably must be something beyond a strict interpretation of the rules of the sport in question. This paves the way for a wider interpretation of acceptable conduct that has been referred to by Williams as a sport's 'working culture' and more recently as its 'playing culture' (see further, chapter 4.4.1.3 and below, 6.4.1), concepts wide enough to encompass not just acts that are within a sport's constituent rules but also some acts of commonly occurring foul play. However no other significant cases were reported over the next hundred years, creating uncertainty about how the criminal law should respond to sports assaults. When these issues were revisited it became clear that the courts were unwilling to impose the full force of the law on those committing sports assaults.

▶ *R v. Billinghurst* **[1978] Crim LR 553**

Following an off-the-ball punch in a rugby union game that fractured his opponent's jaw in two places, the defendant argued that blows of this nature were an expected part of the playing of the game; in other words fighting was one of the practices of rugby union and therefore consented to. Furthermore the victim gave evidence that he had previously both been punched and had himself thrown punches and a former Wales international player gave evidence that punching was the exception rather than the rule in rugby games.

In rejecting these arguments, the judge stated that players consent only to applications of force that are of a kind that could reasonably be expected to occur during a game and that there was no unlimited licence to use force against an opponent. Thus punching may well occur in rugby games but it is not considered by the law to be something which players should expect and therefore protect themselves against. Although this finding lead to the defendant being convicted of inflicting grievous bodily harm contrary to s.20 Offences Against the Person Act 1861 he was only sentenced to nine months in prison which was suspended for two years; the judge had decided that a clear offence of violence was not suitable for a custodial sentence because it had occurred in the course of playing sport.

The continuing lack of reported cases on sports assaults, particularly at appellate level, made it difficult to identify a coherent set of principles that were underpinning the development of the law in this area. In particular the application of the law of consent was at best inconsistent and at worst misunderstood in the sporting context. This was highlighted by the Law Commission in its two Consultation Papers on the law of consent. The first of these, *Consent and Offences against the Person* (LCCP No 134 1994), focuses on determining the reasonableness of the defendant's conduct as the key to determining their criminal liability, though without explaining how this is to be determined across a range of sports.

The second, *Consent in the Criminal Law* (LCCP No 139, 1995), proposes in the light of comments made on the first Consultation Paper that sports participants should be able to consent to all injury inflicted within the rules of the game but not to deliberately inflicted harm or recklessly inflicted 'seriously disabling injury'. The former proposal ignores the developments of the law concerning the playing culture of a sport whilst the latter predicates criminal liability on the degree of injury caused rather than the state of mind of the defendant, meaning that a defendant would have to wait until the outcome of the challenge was known before being able to determine its legality retrospectively. Unfortunately these proposals, although circulated for further comment in 1995, did not result in the promised third and final Paper, leaving the law as it applied to sport in a state of flux.

6.1.2　The role of sports disciplinary tribunals

As the quality of procedural justice in sports disciplinary tribunals has improved (see further, chapter 2), many cases that could in theory be heard before the criminal courts are no longer done so. The more court-like the governing body's tribunals became, the less opportunity there is for the 'defendant' to complain that he has been treated unfairly. Further, the more stringent the penalty imposed, the less cause there was for the victim to complain that the incident had not been treated with an appropriate degree of seriousness by the NGB.

Although more pronounced at the elite level of sport, fewer reported cases are emanating from all levels of the sporting pyramid. The increased robustness of many tribunals' procedures has ensured that many clearly criminal assaults are no longer considered appropriate for the criminal justice system. This raises an important point of discussion: whether self-regulation is more appropriate in these circumstances than legal regulation and whether it is ever appropriate for any form of violent conduct to be dealt with outside of the criminal justice system (below, Hot Topic).

These early cases have left a high degree of confusion about the role of the criminal law in regulating sports assaults. The lack of judicial guidance on how the law should apply and the uncertain relationship between the law and the NGBs have ensured that this topic remains controversial.

6.2　Common assault

The foundations of the law of offences against the person are found in the definition of common assault. This crime can be committed in two ways: by assaulting another person or by battering them. Assault and battery have very specific meanings in the criminal law and these will be used for the rest of this section. However the term 'assault' is generally used whichever of the two technical meanings is actually in issue and in the discussions after this section, assault will be used to refer to all crimes committed including those which are technically batteries.

6.2.1 Definition of common assault

Common assault can be committed by either an assault or a battery. An assault is where the defendant intentionally or recklessly causes the victim to apprehend the immediate infliction of unlawful personal force to their person. In other words it is the threat that unlawful contact will be made with the victim. Battery is the intentional or reckless application of force to the victim; in other words it is the carrying out of the threat (*Fagan v. Metropolitan Police Commissioner* [1969] 1 QB 439).

The aim of the offence is to prevent any unwanted interference with a person's bodily integrity by criminalising the merest touching of another person. However, where the victim has consented to the touching, the defendant will have a complete defence to the charge (below, 6.4.1). Common assaults, in the context of this chapter technically batteries, form the basis of all the other offences against the person that can be committed by sports participants. If the initial common assault cannot be proved then no offence has been committed.

6.2.1.1 The mens rea of common assault by battery

The mens rea of battery is that the defendant acted intentionally or recklessly when making contact with the victim (*R v. Savage; DPP v. Parmenter* [1992] 1 AC 699). Intention means that the defendant desired to make contact with or apply physical force to the victim, for example by pushing or punching them. Alternatively the offence can be committed subjectively recklessly, where the defendant foresaw the risk of making contact with the victim but carried on regardless. For example when attempting to make a tackle, a footballer can foresee that they might not only get the ball but might also come into contact with the opposing player. By carrying on with the challenge regardless of the possibility of making contact with their opponent, the defendant acts subjectively recklessly. The mens rea for battery is the same for all of the assault offences discussed in this chapter, though some of the offences in the Offences Against the Person Act 1861 (OAPA 1861) require additional states of mind regarding the degree of harm caused to the victim.

6.2.2 Application in sport

Common assault will usually be used in situations where the defendant has caused minor injuries such as bruising or grazes to the victim. It is rarely charged in respect of sports assaults either because the contact was consented to or because the degree of harm caused was sufficient to constitute an offence under the OAPA 1861. However in *R v. Brownbill* (unreported) Crown Court (Preston), 4 February 2004, the defendant was charged with common assault despite having repeatedly punched his opponent in an ice hockey game with such force that his two front teeth were knocked out. On conviction Brownbill was fined £250 and ordered to pay £250 in costs. This case can be considered something of an anomaly as the degree of injury inflicted here was at least sufficient to constitute an offence under s.47 OAPA 1861 (below, 6.3.1).

The more usual response of the court would be as happened in *R v. Evans* (unreported) Crown Court (Newcastle), 14 June 2006, where the defendant was accused of having stamped on his victim in a rugby union game. The judge directed the jury to acquit on the basis that the 'slight bruise' on the victim's forehead was insufficient to constitute an actionable injury arising from the normal playing of rugby.

6.3   The Offences Against the Person Act 1861

The vast majority of sports assaults that come before the criminal courts arise from either deliberate foul play or fights and are charged under ss. 47, 20 or 18 OAPA 1861. As there is little need to discuss consent in such cases, because these assaults cannot be said to be an expected part of the playing of the game in question, this issue is discussed separately (below, 6.4.1). Although it is technically possible for an aggravated assault such as those under the OAPA 1861 to be committed during the ordinary playing of the game, this is extremely unlikely to occur as consent will render such contacts lawful.

One of the key issues in these cases can be the choice of offence with which to charge the defendant. Unfortunately the factors affecting this choice are not reported in the cases, which can create some confusion where the same injuries can result in successful charges under either ss.47 or 20 OAPA 1861. There are three main reasons why similar injuries might be prosecuted under either of these two sections. Firstly as there are no formal definitions of the two main levels of harm that a victim might suffer, the determination of whether an injury constitutes actual or grievous bodily harm is not an exact science. Secondly a player may be charged with the more serious offence under s.20 in the hope that he or she will then plead guilty to the lesser offence under s.47 thereby avoiding the need for a trial. Thirdly the defendant might not have the requisite mens rea for the s.20 offence (below, 6.3.2). Although not a serious difficulty, direct comparison of some cases can seem strange at first glance when two defendants are charged with different offences when they have caused the same degree of harm to their victims.

6.3.1   Offences Against the Person Act 1861 s.47 – assault occasioning actual bodily harm

The offence under s.47 is committed where the defendant intentionally or recklessly assaults another person and, as a matter of fact, the assault causes the victim actual bodily harm (ABH). Put simply, it is a common assault that causes the victim ABH. The mens rea is the same as for common assault: the defendant must have intentionally or recklessly made contact with the victim. However no further mens rea is required for the causing of ABH; if the assault causes ABH then the s.47 offence is committed. ABH is not defined in the Act but over the years has come to mean any harm that interferes with the health and comfort of the victim. From a practical perspective this will include serious bruising, concussion and most minor fractures.

6.3.1.1 Application to sport
R v. *Birkin* (1988) 10 Cr App R (S) 303 is a classic example of how and why the law applies to sports assaults. The defendant footballer was the subject of a late foul tackle by his victim that would be considered to have been part of the normal playing of the game. As the two players ran off to take up their positions for the resulting free kick, the defendant punched the victim on the side of his face and broke his jaw in two places. This was an intentional battery that caused the victim ABH. Moreover as it occurred off-the-ball and was clearly retaliatory, it was neither within the 'rules and practices' of football nor was it an act that could reasonably be expected to occur during a football match and therefore the offence was committed.

Offences Against the Person Act 1861 s.20 – assault inflicting grievous bodily harm

In common with s.47, the s.20 offence requires that the defendant intentionally or recklessly assaults another person. However both the degree and/or type of harm caused must be more serious and the mens rea requirements are more stringent than under s.47.

For a charge under s.20 OAPA 1861, the victim must suffer either grievous bodily harm (GBH) or a wound. GBH is not defined in the Act but has been described as being really serious harm, such as major fractures and internal injuries (*R v. Miller* [1954] 2 QB 282). For historical reasons wounds of whatever degree of severity are considered to be a particularly serious type of injury and are therefore specifically included in this section. A wound is any injury that breaks the external skin of the victim (*Moriarty v. Brookes* (1834) 6 C&P 684).

In addition to the initial mens rea that the contact must be made intentionally or recklessly, s.20 also requires that the defendant foresaw that the assault would cause some harm to the victim (*R v. Savage; DPP v. Parmenter* [1992] 1 AC 699). The defendant does not need to foresee that the assault will cause either GBH or a wound, just that some harm will result from the contact. Thus a defendant can commit the s.20 OAPA 1861 offence without intending or even appreciating in advance the precise degree of harm ultimately caused to the victim.

6.3.2.1 Application to sport

In *Billinghurst* (above, 6.1.1) the defendant was charged under s.20 OAPA 1861 having punched an opponent after play had stopped in a rugby union game. Deliberately punching another person is clearly an intentional assault and it is foreseeable that punching someone in the face or head will cause them some physical harm. Even though the resulting injuries, a double fracture of the jaw, were not foreseen at the time by the defendant, they did not need to be to establish an offence under s.20 OAPA 1861; as long as some harm was foreseen, he was liable for the GBH that was actually caused to the victim. As punching is not expected to occur in the normal playing of rugby union, from a legal perspective at least, then this was an act outside of the playing culture of the game and therefore a s.20 assault.

Offences Against the Person Act 1861 s.18 – causing grievous bodily harm or wounding with intent

Section 18 OAPA 1861 is the most serious of the non-fatal offences against the person. It requires that the outcome, the victim suffering GBH or a wound, was intended by the defendant when committing the assault. Thus the offence can be defined succinctly as being where the defendant committed an intentional assault with the intent to cause GBH or a wound to the victim. Where there was no intent to cause GBH or a wound, only to assault, then the defendant must be charged under s.20 OAPA 1861.

The high degree of intent required by s.18 OAPA 1861 means that charges under this section are comparatively rare in sport. Unless the defendant has kicked or stamped on another player's head (*R v. Garfield* [2008] EWCA Crim 130), bitten them (*R v. Johnson* (1986) 8 Cr App R (S) 343), or head-butted them (*R v. Piff* (1994) 15 Cr App R (S) 737), then the appropriate charge will usually be s.20 OAPA 1861. Biting is a particularly unpleasant but clear cut example of a s.18 assault. The initial assault, the bite, can really only be carried out intentionally and by biting through the skin, most commonly the ear lobe, there can be little doubt that the resulting wound and/or GBH was also inflicted intentionally.

6.3.3.1 Application to sport

The mens rea required for a s.18 assault acts as a filter on the number of charges brought for this offence. Thus only rarely will a sports participant be charged with intentionally causing GBH during the course of play.

> ▶ *R v. Blissett* (1992) The Independent, 4 December.
>
> Both defendant and victim were professional footballers who were attempting to head the same high ball. Whilst making his challenge, the defendant's elbow came into contact with the victim's face, fracturing his cheekbone and eye socket. The defendant was sent off for violent conduct as the referee believed that he had deliberately elbowed the victim in the face as opposed to using his arms to try to gain extra momentum to head the ball with greater force. Thus the evidence suggested that the initial assault was intentional and from its nature, an elbow to the face, it could be inferred that the defendant intended to cause his victim the serious physical injury required by s.18 OAPA 1861.
>
> The jury found the defendant not guilty and the incident impliedly consented to on the basis of the 'expert' evidence supplied by the Chief Executive of the Football Association, who claimed that this kind of challenge could be expected to occur at least fifty times in every match. In other words its regularity of recurrence brought it within the playing culture of the game and was therefore the kind of challenge that could be expected to occur.

Although there is much debate about the use of the arms and elbows when attempting to head a football, what the court failed to address here was whether this conduct was legally acceptable. In *Billinghurst* the judge tacitly accepted that fighting did occur in rugby but that even if such conduct was acceptable to the players, it was not acceptable to the court. Here, the court accepted that such challenges did occur in football but did not carry out the further investigation into whether they ought to. Since *Blissett* there have been virtually no reported cases involving assaults so closely connected with the actual playing of the game.

6.4 Defences

As most contacts that occur in the course of playing sport are made either intentionally or recklessly, then for sport to be able to continue in the forms that we currently know it, some legal mechanism must operate to make lawful contacts that would otherwise be criminal assaults. The most important defence in these circumstances is consent, which ensures that those contacts that are truly part of the playing of the game are lawful and cannot form the basis of a criminal charge.

In certain circumstances self-defence may be raised by a defendant where they honestly believed in the need to use reasonable force to prevent an attack upon themselves (*R v. Williams* [1987] 3 All ER 411). As this is really only relevant in the context of fights or where a fight is about to break out, this defence is not discussed further here. In the United States 'involuntary reflex' has been successfully raised to explain why a defendant hit and injured his opponent; however such an argument is unlikely to succeed in the UK (below, 6.4.2.).

Consent

It has long been accepted that sport, particularly contact sports, must be treated differently to other situations in which injury is suffered (*Attorney-General's Reference (No 6 of 1980)* [1981] QB 715). The simple reason for this is that without some kind of exemption to the general prohibition on being able to consent to ABH or greater being inflicted upon oneself (*R v. Brown* [1994] 1 AC 212), many popular sports would be unable to function in the way that they do currently.

The difficulty faced by anyone trying to determine precisely how the applicable law is defined in the context of sports assaults is the paucity of appellate court decisions on the subject and in particular the total lack of any House of Lords or Supreme Court decision that could clarify this area. Outside of sport, the general law on consent to injury is that nobody can consent to the infliction of ABH or greater upon their person (*Brown*). Without further elaboration, a person could consent to a common assault being perpetrated on them but not one of the aggravated assaults contained in the OAPA 1861. As injury of at least ABH is a common occurrence in many sports, thousands of sports participants would be left at risk of prosecution each week for injuries they caused during the course of play. For example if a rugby player tackles an opponent, there is intentional contact between them and therefore an assault. If the tackle breaks the leg of the opponent, injury constituting at least ABH will have been suffered and therefore an assault under s.47 OAPA 1861 is committed. As it would not be in the public interest to criminalise conduct of this nature, the courts have acknowledged that some accommodation for sport needs to be reached.

In *Bradshaw* Bramwell LJ noted that contacts that were within the 'rules and practices' of the sport in question were lawful and could be consented to, regardless of the degree of harm caused to the victim. A hundred years later in *Billinghurst*, the court held that injurious conduct that was 'of a kind which could reasonably be expected to happen during a game' could be consented to. The difficulty for the courts and the players is to determine in advance of play when an act is a necessary, or integral, or an expected part of the playing of the game and when it is criminal violence. It was not until 2004 that the Court of Appeal finally addressed these issues.

> ▶ *R v. Barnes* [2004] EWCA Crim 3246
>
> Towards the end of a football match the victim, a forward, was wasting time by keeping the ball under his control near the corner flag. The defendant attempted a clumsy challenge on the victim, committing a foul, and was warned about his conduct by the referee. A short time later the victim gained control of the ball and ran towards his opponent's goal, shot and scored. After the ball had been kicked by the victim, the defendant tackled him from behind by means of a sliding challenge causing serious injury to the victim's right ankle and fibula. After making the challenge, the defendant was heard to say something to the effect of, 'Have that,' to the victim. The defendant was sent off for violent conduct; the referee considered the challenge to have been a late, high, two-footed lunge as opposed to the defendant's claim that he was attempting to perform a sliding tackle. The judge directed the jury that the defendant could only be guilty of an assault under s.20 OAPA 1861 if the prosecution could prove that the challenge was not done by way of 'legitimate sport' or that it was 'over and above what is generally acceptable in a football game.'
>
> The conviction under s.20 OAPA 1861 was originally justified on the basis that the injury-causing challenge was intentional, in that the defendant intended to make contact with the victim. Furthermore when making the challenge he would have been able to foresee some

harm such as bruising being caused to the victim. The Court of Appeal however allowed the appeal on the basis that the judge had provided the jury with an inadequate explanation of 'legitimate sport' and that the conviction was therefore technically unsafe. It held that only rarely should cases involving sports participants be heard before the criminal courts rather than the relevant governing body's disciplinary tribunal. Where cases were appropriate for prosecution, the jury should consider the type of sport being played, the level at which it was being played, the nature of the act, the degree of force used, the extent of the risk of injury and the state of mind of the defendant when determining whether the defendant's conduct was objectively acceptable in the circumstances.

Although the explanation of the law put forward by the Court provides some much needed clarity in this area, the application of the law to the specific case was not without some controversy in the light of the facts that were found to have occurred by the jury. In allowing the appeal, the Court began by making a very clear policy statement: that because most sports have governing bodies which administer their own internal disciplinary regimes then in the vast majority of cases it will be undesirable to make recourse to the criminal law as well as, or instead of, using these tribunals. Only where the conduct was sufficiently grave should a prosecution be pursued. Ignoring the inherent circularity in this statement and the lack of any further justification of why this specific form of violence should be granted an exemption from prosecution, the Court made it abundantly clear that they did not consider it appropriate for sports assault cases to be heard before the criminal courts. Post-*Barnes* and *Blissett*, it is extremely unlikely that any injury caused by a challenge even remotely connected with the playing of the game will be considered to be a criminal assault. Only where the injuries were caused by a fight or were in some other way 'off-the-ball' or 'behind-the-play' might prosecution be appropriate; in all other cases the Court of Appeal considered that these were matters best dealt with by the sport's governing body.

Having made this statement, the Court then clarified the law that should be applied to sports assaults, taking the opportunity to review the law as it had developed over the previous 130 years. The conclusions of Lord Woolf CJ at para.15 provide a comprehensive and workable series of circumstances that should be taken into account when trying to determine the lawfulness of a sports participant's conduct:

'[The] fact that the play is within the rules and practice of the game and does not go beyond them, will be a firm indication that what has happened is not criminal. In making a judgment as to whether conduct is criminal or not, it has to be borne in mind that, in highly competitive sports, conduct outside the rules can be expected to occur in the heat of the moment, and even if the conduct justifies not only being penalised but also a warning or even a sending off, it still may not reach the threshold level required for it to be criminal. That level is an objective one and does not depend upon the views of individual players. *The type of the sport, the level at which it is played, the nature of the act, the degree of force used, the extent of the risk of injury, the state of mind of the defendant are all likely to be relevant in determining whether the defendant's actions go beyond the threshold.'* [Emphasis added.]

First of all Lord Woolf CJ reiterates that injuries caused by contacts that are an accepted and expected part of the playing of the game, including many contacts that are technically foul play, are part of its playing culture and are therefore lawful and consented to. Instinctive reactions and errors of judgement made in the heat of competition are not considered appropriate cases for prosecution, though could constitute negligence on the part of either the players or those who have trained them to act violently (see further, chapter 5.2). In particular where the governing body of a sport has taken prompt, decisive and meaningful action following an incident of violent conduct, the police and Crown Prosecution Service have been reluctant to take the matter further (below, Hot Topic).

Secondly where a player's conduct is considered to be something other than an error of judgement, then the Court provided a non-exhaustive list of the circumstances surrounding the incident that should be taken into account in order to determine its lawfulness. In doing this, the Court provided a more detailed explanation of the phrase 'legitimate sport' that had been used at trial. By examining these criteria in detail, it should be possible to determine whether a particular act was an acceptable way of playing the game or whether it was so inherently dangerous that it ought to be criminal. It also enables courts to maintain an overview of all sporting conduct, ensuring that the governing bodies of sport are not able to determine unilaterally the extent of a player's consent; vigorous and hard play can be justified but dangerous and violent conduct cannot be.

Applying these criteria to the facts established by the jury in *Barnes*, it must be taken into account that this was a competitive football match and that therefore challenges for the ball were an integral part of the game. Secondly this was a Sunday league game and the players were not highly skilled. Although players cannot use their lack of skill to justify violent play, it is important to take into account whether the challenge in question was one that went beyond the defendant's skill level or for which he had not received prior training. A sliding tackle such as occurred here would be a normal part of play at this level.

The third criterion is key to establishing whether the conduct was criminal: the nature of the act. In *Barnes* the court had to determine whether this was a vigorous but fair challenge for the ball, as the defendant claimed, or a late, high, unnecessary foul tackle from behind, as argued by the prosecution. In reaching a conclusion on this point, the remaining circumstances will also have to be considered: the degree of force used; the extent of the risk of injury and the state of mind of the defendant. At trial, the jury appeared to consider that the degree of force used was excessive as the chances of the defendant playing the ball were remote, that the risk of injury was high as the defendant appeared to have stamped on the back of his victim's leg and that he had done so deliberately, or at least recklessly, as evidenced by his reaction.

The Court of Appeal held that the trial judge's failure to provide a fuller explanation of the meaning of 'legitimate sport' was a misdirection on the law which rendered the conviction unsafe. This conclusion is explicable on the basis that the judge had not provided examples of what he meant by 'legitimate sport' in response to specific questions from the jury. Somewhat strangely however, having provided the fuller explanation of 'rules and practices' or 'expected conduct' or 'legitimate sport' or 'playing culture' that the law required, the Court then failed to apply this new test to facts that had been found by the jury, allowing the defendant's appeal and quashing his conviction. In doing this in the face of what appears to be a case that satisfies its own criteria for establishing criminal liability, it is unlikely that anything other than the most obviously deliberate foul will be considered by a court to be a criminal assault in future. If the Court of Appeal's aim was not only to clarify the law but to discourage during-the-game incidents from being prosecuted, then the dearth of reported cases since *Barnes* would indicate that it has been successful.

Involuntary reflex

In *Barnes* the Court of Appeal referred to a player's 'instinctive reaction' as being an insufficient basis for establishing criminal liability. The strict legal explanation for this is because where a defendant has acted without thinking, instinctively, they will be trying to establish that they did not have the requisite mens rea at the time the assault was committed. If this is a denial of having acted unlawfully, then there is nothing inherently wrong with such a claim. If it is an attempt to establish the defence of automatism however, then it will fail.

Automatism is a complete defence to a criminal charge only where the defendant can prove that they were acting without any voluntary control over their actions, not just that their ability to control their actions was diminished (*Bratty v. Attorney-General for Northern Ireland* [1963] AC 386). Further, the cause of their involuntary conduct must be something external to them, such as a blow to the head that leads to concussion. Where sports participants are concerned it is extremely unlikely that they will be able to claim that they had no control whatsoever over what they were doing; their training may have caused them to react in a certain way, but they still have control over what it is that they are doing. It is equally unlikely that they will be able to claim that their training regime is sufficiently external to constitute the necessary cause for a claim of automatism to succeed. From a practical perspective, if the club has trained the defendant to react in a dangerous manner, then the more appropriate legal response would be to sue the coach and/or employing club for having acted negligently in the provision of training to the defendant (see further, chapter 5.2). In Minnesota, USA however a claim of involuntary reflex helped to raise a sufficient doubt in the minds of the jury that a mistrial was declared.

▶ *State v. Forbes* (unreported) Case 63280, Minn Dist Ct, 12 September 1975

The defendant and his victim were opposing professional ice hockey players in an NHL game. Following an on-ice altercation between them, both were sent to the penalty box for seven minutes. Throughout the period of the penalty, the defendant threatened his opponent. As they returned to the ice, the victim skated up behind the defendant causing the defendant to hit the victim in the face with the butt end of his stick. He then fell upon his prone victim and repeatedly punched him in the face, fracturing his eye socket and causing a wound that required 25 stitches. The defendant was banned from playing professional ice hockey for ten games and charged with aggravated assault by use of a dangerous weapon.

In his defence counsel claimed that it was, 'hockey, not Dave Forbes, [that] should be on trial.' The defendant argued that his initial assault was an instinctive reaction to the training that he had received throughout his career and that in situations like the one he found himself in, an opponent approaching him from behind, his actions were defensive as they would prevent an attack being carried out on him. This argument was sufficient to result in a hung jury with a mistrial declared, despite Forbes having caused serious facial injuries to his victim. A retrial was not sought by the prosecutors as it was considered that if conviction could not be secured on these facts, then it was unlikely that any court would ever convict for a sports assault, a prediction that has proven to be true by the dearth of prosecutions since *Forbes*.

Although this line of argument is unlikely to succeed in the UK for the reasons mentioned above, it is a clear indication of how the seeds of doubt can be sown in the minds of a jury in a criminal trial. In the Canadian case of *R v. Green* (1970) 16 DLR 3d 137, the judge relied on a similar justification for finding that no assault had been committed when an ice hockey player hit an opponent on the upper arm with an ice hockey stick; it was simply an instinctive warning to his opponent to keep away not a deliberate or reckless assault.

6.5 Homicide

From a practical perspective, there are only two forms of homicide that are relevant where a person has been killed whilst participating in sport: unlawful act manslaughter and corporate manslaughter. To establish a murder charge the court must be satisfied so that it is sure that the defendant intended to kill their victim, or that the defendant intended to cause them GBH and that the victim died as a result of the intentional assault (*R v. Cunningham* [1982] AC 566). In other words if a defendant commits a s.18 OAPA 1861 assault against a victim who later dies from their injuries, then murder is established. The high standard of proof and the need to prove intention to kill or cause GBH means that murder charges will be extremely rare in the sports context unless there is a fight that results in fatal consequences. To date there have been no convictions of murder arising from sports assaults.

6.5.1 Unlawful act manslaughter

Although charges of manslaughter are likely to be rare in sport, they are not unheard of. Manslaughter occurs where the defendant commits an unlawful and dangerous act that causes the victim's death. In this context dangerous means that all sober and reasonable people would inevitably recognise the risk that some harm (not death) would be caused by the defendant's act (*R v. Church* [1966] 1 QB 59). Usually the unlawful act that forms the basis of the charge will be an assault under either s.47 or s.20 OAPA 1861. The test is objective so that it is unnecessary to prove that the defendant was aware that their actions were dangerous; if the reasonable person would have recognised that there was a risk of harm being caused to the victim then the act is dangerous.

6.5.1.1 Application to sport

Two of the earliest sports assault cases provide a useful comparison of how an assault can result in a charge of manslaughter.

▶ *R v. Bradshaw* (1878) 14 Cox CC 83, Court of Exchequer Chamber

The deceased was attempting to dribble the ball towards his opponent's goal when the defendant attempted to either challenge him for possession or intercept the ball. In making the challenge, the defendant charged the deceased by jumping at him with his knees raised and pointing towards the deceased's midriff. The deceased died the following day from a rupture to his intestines. The judge directed the jury that football was a rough game but was one that was lawful and in which participation should not be decried. He further noted that the rules and practices of a game cannot make lawful that which is unlawful and that where a defendant is playing a lawful sport in accordance with its rules and does not intend to cause injury by his actions, then it could be inferred that no offence had been committed. Only where the defendant intended to cause, or was reckless as to causing serious injury would a conviction be appropriate. In acquitting the defendant of manslaughter it would appear that the jury considered that the defendant had committed a rough but ultimately fair challenge that was within the rules and practices of football as then understood. In other words the challenge was lawful and therefore consented to by the deceased.

In contrast the defendant in *R v. Moore* (1898) 15 TLR 229 was found guilty of manslaughter having charged the deceased from behind, throwing him violently against the knee of the goalkeeper. Again the deceased died from internal injuries a few days later. In this case, presumably because the defendant had no chance of getting to the ball and had deliberately and violently charged the deceased, the jury considered the challenge to be both unlawful and dangerous and therefore incapable of being consented to.

In both cases it can be seen that there was at least a reckless, if not an intentional assault committed on the deceased players and that it was objectively foreseeable to the reasonable person that some harm may have been caused to them as a result of the challenges. However *Bradshaw*'s act was within the rules and practices of football, because it was a rough challenge for the ball, whereas *Moore*'s was not as there was no attempt to play the ball, only the opposing player.

6.5.2 Corporate manslaughter

Prior to the enacting of the Corporate Manslaughter and Corporate Homicide Act 2007 (CMCHA 2007) there had always been significant difficulties in bringing manslaughter actions against corporate entities. The main problem was identifying the person who was the 'controlling mind and will' of the company who would be the person that formed the mens rea of the offence on its behalf.

Under the common law a company would have to be charged with gross negligence manslaughter. The offence follows the same basic pattern as the tort of negligence (see further, chapter 4.3) except that the breach must be gross and the only relevant harm is death. Thus the requirements of the offence were that the defendant owed the deceased a duty of care, that the duty was breached by the defendant's conduct, that the breach caused the deceased's death and that the breach of duty was so gross as to justify conviction (*R v. Adomako* [1995] 1 AC 171).

However in trying to establish that a company had acted grossly negligently, the court could not aggregate the conduct of two or more employees; instead, a single controlling mind and will had to be identified and that person alone had to have acted with gross negligence (*Attorney-General's Reference (No2 of 1999)* [2000] QB 796). Thus there were virtually no prosecutions for corporate manslaughter, not just in the context of sport, because the larger and more complex the management structure of the company the more difficult it was to identify its controlling mind and will (*R v. P & O European Ferries (Dover) Ltd* (1991) 93 Cr App R 72).

Section 20 CMCHA 2007 abolishes the common law offence of gross negligence as it applies to corporations and s.1 of the Act replaces it with a new offence known as corporate manslaughter in England, Wales and Northern Ireland and corporate homicide in Scotland. The new offence is very similar to the one that it replaces except that it no longer requires the identification of a single directing mind and will of the corporation.

Corporate manslaughter is defined in s.1 CMCHA 2007 as being committed where the activities of a corporation cause a person's death by a gross breach of a duty owed to the deceased. The existence of a duty of care is indentified in much the same way as it is for the law of negligence (see further, chapter 4.3) and includes the duties owed under the Occupiers' Liability Acts, s.2 CMCHA 2007. Under s.4(b), a breach of the relevant duty is considered to be gross where the conduct of the corporation falls far below what could reasonably be expected of it in the circumstances in which it operates. Finally the grossly negligent conduct is attributable to the corporation only if its senior management, defined in s.4(c) as being the persons who play significant roles in making decisions, managing and/or organising the whole or a substantial part of the corporation, played a substantial role in breaching the duty.

In theory the new offence makes it easier to establish criminal liability against corporations that have caused deaths by their activities. To date the lack of prosecutions under the Act makes it unclear whether or not this will actually be the case. Until a clearer picture of how the CMCHA 2007 will be used to regulate corporate conduct, this field of litigation will continue to be as controversial as it always has been.

6.5.2.1 Application to sport

One of the very few successful prosecutions for corporate manslaughter under the old common law was against a company that organised outdoor adventure pursuits for children.

▶ *R v. Kite and OLL Ltd* **[1996] 2 Cr App R (S) 295**

The defendant was the sole director of a company that provided outward bound and adventure activities to groups of children. Eight schoolchildren, a teacher and two of his instructors embarked on a sea canoeing expedition across Lyme Bay. Contrary to British Canoe Union guidelines, all members of the group were inexperienced novices and should not have been out on the open sea and the instructors were not sufficiently experienced to be guiding an expedition of this nature. The entire group got into difficulties and four of the children drowned before they could be rescued. The defendant was found to have acted grossly negligently in causing the deaths and was therefore guilty of manslaughter. He was under a duty to provide a safe system of management that would ensure the safety of those taking part in the activities that he was providing. His failure to adhere to relevant NGB guidelines, failure to provide sufficiently qualified expedition leaders and his failure to respond to the safety concerns brought to his attention by two former employees was evidence of his having fallen far below the expected standard of care owed to the children and was sufficient to amount to gross negligence.

The corporation, of which the defendant was the sole director and therefore the controlling mind and will, had breached its duty to take reasonable care of those who were taking part in its activities by failing to have in place an adequate system to ensure their safety. This was evidenced by his allowing inexperienced instructors to lead canoeing trips and allowing novices to take part in sea expeditions. The breach was gross because of the high risk of danger to all involved in the trip and previous warnings that he had received concerning lapses in safety procedures. The company was convicted of gross negligence manslaughter and its managing director, Kite, was imprisoned.

This case highlighted that it was much easier to bring cases against small companies because the controlling mind and will was clearly identifiable and was one of the reasons for the eventual enactment of both the Activity Centres (Young Persons' Safety) Act 1995 (see further, chapter 8.5.1) and the CMCHA 2007. The new Act should ensure that even a large corporation could now be found guilty as long as it can be proved that mismanagement by its senior managers contributed significantly to the deaths that its activities caused.

6.6 Sentencing

Athletes who are convicted of offences of violence that occur during the course of a game can usually expect to receive a significantly lower sentence than for corresponding offences committed in other circumstances. Despite stating that 'sport is not a licence for thuggery' the court in *R* v. *Lloyd* (1989) 11 Cr App Rep (S) 36 only imposed an 18-month prison sentence for a conviction under s.18 OAPA 1861 arising from an incident in a rugby game where the defendant had deliberately kicked his opponent, who was lying on the ground, so hard that it fractured his cheekbone. Moreover where sports assaults are concerned the courts seem more willing to accept a much wider range of arguments in mitigation of sentence than would usually be the case.

In *R* v. *Birkin* [1988] Crim LR 854, the court took into account that the degree of harm caused, a broken jaw, was neither expected nor intended when the defendant threw his punch. The mens rea of a defendant generally determines which of the offences under the OAPA 1861 the defendant should be charged with, rather than the length of sentence eventually imposed, especially as the punch thrown here was whilst the ball was out of play. In *R* v. *Lincoln* (1990) 12 Cr App Rep (S) 250, the defendant's argument that there had been a degree of provocation from the victim led to his sentence being reduced from four months to 28 days' imprisonment. The provocation in this case was the victim's standing just inside the touchline whilst the defendant took a throw in during a football match. Even though the victim's actions were completely within the rules of the game, this was considered to be sufficiently provocative to reduce the sentence significantly. Finally in *R* v. *Goodwin* (1995) 16 Cr App Rep (S) 885, a 14-month playing ban imposed by the Rugby Football League was used to justify a four month prison sentence despite the defendant elbowing his victim so hard that his cheekbone, jaw, palate and two molars were fractured by the assault.

These examples appear to demonstrate a prevailing attitude amongst the judiciary that sports violence is not real violence. Despite their comments that sports assaults are serious acts of violence and that they should be treated as such, the sentences imposed on sports participants rarely reflect the severity of the attack perpetrated on the victim. *Barnes* only appears to reinforce this belief by declaring specifically that the most appropriate venue for the punishment of those acting violently on the field is the governing body's own disciplinary tribunal, not the criminal justice system.

6.7 Sexual offences and child abuse

There is a growing body of research into the relationships that exist between coaches and sports participants, particularly where those participants are children. The main concern of this research is that sport can provide an opportunity for the exploitation of the relationship and that physical and sexual abuse of the young athlete can occur. This was particularly highlighted in the 1990s when there was a series of high-profile prosecutions for sexual offences committed by coaches on athletes in their care.

Where an athlete has been sexually or physically abused, criminal charges under the Sexual Offences Act 2003 (SOA 2003) and the OAPA 1861 (above, 6.3) will be laid against the abuser. The SOA 2003 applies to sexual offences committed in sport as it would in any other setting. For example in *R* v. *Hickson* [1997] Crim LR 494, a British Olympic swimming coach was convicted of two counts of rape, two counts of anal rape (both now under s.1 SOA 2003) and 11 counts of sexual assault (now s.3 SOA 2003) against female swimmers that he had coached over the course of his career. The fact that these incidents took place in the context of sport was only relevant in that it provided the defendant with the opportunity to commit the offences. The applicable law is not varied in any way where abuse of this nature is concerned because it is impossible to claim in any way that sexual abuse is an expected or accepted part of participation in, or training for sport.

The SOA 2003 was a comprehensive overhaul of the law relating to sexual offences. Of particular note in the context of sport is the range of offences that can be committed against children (ss.9-21 SOA 2003) including abuse of a position of trust by engaging in sexual activity with a child (s.16). For these purposes a child is under the age of 16 and the defendant must be over the age of 18. Inexplicably s.16 SOA 2003 only applies to adults working in the public sector such as teachers, and not those working in the private sector such as many sports coaches.

Further safeguards are provided by extra-legal bodies and the extensive documentation that they have developed. In particular the work of the Child Protection in Sport Unit (CPSU), a cooperative venture established in 2001 by the National Society for the Prevention of Cruelty to Children and the UK's four regional sports councils, has ensured that child protection has become an important focus of the work of many NGBs. The CPSU provides advice and guidance to governing bodies, coaches, athletes and parents on a wide range of child protection issues. It also produces the 'Standards for Safeguarding and Protecting Children in Sport' which provides guidelines to and sets benchmark standards of good practice for governing bodies including a child protection policy template. The aim of these benchmarks is to ensure that certain minimum standards have been reached in respect of their child protection procedures and that these are being implemented by NGBs.

6.8 Violence towards spectators

Although extremely unusual, a few participants have been convicted of assaulting the spectators at events at which they were performing and others have been accused of engaging in behaviour with the potential to incite the crowd to violence. As these actions are unconnected with the actual playing of sport, no special consideration is made for the players who react in this way.

6.8.1 Assaulting a spectator

The most infamous incident of a player assaulting a spectator is *R v. Cantona* (1995) The Times, 25 March. Having been sent off for a foul challenge on an opponent, the defendant was verbally abused by an individual in the crowd who had run down to the front of the stand specifically to throw his insults. The defendant reacted by performing a flying kick which caught the spectator in the chest and caused him minor bruising. The defendant was convicted of common assault and sentenced to 120 hours of community service. As can be seen from this example, the courts will treat attacks on spectators as 'ordinary' acts of violence and deal with them as either common assault (above, 6.2) or an offence under the OAPA 1861 (above, 6.3).

6.8.2   Inciting crowd violence

The on-field conduct of sports participants is capable of being particularly provocative to those who are watching the game. Where the behaviour of the players causes a threat to another person or their property, in this case by causing crowd disorder, then the court will consider a breach of the peace to have occurred and use their powers under s.115 Magistrates' Court Act 1980 or the Justices of the Peace Act 1361. In *Butcher* v. *Jessop* (1989) SLT 593, the former Glasgow Rangers and England football captain was bound over to keep the peace following an on-field altercation between him and the Glasgow Celtic centre forward Frank McAvennie, which resulted in Butcher pushing McAvennie over. The court bound over Butcher to keep the peace and fined him £250. The basis of the breach of the peace was that in the highly charged environment of a Glasgow derby game, pushing a Celtic player directly in front of the Celtic fans had the potential to cause serious crowd disorder, in this specific case a pitch invasion. Although rarely used, breach of the peace is evidence of the range of legal tools available to the police and courts to ensure that players' behaviour does not, whether directly or indirectly, result in serious public disorder.

6.8.3   Causing harassment, alarm and distress to those present at the event

Section 5 of the Public Order Act 1986 contains the offence of using threatening, abusive or insulting words or behaviour within the hearing or sight of a person likely to be caused harassment, alarm or distress by the defendant's conduct. Section 4A creates an aggravated version of the offence where the defendant intends to, and does actually cause harassment, alarm or distress to another person. As with breach of the peace, these offences would appear to be most appropriate to punish a participant's behaviour where it has caused, or was likely to cause, some kind of reaction in the crowd (see further, chapter 10.5.1.1).

In *R* v. *Bowyer* (unreported) Magistrates' Court (Newcastle), 5 July 2005, the defendant pleaded guilty to a charge under s.5 Public Order Act 1986 following an on-field scuffle with a member of his own team, Kieron Dyer. As Bowyer pleaded guilty, there was no explanation why this charge was proffered, as opposed to a charge of common assault, and no explanation of who was likely to have been harassed, alarmed or distressed by his conduct. Dyer was not keen to pursue charges against Bowyer, so perhaps those who were harassed, alarmed or distressed by the altercation were spectators or police officers on duty at the ground.

Hot topic . . .

DOES THE LAW OF THE LAND STOP AT THE TOUCHLINE?

There has been a longstanding debate, encompassing lawyers, academics, governing bodies, referees, players and the media, about the appropriateness of resorting to the criminal law to punish during-the-game conduct. On one side are those who consider sports assaults to be the same as any other form of violent conduct and therefore that resort to the criminal law is both necessary and appropriate. On the other are those who consider that all in-game issues should be the subject of internal, self-regulatory disciplinary procedures operated by the relevant governing body. Following the sentiments of Lord Denning MR, they believe that, 'Justice can often be done in domestic tribunals better by a good layman than by a bad lawyer' (*Enderby Town Football Club Ltd v. Football Association Ltd* [1971] 1 All ER 215).

The former school of thought is best represented by Edward Grayson, whose views on this subject were greatly influenced by the values of fair play and sportsmanship epitomised by Corinthian-Casuals FC. He considered that all deliberate or reckless foul play was outside of the normal and acceptable playing of sport and therefore could not be consented to by the participants. To him, the notion of the professional foul was anathema: it could only ever be a criminal assault. His views can be best summed up by his proposed Draft Safety of Sportspersons Act:

'1. Any person deliberately or recklessly causing any harm or injury in any manner whatsoever to any person concerned with, before, during or after any sporting or other recreational activity shall be guilty of an offence.
2. The said offence shall be committed by any participant during the course of any authorised sporting or recreational activity when it occurs in breach of the rules of laws of such sporting or other recreational activity.'

The counter-argument is that what occurs during the course of the game should be dealt with by the internal mechanisms of the governing body of the sport alone. Only clear acts of violence that take place off-the-ball or in retaliation should be subject to prosecution and even then only where the response of the governing body has been inadequate.

The reality is of course somewhere between these two points of view. However exactly where the line is to be drawn between acceptable sporting conduct and criminal violence is blurred and constantly varying. Ideally, or perhaps idealistically, all sport should be played without any intentional or dangerous fouls being committed. Pragmatically, deliberate, reckless and dangerous foul play occurs at all levels of many sports. An understanding of the reactions of the governing bodies of sport and the criminal justice system is key to establishing whether or not the law of the land does indeed stop at the touchline. Where a short playing ban is imposed, the injured player may consider that an inadequate punishment has been handed down to the person who caused their injuries; this may in turn explain their resort to the criminal law. However *Barnes* appears to discourage prosecution of sports assaults in all but the most extreme of cases; a fatal blow perhaps to Grayson's ideals.

Two incidents illustrate the problem of deciding whether or not resort to the criminal justice system is appropriate: *R v. Bowyer* and *FA v. Thatcher* Independent Disciplinary Commission, 12 September 2006. Following a scuffle with Kieron Dyer, a member of his own team, Bowyer was charged with and eventually pleaded guilty to causing harassment, alarm and distress to another person under s.5 Public Order Act 1986. No physical injury was caused to Dyer nor was there any significant reaction from the crowd, short of disbelief at what they were witnessing. Bowyer was fined £600 and ordered to pay £1000 in costs. The total costs of his court appearances, especially as he attempted to judicially review the decision to prosecute him, amounted to many tens of thousands of pounds. Prior to his trial he had been fined approximately £200,000 by his club (six weeks' earnings) and had been banned for seven games and fined £30,000 by the FA following his admission of violent conduct.

In contrast Thatcher was neither charged nor prosecuted for a deliberate forearm smash to the head of an opponent where there was no attempt to play the ball. The blow left Pedro Mendes unconscious, though he suffered no lasting injuries, and easily satisfied the requirements of s.47 OAPA 1861. Thatcher was fined around £80,000 by his club (four weeks' earnings) and was banned for eight games by the FA, with a further 15-game ban suspended for two years after he admitted serious foul play. The decision not to prosecute Thatcher was taken shortly after the ban was handed down by the Independent Disciplinary Commission.

It is unclear from any of the reports why the reaction of the police and Crown Prosecution Service was so different in these two cases. At great cost to the public purse, Bowyer was prosecuted for a very minor public order offence and punished by a fine that represented a fraction of that imposed by his club and the FA. Thatcher, who committed an unprovoked violent assault, escaped prosecution because it was felt that the football authorities had dealt with the matter adequately. Perhaps this is the true impact of *Barnes*; that if there is any connection between the assault and the game, then it will not be appropriate for the criminal law to intervene.

It remains a truism that the law of the land does not stop at the touchline and that, outside of the combat sports, the rules of a sport cannot turn unlawful violence into lawful sporting conduct. However it would appear that the law is more reluctant to cross the touchline than in the past and will stop to consider the reaction of the governing body before deciding on whether prosecution is also an appropriate response.

Summary

6.1 Despite the longevity of the jurisprudence in this area, an uneasy relationship continues to exist between the criminal law and sports participation. The courts' aim is to punish all acts of violence, including that which occurs in sports. However the judiciary also appears to consider that NGBs should be playing a more proactive role in keeping their own houses in order. These mixed messages have led to much confusion about whether or not the criminal law ever has a role to play in the punishment and control of sports violence.

6.2 Common assault is the foundation stone of all offences against the person. Although it is rarely used to prosecute sports participants, as most common assaults that occur in sport will be consented to, it can be resorted to where the court is uncomfortable with convicting a sports participant of a more serious crime, as in *R* v. *Brownbill*.

6.3 Sections 47 and 20 OAPA are the most common charges brought against athletes accused of acting violently. Players are much less frequently charged with intentionally causing GBH under s.18 OAPA because of the much more stringent mens rea requirements. As a general rule, after *R* v. *Barnes* it is likely that the offences found in the OAPA will only be used to prosecute acts of violence that are completely unconnected with the playing of the game in question.

6.4 The vast majority of contacts that take place in the name of sport are not criminal offences because they are consented to. Simply by taking part in a contact sport, a person is deemed to have consented to all contacts that are necessary and inherent in the normal playing of that game. Without consent acting as a defence to these commonplace physical interactions, contact sports would be unplayable and the courts would be overburdened with sports assault cases. *R* v. *Barnes* has provided the law with a workable approach to determining when the victim's consent can be said to be operative, though this test is perhaps undermined by the Court of Appeal's policy statement that the criminal courts should only rarely be resorted to in cases of sports violence.

6.5 Homicide charges arising out of sport will be extremely rare. They will usually only be appropriate following a deliberate or reckless criminal assault that has resulted in the death of the victim, as in *R* v. *Moore*, or where corporate or gross negligence manslaughter can be established against the organiser of a sports event, as in *R* v. *Kite*.

6.6 The policy of non-prosecution in *R* v. *Barnes* has long been reflected by the courts' approach to sentencing. Many sports participants convicted of a sports-related assault will receive non-custodial sentences and those that are imprisoned generally receive sentences of around one third of that which could be expected outside of the sports setting. It is unclear whether, after *Barnes*, the courts' approach to sentencing will change where only the cases that the CPS considers to be really serious instances of violent conduct are prosecuted.

6.7 Sexual assaults have very little to do with the actual playing of sport. What sport does provide is the setting in which sexual abuse and the abuse of relationships of trust can take place. The leadership and advice provided by the Child Protection in Sport Unit and the policies that it is helping to develop with many NGBs will hopefully raise awareness of the threats posed to athletes, particularly those who are young and vulnerable.

6.8 Prosecutions for public order offences are likely to be extremely rare. It will only be where the behaviour of the player is likely or intended to incite disorder in the crowd that such offences will be committed. In most other cases a prosecution for common assault would be more appropriate.

Further reading

Grayson, *Sport and the Law* (3rd edn, 2000, Butterworths) appendix 6

Herring, *Criminal Law: text, cases and materials* (3rd edn, 2008, Oxford University Press) ch 6

Law Commission, *Consent and Offences against the Person*, LCCP No 134 (1994, HMSO)

Law Commission, *Consent in the Criminal Law*, LCCP No 139 (1995, HMSO)

Lewis and Taylor (eds), *Sport: Law and Practice* (2nd edn, 2008, Tottel) ch D6

Anderson, 'Policing the sports field' [2005] 2 ISLR 25

Anderson, 'No Licence for Thuggery: Violence, Sport and the Criminal Law' [2008] Crim LR 751

Gardiner, 'The law and hate speech: "Ooh aah Cantona" and the demonstration of the other' in Brown (ed), *Fanatics! Power, Identity and Fandom in Football* (1998, Routledge)

Gardiner, 'Not playing the game: is it a crime?' [1993] *Solicitors Journal* 628

Grayson and Bond, 'Making foul play a crime' [1993] *Solicitors Journal* 693

James and Gardiner, 'Touchlines and guidelines: the Lord Advocate's response to sportsfield violence' [1997] *Criminal Law Review* 41

Williams, 'Consent and public policy' [1962] *Criminal Law Review* 74

Links to relevant websites can be found at www.palgrave.com/law/james

Chapter 7

The legality of fighting sports

7.1 Context

Fighting sports are amongst the oldest, most established and most popular sporting disciplines in the world. Of the 28 sports currently included in the Olympic Summer Programme, five are modern forms of traditional fighting sports: boxing, fencing, judo, taekwondo and wrestling. Most of these sports and many others of a similar type can trace their origins to military training regimes. However as warfare became increasingly mechanised and the need for these skills became less important for battle, a number of these activities evolved into the recognisable fighting sports of today.

This category of sport has always received a significant degree of protection from the normal operation of the law. Without this protection all fighting, whether or not in the name of sport, would constitute a criminal assault and possibly homicide (see further, chapter 6.2–6.5) Thus the law of consent has developed to exempt fighting sports from its ambit. The classic explanation of the law is in Foster's *Crown Law*, where it is stated in relation to wrestling and cudgelling:

> 'Here is the appearance of combat, but it is in reality no more than a friendly exertion of strength and dexterity. They are manly diversions, they tend to give strength, skill and activity, and make fit people for defence … I would not be understood to speak of prize-fighting and public boxing-matches, or any other exertions … of the like kind … which are exhibited for lucre, and can serve no valuable purpose; but on the contrary encourage a spirit of idleness and debauchery.'

Not only does Foster explain why these sports should be protected, he also identifies the key issue that has troubled the courts ever since: whether, apart from creating 'fit people for defence', there are any legal, moral or public policy reasons why fighting sports should be exempted from the normal operation of the criminal law. He clearly feels that anyone fighting for money should not benefit from the exemption granted to those who are simply testing their skill, strength and dexterity. This distinction and its specific manifestation in respect of prize-fighting and sparring came before the courts on a number of occasions throughout the eighteenth and nineteenth centuries and continues to influence legal discussions on consent to the present day.

As sport became more organised and less tolerance was shown towards bloodshed for the sake of entertainment, the legality of fighting sports began to be questioned more frequently. Although there is no doubt that some of these sports are completely lawful, the legal status of others occupies a somewhat greyer area, where public policy, morality and legal theory collide with equal force.

7.2 The legal status of traditional fighting sports

Without some measure of exemption from the operation of the law of offences against the person and homicide, participation in any fighting sport would be at least a series of criminal assaults. From before Foster's time it had been acknowledged that in limited circumstances it was possible to provide a valid consent to blows that were struck in the name of sport or for the purposes of military training but that all prize-fights were illegal. The only real question was where precisely to draw the line between what Foster refers to as 'manly diversions' and criminal assaults.

7.2.1 Distinguishing between sparring and prize-fighting

Throughout the 1800s, a number of cases focused their discussions on where to draw this line by creating a distinction between sparring, which was lawful, and prize-fighting, which was not. Sparring is described variously as being an exercise of pugilistic skill, a demonstration of the ability to attack and defend oneself, that promotes strength and agility and where violence was not the aim of the participants who would fight wearing padded gloves for a pre-determined number of rounds. Prize-fighting on the other hand involved bouts that were accompanied by violence and personal danger to the participants and the threat of a breach of the peace amongst the spectators. The threat of violence posed to the fighters was created by the bouts often being bare knuckle and their continuing until one or other of the participants was physically incapable of fighting any longer. The threat of a breach of the peace came from disorder in the crowds that was usually associated with the gambling that accompanied prize-fights.

Not only was prize-fighting itself illegal, so was the training of fighters to compete in prize-fights (*Hunt v. Bell* (1822) 1 Bingham 1) and the organisation of prize-fighting contests (*R v. Coney* (1881–82) 8 QBD 534) (below, 7.2.1.1). There are therefore two strands to the distinction between lawful and unlawful fighting sports: the dangerousness of prize-fighting to the protagonists themselves when compared to the comparative safety of sparring and the potential of prize-fights to cause a breach of the peace. Whether or not the fight was for money appears not to have been considered as important a concern as the risk of injury and disorder.

7.2.1.1 Causing danger to the participants

The potential dangers to which the participants in a prize-fight are exposed range from minor cuts and bruises to death. The seriousness of the harm that could be caused to a prize-fighter was exacerbated by bouts being fought bare knuckle and over an unlimited number of rounds. Conversely, sparring was not considered to be dangerous.

▶ *R v. Young and others* (1866) 10 Cox CC 371

The defendants were charged with manslaughter following the death of Young's opponent in an organised fight. The remaining defendants were the organisers of and seconds at the contest. In the final round the deceased lost his balance and fell, hitting his head against a post that ran up through the centre of the ring. The court considered that it was important to take into account that the fight took place in a private room containing a boxing ring, that the fighters were both wearing padded gloves and that the only other people present were friends of the fighters and their seconds. In directing the jury, the judge noted that where a contest began as lawful exhibition of sparring, it was possible for it to become a criminal assault where the participants continued to fight until they were in such a state of exhaustion that it was *probable* that one would fall and might as a result be injured and die.

All of the defendants were acquitted on the basis that this was an accident caused during the course of a lawful sparring contest. The jury reached this conclusion by relying primarily on the expert evidence of the house-surgeon from Charing Cross Hospital, who stated that sparring with gloves in this manner would be very unlikely to cause injuries that would lead to death. Furthermore the presence of the seconds to look after the participants reduced the inherent dangers of the fight to both of them.

The key distinction identified in *Young* that led to sparring being held to be a lawful activity is that there was some form of regulation in place. Where the activity is inherently dangerous, it is important that there are safety systems and rules in place to make it as safe as is reasonably possible. Unlawful prize-fighting however has few of these safeguards in place, creating a high risk of serious injury being caused to the participants. This reasoning was developed further to require the court to examine the true aim of the fight not just its form.

▶ *R v. Orton* (1878) 14 Cox CC 226

The defendants had paid to enter premises to watch a fight. The fighters each wore padded gloves, fought in a ring and were attended to by seconds. The Court held that where a fight is organised to be an exhibition of skill in sparring, then the contest was lawful. However if the parties intended that the fight would continue until one or other of the participants could not continue either because of the severity of the injuries that they had received or through exhaustion, then the contest was an unlawful prize-fight. The court held that it was not the existence of safety measures, such as the wearing of protective equipment and the attendance of seconds that determined the lawfulness of the event; the focus should instead be on the intentions of the participants and of those who had organised the contest.

Where the aim was to fight until one of the participants was so exhausted or so injured that they could not continue, then the fight was a series of unlawful assaults. Furthermore if the fight was for money it was an unlawful prize-fight. If it was a test of attacking and defensive skill, and after 1865 preferably in accordance with the Marquis of Queensbury's Rules, then it would be a lawful bout of sparring regardless of whether the spectators had paid an entrance fee to watch the event.

7.2.1.2 The tendency of prize-fighting to cause a breach of the peace

In neither *Young* nor *Orton* was it necessary to discuss in any detail whether there had been a breach of the peace as the activities taking place were held to be lawful sporting contests. It would appear from the charges laid against the defendants that where the spectators are at a private venue and have not paid to view the bout there is no breach of the peace as there is no threat to public order (*Young*). However where the spectators have paid to gain entry to the event, then a breach of the peace is at least a possibility because of the public nature of the event (*Orton*) (see also *Butcher* v. *Jessop*, chapter 6.8.2).

> ► *R v. Coney and others* (1881–82) 8 QBD 534

The defendants were prosecuted for being involved in various roles connected with a prize-fight, including in particular the competitors, the organisers and some of the spectators. The fight itself had taken place on private ground in a ring where the participants were separated from the spectators by a rope. Although a crowd of over a hundred people were present and betting was taking place, there was no evidence of crowd disorder. The defendants were found guilty of aiding and abetting an assault and appealed against their convictions.

The Court for Crown Cases Reserved, where an almost unprecedented 11 judgments were handed down, held that participation in a prize-fight is illegal because of the inherent risk of serious injury being caused to the participants and the additional risk of a breach of the peace occurring amongst the onlookers; the consent of the participants is irrelevant and cannot make lawful that which is unlawful. Further the Court held that all those who were aiding and abetting the prize-fight, in particular those who had organised it and those who were acting as seconds for the fighters, were also guilty of an offence. In line with the previous authorities on these issues these convictions were upheld.

The defendants who had been spectators in the crowd that had been watching the prize-fight had originally been convicted on the basis that their voluntary presence at an illegal activity was sufficient evidence that they were guilty of having encouraged it, and therefore aided and abetted it, to take place. In setting aside the convictions a majority of the Court (8–3) held that mere presence at an illegal activity was not sufficient of itself to constitute aiding and abetting the crime to have taken place. Their presence at the contest could only constitute evidence that the defendants *may* have been aiding and abetting the unlawful prize-fight by watching it; to secure a conviction against them it was still necessary to prove that the defendants had actively encouraged or assisted the unlawful fight to have taken place.

The court was unanimous in holding that prize-fights were illegal, that the participants in prize-fights commit a criminal assault with every punch thrown and that anyone who actively encourages the fighters, or who assisted with the organisation of the fight, is guilty of aiding and abetting the assaults committed by the fighters. In coming to these conclusions a variety of explanations were given for why prize-fighting itself was a criminal activity.

Firstly it was considered that where the blows were intended or likely to cause physical injury then a criminal assault had been committed. As prize-fights were usually contests that were fought until one of the participants was physically incapable of continuing, injury was at least highly likely if not actually intended. This was contrasted with blows struck in the course of sporting or sparring contests where it was assumed that there was no intent to cause harm only to exhibit one's skill, and little or no likelihood of causing harm to an opponent because of the safety rules and precautions that were in place.

Secondly that assaults of this nature were breaches of the peace, particularly where a crowd of spectators was watching the event. Prize-fights were referred to as being disorderly exhibitions that were mischievous on many obvious grounds. Nobody is allowed to consent to injuries being inflicted on them where they are likely to be productive of a breach of the peace as it is not in the public interest to cause violent disturbances in the name of sport or entertainment. Therefore prize-fights are criminal assaults that are incapable of being rendered lawful by the consent of the participants because they have the potential to incite violence in others.

Thirdly the harm inflicted on the participants had the potential to be of such a high degree that it was not in the public interest to allow prize-fights for the protection of those taking part in them. As Matthew J pointed out at p.547, 'The fists of trained pugilists are dangerous weapons which they are not at liberty to use against each other.' By highlighting the similarities between the fists of trained fighters and weapons, the court was drawing a distinction similar to that which could be drawn between fencing and duelling. Both activities involve the use of swords, but the aim of the former is a test of skill based on a scoring system whereas the aim of the other is to inflict injury and/or death. Likewise where fists are used in a controlled environment with a scoring system and safety procedures in place, then the event is a bout of lawful sparring. But where the aim is to inflict injury and where there is an attendant risk of death then the punches thrown are unlawful assaults.

7.2.1.3 An alternative approach – the reasonableness of the rules of the game

The approach of the English courts is in contrast to that used by the courts in the USA through a decision of the New York State Supreme Court.

▶ *People v. Fitzsimmons* **(1895) 34 NYS 1102**

The defendant had killed his opponent by punching him during an exhibition of boxing. In directing the jury, the judge stated that where the rules and practices of the game are reasonable, are consented to by all engaged in the activity and are not likely to cause serious injury or death, then no offence is committed if the injury-causing blow is landed within those rules and practices. The focus of the American courts is on whether the rules and practices of the sport in question are reasonable; if they are then all injury-causing contacts that occur during the playing of the game are lawful. However where the rules and practices are not reasonable then all contacts made are criminal.

In *Fitzsimmons* the rules of boxing under which the event took place were considered to be reasonable and that therefore no criminal assault that could form the basis of the manslaughter charge had been committed. Had the event been a prize-fight as defined by the English courts, then the court may have held that the rules of the game were unreasonable and that manslaughter had been committed by the defendant. This is a much simpler approach to the determination of the legality of an activity and would have allowed English law to have developed incrementally in a more structured manner than it has when confronted by some of the less traditionally British fighting sports that are currently popular.

7.3   The legal status of modern fighting sports

By the 1880s a clear distinction had been drawn between lawful sparring and unlawful prize-fighting. The challenge for the law would be to see how it would respond to the emergence of professional fighting sports, particularly with the increasing popularity of professional boxing, and later the evolution of hybrid and mixed-discipline sports; post-*Coney* the only fighting sports specifically referred to as being lawful activities were sparring, wrestling and fighting with single-sticks or cudgels. Two arguments are at the centre of this debate. Firstly some commentators have argued that as modern fighting sports in general and boxing in particular have never been declared lawful as part of the *ratio decidendi* of a case, then these too are unlawful activities.

In response to this claim, the lack of case law on the legality of fighting sports would appear to suggest that most of the more common disciplines are lawful activities, as under English law an activity is lawful until it is declared by either Parliament or the courts to be unlawful. In the light of the many comments made by the appellate courts on the legality of boxing over the years, the exemption for fighting sports must extend beyond the three activities named in *Coney*, though how far is not entirely clear. This lack of judicial and Parliamentary analysis also means that there is no framework provided for determining whether a new sport should or should not be lawful.

A second claim draws on Foster's statement of the law and argues that where professional boxing is concerned, as the participants are fighting for money the bouts are in legal terms prize-fights and therefore unlawful. This argument also struggles to withstand closer scrutiny as it focuses unduly on the financial element of the bout at the expense of analysing the intentions of the fighters. It is in the context of arguments such as these that the legality of fighting sports must be examined.

7.3.1   The anomalous position of fighting sports

The almost unquestioning acceptance of the legally anomalous position of fighting sports is epitomised up by the comments of Lord Lane CJ in *Attorney-General's Reference (No6 of 1980)* [1981] QB 715 in the context of a fight between two young men trying to settle an argument, where he stated at p.719:

> 'It is not in the public interest that people should try to cause … each other actual bodily harm for no good reason … [It] is immaterial whether the act occurs in private or in public; it is an assault if actual bodily harm is intended and/or caused. This means that most fights will be unlawful regardless of consent. Nothing which we have said is intended to cast doubt upon the accepted legality of properly conducted games and sports … [This apparent exception] can be justified as … needed in the public interest.'

Thus 'properly conducted sport' is exempted from the normal operation of the law of assault because it is accepted as being in the public interest to afford such activities some protection from the law. No further explanation is provided beyond this but also no limits are put on the sports to which the exemption extends. Presumably if similar reasoning to that used in *Fitzsimmons* is applied then other established and properly conducted sports, such as the Olympic sports of judo and taekwondo, are also protected by the exemption. Although participants in sports such as these, and many others besides, are undoubtedly covered by this exemption, there is nothing in the case law that definitively justifies such a conclusion.

This was reiterated in *R v. Brown* [1994] 1 AC 212, the leading case on the general application of consent in the criminal law, where Lord Mustill regarded an intellectually satisfying account of the immunity of boxing as being impossible to achieve. Instead his Lordship stated simply that boxing is a special situation which stands outside the ordinary law of violence because society chooses at present to tolerate it.

The Law Commission's analysis in its two consultation papers on consent also failed to provide a convincing analysis of the legality of fighting sports. In *Consent and Offences against the Person*, the Law Commission stated that the immunity of boxing from the reach of the criminal law was so firmly embedded that only Parliamentary intervention could change its legal status. In respect of other fighting sports the Commission again thought that legislation was the most appropriate means of clarifying their legal position.

In its follow up paper, *Consent in the Criminal Law*, the Law Commission recommended that a scheme should be established under the auspices of what is now UK Sport that would 'recognise' lawful sports. If injury was inflicted during a recognised sport the conduct would be lawful, but if the same harm were caused during an unrecognised sport then a criminal assault would be committed. As the consultation papers have not been acted on and the proposed scheme never developed into a workable set of criteria, they provide little further guidance on whether or not participation in a fighting sport is actually lawful. The intellectually satisfying justification for the immunity of fighting sports from the criminal law remains elusive.

Without a binding precedent to justify the legality of fighting sports and in the absence of a convincing theoretical justification for the exemption extending beyond the activities referred to in *Coney*, the suggestion remains that sports whose object is to inflict harm rather than score points in a test of skill should be illegal. In particular the legality of modern professional boxing has been questioned by a number of academic commentators on the basis that it bears a greater resemblance to unlawful prize-fighting than to the lawful sparring referred to in *Coney*. It has been argued that a combination of over-hyped grudge matches, the emphasis on the knockout punch, the lack of protection for the main target area (the head) and that because injury is an integral and necessary part of participation, these points all demonstrate that professional boxing is about fighting until one party can no longer physically continue rather than being a test of skill based on point-scoring. In other words, professional boxing is the modern equivalent of prize-fighting and should be illegal. In contrast amateur boxing, with its low number of short rounds, the requirement to wear head guards and its emphasis on point-scoring, is the true inheritor of the exemption afforded to sparring.

This argument is of course refuted by those who see boxing as the noble art of self-defence and professional boxers as its elite exponents. Those in favour of boxing remaining a lawful activity point out that even in the professional arena most bouts are decided on points not by a knockout. Moreover the training undergone by all boxers but particularly by professionals means that they are able to dodge or cushion the impact of the blows struck, have to wear padded gloves and can be forced to retire by either the referee or their seconds if it appears that they are physically unable to continue to defend themselves. In other words although a knockout is the most decisive way to secure victory, professional boxing is still a test of skill, strength, stamina and ability, as was sparring and as is amateur boxing.

Despite the lack of specific appellate authority, the legality of boxing was confirmed where contests were conducted in accordance with a set of rules that had been designed to measure the comparative skill of the fighters.

▶ *R v. Roberts* **(unreported) Central Criminal Court (London), 28 June 1901**

The defendants were charged with manslaughter following the death of Roberts' opponent in a fight organised in accordance with the rules of the National Sporting Club, which in turn were based on the Marquis of Queensberry's Rules. The remaining defendants included the seconds at the fight, the referee, the timekeeper and the manager of the National Sporting Club on whose premises the contest took place. The prosecution argued that the rule that awarded the contest to a participant whose opponent could not resume fighting after having been knocked down for a count of ten seconds encouraged boxers to attempt to knock each other out. If this was the case, the fight was unlawful as its outcome was to be decided on the basis of the ability of one of the participants to continue fighting as opposed to their skill and ability at boxing. The defence argued that the ten second rule was there to protect the safety of participants by preventing them from fighting when they were concussed and therefore unable to protect themselves properly. In directing the jury, the judge stated that if they believed that the contest was carried on with the intention that one of the parties should fight until the other gave in because of injury or exhaustion then they had been acting criminally. However if this was a case of fighting in accordance with rules that were designed to measure the comparative skill of the participants, not simply to enable them to fight until one or other of them was physically unable to continue, then this was a lawful sporting contest.

The jury found the defendant boxer not guilty of manslaughter on the basis that the participants had not intended to fight until one or other of them was physically incapable of continuing. Instead the fight had been to determine who was the more skilful according to the number of points awarded by the referee. Further, the injury appeared to have been caused by the deceased's head hitting the ropes around the edge of the ring, not from a blow landed by the defendant and was an accident that had occurred in the course of a lawful sporting contest. As the primary liability of the defendant boxer could not be established, the cases of secondary party liability against the remaining defendants also failed as there was no crime committed for them to have aided and abetted.

Thus where the aim of the fight is to determine who is the more skilful exponent of the noble art rather than to batter the opponent into submission or unconsciousness, then the fight is a lawful sporting contest. Although it could be argued that some professional boxing matches place too great an emphasis on the knockout blow, the further judicial acceptance of its legality in cases up to and including *Brown* indicate clearly that both professional and amateur boxing, and by analogy other 'properly conducted sports,' are exempted from the operation of the criminal law. Furthermore these sports will continue to benefit from this protection unless and until they are declared by Parliament to be otherwise.

7.3.2   Properly conducted sports

In the absence of a definitive list of lawful sports, some link needs to be found between the various decisions that will indicate how and why a fighting sport will be considered to be a lawful activity. For this to occur, it would appear that the most important criterion is that the sport be 'well-organised' or 'properly conducted.' Although there is no explanation of what is meant by these terms, certain basic requirements can be identified as being necessary in the sport's administration. For example they will need to be contested according to a predetermined set of rules, where each contest is overseen by appropriately qualified referees or judges, and possibly organised under the auspices of an appropriate NGB and/or ISF.

The necessary level of organisation will go beyond the drafting of the playing rules and administering fixtures to include the drafting of safety rules and protocols, including the provision of medical staff and facilities where appropriate. Where these are not provided, the governing body of the sport or the organiser of the event may find themselves not only guilty of organising an illegal event where they have aided and abetted the commission of criminal assaults and breaches of the peace, but that they are also liable in negligence to an injured participant (*Watson* v. *British Boxing Board of Control* [2001] QB 1134, Court of Appeal, chapter 3.4.1.1.2). If these safeguards are in place and there is some inherent worth in the sport that justifies its protection as being in the public interest, usually that it is a test of strength, skill and dexterity not just the infliction of violence and pain for the purposes of entertainment, then it is likely that the sport will be found to be a lawful activity. In the cases of boxing and other high-profile, universally recognised sports there is little doubt that their levels of organisation and conduct are sufficient to ensure that they will continue to be lawful activities for as long as society sees fit to tolerate them.

The position of less well-organised, perhaps poorer or newly emergent disciplines is less clear. Their lack of an agreed set of playing rules or their inability to secure an appropriate level of medical support could mean that participation in such sports is significantly more dangerous than it is in the richer, higher-profile and more established sports. For example despite its popularity as a participation sport, none of the major forms of kick boxing have ever been recognised by UK Sport for funding purposes. One of the main reasons for this is that there is no universally recognised governing body within the UK that oversees the sport. This means that the sport cannot be recognised as an activity by UK Sport as there is insufficient agreement on what the sport actually entails, no unified set of rules and no single entity in charge of regulating the activity. This lack of agreement makes it difficult to argue that the sport is properly conducted, not whether it has the ability to cause shock or disgust.

Mixed Martial Arts competitions have attracted a significant amount of controversy in recent years because of their apparent lack of rules. These events pit exponents of different fighting disciplines against one another and therefore require a limited set of rules to ensure that fighters from different traditions can compete against one another (see below, Hot Topic). It is possible that competitions of this kind are lawful as they are based on what are generally recognised as lawful sports rather than being completely unregulated brawls. Provided that each contest has a pre-defined set of playing rules and appropriate safety protocols and medical support in place it is difficult to see how it could be declared unlawful just because it is new to the UK and distasteful to some. The key to an activity's legality rests on whether or not it can demonstrate that it is properly conducted.

The requirement that a fighting sport must be properly organised ensures that there is in place at least a basic set of criteria against which its legality can be judged. The courts are then able to apply what they consider to be appropriate public interest arguments to prevent the emergence of any unnecessarily violent activities that they feel are masquerading as lawful sports. The Law Commission suggested that a validating body, perhaps UK Sport, would be able to accredit sports as lawful to avoid further litigation on this subject. In other countries, for example Australia, this function is performed by the state. However since the Law Commission's proposals were put forward there have been no further developments on such a scheme. Regardless of the actual legal status of emergent and/or less organised fighting sports, the reality is that they are protected by the participants on a day-to-day basis. The factual consent of these participants and their desire to ensure the continuation of their chosen discipline ensures that it is extremely unlikely that legal action will be taken by any of them against anyone else connected with their sport except in the most extreme of cases.

7.4   Justifying the legal status of fighting sports

When seeking to justify their views on the legal status of fighting sports, a wide range of public policy, legal and jurisprudential arguments are frequently referred to. What follows is not an attempt to provide a definitive proof that one side of the argument is more convincing than the other. Instead it provides a basis upon which a justification for either point of view can be built. The focus of this discussion is the legal status of boxing rather than all fighting sports. Its traditional and well-established place within British sporting culture and its centrality to legal and medical debates on whether fighting sports are acceptable activities mean that boxing can be used as a benchmark against which the legality of other sports can be judged.

The starting point of any analysis of this area has to be that regardless of one's personal views on the matter, boxing is lawful. The twin bases for this claim are the judicial comments on the accepted legality of boxing referred to above and the failed attempts by Parliament to outlaw professional boxing that have taken place on several occasions over the past 50 years. If the House of Lords or Supreme Court considers that an activity, if properly conducted, is legal then it can be assumed that it is. Furthermore if Parliament considers it necessary to debate the possibility of outlawing certain forms of boxing, then it can be assumed that the activity is lawful and will continue to be so until sufficient numbers of MPs vote to implement a ban.

7.4.1 The public policy arguments

A wide range of public policy arguments have been put forward to justify both sides of the argument about whether boxing should be a lawful activity. Although there is an element of validity contained in most of them, none deliver the decisive blow for either side.

7.4.1.1 Boxing should be lawful because it is a sport

Although the appellate courts have stated that 'properly conducted sports' are lawful activities, a simple statement that boxing is a sport is not sufficient for it to gain legal acceptance. As has already been discussed (above, 7.3.2), there appears to be a series of criteria that must be fulfilled before an activity can be considered to be a properly conducted sport; a simple declaration that it fulfils these is not sufficiently legally robust to justify that status. Although being a properly conducted sport enables boxing to clear the first hurdle to becoming a lawful sport, it still relies on the goodwill of Parliament and the courts for its continued protection.

7.4.1.2 Boxing should be lawful because it promotes fitness

It is undoubtedly true that the training regimes undergone by boxers create extremely fit and healthy athletes. However it is the training rather than participation in the sport that promotes health and fitness; actual participation in a boxing bout can be seriously detrimental to a boxer's health because of the blows received to the head and body. If fitness was the sole justification, then only training to box, rather than actually boxing, can be justified as being in a person's best interests.

7.4.1.3 Boxing should be lawful because it instils discipline

There are several facets to this argument. Firstly the physicality of the training regime ensures that a boxer must exhibit a high degree of self-discipline by turning up for sessions, not drinking or smoking and generally looking after their physical well-being, otherwise they will not be physically or mentally prepared to fight in the ring. Secondly it teaches boxers to be disciplined in the use of their fighting skills and encourages them not to use violence in any other setting except the boxing ring. Thirdly it is often argued that the discipline and self-respect instilled by the training regime and camaraderie of the boxing club has prevented some young boxers from pursuing a life of crime. As with the previous argument, these arguments struggle to justify why boxing, as opposed to the training regime to which boxers are subjected, should be lawful.

7.4.1.4 Boxing should be lawful because it offers financial security
This much used justification, that boxing enables people from poor backgrounds to work their way out of poverty, is one that has little evidence to back it up. Although many of the world's most successful boxers have come from poor backgrounds, and those that become successful are financially secure for life, the vast majority of boxers make comparatively little money from participation in the sport. An opportunity to earn substantial sums of money is undoubtedly available to all boxers, but the reality is that very few are ever able to take full advantage of it.

7.4.1.5 Boxing should be lawful because it is popular
It has often been stated in the courts that what is of interest to the public is not necessarily in the public interest. Thus, just because an activity is popular does not automatically mean that it will be, or even ought to be, lawful. Boxing is not only popular but is important in economic terms, providing employment to many boxers, coaches and an entire supporting industry. Although it would be difficult and controversial to outlaw the sport because of its entrenchment within the UK's sporting and social fabric, Parliament has not always shied away from banning popular activities that it no longer considers to be socially acceptable, as was the case with some shooting sports and fox hunting. Popularity alone is not enough to guarantee the continued legality of boxing.

7.4.1.6 Boxing should be lawful because it is traditional
As with the previous point, the longevity and traditions of a sport are not enough to guarantee its legality. Both shooting sports and fox hunting can trace their roots back many centuries, though both have been regulated and/or outlawed by statute on the basis that their traditional position in British sport could no longer be justified.

7.4.1.7 Boxing should not be lawful because it is too dangerous
Perhaps the strongest argument against the continuing legality of boxing is the growing weight of medical evidence that it can be a very dangerous activity in which to participate. This may sound obvious considering that this is a sport where points are scored for punching an opponent, but the difficulty that the medical profession has encountered has been in creating an evidence base for some of its claims. In particular, until comparatively recently it had been difficult to prove a specific link between boxing and chronic brain injury, which is the cumulative brain damage caused by repetitive blows to the head over a prolonged period of time. This kind of harm is distinguished from acute brain injury which is caused by individual traumatic blows to the head, such as the knockout punch.

However despite the specific risk of serious harm associated with boxing, serious injury and death are amongst the potential outcomes of participation in many sports. To single out boxing is to fail to take into account the dangers inherent in these other sports, the measures taken by boxing to make it as safe as is reasonably practicable and that the inherent dangers of boxing are known to all boxers in advance of entering the ring. The risk of serious injury alone is not sufficient justification for outlawing boxing.

7.4.1.8 Boxing should not be lawful because it encourages violence

In direct contrast to the claim that boxing enables people to control their violent tendencies and only to let off steam inside the ring is the argument that training people to box encourages them to use violence in other less well-regulated contexts. There is no definitive evidence that proves which of these claims is true and it is possible that to some extent, and for different people, both are. Without the necessary proof, this argument alone cannot justify outlawing boxing.

7.4.1.9 Boxing should not be lawful because it encourages gambling

There is little doubt that boxing is a sport that is heavily gambled upon and that this has always been the case. One of the main reasons for the outlawing of prize-fighting was because of the fear of outbreaks of public disorder that often occurred because of disagreements over the settling of gambling debts arising from the matches. However the growth in sports betting in recent years and the much greater degree of social acceptance of gambling means that this argument is now rather outdated. If gambling was to be a key determinant in the legality of sporting activities, then other sports would be at a greater risk of being banned than boxing.

7.4.1.10 Boxing should not be lawful because it creates public disorder

As with the previous argument, this claim is to a great extent outdated. One of the reasons for outlawing prize-fighting was because of the potential for crowd disorder. Although outbreaks of crowd violence do occasionally occur, they are by no means as frequent and are not of the same scale as those which used to occur at prize-fights. If this was a genuine reason for outlawing a spectator sport, then football would be at much greater risk of being banned than boxing.

7.4.1.11 Summary of the public policy arguments

Whether individually or collectively, each of these claims have been used to explain why boxing either is or is not in the public interest. Although they can help to justify claims for either position, none of them provides a conclusive or robust explanation for what the legal status of boxing ought to be. As Lord Mustill observed, the best explanation would appear to be that boxing is lawful for the present because society chooses to tolerate it.

7.4.2 The legal arguments and *R* v. *Brown*

In the wide-ranging discussions of the law of consent in *R* v. *Brown*, the five members of the House of Lords provided a number of explanations for why an activity might be considered to be unlawful. As with the public policy arguments above, none provide a definitive explanation of how to determine the lawfulness of an activity and the disparate views of their Lordships mean that none of these arguments can be said to form the ratio of the case. However an analysis of them provides an insight into how the courts might approach the question of the legality of boxing.

7.4.2.1 The extent of the injuries caused is unknown in advance

This claim goes to the heart of the question of consent. It is argued that if a person does not know the extent of the harm that will be caused to them prior to contact being made with them, then they cannot know to what it is that they are consenting. In boxing when a fighter is punched it is impossible for them to know in advance whether they will be bruised, cut, concussed, suffer a serious facial injury or perhaps even die. If they are unaware of the precise nature of the harm that will be caused to them then, so the argument goes, they cannot provide a valid consent to its occurring.

The law of consent is supposed to enable a person to permit another to make specific contacts with them without the interference of the criminal law. In most cases, for example where a person consents to undergo a surgical procedure, consent to the act being performed on them will necessarily mean that they have consented to a specific harm being caused to them. In contact sports in general and fighting sports in particular, the nature of the interpersonal contacts between the participants means that it is impossible to know the outcome of any specific contact in advance; at best, a range of potential outcomes can be speculated on.

Use of this argument to justify outlawing boxing is somewhat disingenuous. Under the criminal law it is the contact that one consents to, not its consequences. If the contact is lawful then all of the harm flowing from it will, of necessity, also have to be lawful. Thus as boxers consent to be being hit by punches that are thrown within the rules of the sport, the full range of potential outcomes, all of which are possibilities known to the participants in advance, are lawfully inflicted. If however a punch is thrown outside of the rules or after the bell has rung to indicate the end of a round, then the punch itself is not consented to and all injury that flows from it is unlawful.

7.4.2.2 There is insufficient regulation of the causing of serious injury

The British Medical Association (BMA) has been a long-time opponent of the legality of boxing, particularly the professional format. In particular it is concerned that sufficient steps to prevent serious injury, specifically serious cumulative brain injury, are not taken by the boxing authorities. The BMA claims that as the unprotected head is the primary target in boxing, serious brain injury is the inevitable outcome of participation in the sport and that it should therefore be banned. Alternatively if boxing is to be allowed to continue as a lawful activity, then the BMA suggests amongst other proposals removing the head from the target area.

The response of the boxing fraternity is that all reasonable steps have been taken to ensure that the sport is as safe as it can be without destroying its very essence. The requirement that boxers wear padded gloves, fight for a pre-determined number of rounds with breaks in between, have assistants present ringside who can provide advice and first aid and doctors who can provide more specialised medical assistance mean that the boxing match itself is as safe as it can be. The boxer's seconds and the referee can bring the fight to a premature end if they feel that the boxer is no longer able to defend themselves and pre-fight medical checks and regular brain scans all ensure that professional boxers are as well-protected as it is possible for them to be without significantly changing the rules and nature of the sport.

The two views expressed here go to the very heart of the argument about the legal status of boxing. There is no doubt that boxing has the potential to cause serious injury, brain damage and death. Post-*Watson* the BBBC has created a sport that is probably as safe as it can get. At present that appears to be sufficient to ensure the continued legality of the sport.

7.4.2.3 There is a potential for the cross-infection of blood-borne diseases

In *Brown* the House of Lords was concerned that where an activity could create an open wound and where close interpersonal contact also occurs, then there is an increased risk of the transmission of blood-borne disease from one participant to another. The combination of facial cuts and grappling that frequently occur in boxing could therefore be of concern to the courts. A combination of pre-fight medical checks to ensure that boxers are not carrying infectious diseases that can be transmitted in this manner and in-fight medical treatment to stop any bleeding that is occurring mean that the risk of cross-infection is very low. As with the previous argument the analysis of whether the risk of harm or infection is an acceptable one will determine the law's response to the legality of the activity. It would appear that at present the steps taken by the governing bodies of boxing ensure that the risk is low enough for the sport to maintain its lawful status.

7.4.2.4 The activity promotes a cult of violence in society

The House of Lords was also concerned that if violent activities were capable of being consented to, then this would create a society in which the use of violence was normalised and therefore resorted to more frequently. The lack of conclusive empirical evidence on this point makes it almost impossible to rely on this argument alone when determining whether or not boxing should be lawful (above, 7.4.1.8). The ethos inculcated into boxers is that fighting should only take place in the ring, not outside of it. Further, those watching a boxing match are rarely incited to commit acts of violence themselves. Alternatively those who consider all fighting to be unjustifiable and that fighting for sport and entertainment purposes encourages the use of violence in the wider society, feel that there is a strong justification for outlawing boxing. Until such a link can be either proved or disproved however, this remains an unconvincing point to justify either side of the argument.

7.4.2.5 Summary of the legal arguments

As the leading case on consent, *Brown* is of paramount importance to the discussion of the legality of boxing and other fighting sports. The difficulty that it presents however is its factual context: *Brown* concerned the legality of sado-masochistic homosexual activity not fighting sports. The judgments of the majority in the House of Lords demonstrate clearly their moral disapproval of conduct of this kind and their determination to find reasons for outlawing it. Boxing was mentioned only when their Lordships noted the existence of certain exempted activities; its exemption was neither justified in detail nor seriously questioned. As has been shown, the same arguments that were used to justify the illegality of sado-masochism can be used to justify outlawing boxing; however robust counter-arguments can also be put forward to explain why boxing is different, why these arguments do not apply to boxing and why its continuation as a lawful activity is in the public interest.

The jurisprudential arguments

The search for Lord Mustill's 'intellectually satisfying' justification for the legality of boxing is a difficult one. Perhaps the most under-explored field that could provide such an explanation is jurisprudence. The theories that underpin the reasons why the law regulates certain forms of conduct should at least provide the foundations upon which a justification could be built. However the cases on consent have avoided any real engagement with legal theory and have instead focused on less well-developed public interest and public policy arguments.

7.4.3.1 Liberalism

English law is founded upon the general principles of liberalism. All activities are lawful unless declared to be illegal by Parliament or the courts and state intervention in a person's private life is only justifiable to prevent non-consensual harm being caused to other people. For the state to intervene it would have to be proved that either the consent of the participants was invalid or that harm beyond that which had been consented to had been inflicted on the participants. Therefore as no Act of Parliament or decision of the House of Lords or Supreme Court has ever outlawed boxing and because the only people likely to be physically harmed are the participants who have given their full, free and informed consent to participate in the sport, boxing is lawful.

It has been argued that harm is caused to the wider society by the glorification of violence inherent in boxing and because it is a degrading spectacle to watch fighting for the purposes of sport and entertainment. Moral repugnance is not the kind of harm that liberal theory is concerned with; that is the central tenet of legal moralism. Unless those who seek to have boxing outlawed can prove a specific link between the existence of boxing and an increased use of violence in society as a whole, then the kind of harm that liberalism would allow the state to step in to regulate has not been caused.

Liberalism best explains the current legal status of boxing and the law's reluctance to change that on behalf of a vocal and well-organised minority. It places a premium on the consent of the participants and justifies the legality of boxing as a sport on the basis that the boxers' consent to fight according to the rules of the sport has been given validly. If the state was to consider that boxing could no longer be tolerated as being in the public interest, then it would be difficult to justify such regulation on liberal grounds.

7.4.3.2 Paternalism

Paternalism is often used to justify the introduction of protective legislation. The basis of the theory is that where people fail to look after their own safety adequately and suffer preventable harm as a result, then the state should intervene and force safe practices to be observed by everybody. Anyone who fails to adhere to the imposed safety regime created by Parliament will then be guilty of a criminal offence. The requirement to wear seatbelts in cars is a classic example of paternalistic legislation; if people will not make themselves safe by wearing seatbelts voluntarily then the state will force them to be worn or will impose a criminal sanction for the failure to do so (Road Traffic Act 1988 ss.14 and 15). On occasion the courts have also justified their decisions on paternalistic grounds; Stephen J in *Coney* argued that prize-fighting should be outlawed because the severity of the injuries caused to the participants could not be justified. Building on these arguments the BMA has consistently argued that boxers need protecting from themselves and that they should not be allowed to subject each other to the risk of such serious injury as can be caused when boxing.

Any legislation introduced to outlaw boxing would almost undoubtedly be based on paternalistic justifications. If the body of evidence linking boxing with cumulative chronic brain injury, rather than acute traumatic harm, continues to grow then the basis for the state to intervene and regulate the sport by requiring a higher level of protection for the boxers, for example by changing the target area and banning blows to the head or by outlawing boxing altogether, becomes much firmer. Without such evidence it is difficult to justify banning boxing whilst allowing other dangerous activities to continue and it is difficult to justify introducing paternalistic legislation that overrides UK law's generally liberal legal tradition and the participants' specific and validly given consent to box.

7.4.3.3 Legal moralism

The final theoretical standpoint that is relied on by some of those who are seeking to outlaw boxing is legal moralism. In accordance with this theory the state is justified in introducing legislation to regulate spheres of activity on the basis of upholding community morality; if the majority of citizens consider that an activity is morally repugnant then state intervention is justified to regulate or outlaw it.

The unfashionableness of legal moralism as a theory of state intervention comes more from its potential to justify oppression by the majority of the populace of any group that is 'different' for no other reason than distaste rather than for its specific application to boxing. At present there is undoubtedly not enough widespread distaste of or moral repugnance felt towards boxing to justify banning it on these grounds. Furthermore liberal theorists would argue that no amount of distaste could ever justify state intervention without specific identifiable harm being caused to someone other than the participants. However legal moralism has been behind Parliamentary responses in the past, including the passing of the Firearms (Amendment) Act 1997 that led to shooting sports becoming more heavily regulated, and in some cases unlawful activities. The next death in the ring will undoubtedly lead to these arguments being brought out once again for debate.

7.4.3.4 Summary of the jurisprudential arguments

Only three theories of state regulation have been discussed in brief here as they are the ones most frequently called upon when the legality of boxing is debated. Of the three, liberalism probably best sums up the current attitude of both Parliament and the courts to boxing; that as long as only consensual harm is caused to the participants, then there is no justification for state intervention to regulate a 'properly conducted' sport such as boxing. If state intervention were ever to be justified, then a paternalistic approach based on medical evidence that society should no longer allow injuries of such severity to be caused in the name of sport would appear to be the most appropriate. Legal moralism will continue to feature in the moral panics that follow all serious incidents and deaths that occur in the ring. Although it is unlikely that boxing will be banned on the basis of such intolerance, as has been seen with some shooting sports it is not completely impossible for this to occur.

Conclusion

All of the legal, public policy and theoretical arguments are to a greater or lesser extent relevant to a coherent justification of the legal status of boxing and all other fighting sports. However none of them can be said to provide a definitive, objective and intellectually satisfying justification. The responses of Parliament, the courts and society appear at present to favour a liberalist approach to boxing. Any change in the legal status of boxing would need justifying on clearly defined theoretical and evidential bases. It would appear that the current legal status of boxing is safe until either there is a significant groundswell of opinion in favour of banning it, or until there is sufficiently clear evidence of the lasting harm caused to boxers through participation in their chosen sport. On an individual level, it is important to be aware of all of the issues that need to be taken into account and that can be used to justify a more personal position on the status of all fighting sports, not just boxing. The focus of any future discussions is likely to be on the degree of injury caused to the participants either because too much harm appears to be being inflicted on them for the purposes of entertainment or because the apparent lack of safety protocols mean that the sport is not being properly conducted.

Hot topic . . .

THE LEGAL STATUS OF MIXED MARTIAL ARTS

Of the many new and increasingly popular forms of combat sport that have emerged in recent years, one category stands out as being more controversial than all the others: mixed martial arts (MMA). MMA is becoming a generic term for all sports that have limited rules or which advertise themselves as being 'no holds barred'. The aim of these modern hybrid sports is to enable inter-disciplinary contests to take place where exponents of different fighting traditions compete against one another without undue restriction on their individual skills.

For such contests to take place, the applicable rules need to be pared down to a minimum so that wrestling holds, punching, martial arts throws and kicking are all allowed. This enables, for example an exponent of karate to take on a boxer. The rules of the various forms of MMA are in reality safety rules. These ensure that any moves, holds or blows that are intended to cause serious injury or which are particularly dangerous are banned; for example eye-gouging, blows to the windpipe and the back of the head and

the breaking of fingers and toes are almost always considered to be unlawful moves.

The controversy surrounding these sports is that to some viewers they appear to be little more than unregulated brawls where the infliction of pain and injury is the main goal of the bout and the publicity surrounding many of these events does little to dispel this concern. To others however this is a contest between two highly trained athletes where each is trying to demonstrate that their particular discipline, or disciplines as many are proficient in more than one martial art, and their skill as a fighter is more effective than their opponent's. The difficulty for the law and for legal commentators is to determine whether MMA and related activities can justifiably claim that they are deserving of the same exemption that is afforded to more traditional British combat sports such as boxing and wrestling.

The first difficulty that these activities encounter is that simply calling an activity a sport, whether it is a generic name like MMA or a trade name such as 'Ultimate

Fighting Championships' or 'Cage Wars', does not mean that the activity will be legally recognised as a sport. Therefore to be able to benefit from the same exemption from the criminal law that boxing enjoys, it must also be properly conducted and in the public interest to allow participation in these kinds of sporting activities.

Secondly there is a lack of a universally accepted, standardised set of rules. This makes it almost impossible to determine whether participants in different events are actually competing in a sport rather than simply fighting. Thirdly there is no single licensing authority, governing body or international federation that oversees these activities that can enable a standard set of rules and safety protocols to be developed. Fourthly this lack of standardisation, coordination and administration leads some groups to claim that this is brutality masquerading as sport, that MMA events are not properly conducted sporting contests and that all MMA bouts are therefore unlawful and criminal.

Much of this unease comes from the hype surrounding many MMA contests. Describing a contest as 'no holds barred' where 'anything goes' in 'a competition to find the hardest man in the world' do little to allay the fears of those who consider these contests to be at best a modern incarnation of prize-fighting and at worst little more than unregulated brawling. When these concerns are coupled with images of fighters bleeding, nursing fractures and being carried unconscious from a caged ring, the case against MMA appears to be a strong one.

However the counter-arguments are equally robust. Firstly a set of rules, exemplified by the New Jersey State Athletic Control Board's *Mixed Martial Arts Unified Rules of Conduct*, have become the standard for most high-profile limited rules fighting contests. These are the legal requirements that any contest must adhere to in order to stage an event in the American states where MMA is recognised as being a lawful activity and have been adopted by many other countries and fight organisers worldwide. Thus a set of rules and safety requirements overseen by an independent body is emerging.

Secondly although there is no governing body structure in place, the contests themselves are still well-organised or properly conducted. The difference between how sports are traditionally organised and how MMA is currently administered differ only in that most MMA bouts are run by purely commercial entities rather than by domestically, regionally or internationally recognised governing bodies that fulfil administrative, licensing and commercial roles. Further, professional boxing has experienced so many schisms over the years that its seven world championship sanctioning bodies can hardly be said to provide a template of good governance for other fighting sports.

Thirdly as these events are based upon fighting disciplines that are already generally recognised as being lawful then MMA as a concept should also be lawful. If this were not the case then where a fighter competed against someone trained in the same discipline as he or she was, then all contacts would be lawful; but where they competed against someone who was trained in a different discipline then the entire fight would be unlawful. There appears to be no logical justification for why this should represent the law's response to inter-disciplinary bouts that occur under the umbrella of MMA.

Fourthly the chances of lasting serious injury are arguably lower than in more traditional sports such as boxing. In MMA the entire body, not just the head and torso, are the target area. This ensures that there are much fewer blows to the head and therefore a much lower risk of being caused either chronic or acute brain injury. The majority of MMA contests are decided by a hold resulting in a submission rather than retirement through injury or concussion. Where injury does occur it is usually to a part of the body that can heal rather than to the brain. Thus although the associated imagery may make some bouts seem more violent than they are, the organisers can make a strong claim for MMA being less dangerous than boxing.

Finally if the main issue is that a sport must be properly conducted to enable it to take advantage of the exemption afforded to boxing, then each individual event organiser's rules and medical procedures ought to be examined to determine whether or not they reach appropriate standards of administration and safety. Provided that it has sufficient rules in place that are robustly enforced by independent referees, that necessary safety and medical protocols are in place and are followed and that an appropriate level of ringside medical assistance is provided, then it becomes easier to draw an analogy between 'properly conducted' MMA contests and 'properly conducted' boxing matches.

Many of the policy and theoretical arguments used against boxing are equally valid against MMA. Moreover its apparent glorification of the fight itself can make contests appear more violent than skilful. However provided that similar standards of safety are adhered to, then arguably it is a sport that can be at least as safe as boxing as it places so much less emphasis on the blows to the head that so concern the BMA. Until there is an agreed set of rules and perhaps a governing body MMA will continue to face criticism. If MMA as a whole, and its dominant commercial event organisers in particular can develop measures to ensure the quality and integrity of their competitions and the safety of the competitors over the glorification of violence, then it will not only survive the legal, moral and policy challenges thrown at it but may even find its way into the mainstream of British sport.

Summary

7.1 Historically fighting sports needed to be protected by the law to ensure that the citizenry could be trained to be fit and able to defend the realm. As warfare evolved from hand-to-hand combat to more mechanised means of fighting, the learning of these skills became less important. In place of the training regimes that prepared people for war, activities such as boxing began to evolve into the modern forms of combat sports that we can see today. As this evolution took place, it fell to the courts to determine which forms of fighting, if any, should be protected by the law and which should not.

Summary cont'd

7.2 Eventually the courts determined that only those fighting sports that were tests of skill were lawful activities that could be organised, watched and participated in without fear of prosecution. However those sports that were more a test of how long a person could endure a physical battering were criminal assaults: anyone organising or actively encouraging participation in one of these unlawful prize-fights was guilty of aiding and abetting the criminal assaults perpetrated by the fighters on one another (*R* v. *Coney*). When establishing the legality of a specific activity, the court must look to the aim of the organisers and the fighters, not just the form of the fight, to determine whether its true object is a test of skill or a fight until one or other of the participants is physically unable to continue.

7.3 *R* v. *Roberts* established that fighting for sport that took place according to a pre-determined set of rules that was designed to measure the skill of the protagonists and which provided them with safety systems that could minimise the degree of harm suffered by them were not criminal activities. Despite occasional attempts by Parliament to outlaw boxing, particularly in its professional form, the Law Commission stated that boxing and other similarly regulated fighting sports are, and should remain, lawful activities until such time as society no longer chooses to tolerate them.

7.4 There is a wide range of legal, jurisprudential, social, medical and policy arguments that attempt to justify the current legal status of combat sports or why their current status should be changed. It is important to be aware of these in order to be able to justify a position on whether or not sports of this kind should continue to be tolerated by the law.

Further reading

Anderson, *The Legality of Boxing* (2007, RoutledgeCavendish)

Bettinson and Tristram, *The National Sporting Club past and present* (1902, Sands and Co) available at: http://openlibrary.org/details/nationalsportin00trisgoog

Law Commission, *Consent and Offences against the Person*, LCCP No 134 (1994, HMSO) paras 10 and 35–47

Law Commission, *Consent in the Criminal Law*, LCCP No 139, (1995, HMSO) paras 12–13 and appx C

Foster, *Crown Law* (1762) 260, quoted in Williams, 'Consent and public policy' [1962] Crm LR 74

Gendall, 'The sport of boxing: freedom versus social constraint' [1997] *Waikato Law Review* 5

Gunn and Omerod, 'The legality of boxing' (1995) 15(2) *Legal Studies* 181

Sithamparanathan, 'Noble art of self-defence or unlawful barbarism?' [2002] *Entertainment Law Review* 183

Links to relevant websites can be found at www.palgrave.com/law/james

Part 3

Spectators, stadiums and the law

Chapter 8

Liability for dangerous premises and dangerous events

Key words

▶ **Occupier** – the person or body having sufficient control over premises to ensure that they are safe to use by those invited on to them.

▶ **Visitor** – a person who is invited on to the occupier's premises and who has permission to be there.

▶ **Trespasser** – a person who is on the occupier's premises without their permission or who is acting in excess of the original permission granted to them.

▶ **Private nuisance** – an unlawful and continuing activity that unreasonably interferes with the claimant's right to quiet enjoyment of their own property.

▶ **Public nuisance** – an activity that materially affects the reasonable comfort and convenience of a section of the community but which causes special damage to the claimant above and beyond that suffered by their neighbours.

▶ **Injunction** – an order of the court requiring the defendant either to stop doing something (prohibitory injunction), or to do something in a particular manner (mandatory injunction).

8.1 General tortious liability of organisers and hosts of sports events

The potential liability of those who organise sporting events and manage sports facilities is extremely wide. Injuries can be caused to the participants and spectators because of the state of the premises, to the spectators because of the management of the facility, or to neighbours and passersby by things, usually balls, being hit out of the playing area or stadium. The causes of action that can be relied on by claimants are equally diverse, including breach of contract, negligence, occupiers' liability and nuisance.

As spectator sports grew in popularity throughout the Victorian era, event organisers became aware of the need to construct facilities in which the competitions could take place. These new venues served two main purposes: firstly to demarcate the playing area from the onlookers and secondly to regulate entrance to the event, thereby facilitating the ability to charge spectators to watch the fixture. Later, facilities such as seating were provided to spectators who were willing to pay a premium to watch an event in comfort. A recurring feature of the early cases is the poor quality of the stadiums and grandstands that were constructed to host major sports events and the lack of appropriate regulation of these venues. This chapter will focus on the civil law remedies available to those caused harm by a sporting event.

8.1.1 Historical background

Before the development of the modern law of negligence in *Donoghue* v. *Stevenson* [1932] AC 502 and the passing of the Occupiers' Liability Acts in 1957 and 1984, actions against the organisers of sporting events were particularly complex.

► *Francis* v. *Cockrell* (1870) LR 5 QB 501, Court of Exchequer Chamber

The claimant was injured following the collapse of a temporary grandstand at the 1866 Cheltenham Races. The defendant, with others, had engaged a competent independent contractor to construct the grandstand, which enabled those who paid an entrance fee of five shillings to gain a better view of the races. The grandstand had been built negligently and collapsed, injuring the claimant.

The Court held that there was a contract between the claimant spectator and defendant organiser that allowed the claimant entry to the grandstand. This contract included an implied term that the grandstand was reasonably fit for the purpose of watching the races but did not cover unseen or unknown defects that could not reasonably be discovered. However, because the independent contractor had acted negligently in the construction of the grandstand, the defect that lead to its collapse could not be considered to be unseen or unknown as a reasonably competent constructor would have identified it. Therefore, the implied term that the grandstand was fit for its purpose was breached, even though there was no fault on the part of the defendant-organiser.

Two of their Lordships also held that the defendant owed two tortious duties to the claimant. The defendant had discharged his first duty, to employ a reasonable and competent independent contractor, but breached the second, which was a duty to provide a reasonably safe place from which to watch the race meeting.

Although some of the reasoning behind this case has been superseded by s.2(4) of Occupiers' Liability Act 1957 (OLA 1957), which would require the claimant to seek relief from the constructor if similar facts were to arise today, it still sets the scene for the cases that followed and for how spectators would continue to be treated in the future.

This apparent disregard for spectator safety was reinforced when a grandstand collapsed at Blackburn Rovers Football Club's home ground, Ewood Park. In *Brown* v. *Lewis* (1896) 12 TLR 455, the directors of the club were held personally liable in negligence for the injuries caused to the claimant. Their breach of duty was the failure to engage a competent independent contractor to carry out work on the grandstand. This finding meant that each of the individual directors had to pay a proportion of the claimant's compensation. Rather than leading to an improvement in stadium safety or a change in the law regulating major events, the case resulted in the majority of professional sports clubs incorporating to ensure that in future the club, rather than its directors, would be liable in a similar situation (see further, chapter 9.1.1).

Over time, the law evolved to impose duties for the benefit of sports participants as well as the spectators. *Gillmore* v. *London County Council* [1938] 4 All ER 331 held that the defendant council owed a duty of care to the claimant who was taking part in a physical training course on its premises. The duty was to ensure that the flooring on which the activity was taking place was reasonably safe for this purpose. As the lesson was taking place on a highly polished dance floor, instead of in a purpose built sports hall, the flooring was too slippery for the participants to maintain their footing. When the claimant slipped and injured himself, the defendant was liable for conducting an activity in an unsafe environment.

These cases show that as the law of negligence was developing generally, it was also developing specifically to ensure that those who were organising sports events, or who ran sports facilities, were doing so safely. Although the vast majority of cases will now be based on the Occupiers' Liability Acts 1957 and 1984, these early cases illustrate how the law was to develop and still plays a significant role in the limited circumstances where the Acts do not apply.

8.2 The Occupiers' Liability Acts 1957 and 1984

The OLA 1957 partially codifies this area of the law and in particular defines the duty of care owed by an occupier of premises to its visitors. The OLA 1984 deals specifically with situations where the claimant is a trespasser on the premises as opposed to someone who has permission to be there. As a preliminary to any claim, it must be established that the injury was caused by the state of the premises and that the defendant was the occupier of those premises at the time the injury occurred. It must then be determined whether the claimant was a lawful visitor with permission to be on the premises or was a trespasser on the premises without, or in excess of, the occupier's consent.

8.2.1 Liability for occupancy or liability for the activity

The preliminary factual investigation must establish whether the harm was caused because of the state of the premises or the nature of the activity taking place on them. Where the harm is caused because of the state of the premises, the cause of action is for the breach of the duty imposed on an occupier by s.2(2) OLA 1957 (below, 8.2.5). For example, the injuries caused in *Gillmore* were because of the inappropriate and unsafe nature of the flooring where the activity took place; if similar facts were to reoccur today, the claim would be made under the OLA 1957. However, where the injury is caused as a result of the activity taking place on the premises, then the only cause of action open to a claimant will be in negligence.

> ▶ *Poppleton v. Trustees of the Portsmouth Youth Activities Centre* **[2008] EWCA Civ 646**
>
> The claimant was an inexperienced rock climber who was using an artificial climbing wall operated by the defendants. He had not asked for, nor had he been offered, training or instruction on the use of the climbing wall and had not seen, nor had his attention drawn to, a sign prohibiting jumping from the wall and climbing on the roof beams. In trying to emulate a more experienced friend, the claimant jumped from the wall and attempted to grab hold of one of the roof beams, from where he intended to drop on to the safety matting below. He lost his grip midway through his attempt, somersaulted in the air and landed on his neck, rendering him tetraplegic.
>
> It was held that the risk of injury from such an inherently dangerous move was obvious to any user of the climbing wall, even one with little climbing experience. It was also obvious that no amount of matting could prevent serious injury from occurring in a situation such as this. As the claimant's injury was caused by his unsafe use of the climbing wall, not because the climbing wall itself was unsafe, the only claim that he could make was that he had been negligently trained or supervised by the defendant; the OLA 1957 was not engaged. The defendant had not breached its duty to provide a safe climbing facility; the accident was caused by the claimant running an obvious risk of injury by acting in a manner wholly inappropriate to his level of experience.

8.2.2 The premises

'Premises' is given a wide meaning and includes not only land and any permanent or movable structures on it, but also includes vessels, vehicles and aircraft (s.1(3)(a) OLA 1957). The width of the definition is important as it will extend to all sporting premises of whatever nature including temporary structures, such as the grandstand in *Francis* v. *Cockrell*, and movable structures such as goalposts, as was the cause of the claimant's injuries in *Hall* v. *Holker Estate Co Ltd* [2008] EWCA Civ 1422 (below, 8.2.5.1). Although there has not been any litigation on the point to date, the Act would also appear to cover participants who are injured whilst travelling in any vehicle, including cars, yachts and planes that are being used for racing.

8.2.3 The occupier of the premises

Perhaps surprisingly, who or what constitutes an 'occupier' of premises is not defined in either of the Acts; s.1(2) OLA 1957 states specifically that reference to the previous common law should be made to determine the identity of this central character. An occupier is someone who has sufficient control of the premises to enable them to discharge the common duty of care owed to visitors under s.2(2) OLA 1957 (below, 8.2.5). In other words, they must be in a position to ensure that the premises are reasonably safe to be used by their visitors.

The most obvious occupiers of the premises will be the owner or tenant who is in possession of them. However if another person is in day-to-day control of the premises, for example, because they have been hired to a third party, then the operator or organiser of the event can also be the occupier. In certain circumstances it is also possible for more than one person to be the occupier of the same premises. The fluidity of the concept provides the claimant with the best opportunity to identify the person or persons who were actually in control of the safety of the premises and to bring their action against any or all of them as appropriate (*Wheat* v. *E Lacon and Co Ltd* [1966] AC 552).

8.2.4 Visitors and trespassers

The final preliminary issue is to determine whether the claimant was a lawful visitor to the premises or a trespasser on them. This point is key to the rest of the claim as it determines whether the action will be brought under the OLA 1957 or the OLA 1984. As with 'occupier', neither 'visitor' nor 'trespasser' are defined in the Acts.

A visitor is a person who has been invited on to the occupier's premises for a specific purpose, or who has the occupier's consent to be on them. Such permissions can be granted either expressly or impliedly by the occupier. Express permission would include, for example, where the participants have paid to use a sports facility, as where the claimants in *Roddie and Roddie* v. *Ski Llandudno Ltd* [2001] PIQR P5 had paid to go down a concrete toboggan run, or where spectators have paid an entrance fee to watch a sports fixture (*Murray* v. *Harringay Arena LD* [1951] 2 KB 529) (below, 8.2.5.4.1). Implied consent would include where the occupier has allowed an activity to take place without specifically granting permission to the claimant or where the activity has been tacitly encouraged (*Hall* v. *Holker*) (below, 8.2.5.1).

A trespasser is a person without the requisite permission to be on the premises, or someone who is acting in excess of their permission. The former is what most people would consider to be a trespasser; a person on someone else's property without their permission (*Ratcliffe* v. *McConnell* [1999] 1 WLR 670) (below, 8.2.6). The latter definition enables a person to change their status from being a lawful visitor to an unlawful trespasser by doing something, or by going somewhere, that they are not permitted. This, and a number of related issues, were analysed in *Tomlinson* v. *Congleton Borough Council* [2003] UKHL 47 (below, 8.2.6). By diving into a lake contrary to an express prohibition on swimming, the claimant's classification as a visitor to the defendant's park changed to his being a trespasser as he was doing something that he was not permitted to do on the premises. Thus, his claim was tried under the OLA 1984, not the OLA 1957.

8.2.5 Occupiers' Liability Act 1957

Once it has been established that the claimant is a lawful visitor to the premises, then the common duty of care is owed to them by the defendant-occupier.

> ▶ **Occupiers' Liability Act 1957 s.2(2) – the common duty of care**
>
> The common duty of care is a duty to take such care as in all the circumstances of the case is reasonable to see that the visitor will be reasonably safe in using the premises for the purposes for which he is invited or permitted by the occupier to be there.

As a codified version of common law negligence, it is a duty to take only reasonable steps to ensure that the visitor is safe; it is not a standard of absolute safety. As with negligence, the degree of safety provided will depend on the type of activity taking place and greater care must always be taken where children are concerned.

The OLA 1957 contains specific reference to ways that the common duty of care can be discharged and to defences that an occupier can raise to any claim made against them. Firstly in s.2(4)(a) OLA 1957, the duty is discharged where a warning has been given that is sufficient to enable the visitor to make themselves reasonably safe. Consideration of this provision is often relevant where the claimant has been injured whilst swimming. Secondly, in s.2(4)(b) OLA 1957, the defendant is absolved from liability where they have chosen competent independent contractors to carry out works on the premises. Thus, if *Francis* v. *Cockrell* were to occur today, the claimant would have to bring their action against the constructors of the grandstand, subject to the common duty of care being imposed by virtue of s.5(1) OLA 1957. Thirdly, s.2(5) OLA 1957 states that the occupier will not be liable for harm caused by risks willingly run by the claimant. This will include the inherent risks associated with dangerous activities, for example, losing control of a toboggan on a downhill run, as in *Roddie* v. *Ski LLandudno*.

8.2.5.1 Participants v Occupiers – establishing a claim

An occupier will be liable for the injuries caused to a sports participant where the injury has been caused by the dangerous state of the playing arena or the equipment that is used to play the game in question.

> ▶ *Hall* v. *Holker Estate Co Ltd* **[2008] EWCA Civ 1422**
>
> The claimant had been playing football with his son and one of his son's friends when his foot became entangled in the net of the goal. As he fell to the ground, the goal posts, which had not been adequately secured, fell on to him and the crossbar hit him in the face causing injuries to his teeth and jaw. The defendant was aware that from time to time the pegs that should have secured the goalposts to the ground were removed by users of the campsite on which the football pitch was situated and that as a result, the goalposts were not be as safe as they should have been.
>
> The Court of Appeal held that where an occupier allows or encourages an activity to take place on its land and/or where it provides the equipment for such an activity, it must ensure that both the playing area and the equipment are reasonably safe for the purposes of playing the game in question. This will require the occupier to carry out risk assessments of the facilities and to ensure that the equipment is properly maintained. An occupier will only be able to avoid liability in circumstances such as these where it can prove not only that there is an adequate system in place for inspecting the facilities and eliminating any dangers but that this system was being implemented effectively. As the defendant was aware that the pegs securing the goalposts were often missing, the common duty of care was breached by the failure to take proactive steps to remedy this dangerous situation.

In *Simms* v. *Leigh Rugby Football Club Ltd* [1969] 2 All ER 923, the Court of Appeal discussed obiter the ways in which an occupier could discharge the common duty of care towards the claimant rugby league player. The claimant claimed to have broken his leg by colliding with a concrete fencing post and that, in breach of s.2(2) OLA 1957, this was too close to the edge of the pitch. He claimed that it was obvious that when rugby players were tackled into touch their momentum could carry them several metres beyond the touchline and that there should, therefore, be a much greater distance between the playing area and the fencing.

The Court noted that the distance between the touchline and the post was 2.2m; this was some 8cm beyond the recommended minimum distance required by the relevant bye-laws of the Rugby Football League, the sport's NGB. As the governing body thought that this was a sufficient distance to make the players safe, and the defendant had complied with this requirement and there was no evidence to suggest that injuries of this kind were occurring because this distance was too short, the common duty of care was discharged.

If a similar case were to come before the courts today, the claimant would be well advised to sue the appropriate NGB in negligence to test whether there was any logical justification for choosing the prescribed minimum distance (see further, chapter 5.4). As can be seen from *Hall* v. *Holker* and *Watson* v. *British Boxing Board of Control* [2001] QB 1134 (see further, chapter 5.4.1.1.2), not only must a risk assessment be carried out, it must also be reviewed to ensure that safety is maintained. Where an NGB has laid down safety guidelines, it must be able to justify why they are being imposed, assess their effectiveness and review them in the light of any new evidence of injuries that are occurring despite, or because of, their recommendations.

8.2.5.2 *Participants v Occupiers – defences*

As with negligence at common law, the main defences to claims under the OLA 1957 are voluntary assumption of risk and contributory negligence (see further, chapter 4.6.2).

Voluntary assumption of risk is specifically restated in s.2(5) OLA 1957 and the role of warnings in bringing the claimant's attention to any risks of injury is defined in s.2(4)(a) of the Act.

8.2.5.2.1 Voluntary assumption of risk and inherent dangers

▶ **Occupiers' Liability Act 1957 s.2(5) – voluntary assumption of risk**

The common duty of care does not impose on an occupier any obligation to a visitor in respect of risks willingly accepted as his by the visitor (the question whether a risk was so accepted to be decided on the same principles as in other cases in which one person owes a duty of care to another).

Despite reiterating the existence of the defence, the Act then refers back to the common law for the means of determining whether or not the claimant had in fact run the risk of injury to which they had been exposed by the defendant. The key point here is to determine whether the risks to which the claimant was exposed can be said to be inherent in the activity, and therefore of necessity run by him or her, or are because of a particular problem with the premises on which the activity was taking place. For example, it is an inherent risk of playing football that goalkeepers might collide with the goalposts and be caused serious injury. However they would not expect the goalposts to fall on them during the course of play. The former is an inherent risk willingly run by the injured player; the latter is neither an inherent risk of playing football nor one that is willingly run by goalkeepers.

When determining whether a claimant has willingly run the risks inherent in an activity, the court must perform a balancing act that weighs the risk of harm to which the participants were exposed against the nature of the activity in which they were involved. For example, in *Tysall Ltd* v. *Snowdome* [2007] CLY 4196, the claimant was injured whilst tobogganing at an indoor snow centre. She claimed that there was insufficient time for those in her group that were following her down the slope to take evasive action and avoid colliding with her once she had fallen from her toboggan. The court held that the element of risk inherent in sports such as tobogganing is often part of the reason why participants engage in such activities. The inherent risks, such as falling off, have to be weighed against the nature of the activity, including that this was a group social event involving a number of friends, the gravity of the injury sustained and the social value of the exercise. To make the activity safe so that this injury could not have occurred would have compromised its nature to such an extent that either the group could not have participated together at the same time or would have removed the 'thrill' element of participation. Thus, following the briefings on safety and how to use the toboggan, the claimant had willingly run the inherent risks of the activity by taking part in it with her friends.

8.2.5.2.2 Warnings

The OLA 1957 also establishes the circumstances in which occupiers will be able to avoid liability by providing warnings to their visitors.

> ▶ **Occupiers' Liability Act 1957 s.2(4) – discharging the common duty of care**
>
> In determining whether the occupier of premises has discharged the common duty of care to a visitor, regard is to be had to all the circumstances so that …
>
> (a) where damage is caused to a visitor by a danger of which he had been warned by the occupier, the warning is not to be treated without more as absolving the occupier from liability, unless in all the circumstances it was enough to enable the visitor to be reasonably safe.

Thus the simple provision of a warning is unlikely to discharge the common duty of care; telling someone to be careful or installing a sign proclaiming only that there is 'Danger' will rarely be sufficient. The warning must be in sufficient detail to enable the visitor to make themselves safe or to enable them to make an informed decision that the risk is one that is worth running in the circumstances. In *Roddie and Roddie v. Ski Llandudno,* the Court of Appeal considered that the warnings that were installed throughout the length of the toboggan run reminding users to brake as they turned into corners were sufficient to have discharged the common duty of care. Firstly the warnings brought the inherent risks of the activity to the notice of the claimant by highlighting that it was dangerous to go too fast round the corners. Secondly the warnings enabled the claimant to make himself reasonably safe by reminding him to apply the brakes at appropriate points during his descent. Only if the toboggan or the track were defective would a claim under the OLA 1957 have been sustainable.

8.2.5.2.3 Contributory negligence

Under s.1(1) Law Reform (Contributory Negligence) Act 1945, a defendant can seek a pro-rata reduction in the amount of compensation payable where the claimant has contributed by his own fault to the injuries that he has suffered (see further, chapter 4.6.2.2). This provision enables the court to balance the negligence of the defendant against the claimant's own carelessness and ensures that claimants cannot abdicate all responsibility for their own safety.

There are many cases involving injuries of varying degrees occurring at swimming pools, with one of the more unusual being *Greening v. Stockton-on-Tees Borough Council* (unreported) Court of Appeal, 6 November 1998, where the claimant swam into the edge of a swimming pool and was caused facial injuries as a result. He claimed that the edge of the pool was not clearly visible because of the murkiness of the water and the inadequate depth of the contrasting line of tiling that delineated the pool's edge. In establishing the primary liability of the defendant, the Court held that both of these factors contributed to the claimant's inability to see the edge of the pool sufficiently clearly. The court also held that there were two factors that should have alerted the claimant to the possible dangers of swimming in this pool and that he should have taken greater care of himself whilst he was in it. Firstly as this was an irregularly shaped 'deck level pool', where the water is at the same level as the edge of the pool, he should have paid greater attention to his position in relation to its edge. Secondly that as he was aware of the murkiness of the water (he claimed to have been unable to make out his own feet in only 95cm of water) he should again have been paying greater attention to his whereabouts in the water. His failure to notice the edge of the pool and his taking an additional unnecessary stroke contributed significantly to the cause of the accident and his damages were reduced by 50 per cent.

This case highlights clearly that even where the occupier has provided a potentially dangerous facility, the claimant cannot ignore the dangers that have been created. The greater the degree of knowledge of the dangers exhibited by the claimant, the greater the chance that the court will find either that they have contributed to the cause of their own injuries or that they have willingly run the risk of being injured whilst using the defendant's premises.

8.2.5.3 Spectators v. Occupiers – establishing a claim

To bring an action under the OLA 1957, as opposed to the common law of negligence, the claimant must be able to prove either that their injuries were caused by the state of disrepair of the premises or that they were unsuitable for hosting the kind of event that was taking place. Where there is a fault with the fabric of the venue, liability will be relatively easy to establish. In *McDyer* v. *Celtic Football and Athletic Co Ltd (No 1)* 2000 SC 379, a piece of timber that had been used as part of the framework from which banners were hung became dislodged and fell onto the claimant. Although the case was brought under the similarly worded s.2(1) Occupiers' Liability (Scotland) Act 1960, the principle that it establishes is the same; injuries caused by defects in the stadium which make it unsafe for the purposes of viewing an event will be the responsibility of the occupier.

The distinction between occupancy and activity liability was not so clear-cut in *Cunningham* v. *Reading Football Club Ltd* [1992] PIQR P141, where the claimant, a police officer on duty at a professional football match, was injured by a piece of concrete thrown at him by one of the spectators. It could be argued that the claimant was not injured by the state of the premises but by the activity that was occurring on them; in this case, an outbreak of crowd violence. However, the case was approached on the basis that the premises taken as a whole were not reasonably safe for the police to carry out their duties effectively. In coming to this conclusion, the court took into account that spectator disorder of this specific kind was reasonably foreseeable because pieces of concrete had been thrown by fans at the defendant's stadium on a previous occasion four months earlier. The football club's awareness of this danger, especially in the light of assurances given by it to the Football Association that measures would be taken to correct this problem, and its failure to take any such action meant that the stadium was not reasonably safe for the purposes for which the claimant had been invited into it. Thus, once the defendant is aware of the specific danger, it must take specific steps to negate it or be held in breach of duty.

Defendants must also ensure that any risk assessment or licensing inspection that is undertaken addresses the needs of all users of the premises. In *Fenton* v. *Thruxton (BARC) Ltd* (unreported) County Court (Basingstoke), 12 December 2008, the occupiers of a motor racing track were held not to have discharged the duty owed to spectators at a race meeting by relying on a safety inspection carried out by the NGB of motorcycle racing in the UK as this only addressed the safety of the competitors and race officials present at the event. A risk assessment that had been aimed at the safety of spectators would have identified the specific danger that led to the death of the deceased and enabled the occupier to take the necessary remedial action (below, 8.4.2).

8.2.5.4 *Spectators v Occupiers – defences*

There are two categories of defences that can be raised by an occupier of sports premises; that the harm was caused by an inherent risk of the sport and/or that the spectator has voluntarily run the risk of being injured and that the occupier has excluded its liability under s.2(1) OLA 1957. It must be noted that the ability of an occupier to rely on s.2(1) OLA 1957 has been limited significantly by s.2(1) Unfair Contract Terms Act 1977 (UCTA 1977).

8.2.5.4.1 Inherent and voluntarily run risks

The occupier of premises will not be liable for injuries caused by the inherent risks of watching a sporting event, providing that they have taken reasonable care to ensure the safety of the spectators. It must be remembered that the duty under the OLA 1957 is only to ensure that the premises are reasonably safe; it is not to insure against all harm absolutely.

In determining what steps, if any, should have been taken by the occupier to discharge this duty, a balance must be struck between spectator safety and spectator culture. For example, a spectator at a cricket match would not be able to claim for injuries caused by a cricket ball being hit for six runs into the crowd as it is an inherent risk of the game that the batting side will attempt to score as many runs as possible, which includes hitting sixes. The balance that has to be struck is between making the spectators reasonably safe and allowing them to view the game unhindered against making them absolutely safe by erecting netting and posts that could stop the balls from entering the crowd but which may obstruct their view of the game. Thus it is reasonable to provide no protection to spectators at a cricket game beyond their sitting at an appropriate distance from the action.

The closer to the action that a spectator is positioned, and the faster moving or more dangerous the game is, may mean that a greater degree of protection should be provided by the occupier.

> ▶ *Murray v. Harringay Arena LD* [1951] 2 KB 529
>
> The claimant was watching an ice hockey match from a front row seat along the side of the rink. He was hit in the face by a puck that had unintentionally been hit out of the playing area and was caused a serious eye injury. In balancing spectator safety against spectator culture, it was considered necessary to provide protective netting at the ends of the rink behind the goals to prevent mishit attempts to score from entering the crowd on a frequent basis, at high speed and with the potential to cause serious injury. However, it was not considered to be necessary to install similar netting down the sides of the rink because of the infrequent, low velocity and accidental nature of the puck entering the crowd at this point and further, because the netting would have unreasonably and unnecessarily obstructed the spectators' view of the action.
>
> It was held that there was no duty to protect spectators from the incidental risks of watching the sport in progress and that the claimant had willingly run a risk of injury that was reasonably foreseeable to any spectator by choosing to sit where he did. As occupiers only have to provide a reasonably safe environment, not one that is absolutely safe, the claim was dismissed.

Murray demonstrates that as long as a risk assessment has been carried out and the decision regarding the level of protection can be rationally justified, then the defendant may be able to escape liability. Different protections will be required for different sports based on the nature of the sporting activity taking place, the expectations of the spectators and the risk of something leaving the playing area and entering the crowd. It is also important to note that changes in perceptions of what is reasonably safe can and do change over time; what was acceptable in some of the older cases would not be considered to be reasonably safe today.

8.2.5.4.2 Exclusions of liability

> ▶ **Occupiers' Liability Act 1957 s.2(1) – extent of occupier's ordinary duty**
>
> An occupier of premises owes the same duty, the 'common duty of care', to all his visitors except in so far as he is free and does extend, restrict, modify or exclude his duty to any visitor or visitors by agreement or otherwise.

This extraordinarily wide-ranging section appears to allow occupiers to avoid owing the common duty of care altogether if they can impose a sufficiently specific exclusion of liability on their visitors. This is precisely what happened in *White* v. *Blackmore and Others* [1972] 2 QB 641 in respect of injuries caused to a spectator at a stock car racing event. However the ability to disclaim liability in these circumstances is now significantly restricted.

> ▶ **Unfair Contract Terms Act 1977 s.2(1) – negligence liability**
>
> A person cannot by reference to any contract term or to a notice given to persons generally or to particular persons exclude or restrict his liability for death or personal injury resulting from negligence.

Under s.1(1)(c) UCTA 1977, negligence includes the common duty of care, thereby limiting severely what had become a significant loophole in the OLA 1957's protections. These provisions of UCTA 1977 apply only to business liability, which is defined in s.1(3) as being where the harm is caused in the course of business or on premises occupied for the purposes of the business. Thus, wherever sport is conducted as a business, the occupier will be unable to exclude liability for personal injury that is caused as a result of a breach of the common duty of care.

From a practical perspective, unless the injuries are caused during informal sports or games, or where the use of the land is gratuitous, then liability cannot be excluded. Where the sporting event is not organised in the course of a business, then liability can only be excluded by a clearly worded exclusion clause that is brought to the attention of the spectator prior to their entry to the event.

8.2.6 Occupiers Liability Act 1984

Occupiers do not only owe a duty of care to the visitors who are permitted to be on their premises; they also owe a limited duty to trespassers who are on their premises without permission, or in excess of the permission that was initially granted to them. This is particularly important as it is possible for a visitor to become a trespasser by going somewhere on the premises, or by doing something on them, that they are not supposed to. If it is established that the claimant was in fact a trespasser, then the claim must be brought under the OLA 1984 instead of the OLA 1957. Before a claimant can rely on the protection of s.1(4) OLA 1984, three preconditions must be satisfied.

> ▶ **Occupiers' Liability Act 1984 s.1 – duty of occupier to persons other than visitors**
>
> (3) An occupier of premises owes a duty to another (not being his visitor) in respect of any [risk of their suffering injury on the premises by reason of any danger due to the state of the premises or to things done or omitted to be done on them] if –
>   (a) he is aware of the danger or has reasonable grounds to believe that it exists;
>   (b) he knows or has reasonable grounds to believe that the other is in the vicinity of the danger (in either case, whether the other has lawful authority for being in that vicinity or not); and
>   (c) the risk is one against which, in all the circumstances of the case, he may reasonably be expected to offer the other some protection.
> (4) Where, by virtue of the section, an occupier of premises owes a duty to another in respect of such a risk, the duty is to take such care as is reasonable in all the circumstances of the case to see that he does not suffer any injury on the premises by reason of the danger concerned.

The duty in s.1(4) OLA 1984 is often referred to as the 'common duty of humanity' in that it is the lowest level of protection that anyone on the occupier's premises would expect to receive. The very nature of sports facilities, particularly for swimming, will often mean that some element of danger is associated with them and that the occupier will be aware of this danger; in reality, the danger will often be an integral component of a facility such as a swimming pool, climbing wall or motor racing track. Although these preconditions may be relatively easily satisfied, the corollary is that the duty imposed under s.1(4) OLA 1984 can often be easily discharged by a warning or notice of the dangerous nature of the premises, provided it fulfils the requirements of s.1(5):

'Any duty owed by virtue of this section in respect of a risk may, in an appropriate case, be discharged by taking such steps as are reasonable in all the circumstances of the case to see that he does not suffer injury on the premises by reason of the danger concerned.'

In *Ratcliff* v. *McConnell and Others* [1999] 1 WLR 670, the Court of Appeal held that because of the obvious danger associated with diving into the shallow end of an outdoor swimming pool, the claimant had willingly accepted the risk of harm, in this case tetraplegia, under s.1(6) OLA 1984. It was also noted that the protections and warnings provided by the college about the pool would have been sufficient to discharge the duty owed under the OLA 1984. The pool was surrounded by walls and fences of at least 2.2m in height, there was a prohibition on the use of the pool between 10pm and 6.30am situated at the entrance to the pool and a substantial notice in red lettering on a white background identifying its shallow end. Further, the obviousness of the inherent danger of diving into the shallow end of a pool meant that there was no need to warn the claimant specifically that he should not do so.

▶ *Tomlinson v. Congleton Borough Council* **[2003] UKHL 47**

The defendant was the owner and occupier of a country park and lake that were used as a leisure facility. Members of the public were permitted to use the park for recreational purposes but were specifically prohibited by prominent signage from swimming in the lake. Ignoring this prohibition, the claimant ran down to the water's edge and dived in. At this point the water was extremely shallow and he hit his head on the bottom of the lake, fracturing his neck, and was rendered tetraplegic as a result. Firstly it was held that as his actions were in direct contravention of an express prohibition of the occupier, he was a trespasser from the point that he entered the water and that, therefore, he was owed the duty of care under s.1(4) OLA 1984 and not the more extensive duty under s.2(2) OLA 1957. Secondly that under s.1(5) OLA 1984 the duty was discharged by providing warnings discouraging the defendant from incurring the risk. Thirdly and in the alternative, the risk of injury from diving into water of unknown depth was so obvious as to have willingly accepted by the defendant, s.1(6) OLA 1984. Thus, although it is technically possible for a claimant to bring an action under the OLA 1984, their chances of success are likely to be low.

There is a clear distinction between the duties owed by an occupier under the two Acts. The OLA 1957 ensures that where the occupier has permitted a person to be on their premises for a specific purpose, then they must take positive steps to make them safe for the purpose of the visit. The OLA 1984 requires only that the occupier take reasonable steps to see that the trespasser does not suffer harm from a known danger. For example, if an occupier invites people to swim on their premises, he must ensure that the area is safe for them to do so; warnings about the depth of the water must be provided and it must be free from hidden dangers. Where an occupier does not want people to swim on his premises, then they need only take steps to ensure that this is made clear to anyone who is present on them and to provide a warning of any known dangers. There is no need to warn of specific hidden dangers if a complete ban on swimming is in place, as was the case in *Rhind* v. *Astbury Water Park Ltd* [2004] EWCA Civ 756. Thus, the positive duty owed to those with permission to be on the premises is replaced by a negative duty to avoid causing harm to those without the requisite permission to be there.

8.3 Nuisance

The aim of the tort of private nuisance is to protect a person's right to enjoy their own property without undue interference. Such a claim cannot be brought under the Occupiers' Liability Acts as the claimant must be physically present on the defendant's land to benefit from the protections of those statutes. Where sport is concerned, private nuisance ensures that the organisers of a sporting event, or those with a legal interest in the land on which an event is taking place, do not produce an unreasonable level of noise or cause physical damage to the neighbouring properties. An action could lie in public nuisance where a section of the community is affected by an activity but the claimant has suffered harm above and beyond that caused to other affected properties. Although difficult to prove and requiring the permission of the Attorney-General to bring the case, public nuisance actions can be of assistance to physically injured claimants in certain limited circumstances.

The aim of nuisance claims will depend on the nature of the inconvenience suffered and the means by which it was caused. Where the interference is by noise, the claimant will usually seek an injunction to stop the activity or reduce its frequency. Where physical harm is concerned, the claimant will want both an injunction to stop the activity and compensation for the harm caused. In balancing the reasonableness of a defendant's conduct against the rights of the claimant to enjoy their property without interference, the court can decide that the defendant should be allowed to continue their activity, or that the activity be allowed to continue but that compensation be paid to the claimant to reflect the reduction in the value of the claimant's property, or that the activity be restricted in some way or stopped altogether.

8.3.1   Private nuisance

Private nuisance is where the defendant has created an unlawful and continuing interference with the claimant's use or enjoyment of their land, that has caused damage to the claimant's legal interest in the land and which is, on balance, unreasonable. An action in private nuisance can only be brought by a claimant who has a legal interest in the affected land, usually as either the owner or tenant of a neighbouring property (*Hunter v. Canary Wharf Ltd* [1997] AC 655).

An interference is continuing where it is repeated sufficiently frequently; where it only happens occasionally, then it is not 'continuing'. This is one of the reasons why *Bolton v. Stone* [1951] AC 850 (below, 8.4.4) had to be brought in negligence rather than nuisance. The interference with the legal interest can be either direct or indirect. A direct interference will be where the defendant's conduct has caused physical harm to the claimant's land by, for example, hitting a ball on to it. Indirect interference is where there is no physical harm caused but the claimant's enjoyment of his land is interfered with by, for example, excessive noise.

In determining the reasonableness of the defendant's conduct, and therefore whether or not it is a nuisance, the court will take into account the type of interference, the locality in which it takes place, its duration, its public utility, the sensitivity of the claimant's land and whether the defendant was acting deliberately to annoy the claimant. The most common complaints from neighbours of sports facilities are that their property is being physically damaged by things exiting the stadium or that the noise is so excessive that they cannot live peacefully in their homes.

8.3.1.1 Physical injury

Where direct physical harm is caused to the claimant's land, an actionable nuisance will almost always have occurred. However that does not mean that the activity causing the harm will be forced to stop.

> ▶ *Miller v. Jackson* [1977] QB 966
>
> This case has become a benchmark for discussions on whether or not an activity is a nuisance and is famous for Lord Denning MR's robust defence of village cricket as an integral part of the social fabric of a community. The claimant bought a house on the edge of a village green where cricket had been played by the local club for over 70 years. His back garden was separated from the playing field by a fence 1.8m in height. His complaint was that balls were being hit from the green on to his property, interfering with his right to enjoy his property and damaging his house on a regular basis. The club had increased the height of the fence to 4.5m, which had prevented the vast majority, but not all, of the balls from being struck onto his land, but this was not considered to be acceptable by the claimant.

The Court of Appeal was left with the difficult task of balancing the competing interests of the householder and the cricket club in reaching an appropriate solution. On the one hand the type of interference, direct physical harm, was one that would usually be prohibited by an injunction; on the other was the public interest in allowing the cricket club to continue to play where it had done for over 70 years. The majority of the Court held that playing cricket on this piece of land was a nuisance as there was a degree of inevitability associated with the risk of balls being hit on to neighbouring properties and causing them physical harm. It was further held that the defendant cannot avoid liability by arguing that the claimant had placed himself in danger by moving into a house adjoining the pitch. It is not a defence to say that the claimant has 'come to the nuisance'; either the activity was a nuisance or it was not and in this case it was.

However, in determining the appropriate response to this nuisance, the Court took into account the character of the neighbourhood, the public or social utility of the activity and the conduct of the parties. Firstly it is to be expected that part of the character of rural villages is provided by having sports and other activities taking place on their greens. By purchasing a property overlooking the cricket ground, the claimant was not 'coming to the nuisance' but buying into the character of the village as a whole. This included that activities in general, and cricket in particular, would take place there. Secondly the greater interest of the local community in maintaining the cricket club as a focal point of the village's life should take precedence over the occasional hardship caused to an individual householder. Thirdly the club had paid for a higher fence to be installed, which had eliminated most of the harmful shots, but the householder was not prepared to accept any inconvenience whatsoever. In other words, by accepting the benefit of overlooking the green, the claimant also had to accept the burden of the activities taking place on it. Thus, compensation was awarded to reflect the claimant's past and future inconvenience.

8.3.1.2 Excessive noise

The noise created by certain sports, particularly motor sports, has been the focus of a number of cases over the years. Key to determining the existence of a nuisance in these cases will be the level of noise, its regularity and the character of the area where the activity is taking place. In *Stretch v. Romford Football Club Ltd* (1971) 115 Sol J 641, an injunction was granted to prevent speedway events from taking place at Romford FC's football ground. Although fixtures only took place for two hours, once each week from May to October, the amount of noise generated was held to be so far in excess of that which occurred at football matches held at the same venue as to constitute an unreasonable interference with the club's neighbours' quiet enjoyment of their property. The speedway club was banned from competing in Romford from the end of that season's competition.

In contrast to *Stretch v. Romford*, a judicially imposed compromise saw the activities of the Cotswold Motor Boat Racing Club restricted rather than stopped altogether.

▶ *Kennaway v. Thompson* [1981] QB 88

The Club had expanded its activities, including organising power boat races and water skiing sessions, without restriction until the amount of noise became unbearable to local residents. Each race day was preceded by practice days and water skiing took place at every available opportunity. This meant that the lake was in use by high-powered boats from 9am until dusk on most days, and especially on weekends, from March to November each year. The Court of Appeal held that the Club's use of the lake was unreasonable and imposed an injunction on it limiting the number and type of race days per year, enforced gaps between each of these race days and limited the number of boats that could be involved in water skiing at any one time. These limitations balanced the rights of local residents to enjoy the benefit of living in a peaceful lakeside environment against the Club's right to continue its activities in a responsible manner.

It is possible that similar reasoning could be applied to noxious fumes and smells emanating from a stadium. This is most likely to occur in respect of motor sports and was one of the lines of argument put forward in *Stretch* v. *Romford*, although it was rejected by the court. The likelihood of success of such a claim is again likely to focus on the character of the neighbourhood; the more residential the area, the less likely that interferences of this kind will be acceptable.

8.3.2   Public nuisance

The tort of public nuisance has two discrete forms. The more common of the two versions is where the defendant's activity materially affects the reasonable comfort and convenience of a section of the community but the claimant suffers special damage above and beyond that suffered by everyone else. The second version is where a series of individual private nuisances are amalgamated into one generic public nuisance. Although not commonly used, partly because the action must be brought by the Attorney-General on behalf of the injured party, it can provide additional protections to the neighbours of sports facilities.

Public nuisances include unlawful acts or omissions which endanger the lives, safety, health or comfort of a section of the public, or by which the public is obstructed in the exercise of some common right, for example using the highway. Unlike claims for private nuisance, the claimant does not need to possess a legal interest in the land to bring the claim; whereas private nuisance protects the claimant's interests in their land, public interest protects the public in general from annoyance.

8.3.2.1 Special damage

Castle v. *St Augustine's Links Ltd* (1922) 38 TLR 615 exemplifies the case where the claimant has suffered harm above and beyond that suffered by the rest of the public. The defendant was aware that golf balls were occasionally hit on to a busy road adjacent to its course. Thus, the class of affected members of the public extended to anyone who drove down this particular road. The claimant was the driver of a car who was blinded by a golf ball that had been hit from the defendant's course and which went through his windscreen. The claimant had, therefore, suffered above and beyond other members of the affected group; he had suffered a specific personal injury whereas the other road users had suffered only the risk of personal injury.

8.3.2.2 Amalgamated private nuisances

Where a section of the community is affected by the same activity, then public nuisance can be established on the basis of amalgamating the individual private nuisances that are occurring. In *East Dorset District Council* v. *Eaglebeam Ltd and Others* [2006] EWHC 2378 (QB), the defendants operated a motocross course in a large park. The noise this generated interfered with local residents' right to enjoy their own premises, particularly as it prevented them from being able to use their gardens peacefully in the summer. Despite the alterations that had been made by the defendant to his course in an attempt to abate the nuisance, the noise was still considered to be of a sufficient level of interference to constitute a public nuisance.

8.4 Actions in negligence

There are several situations where an action in negligence survives either alongside of or instead of a claim under the Occupiers' Liability Acts. Despite the Acts not applying in these cases, the duty owed by the defendants has been held to be coextensive with the common duty of care (*Craven* v. *Riches and Others and the Knockhill Racing Circuit Ltd* [2001] EWCA Civ 375). From a practical perspective, this means that there will be no difference in how the case is argued and its ultimate outcome will be the same whether the action is brought under the OLA 1957 or the common law. As with any claim in negligence, it must then be established that a breach of the duty owed caused the claimant's injuries (see further, chapter 4)

8.4.1 Participants v. organisers

Where the claimant's harm is not caused because of the state of the defendant's premises but by the nature of the activity taking place on them, then the action must be brought in negligence. In *Poppleton* v. *Trustees of the Portsmouth Youth Activities Centre* [2008] EWCA Civ 646 (above, 8.2.1), the claimant alleged that in failing to train him before allowing him on to the climbing wall, to supervise him whilst he was taking part in the activity, to warn him of the dangers of leaping from the wall in the way that he did and to inform him that the matting would not save him from injury in all cases amounted to a breach of the duty of care owed to him. The Court of Appeal held that the defendants were only under a duty to warn the claimant about dangers that were not obvious; the other duties would only have been engaged where training was requested and carried out negligently. As his injuries were caused by his voluntarily running an obvious risk by leaping from the wall in the way that he did, his claim failed.

In several cases, the courts discuss negligence and occupier's liability at the same time, making no clear distinction as to which cause of action is ultimately at issue. As the duties owed to the claimant are the same, this is not a significant problem; the main difficulty that these cases raise for the reader is that by combining the discussions in this way, the courts will often avoid identifying who is the occupier.

Where the distinction is not made specifically, organisers of an event, as opposed to occupiers of the premises, owe a duty to take reasonable care to ensure that the event is run in such a way that it is reasonably safe in all the circumstances for the claimant to participate in it (see also, chapter 5.4.1.1.1). In *Craven*, there was nothing wrong with the state of the racing track only with the way that the first defendants had organised the event. They were under a duty to ensure that they had designed out any unnecessary dangers, which they had attempted to do by limiting the number of motorcyclists who were on the track at any one time and by grouping together those who would be riding at similar speeds. The duty was breached by their failure to enforce this grouping. Thus, when the claimant unexpectedly came across two riders who were travelling at a significantly slower speed than him, his being forced to brake suddenly and lose control was held to have been caused by the presence of riders who should not have been on the track at the same time as he was. Although he was found to have been contributorily negligent, because of his failure to keep a proper look out for other track users, the defendant was liable for failing to organise a reasonably safe event.

8.4.2 Spectators v. organiser

As with participants, where the injury is caused as a result of the activity taking place on the premises, rather than their state, then an action can only be brought in negligence. The claimant in *Bottomley* v. *Todmorden Cricket Club* [2003] EWCA Civ 1575 was injured by a firework at a display being hosted by the defendants. The duty owed by the defendant was to take reasonable care in choosing a competent pyrotechnic contractor, not that under s.2(2) OLA 1957, as there was nothing unsafe about the cricket ground itself. As the contractor was not competent and did not have the relevant insurance cover, the cricket club was held liable in negligence for the claimant's injuries.

In *Fenton* v. *Thruxton (BARC) Ltd* (above, 8.2.5.3), the NGB was liable in negligence for the death of a spectator for conducting a safety inspection that focused only on the potential risks posed to competitors and officials from the operation of the race track. As danger caused to the spectators by things leaving the track at high speed was reasonably foreseeable, the inspection should also have addressed the safety concerns of this group of users. Although only a County Court decision, this case demonstrates clearly that the duty to ensure that the premises are reasonably safe can fall on a number of defendants, not just the occupier.

8.4.3 Spectators v. participants

The opportunities for participants to cause injury to the spectators at a sporting event are somewhat limited. In most cases where injury can be said to have been factually caused by the participant, it will be the occupier or organiser who will actually be at fault for allowing the incident to have occurred (*Murray* v. *Harringay Arena*) (above, 8.2.5.4.1). A duty of care is undoubtedly owed by the participant to the spectators at the event; the only question is the precise content of that duty. The problems in this area of the law stem from *Wooldridge* v. *Sumner* [1963] 2 QB 43 and the obsession of some commentators with attempting to introduce a standard of reckless disregard into the law of negligence (see further, chapter 4.4.2.3). These discussions distract attention from the Court of Appeal's important analysis of how the determination of the defendant's breach of the duty of care requires the court to examine the case in the context of all of its relevant circumstances.

> ▶ *Wooldridge* v. *Sumner* [1963] 2 QB 43
>
> The claimant was injured when a rider temporarily lost control of his horse during a demonstration event at the Horse of the Year Show. The rider had taken a bend at speed, lost control and on entering the straight part of the track had collided with the claimant who had been standing at the edge of the arena taking official photographs of the event. As the horse approached, the claimant attempted to take evasive action and the collision occurred.
>
> The duty of care identified by the Court was that a competitor should use reasonable care and skill in performing the manoeuvres necessary for participation in the sporting event. In determining whether this duty had been breached, the court held that it was important to take

into consideration the nature of the event, that horses can be unpredictable and can be difficult to control and that the participant would be going all out to win the competition.

The Court also held that mistakes and errors of judgement can and do occur in the heat of competition and that when going all out to win an event, a participant will usually have little or no regard for the safety of the event's spectators. In this situation, the rider had only been doing what was expected of him and his loss of control was simply an inherent risk of competitive horse riding. Therefore, there was no breach of the duty owed by him to the claimant.

In going all out to win, it is possible that the participant may make errors of judgement or exhibit lapses of skill. As anyone who has ever played competitive sport is aware, it is impossible to get everything exactly right all of the time; this dynamic unpredictability is part of what makes sport the spectacle that it is. Such errors or lapses when made in the heat of competition are not negligent; they are simply an integral part of sport.

It was further added that participants are entitled to expect that the spectators will have some knowledge of the risks and dangers inherent in the sport that they are watching. Depending on the sport concerned, that might mean that in attempting to win an event, the competitor need have little or no regard for the safety of the spectator; the safety of the spectators is a concern of the occupier and/or organiser of the event, not the participants in it.

After *Caldwell* v. *Maguire and Fitzgerald* [2001] EWCA Civ 1054 (see further, chapter 4.4.1.2), it is now possible to propose a modernised version of the law that combines the imposition of the duty from *Wooldridge* with the negligence in all the circumstances approach that the judges in both of these cases preferred; that a competitor in a sporting event owes a duty to take all the care that is objectively reasonable in the prevailing circumstances of the contest to avoid the infliction of injury on those present as spectators. Perhaps the most important circumstance to be considered is that the competitor will be, or at least should be, concentrating on their performance, not the safety of the spectators. Taking all of this into account, it will only rarely be the case that a competitor will have acted with a sufficient degree of carelessness to be individually responsible for the injuries caused to a spectator.

8.4.4 Passersby v. organisers

Organisers of sporting events must ensure not only that those who are within the stadium are safe, but must also ensure that harm is not caused to their neighbours. This includes those who are passing by when an event is taking place. Where the injured person is off the organiser's premises, and cannot therefore use the Occupiers' Liability Acts, and the incident is a one-off, or is so infrequent that it cannot constitute a course of conduct necessary to fall under nuisance, then the claimant's only option will be an action in negligence.

▶ *Bolton* v. *Stone* **[1951] AC 850**

The claimant was struck on the head by a cricket ball that had been hit out of the local ground. The ball had been hit with considerable force and had travelled over a fence that was 2.1m high, situated 71m from the wicket, before hitting the claimant who was stood outside of her house about 91m from where the ball had been hit. The evidence suggested that there had not previously been a shot of this magnitude at this ground but that on perhaps six occasions over the previous 28 years, a ball had been hit on to the road in front of the claimant's house, but never as far as on this occasion. Nuisance could not be established as there was insufficient regularity of recurrence to establish a course of conduct, so discussion centred on whether the defendant had acted negligently in their organisation of cricket matches at this ground. The House of Lords held that the duty was to take care to prevent reasonably foreseeable harm from occurring, not all harm. As this incident was not reasonably foreseeable, only an improbable possibility, there was no breach of duty.

The House of Lords concluded that there was no negligent conduct on the basis that the duty owed by the cricket club, which was to prevent balls from being hit into the adjacent road but only in so far as there was any reasonably foreseeable risk of that happening, was not breached. Although it was foreseeable as a possibility that a ball might be hit out of the ground and that, as a result, it was foreseeable as a possibility that a ball might hit and injure someone outside of the ground, such an outcome was not sufficiently probable to establish liability in negligence. For that, there must be a reasonable chance of the ball being hit out of the ground and a reasonably foreseeable risk of the injury occurring to someone in the claimant's position. In this case, the probability of the ball being hit out of the ground was extremely low; when this was coupled with the probability of one of the balls that was struck out of the ground hitting a passerby on a little used path, the risk of injury was considered to be so low that it would not be contemplated by the reasonable person. Therefore, there was no need to guard against such an improbable outcome.

This can be contrasted with *Lamond v. Glasgow Corporation* (1968) SLT 291 where a pedestrian was hit on the head by a golf ball that had been hit from a course on the defendant's land. Although there was no evidence of any previous accident of this kind occurring, the fact that around 6,000 shots each year were hit over the fence behind which the claimant had been walking should have put the defendant on alert that it was reasonably foreseeable that at some point, someone would be injured by one of the shots.

8.5　Outdoor and adventure sports

In general, the normal rules relating to occupiers' liability, negligence and nuisance will apply to the organisers of outdoor and adventure sports in the same way as they would to those organising any other sport. There are, however, two situations where variations on the normal operation of the law occur. The first is in respect of activity centres providing instruction to children and the second is the modified duty of care owed to those who are exercising their right to roam over access land.

8.5.1　Activity Centres (Young Persons' Safety) Act 1995

Following the Lyme Bay canoeing tragedy (see further, chapter 6.5.3), the government reviewed the provision of adventure and outdoor activities to young people with a view to making them better regulated. Section 1 Activity Centres (Young Persons' Safety) Act 1995 creates a licensing regime that applies to all people who wish to provide facilities for adventure activities and s.2(1)(a) makes it an offence to provide instruction, leadership or facilities to those who are under the age of 18 unless a valid licence is held.

The aim of the legislation is to ensure that those providing adventure activities to young people are suitably qualified to lead or instruct the activity in question in an attempt to make provision safer for the participants. Where an adventure activities provider is in breach of this legislation, an action will still have to be brought either on the basis of negligent instruction or organisation, or a breach of the duty owed under the Occupiers' Liability Acts if compensation is to be secured.

8.5.2 Access land

There has been much debate over the extent and meaning of rights of access for recreational purposes to the wilder parts of the countryside. The 'right to roam' was until recently unknown in English law. The National Parks and Access to the Countryside Act 1949 created a framework of access agreements and orders allowing access for open-air recreation to national parkland. The Countryside and Rights of Way Act 2000 allows even greater rights to the public over access land, as defined in s.1 of the Act to include all registered common land, any land over 600m high and any other land designated as such under the Act.

These two provisions have enabled walkers, mountaineers and others engaged in outdoor and adventure sports to have much greater access to land throughout the country. Section 60 National Parks and Access to the Countryside Act 1949 and both s.2 and sch.2 Countryside and Rights of Way Act 2000 contain a number of restrictions on the right to roam. These restrictions are there to ensure that the right is exercised responsibly and does not cause damage to the land or to the plants and livestock that are farmed on it.

Section 1(4) OLA 1957 specifically excludes those on access land from being treated as visitors, meaning that the duty of care owed to those exercising their right to roam is the 'common duty of humanity' found in s.1(4) OLA 1984 (above, 8.2.6). The duty owed to those using access land has had a further gloss put on it by s.1A OLA 1984 to ensure that an undue burden is not placed on occupiers. In particular, s.1A(b) OLA 1984 provides that in determining the nature and extent of the duty owed by an occupier, regard must be had to the importance of maintaining the character of the countryside, including any features of historic, traditional or archaeological interest that are on it. Thus, occupiers must ensure that known dangers are brought to the attention of the users of access land but that the duty must be interpreted sympathetically in the context of the character of the land and its environment.

Hot topic . . .

COMPENSATION CULTURE V. PERSONAL RESPONSIBILITY

In recent years, the media have painted a picture of a litigation-obsessed society that is spiralling out of control. Their use of some of the more extreme and unusual cases that find their way to the courts to try to prove the existence of a compensation culture has caused concern to and a reaction from both Parliament and the judiciary. Although rarely referred to explicitly in court, s.1 Compensation Act 2006 requires judges, when determining liability, to take into consideration the social utility of the activity in question. The perceived need for this provision, which appears simply to restate an exercise that judges would engage in as an integral part of determining liability in the cases discussed in this chapter, was that certain activities were being seen as so high-risk in terms of litigation that nobody would organise them for fear of being sued.

Sport, leisure and recreational activities are without doubt 'desirable activities' within the meaning of s.1 Compensation

Act 2006. Their ability to promote health, fitness and social and physical skills, amongst many other positive attributes should ensure that they receive some protection from the Act. The provision does not enable an occupier or organiser of a sports event to act negligently with impunity. Instead it reinforces that a participant does not have an automatic right to complain about being injured by the inherent risks of participation in physically risky activities.

Society does not want to ban swimming simply because people have been catastrophically injured by diving into a lake having chosen to ignore a warning not to do so (*Tomlinson*), or without knowing whether it is safe to do so (*Rhind*), or into the shallow end of a swimming pool (*Ratcliffe*, *Evans*). What the law expects to see is that swimming activities are organised safely, that signage is adequate and that warnings are provided where necessary. Once an occupier's duties have been discharged, it is the participant's choice to decide whether to run the inherent and/or obvious risks involved with the activity.

This tension between the obligation to provide safe sport and leisure facilities and an injured person's responsibility for their own safety and risk-taking has been the focal point of many cases in recent years. Far from encouraging, or facilitating, the growth of a compensation culture, the courts are requiring sports participants to take greater responsibility for their own safety; a participant cannot voluntarily take part in a dangerous activity, such as tobogganing, and then complain when they lose control and are injured (*Roddie*, *Tysall*). Three cases in particular have highlighted the development of the jurisprudence of personal responsibility for risk-taking: *Tomlinson*, *Poppleton* and *Anderson* v. *Lyotier, Lyotier and Portejoie* [2008] EWHC 2790 (see further, chapter 5.2.2).

Tomlinson had specifically ignored a sign that prohibited swimming in a lake. The occupier did not need to explain what the particular danger was, in this case shallow water, nor did it need to explain what the risks associated with the danger were, in this case suffering a broken neck. It was an obvious risk of diving head-first in to water of unknown depth that it might be shallow and that serious injury might result. Therefore by ignoring the warning Tomlinson was responsible for his own safety when the water turned out to be too shallow to dive into.

Poppleton was trying to emulate a friend's gymnastic dismount from a climbing wall, despite being only a novice climber. Regardless of the obvious lack of prior training that he had received as this was one of the first times that he had used the climbing wall, sports participants cannot expect to perform the advanced skills of their chosen activity before they have mastered the basics. Copying someone else's move may be a good way of learning a skill, however, by attempting an obviously dangerous move for the first time without any training or instruction in how to do it, Poppleton was responsible for his own safety when he mistimed his dismount and landed head-first on the matting.

Anderson was aware that he lacked sufficient skill to ski off-piste on a steep slope that descended through trees. Although his instructor should also have been aware of this, a sports participant cannot assume automatically that this will be the case. A group member who does not want to disrupt the dynamics of the group, or who does not want to be seen to be making a fuss, is not a sufficient reason to transfer all responsibility to the instructor. Anderson knew that he lacked the skill and/or confidence to perform this dangerous activity without close supervision and was partly responsible for his own safety when he went ahead without drawing his instructor's attention to his own lack of competence.

In each case, the courts required the claimant to take responsibility for their own decisions, their own actions and their own level of ability. Where there was no justification for exposing the claimant to a risk of injury, as in *Gillmore*, then liability will be imposed on the activity organiser. However where the decision to act in the manner that caused injury to the claimant was wholly or partly their own, then the claimant will be expected to bear at least some of the responsibility for the outcome.

Far from encouraging the development of a compensation culture, the courts are reinforcing the need for personal autonomy over the decision making process. Requiring personal responsibility for those decisions and attempting to ensure that those providing socially desirable activities do not become so risk averse that they withdraw their services is of paramount importance. Sometimes, unfortunately, accidents do happen and sometimes they are the injured person's fault.

Summary

8.1 The duties owed by the occupiers of sports stadiums and the organisers of sports events were originally governed by the law of contract and the tort of negligence. These two branches of the law still have a role to play in the protection of people affected by the holding of a sports event, though many of these cases will now fall under the Occupiers' Liability Acts.

Summary cont'd

8.2 An occupier owes their visitors a duty to take reasonable care to ensure that their premises are reasonably safe for the purposes of the visit (OLA 1957 s.2(2)). Further, an occupier owes trespassers a duty of care to ensure that they do not suffer any harm from known dangers that the occupier has reasonable grounds to suspect that trespassers will come into contact with (OLA 1984 s.1(3)). Both of these duties can be discharged by providing warnings that there is a specific danger present on the premises or where the visitor/trespasser has voluntarily run the risk of harm being caused to them by the danger.

8.3 Private nuisance protects a landowner's right to enjoy the use of their property without unreasonable interference by others. This tort is most commonly used by people who live close by sports venues to control noise (*Kennaway* v. *Thompson*), and objects (*Miller* v. *Jackson*), emanating from them.

8.4 Where a claimant is injured at or in the proximity of a sports venue but they do not fall under the protection of the Occupiers' Liability Acts or private nuisance, then they will have to resort to an action in negligence. The versatility of this tort means that it can be used in a variety of unusual circumstances, such as *Bolton* v. *Stone* and *Wooldridge* v. *Sumner*.

8.5 Following *R* v. *Kite*, the Activity Centres (Young Persons' Safety) Act 1995 introduced a licensing regime for the providers of sporting and outdoor adventure activities to young people. The Countryside and Rights of Way Act 2000 defines more clearly the 'right to roam' and provides greater access to the wilder parts of the UK for sport and leisure purposes.

Further reading

Dugdale and Jones (eds), *Clerk and Lindsell on Torts* (19th edn, (3rd supplement), 2008, Sweet and Maxwell) chs 12 and 20

Steele, *Tort Law: text, cases and materials* (2007, Oxford University Press) chs 10 and 12

Bale, *Sport, Space and the City* (2001, The Blackburn Press)

Lewis and Taylor (eds), *Sport: Law and Practice* (2nd edn, 2008, Tottel) ch D5

Anderson, 'Countryside access and environmental protection: an American view of Britain's right to roam' (2007) 9(4) *Environmental Law Review* 241

James and James, 'Spectator safety and the liability of governing bodies' [2009] 4 *Sports Law Administration and Practice* 1

McArdle, 'The enduring legacy of reckless disregard' (2005) 34(4) *Common Law World Review* 316

Norris, 'Duty of care and personal responsibility: occupiers, owners, organisers and individuals' (2008) 3 *Journal of Personal Injury Law* 187

Wallinga, 'Effusa vel deiecta in Rome and Glasgow' (2002) 6(1) *Edinburgh Law Review* 117

Links to relevant websites can be found at www.palgrave.com/law/james

Chapter 9

Stadium disasters and spectator safety

Key words

▶ **Terraces** – stepped concrete or wooden standing areas at sports grounds.
▶ **Stands** – seated areas at sports grounds, also referred to as grandstands.

9.1 Background and context

During the late 1800s and early 1900s, as attending live sports events grew increasingly popular, dedicated venues were built throughout the country to host sporting fixtures of all kinds. Many of these were permanent stadiums and they or their successor buildings rank amongst some of the most iconic buildings in the country and in some cases the world. Others were of a more temporary nature with grandstands built specifically to watch an individual game or event. Regardless of whether the stadium was of a temporary or permanent nature, the disasters that subsequently unfolded can generally be blamed on one of two reasons: the negligent construction of the building used to watch the event or mismanagement of the crowd once it was on the premises.

9.1.1 Cheltenham Races, 1866 and Ewood Park, Blackburn, 1894

In *Francis* v. *Cockrell* (1870) LR 5 QB 501, the organisers of the 1866 Cheltenham Races were held liable to an injured spectator for being in breach of contract for failing to provide a safe place from which to watch the event following the collapse of a temporary grandstand that had been negligently constructed by an independent contractor. Thirty years later in *Brown* v. *Lewis* (1896) 12 TLR 455, the directors of Blackburn Rovers Football Club were held personally liable in negligence for the injuries caused to the claimant by the collapse of another temporary grandstand. The directors' breach of duty was their failure to engage a competent independent contractor to carry out work on the grandstand (see further, chapter 8.1.1).

Despite the potential for serious injury or death being caused to countless thousands of sports spectators around the country, these two incidents appear to have been treated as no more than unfortunate accidents. Perhaps this was because the numbers involved were comparatively low and their injuries comparatively minor. Whatever the reason for the complacency there was no inquiry into how or why these grandstands had collapsed, there were no discussions of applicable safety standards that should have been adhered to and there was no mention of the need for a regulatory or licensing regime to be created.

9.1.2 Ibrox Park, Glasgow, 1902

Eight years later at Ibrox Park, Glasgow the UK's first major sporting disaster provided the ideal opportunity for Parliament and the NGBs to investigate stadium safety and create a new set of standards for sports venues. They failed to take it, setting the scene for almost a century of ineffective responses to the needs of spectators.

▶ **Ibrox Park, 5 April 1902**

The first Ibrox disaster occurred during the first fully professional international football match between Scotland and England. A section of the newly erected wooden terracing collapsed, leaving a gaping hole through which hundreds of spectators fell around 15 metres to the ground below. 25 people were killed and over 500 injured as a result of the poor construction of this part of the stadium. Despite the fatalities and the large number of injuries caused by this disaster, no public inquiry into its causes was held. The explanation for this is that the only statutory authority for ordering such an investigation at the time was the Fatal Accidents Inquiry (Scotland) Act 1895 which applied only to deaths caused during the course of the deceased's employment. As none of those who died at Ibrox were working at the stadium there were no grounds for ordering a public inquiry into the disaster.

Unusually however the contractor responsible for the terrace's construction was prosecuted for culpable homicide (a Scottish equivalent of the English offence of manslaughter) on the basis that he had substituted an inferior quality of wood that was weaker than the one specifically contracted for (*R* v. *McDougall*, (unreported) High Court of Justiciary (Glasgow), 28 June 1902). McDougall was eventually acquitted on the basis of a lack of evidence, leaving yet another sporting disaster being registered as an unfortunate accident rather than resulting in a greater degree of safety being provided to those who had paid to watch the event.

Although McDougall was prosecuted for having used substandard materials for the construction of the terracing, two other factors that could have been investigated by an appropriately constituted public inquiry may have contributed to the stadium's collapse. The first was the design of the terrace's structural framework which appears not to have been adequately supported, causing it to become unstable. The second, and one which became a recurrent theme of subsequent official inquiries into stadium disasters, was that there was no accurate measure for calculating the maximum capacity of either the stadium as a whole or its individual terraces. Capacities, it appears, were calculated by no more scientific a basis than how many people could be fitted on to the terrace. Thus the sheer weight of people on Ibrox's western terracing could have had a significant impact on both the cause and the scale of the disaster.

These early disasters were caused in the main part by the inadequate and/or negligent construction of the stadiums in which the sporting event was taking place. However at both Ewood Park and Ibrox Park a contributing factor appears to have been the mismanagement of the crowd that allowed too many people on to a structure that was not strong enough to support the supporters' combined weight. The lack of any inquiry into the causes of these incidents contributed directly to the other major incidents that occurred throughout the twentieth century.

9.2 Empire Stadium, Wembley and The Shortt Report, 1923–24

Although there had been disorder and injuries caused at a number of sporting events after the first Ibrox disaster, the next major incident occurred at the newly constructed Empire Stadium, or Wembley Stadium as it is now known, during the 1923 FA Cup Final. This incident and the genuinely disastrous events that happened at Burden Park, Bolton, in 1946 (below, 9.3) are of particular importance because they were the first of the sporting disasters to be followed by governmental inquiries. The main distinction between these two incidents and those that had gone before is that their sole cause was the mismanagement of the event itself rather than the negligent construction of either of the stadiums.

9.2.1 Empire Stadium, Wembley, 1923

Often referred to as the 'White Horse Final' because a policeman on a white horse has gone down in popular history as the man who single-handedly controlled the fans on the pitch and averted a major disaster, the events at Wembley provided the ideal opportunity for the government to develop an effective licensing regime for sports grounds.

▶ **Empire Stadium, 28 April 1923**

The Empire Stadium at Wembley was completed only days before the 1923 FA Cup Final took place between Bolton Wanderers and West Ham United. The FA had decided that the vast majority of spectators would be admitted to the ground on payment of an admission fee at the turnstiles. Unfortunately the public interest in attending the inaugural game at the new stadium was grossly underestimated and the authorities were totally unprepared for the volume of people who turned up. The stadium had an official capacity of 126,000, though this had not been calculated scientifically despite the events at Ibrox in 1902. Estimates of how many people actually gained entry to the Final reach as high as 300,000.

The ground was full over an hour before kick-off, however people continued to arrive in ever-greater numbers expecting to be able to pay at the turnstiles. To alleviate the pressure on those who were being crushed immediately outside of the ground, large numbers of spectators were admitted onto terraces that were already full. As further crushes developed inside the now overcrowded stadium, spectators were able to escape from the terraces on to the pitch and the track surrounding it. Fortunately there were no perimeter fences in place. Around 900 spectators suffered minor injuries with 22 being treated in hospital.

Despite the scale of the incident and the obvious mismanagement of the crowd at the new stadium the Home Secretary, William Bridgeman did not order a full public inquiry as he considered that the police had dealt with the situation effectively and appropriately. He did however constitute a Committee of Enquiry with a remit to examine 'abnormally large crowds at special occasions.' It was not the Committee's aim to establish fault for what happened at Wembley but to examine how a repeat of what happened there could be avoided.

9.2.2 The Shortt Report, 'Report of the Department Committee on Crowds'

The Committee of Enquiry made a series of recommendations that it felt would make events of this magnitude much safer in the future. These included creating self-contained terraces with individually and scientifically calculated maximum capacities. Further, each of these terraces should be fed by specific and more efficient turnstiles that channelled spectators through dedicated entrances directly on to the standing areas.

It also recommended that more stringent fire precautions should be installed at all stadiums as wood continued to be a major component of these buildings. From a management perspective, the Committee recommended that the police should be in overall control of law and order and that a named officer should be in command of all crowd safety and crowd control measures on the day. Further, trained stewards who had stadium-specific knowledge should be in place to assist with the management of large crowds, particularly where the spectators were at an unfamiliar venue. It was also recommended that in future entrance to popular events such as the FA Cup Final should be by advanced purchase tickets only.

With hindsight each of these recommendations seems to be grounded very much in common sense and would have been an efficient, cheap and effective means of controlling large crowds safely. The Committee considered it to be unnecessary for either national or local government to administer a formal framework of regulations to ensure safety at sports venues because the governing bodies of sport were capable of establishing a system that would be effective in their own sport. This conclusion was reached despite the FA's refusal to attend the Committee's hearings or to engage with the discussions that followed the publication of its proposals. Instead somewhat naively the Committee considered that the threat of the imposition of a licensing scheme, should the governing bodies fail to take safety issues seriously, would be sufficient.

The Shortt Report was never debated in Parliament and only one of its proposals was ever implemented: from 1924, tickets to all FA Cup Finals must be bought in advance. It was clear from its findings that poor organisation and mismanagement of the event had caused the overcrowding and injuries at the Cup Final. Instead of learning from the events at Wembley and imposing basic safety standards that could have prevented each of the following disasters, the lasting image is of a large but well behaved crowd being controlled by single policeman on a white horse.

9.3　Burnden Park, Bolton and the Moelwyn Hughes Report, 1946

The disaster that occurred at Burnden Park provided Parliament with a further opportunity to review the safety and management procedures at major sports events; its failure to do so led directly to the disasters of the 1970s and 1980s.

9.3.1　Burnden Park, Bolton, 1946

The Burnden Park disaster unfolded in circumstances bearing an eerie similarity both to those that led to the overcrowding at Wembley in 1923 and those that would occur 43 years later at Hillsborough.

▶ **Burnden Park, 9 March 1946**

Bolton Wanderers were playing at home to Stoke City in an FA Cup quarter-final tie. In much the same way as the police and football authorities had failed to gauge the popular interest in the 1923 FA Cup Final, so they failed to take into account a number of factors that helped to swell the numbers hoping to get in to see the game at Burnden Park. This was a tie involving two of the biggest clubs in the country at the time in the first FA Cup competition after the end of the Second World War; the weather was unseasonably good and a large number of spectators seem to have turned up in the hope of watching one of the most popular British footballers of all time, Stanley Matthews. Furthermore as this was only a quarter-final tie an entrance fee could be paid at the turnstiles, encouraging spontaneous attendance amongst a number of people who might not otherwise have turned up.

It is estimated that around 85,000 people gained entry to a ground that had a previous highest recorded attendance of fewer than 70,000 spectators. Predictions of the likely crowd size were based on the fact that Burden Park had not hosted a crowd in excess of 45,000 during the preceding season and so just as in 1923 the police and stadium operators were totally unprepared for the huge crowds that turned up. The stadium was closed around 20 minutes before kick-off but many thousands gained entry to the terraces by climbing over walls, breaking through fences and coming in through an open exit gate.

As the crowd surged forward when the teams took to the field, two of the crush barriers on one of the terraces collapsed under the sheer weight of numbers pushing against it, causing a pile up of bodies. In the resulting crush 33 people died and over 400 were injured. Within a few weeks an inquiry chaired by Moelwyn Hughes J had been commissioned by the Home Office.

9.3.2 The Moelwyn Hughes Report, 'Enquiry into the Disaster at Bolton Wanderers' Football Ground on the 9th March 1946'

The Moelwyn Hughes Report began by condemning the Shortt Report for being anaemic and failing to address the needs of football spectators by allowing the football authorities to regulate themselves on issues of safety. It then went on to explain that neither Bolton Wanderers FC nor the police were at fault for the disaster because they had taken proper steps to control the crowd on the day.

The Report then made several specific criticisms of the general framework of safety within which football clubs operated. In particular it was critical of there being no scientific calculation of a ground's maximum capacity. This was compounded by there being no means available to those who were in charge of crowd safety for establishing precisely how many spectators were inside the ground. Thus there were no means of knowing how many spectators could be accommodated safely inside the stadium nor when this number had been reached. Further, there was no effective means of closing the turnstiles when the stadium appeared to be full, enabling many people to climb over them when informed that the stadium's capacity had been reached.

The Moelwyn Hughes Report's recommendations went far beyond those of the Shortt Report and refused to accept that the football authorities were capable of regulating themselves where spectator safety was concerned. The central coordination of crowd safety, the fixing of capacities for each specific part of a ground and the counting of spectators into each of those parts were again recommended as essential elements of ensuring that too many people were not herded into too small a section of the stadium. The Report specifically recommended that a licensing regime operated by local councils should be created by statute. If a stadium did not meet the standards and procedures required to make spectators safe then a licence would not be granted and football matches could no longer be played at that ground.

Once again none of the proposals were acted on by the government of the day. The licensing regime was considered to have the potential to place too great a financial and administrative burden on local authorities whilst the clubs and governing bodies of football were concerned that the cost of making their grounds as safe as the proposals required were prohibitively high. Thus once again the government opted for football in particular and sport in general to operate under an ill-defined system of self-regulation, despite the FA's failure to take a lead on safety issues post-1923.

9.4   Creating the conditions for further disasters

In the Parliamentary debates that followed the 1923 FA Cup Final, Oswald Mosley MP accused those who had attempted to gain entry to the stadium after the gates had been closed of acting like hooligans. Although not supported by other Members of the House of Commons and reprimanded by the Speaker for his comments, it highlights that from the earliest debates on stadium disasters there has always been a small but vociferous group that considers a prime cause of the deaths and injuries to have been the spectators themselves. In deciding that the licensing regime proposed in the Moelwyn Hughes Report should not be implemented, the government pointed out that no legislation could prevent accidents that were caused by spectators who had entered the stadium illegally. Although this statement is true where deliberate vandalism is concerned, it fails to take into account that the purpose of the licensing regime was to ensure that stadiums were constructed and managed in a way that ensured that it was easier to control and regulate the large numbers of people who were trying to gain entry to them. The anticipated result of such a regulatory scheme would have been that fewer spectators would attempt, or be able to enter stadiums illegally in the manner that had been seen at both Wembley and Burnden Park.

Throughout the 1960s a growing concern with and focus on crowd disorder hid the fact that many stadiums had become dilapidated and unsafe, exacerbating the problems that had already been identified by the disasters of 1902 and 1946 and the near miss in 1923. Stadiums and those attending the games at them were now viewed through a 'hooligan lens'. The overriding concern was no longer about making spectators safe but about controlling the anti-social behaviour of the hooligan minority. This change of focus coupled with the failure to develop an effective safety regime led to a situation where all of the previously identified problems were still in existence but policing tactics and stadium design, for example the introduction of perimeter fencing, were aimed at preventing rival fans from coming into contact with each other or getting on to the pitch.

Three further government reports on football were commissioned during the 1960s: the Chester Report of 1966 examined the administration of football and the means by which the game could be developed for the public good and the Harrington and Lang Reports of 1968 and 1969 respectively focused on the issue of crowd disorder (see further, chapter 10). All three reports made recommendations about the need to ensure that spectator facilities were both adequate and safe, though crowd safety was not their primary focus. The Harrington Report also noted that improved facilities at stadiums may make it easier for the police and clubs to control crowd disorder, however they also acknowledged that the costs involved in stadium development meant that it was unlikely that clubs would voluntarily improve their own safety arrangements.

Conflating the issues of spectator safety and crowd disorder in this way ensured that the focus of the discussions in this area shifted and became confused. On the one hand, much greater importance was placed on the need to combat the growing threat to public order posed by crowd disorder than on the need to make what were becoming increasingly outdated and dangerous stadiums safe. On the other, spectator safety and crowd disorder were seen as being inextricably linked; if crowd disorder could be eliminated, spectators would once again be safe almost regardless of the state of the premises in which they were watching the game. This change in focus ensured that the circumstances became ripe for another major disaster at a football stadium.

9.5 Ibrox Park, Glasgow and the Wheatley Report, 1971

Whilst the focus of the government, police and football authorities turned to football hooliganism, football stadiums continued to be mismanaged and increasingly unsafe places to visit. The second Ibrox disaster finally resulted in legislative intervention that created the first licensing framework for sports grounds.

9.5.1 Ibrox Park, Glasgow, 1971

The precise cause of the second Ibrox disaster is unclear, however a combination of poor stadium design and mismanagement of the crowd undoubtedly contributed to the scale of the tragedy.

> ▶ **Ibrox Park, 2 January 1971**
>
> In the 89th minute of a Glasgow derby between Rangers and Celtic football clubs, Celtic scored to take a one-nil lead. A minute later, with almost the last kick of the game, Rangers equalised. As the Rangers fans on Stairway 13 surged forward, one or more people appear to have lost their balance and fallen. With no crush barriers to stop the flow of people down the stairs, those who had fallen were not only crushed but caused others to fall and be crushed themselves. 66 people were killed and 145 were injured on a stairway that had been the cause of three similar incidents over the previous ten years, including having caused two deaths in almost identical circumstances in 1961.
>
> Many reports of the disaster suggest that large numbers of Rangers fans had started to leave the stadium after Celtic had taken a late lead in the game. They go on to say that when Rangers equalised, these fans attempted to return to the terraces to celebrate and that their pushing against the flow of fans trying to leave the stadium caused someone to fall and the subsequent disaster to occur. The Wheatley Report, the official inquiry into the disaster, denies that this can have occurred as the bodies of those killed and injured were all facing in the same direction: towards the pitch. Thus it appears that it was the unrestricted surge of spectators down the stairway towards the pitch that caused someone to fall, not people pushing against one another. Once again stadium design had played a key part in the events.
>
> Stairway 13 stretched from the bottom of the terrace at pitch-side to the top of the terrace at the back of the stadium. It formed an unbroken series of stairs for its entire length, except for three small landings the width of about five stairs. Although there were handrails dividing the stairway into seven lanes, there were neither crush barriers nor changes in the direction of the lanes that could break up the flow of people. This meant that once the surge began, there was nothing to slow it down or stop it until the people at the front reached the bottom of the stairway or somebody fell. As with previous disasters, the lack of any means of calculating the capacity of a terrace and the lack of effective monitoring of the exact numbers of people in any area of the stadium meant that too many people were trying to use a badly designed stairway at the same time.

9.5.2 The Wheatley Report, 'Report on Crowd Safety at Sports Grounds'

The aim of the Wheatley Report was not to establish blame for the disaster but to investigate current standards of crowd safety. The Report did note that lessons had not been learned from the previous three incidents on Stairway 13 and that there was no clear or adequate division of responsibility for crowd safety between the club and the police. This in turn led to a situation where crowd safety fell between the spheres of responsibility of the bodies best placed to ensure that the stadium was in fact safe for the spectators. In *Dougan* v. *Rangers Football Club Ltd* 1974 SLT (Sh Ct) 34, Rangers were held liable in negligence for the death of one of the spectators with the club's failure to ensure that the stadium was reasonably safe being central to the claim.

The Wheatley Report not only made a series of recommendations, it pre-empted the complaints that would be made against them and sought to justify why its proposals should become law. The Report's main proposal was that all sports grounds, and in particular all major football grounds, should be subject to a licensing system. The justification for this was that if a club was charging an admission fee from the spectators then it owed them a duty of care to ensure that they were reasonably safe. It was therefore necessary to impose certain standards on these stadiums and to ensure that these were observed as self-regulation had clearly failed.

The proposed licensing system was not a new idea; it was first mooted in the Shortt Report in 1924. Furthermore the identification of a duty of care being owed by the stadium owners or occupiers to their spectators is simply a restatement of the duty of care found in s.2(1) Occupiers' Liability Act (Scotland) 1960 (the equivalent Scottish duty to that found in s.2(2) Occupiers' Liability Act 1957 (see further, chapter 8.2.5). The novelty in the proposal was that criminal liability should follow from a breach of the safety regime proposed to ensure that these minimum standards were actually achieved.

9.5.3   The Safety at Sports Grounds Act 1975

The Safety at Sports Grounds Act 1975 (SSGA 1975) enacted the proposed licensing system. Further guidance on how to design and build a safe stadium was provided by the *Guide to Safety at Sports Grounds*, more usually referred to as the Green Guide. Section 1(1) enabled the Home Secretary to designate any sports stadium that held more than 10,000 spectators as requiring a safety certificate before events could be held there. During the intervening years, this figure has been reduced to 5,000 spectators for football grounds but remains at 10,000 for all others sports (Safety of Sports Grounds (Accommodation of Spectators) Order 1996/499). The safety certificate is to be issued by the local authority in which the ground is located (s.1(3)) and by s.2(1) can contain any terms and conditions that the authority considers to be necessary or expedient to secure the reasonable safety of the spectators.

The SSGA 1975 was only to apply to 'sports stadia' not 'sports grounds'. Under s.17(1) of the Act, a sports ground was any place where sports or other competitive activities took place in the open air and where accommodation was provided for spectators that consisted of artificial structures or natural structures that had been artificially modified for the purpose. A sports stadium was a sports ground where the accommodation provided for spectators wholly or substantially surrounded the area used for the activities taking place on it. Thus the Act was originally aimed at places where major team sports events were played, not for example horse racing courses, motor sports tracks or sports grounds used by lower league teams.

In addition to this requirement, under s.10 the local authority can issue a prohibition notice preventing any event from taking place at any sports ground, not just those that are designated under the Act, where it considers that the stadium as a whole or a particular part of it poses a serious risk of harm to spectators. The failure to secure a safety certificate and breach of the terms of either a safety certificate or a prohibition notice are offences under s.12.

From 1 January 1977 the Act applied to the major English and Welsh football grounds, Wembley Stadium and the international rugby stadiums at Twickenham, Murrayfield and in Cardiff. Since then, by means of what have become annual updates to the legislation, most professional sports grounds have now been added to the list. This includes all professional football, rugby and cricket grounds and the larger grounds used in most other major sports. However the licensing regime initially created by the SSGA 1975 did not promote the culture of safety that was its aim. Firstly the inspections carried out by the local authorities were not as thorough as had been originally intended. Secondly because of concerns about the cost to clubs of meeting any conditions imposed on their grounds the Act did not apply to lower division football grounds for another eight years. This simple concession led directly to the disaster at Bradford City's ground, Valley Parade.

9.6 Valley Parade, Bradford and The Popplewell Reports, 1985–86

The end of the 1984–1985 football season saw three very different disasters unfold. At Valley Parade, Bradford City's home ground, a fire broke out in the wooden main stand leading to 56 deaths and many hundreds of injuries. On the same day at Birmingham City's stadium, St Andrew's, a fan was crushed to death when a wall collapsed on him during widespread violent disorder involving City supporters and fans of their opponents, Leeds United. Two weeks later a riot at the European Cup Final between Liverpool and Juventus at the Heysel Stadium, Brussels resulted in 39 deaths and hundreds of people being injured.

The combined reactions to these three tragedies could not have been more confused. Where the fire at Valley Parade was a classic case of a disaster based on stadium mismanagement and a failure to recognise the need to secure spectator safety, the fatalities in Birmingham and at Heysel were caused by crowd disorder descending into full-blown riots. The disaster at Heysel had the additional complicating factor of occurring in a stadium completely unfit for the level of game being played at it. Under normal circumstances, three separate inquires would have been appropriate because of the very different underlying causes of the deaths at each of these venues. Instead a single Committee of Enquiry was convened under the chairmanship of Popplewell J with a remit to investigate issues of both crowd safety and crowd control. Although both safety and control were relevant at all three of these disasters, the focus of much of what followed, particularly of the government of the time, was on how to eradicate football hooliganism.

In an attempt to unpick the two lines of investigation that were pursued by the Committee, which although closely linked are separate and distinct problems for stadium operators, only the issues related to spectator safety will be examined here; those relating to spectator disorder, including analyses of the disasters at St Andrew's and Heysel, are examined in Chapter 10.3. In this way it is possible to focus on the important conclusions drawn by the Popplewell Report on stadium safety that have, to a certain extent, been lost in the panic to promote the anti-hooligan agenda that still prevails.

9.6.1 Valley Parade, Bradford, 1985

The Bradford fire was caused by an unfortunate coincidence of events. The failure to acknowledge the importance of spectator safety in an old wooden stadium was a key factor in this avoidable tragedy.

▶ **Valley Parade, 11 May 1985**

During the last game of the 1984–85 football season a fire broke out underneath the main stand at Valley Parade. The direct cause of the fire was the ignition by a discarded match or cigarette of around 20 years' worth of rubbish that had accumulated in a void under the largely wooden stand. The shape of the structure caused the fire to intensify rapidly and to increase temperatures to around 1000°C. The entire stand was completely ablaze within five minutes of the first sighting of flames appearing under the stand, killing 56 people and injuring hundreds more. Old newspapers dating back to 1968 were found in the debris of the disaster demonstrating quite clearly the club's failure to keep its stadium safe to the extent that spectators were paying a premium entrance fee to sit on top of what was known to be a fire hazard. The scale of the disaster was exacerbated by the club locking most of the exit gates during the course of the game so that many people who might otherwise have survived were trapped at the back of the stand and unable to escape.

Bradford City had been made aware of the existence of this fire risk on at least two previous occasions. In 1980 a Principal Inspector of the Health and Safety Executive (HSE) had visited the ground to investigate a complaint that one of the concrete terraces had become unsafe. In the course of his inspection, he noticed that there was a build up of rubbish in the void under the main stand and that this constituted a fire risk. This was reported to the club in a letter outlining issues to which further consideration should be given to improve health and safety.

In 1984 a chartered engineer from the Engineering Department of the West Yorkshire Metropolitan County Council (WYMCC), who was also a member of the Council's Safety Team that was responsible for conducting licensing inspections for sports grounds designated under the SSGA 1975, noticed and reported the same risk of fire to the club whilst inspecting the condition of the main stand's roof. He also noted that those using the main stand should be able to exit it in the case of an emergency in two and a half minutes, a speed that he did not at that time consider to be possible. His report to the club pointed out that these were health and safety considerations that would need to be addressed should Valley Parade ever require to be designated under the SSGA 1975.

Although both of these inspections drew attention to the precise risk that eventuated, their main aim was to examine other issues in other parts of the ground. In neither of the reports to the club was the risk of fire prioritised nor was the club required to do anything more than 'consider' how this could be addressed. Despite the clear concerns of the inspectors, the lack of forcefulness in the tone of the two reports led to the risk of fire in the main stand never being addressed by the club.

In *Fletcher and others* v. *Bradford City Association Football Club (1983) Ltd, Health and Safety Executive and West Yorkshire Metropolitan County Council,* (unreported) High Court (QBD) (Bradford), 23 February 1987, compensation for injuries caused to spectators and police who were injured in the main stand and for dependency by relatives of those who had died in the fire was sought. Bradford City was found to be in breach of the common duty of care owed under s.2(2) Occupiers' Liability Act 1957 (see further, 8.2.5) because it had failed to provide premises that were reasonably safe for watching football matches. This was specifically evidenced by its failure to address the clear risk of fire that had been drawn to its attention by the two inspections, its lack of any evacuation plan and because the exit gates at the back of the stand were both locked and unmanned.

WYMCC was found liable in negligence for its failure to investigate a known fire risk more fully. Following the inspection by one of its officers in 1984, WYMCC should have utilised its powers under one of two Acts. Firstly for the purposes of the Fire Precautions Act 1971, WYMCC was identified as the relevant Fire Authority. Under this Act WYMCC had the power to investigate premises to ensure that people using them were adequately protected from the risk of fire. Under s.10 the Council had the power to apply to the Magistrates' Court for an order to close or restrict the use of the ground where it was satisfied that the risk of fire was so serious that it could no longer continue to be used in its current state. Further, under the emergency procedure contained in s.10 SSGA 1975, WYMCC could apply to the Magistrates' Court for a prohibition notice to prevent the use of Valley Parade if it was considered that the risk to the safety of the spectators was too great; as already noted above, this provision applies to all sports grounds whether or not they are designated. The court held that once a copy of the WYMCC's engineer's report had been forwarded to the Chief Fire Officer in 1984, no reasonable Fire Officer could have failed to realise the gravity of the risk posed by the rubbish that had accumulated in the void under the main stand.

The HSE were cleared of having acted negligently by failing to require the club to take immediate steps to eliminate the risk of fire. Although the initial report in 1980 had identified the risk posed by the build up of rubbish in the void under the main stand and subsequent reports had failed to follow up on whether the club had taken any remedial action, this was considered to be only an error of judgement on the part of the Inspector. The prioritising of other safety issues above the fire risk was not so careless as to be a failure to utilise the HSE's powers under the Health and Safety at Work Act 1974. Thus liability was apportioned between the first and third defendants so that the club was two-thirds responsible and WYMCC one-third.

The indirect causes were more varied and included the club and police viewing the crowd and its behaviour through a hooligan lens and the ongoing governmental failure to take spectator safety seriously. By focusing on the potential for crowd disorder, Bradford City had exacerbated the risk of harm from fire by removing the fire extinguishers from the stand because they were concerned that they would be used as missiles by hooligans. Furthermore most of the exit gates at the back of the grandstand, where many of the bodies were found piled up and trying to escape, were locked shortly after the game began to ensure entry to the stadium was easier to control. The justification for this decision was that if the gates were left unlocked then people would either try to get into the stadium for free or would undermine the club's segregation policies; no thought was given to the possibility that the spectators may need to escape from a dangerous situation. Fortunately the club had not installed perimeter fencing as many other clubs had, otherwise the death toll could have been considerably higher.

The failure of any government from 1924 onwards to enforce an effective safety regime on sports grounds compounded the problems at Valley Parade. The Shortt Report had recommended that more stringent fire safety regulations should be applied to sports grounds in 1924 but the government had preferred to rely on the governing bodies of sport regulating their own members' safety. Following the second Ibrox disaster the government decided that the SSGA 1975 would not apply to Third and Fourth Division clubs because of the cost of implementation and monitoring. Thus if the recommendations of a 60 year-old report had been implemented or the 1975 Act taken seriously and applied to all sports grounds then this disaster could not have happened as Valley Parade would have been closed for failing to meet the relevant safety criteria.

9.6.2   The Popplewell Reports

Popplewell J authored two reports on the disasters that took place in 1985. The Interim Report, which focused on the events at Bradford and Birmingham, was published in July 1985. It ensured that at least some recommendations could be made prior to start of 1985–86 football season that August. The Final Report, published in January 1986 contained an analysis of the events at Heysel and further consideration of a number of the issues that had been raised in the Interim Report.

9.6.2.1 The Popplewell Interim Report, 'Committee of Enquiry into Crowd Safety and Control at Sports Grounds'

Popplewell made 25 recommendations and a further eight provisional recommendations that were to be considered further in the Final Report. In respect of safety, the main recommendations were that police and stewards should be trained in evacuation procedures and that stewards should also receive fire-fighting training, that new permanent stands should not be made of combustible materials and that all sports grounds should have adequate and suitable exits including exits in perimeter fencing. Several additional, though weakly phrased proposals suggested that there should be a greater degree of consultation between clubs and the emergency services in devising major incident plans, that a local registration system be established to monitor sports grounds and that the *Green Guide* should be followed more explicitly by stadium owners. These proposals were eventually developed into the criteria that are applied by the Football Licensing Authority when determining whether or not to grant a licence to a football stadium (below, 9.6.2.4).

Immediate legislative action was taken on one of the report's provisional recommendations: from 9 August 1985 the football grounds of all clubs in the top four English divisions and the Scottish Premier League and all major rugby league grounds became designated sports grounds that required a safety certificate in order to hold a sports event (Safety of Sports Grounds (Association Football Grounds) (Designation) Order 1985/1063 and Safety of Sports Grounds (Rugby Football Grounds) (Designation) Order 1985/1064).

9.6.2.2 The Popplewell Final Report, 'Committee of Enquiry into Crowd Safety and Control at Sports Grounds'

After further consideration of the efficacy of the regulatory framework for spectator safety, how best to control disorderly crowds and a specific analysis of the Heysel disaster, Popplewell J's Final Report contained 15 specific recommendations to the government. Of these, ten referred to issues concerning spectator safety (the remaining five concerned issues of crowd control, see further chapter 10.3). The Report makes it clear from the outset that responsibility for the safety of the spectators lies with the club whilst responsibility for law and order is the primary concern of the police.

The most important of these recommendations were implemented in primary and secondary legislation that was produced over the 18 months following the publication of the Final Report. Firstly having already designated all English Third and Fourth Division football grounds and all First and Second Division Rugby League grounds (9.6.2.1), the Safety of Sports Grounds (Designation) Order 1986/1296 added all major rugby union, cricket and athletics grounds to the licensing regime governed by the SSGA 1975. The age and state of repair of most stadiums in all parts of the UK was a clear indication that any subsequent disaster could occur at any sports stadium, not just one that hosted football matches.

9.6.2.3 The Fire Safety and Safety of Places of Sport Act 1987

The Fire Safety and Safety of Places of Sport Act 1987 enacted the most important of the remaining recommendations on spectator safety from the Final Report. The distinction between sports stadiums and sports grounds was abolished by amending s.17 SSGA 1975, ensuring that any premises where sport took place outdoors and accommodation was provided for 10,000 or more spectators would now be covered by the Act. The simple justification for this amendment was that a sports ground that was only partially surrounded by dangerous spectator accommodation was just as likely to cause death and/or serious injury as a dangerous sports stadium, as originally defined in the SSGA 1975.

The lack of any adequate safety regime and the failure of sports governing bodies to self-regulate effectively on matters of safety had led to many smaller sports grounds providing particularly dangerous accommodation to their spectators. Parts II and III of the Fire Safety and Safety of Places of Sport Act 1987 provided that all stands that were wholly or partly covered by a roof, with a capacity of 500 spectators or greater and which were located in sports grounds that were not designated under the SSGA 1975 should be individually designated. Thus the safety framework originally anticipated by the Wheatley Report was finally brought a step closer to reality.

Part IV of the Fire Safety and Safety of Places of Sport Act 1987 created a licensing framework for indoor sports premises. Although these provisions have subsequently been replaced by the Licensing Act 2003 in England and Wales, the 1987 Act ensured that local councils would now be in control of licensing all sports premises, regardless of size and whether the sporting event was taking place indoors or outdoors. By placing responsibility for licensing on one body in this way, it was anticipated that councils would be able to take an overview of the most effective way of licensing all sports premises and develop a high degree of expertise in matters of safety at sports events.

9.6.2.4 Football Spectators Act 1989

The Final Report recommended improvements be made to the procedures by which licences were issued to designated sports grounds and that annual inspections be carried out as an integral part of the licensing procedure. Although the recommendation applied to all sports grounds, a new licensing procedure was only established for designated football grounds. The Football Licensing Authority (FLA) was established by s.8 and Sch.2 Football Spectators Act 1989 (FSA 1989) with its powers further defined in s.13.

The primary functions of the FLA are to implement the government's policies on the safety management of spectators at football grounds and to review whether local authorities are discharging their duties to inspect football grounds under the SSGA 1975. The FLA also conducts annual inspections of all designated football stadiums to ensure that the grounds continue to provide safe accommodation to all users and that there are adequate and effective evacuation procedures and major incident plans in place. A failure to comply with the conditions imposed by the FLA can result in a ground's license to host football matches being withheld or withdrawn; hosting a football game at a designated football ground without a valid licence is an offence under s.9 FSA. By requiring best practice as a condition of the licence, it is to be hoped that the lack of a coordinated response that was seen at Hillsborough cannot be repeated.

On top of its regulatory functions, the FLA also provides advice and guidance materials to football clubs on spectator safety and how to implement best practice. Its only drawback is that its remit does not extend beyond designated football stadiums to all designated sports grounds.

9.6.2.5 The impact of the Popplewell Reports

The Popplewell Reports made it their conscious aim to try to create a more effective and more uniform approach to spectator safety at all sports grounds. The creation of the FLA has gone a long way to achieving that aim in respect of football stadiums. Having noted that many operators of sports grounds that were not designated did not take the recommendations of the Green Guide sufficiently seriously, it is perhaps strange that the Final Report recommended that its provisions should remain only a voluntary code without any further explanation. However, that the government of the time was prepared to take swift and, in the context of previous failures to act, dramatic action following the publication of the Final Report is testament to the forcefulness of the main recommendations made by Popplewell J and his team. Unfortunately, during the passage of the FSA 1989 through Parliament and therefore before the creation of the FLA, events once again overtook the legislative action that was being taken.

9.7   Hillsborough Stadium, Sheffield and The Taylor Reports, 1989–90

The worst British sporting disaster to date occurred when 96 people were crushed to death on the terraces at Hillsborough during an FA Cup semi-final between Liverpool and Nottingham Forrest. The striking similarities with the disaster at Burnden Park in 1946, reflected in the opening comments of Taylor LJ at para.19 of *The Hillsborough Stadium Disaster (Final Report)*, demonstrate quite starkly that these events would never have happened if spectator safety had been taken as seriously as it ought to have been:

> 'It is a depressing and chastening fact that mine is the ninth official report covering crowd safety at football grounds. After eight previous reports and three editions of the Green Guide, it seems astounding that [96] people could die from overcrowding before the very eyes of those controlling the event.'

Despite the recommendations of these eight previous reports, four of which specifically focused on spectator safety, three on crowd disorder and safety and one on the lack of effective leadership and administration of football, the Hillsborough disaster occurred at what was generally considered to be one of the safest grounds in country. It also occurred at a time when the focus of the police was almost entirely on crowd disorder and preventing acts of hooliganism. Despite the recommendations contained in the two Popplewell Reports, safety was not high on the agenda of the main contributors to the deaths at Hillsborough. In the immediate aftermath of the disaster, Taylor LJ was appointed to head an inquiry whose remit was to examine the causes of the deaths and to make recommendations on the needs of spectator safety and crowd control. The Interim Report specifically focuses on the events of 15 April 1989 and the recommendations to be implemented before the start of the next football season. The Final Report was a much more wide-ranging analysis of how football spectators and football grounds could be made safer.

The focus of this section is the impact of the disaster on stadium safety and Hillsborough's place at the end of a long period of inaction on the part of Parliament, the football authorities, the clubs and local authorities in the face of specific recommendations from the reports and inquiries commissioned over the previous 66 years. There were many other controversial aspects of the disaster: the use of the stadium gym as a temporary morgue, the misinformation supplied to the press by the police match day commander, Chief Superintendant Duckenfield, the presumption of the coroner that all of the victims had died by 3.15pm and his use of generic rather than individual inquests, the editing of the first hand accounts of many of the officers who were on duty at the stadium by South Yorkshire Police's solicitors, the decisions of the House of Lords restricting who could claim for Post-Traumatic Stress Disorder as a result of witnessing the disaster and its aftermath and the lack of coordination of the various investigating authorities into the disaster leading to the failure to prosecute those in command on the day.

In 1997 the newly-elected Labour government announced that Stuart-Smith LJ was to conduct a scrutiny of the evidence that had not been available to or was not presented at previous enquiries or investigations. Its purpose was to establish whether a further judicial inquiry, or coronial inquest, or prosecution should be ordered; it was not to be a further inquiry into stadium safety after the implementation of Taylor LJ's recommendations. Stuart-Smith LJ's conclusion was that there was no basis for ordering a reopening of any of the previously examined issues.

9.7.1   Hillsborough Stadium, Sheffield, 1989

The Hillsborough disaster could have happened at almost any major English football stadium. Their general state of disrepair and the unrelenting focus on crowd disorder saw a disaster unfold that, in the light of the findings of the previous official enquiries, should not have occurred.

▶ **Hillsborough Stadium, 15 April 1989**

The direct cause of the deaths at Hillsborough was the chronic overcrowding of pens three and four in the middle of the Leppings Lane terraces, directly behind the goals. This overcrowding was in turn caused by mismanagement of the stadium itself and entry into it on the day. Firstly although the entire standing area was recorded as having a maximum capacity of 10,100 spectators, no individual capacity had been calculated for each of the six pens into which the terrace had been divided. Secondly as the seven turnstiles servicing the terrace did not feed directly into specific pens, there was no means of monitoring effectively exactly how many people were in each individual pen. The Shortt Report had recommended as early as 1924 that steps should be taken to ensure that adequate means of counting spectators into each part of the ground were installed at all major sports grounds.

Thirdly the police operated a policy of allowing the spectators to 'find their own level' as a means of determining when a pen was full. By this method the police assumed that when a pen became uncomfortably full spectators would use one of the emptier pens instead. Thus instead of managing entry onto the terraces pro-actively, the police allowed events to unfold before them unchecked. Fourthly the police failed to notice, when it should have been obvious to them, that pens three and four had become dangerously overcrowded. Fifthly they failed to take any effective action to alleviate the crushing by barring further entry to pens three and four or allowing those at the front of the pens to escape onto the pitch and into the less crowded areas of the Leppings Lane terracing.

Finally in response to the crushing that had begun to occur outside of the stadium after CS Duckenfield's refusal to delay the game's kick-off, an emergency exit gate, Gate C, was opened and 2,000 further spectators were allowed entry onto the Leppings Lane terraces. The layout of the ground channelled the entirety of this large group of spectators into the already overcrowded pens three and four, to which the police had failed block entry and redirect spectators to the emptier pens. The volume of spectators in the pens, followed soon after by a surge forwards, caused a number of crush barriers to collapse and many people to be crushed to death as bodies piled on top of those who had fallen. Further crushing occurred at the front of the terrace against the perimeter fencing as the mass of bodies pushed down the slope towards the pitch. It was only after some spectators got through the fencing and onto the pitch to talk to the players that the police became aware of the gravity of the situation and the match was abandoned.

Taylor LJ was clear that although there were other contributory causes, the main reason for the disaster was the failure of senior police officers to manage the crowd both outside and inside the stadium and the breakdown of effective policing on the day. In particular he criticised the performance of CS Duckenfield for failing to draft an effective Operational Order, for failing to notice the overcrowding in pens three and four which were clearly and dangerously overfull from about 2.30pm, for perpetrating 'a blunder of the first magnitude' by failing to foresee the consequences of opening Gate C, for failing to show effective leadership and for freezing in the face of the unfolding disaster. Taylor LJ's damning conclusion that the overwhelming cause of the disaster was the fault of the police goes significantly further than any of the previous enquiries had done in specifically apportioning fault. It also provided him with the justification for insisting that his recommendations be acted upon rather than being filed away.

9.7.2　The Taylor Interim Report, 'The Hillsborough Stadium Disaster'

Having identified the police as the main cause of the disaster, chapters 16–22 of the Interim Report explain how its scale was compounded by a series of indirect causes attributable to many other actors. Taylor LJ identified an institutionalised lack of care for the safety of spectators amongst each of the organisations that should have been acutely aware of the danger to which old, and in many cases decrepit, stadiums posed to those who paid to use them and an over-concentration on the threat posed by spectator disorder.

9.7.2.1 The Football Association

The FA was criticised for choosing Hillsborough as an appropriate venue for a match of this magnitude. Although the previous year's semi-final between the same two clubs had been held there, complaints had been made that the ground was neither suitable nor big enough to host the game again; these complaints were ignored. Although not causative of the disaster of itself, the choice of venue was a significant contributory factor. The FA had no specific criteria against which a stadium could be judged to be suitable to host a game of this importance, a fact mentioned in the Final but not the Interim Report. If the FA had inspected the ground or had required production of the ground's safety certificate then the game would not have been awarded to Hillsborough. This failure to have any objective criteria for determining the suitability of a ground to host this game led the FA to choose Hillsborough when it should not have done so.

9.7.2.2 Hillsborough did not have a valid safety certificate

The importance of demanding a copy of the safety certificate is that Hillsborough did not have one that was currently valid. According to the Interim Report, Sheffield City Council had been 'inefficient and dilatory' in the performance of its duties to inspect and license football grounds under the SSGA 1975. The failure of the Council to inspect and amend the safety certificate following alterations to the ground that had been made in 1981 and 1985 was a serious breach of duty. If an inspection had been carried out, it would have found numerous breaches of the Green Guide and problems with the siting and physical condition of the crush barriers, some of which were seriously corroded around their base. Further criticism was made of the informality with which the Safety Advisory Group, the body responsible for ensuring that the ground was safe enough to be awarded a safety certificate, operated. If an inspection had been made then the safety certificate could have been withheld until appropriate changes to the stadium had been made. The failure of the Council to undertake its duties with sufficient vigour led to Hillsborough being chosen to host a game that, legally, should not have been played there.

9.7.2.3 Sheffield Wednesday Football Club

As part of its ongoing safety consultations with the police, Sheffield Wednesday Football Club had undertaken a number of developments to Hillsborough and was also aware of the need to make further alterations to the stadium. The club retained a consultant engineer who in 1985 had recommended that each of the six pens on the Leppings Lane terrace should be completely separated from the others. To enable the effective monitoring of the number of spectators in each pen, it was also recommended that each pen should have at least four dedicated turnstiles to enable safe entry into the ground. Following the fire at Valley Parade the club had to make alterations to other parts of the ground to ensure that it complied with the recommendations of the Popplewell Reports, leaving the engineer's recommendations ignored on the basis of cost. The failure to implement these recommendations left the club and the police unable to know precisely how many people were in each pen at any one time, causing massive overcrowding to occur in a very short period of time. The poor layout of the ground, accompanied by poor signposting inside it, meant that entry into pens three and four appeared to be the only choice for those entering the Leppings Lane terraces.

Further, the club operated and could view the CCTV images of the terraces and knew exactly how many spectators had gone through the turnstiles. Thus although it did not know how many people were in each pen, the club was aware of the total number of people on the terrace as a whole and so should have been in a position to alert the police of the uneven distribution in the pens. For these reasons the club was at fault under the Occupiers' Liability Act for failing to provide a reasonably safe stadium for spectators paying to watch the game.

9.7.2.4 The recommendations

The Interim Report rebutted suggestions that the emergency services, including the South Yorkshire Ambulance Service, the fire brigade and the St John's Ambulance Brigade were in any way to blame for delays in attending the ground or treating the injured. It did point out that there was insufficient cooperation between the police and the other emergency services and recommended that more effective major incident planning should be undertaken in the future, but that this would not have prevented the disaster from occurring.

The Interim Report's recommendations were for immediate implementation, where possible before the start of the next season, with the aim of preventing overcrowding and crushing on terraces generally improving safety procedures at football grounds. The vast majority of the recommendations had in one form or another been made in one or more of the previous eight government commissioned reports. The only radical difference with the recommendations in the Interim Report was that Taylor LJ insisted that they be implemented.

The recommendations ensured that there would need to be an upgrading of the quality of accommodation provided for spectators, an overhaul of the licensing procedure for all sports grounds, better training for and planning by the police and stewards and clearer coordination between the various emergency services. The first group of recommendations were to ensure that the specific conditions that gave rise to the Hillsborough disaster could not occur again. Firstly all self-contained pens were to have individually set maximum capacities that were calculated in accordance with the Green Guide; this maximum was then to be reduced by 15 per cent to improve the margin of safety. Secondly on entry into the stadium spectators must be counted into each pen and a means to shut down turnstiles and close off pens that were full would have to be employed. Finally to enable easy escape from these pens, all perimeter fencing must have a clearly marked emergency exit which should remain open for the entire period during which spectators were using it.

It was then recommended that an immediate review of all safety certificates should take place as a matter of urgency and that an Advisory Group consisting of representatives of the Council, the club and the emergency services should be established. Having reviewed the safety certificates already issued, these should then be reviewed and where necessary renewed each year. In particular the Interim Report recommended that all crush barriers be inspected as soon as possible because of the serious state of disrepair that had been found in those that had collapsed at Hillsborough. Thus the procedure outlined in the Safety at Sports Grounds Act 1975 was finally being forced into a coherent framework for determining the safety or otherwise of major football grounds.

In addition to these major recommendations clubs were required to review entry rates through their turnstiles to determine whether more should be installed or the capacity of a part of the ground should be reduced. Additionally the information provided to spectators on tickets and around the ground was to be improved. The police and stewards were to be trained in crowd safety and how to identify whether overcrowding was occurring and a major incident plan was required to ensure that all organisations attending a disaster should know the relevant chains of command, lines of communication and roles which they were supposed to fulfil.

There was no real need for any new legislation to implement these recommendations as they were either instances of best practice that could not be rationally contradicted or could be enforced by imposing conditions on a stadium's safety certificate. For the first time all interested parties were willing to engage with the recommendations of a Committee of Enquiry.

9.7.3　The Taylor Final Report, 'The Hillsborough Stadium Disaster'

Taylor LJ's final report focused on improving spectator control and crowd safety more generally; it was not to revisit the issues concerning the disaster itself. As the Football Spectators Act 1989, which contained the framework for the implementation of many of Popplewell J's recommendations, had made its way onto the statute books during the course of the Hillsborough inquiry, Taylor LJ also took the opportunity to revisit the efficacy of some of its provisions.

In the course of the opening chapter Taylor LJ identified an institutional failing on the part of every group of people who were associated with football to take spectator safety seriously. He criticised the long line of governments that had failed to implement the recommendations of previous Committees of Enquiry and the football authorities for failing to show any leadership to the clubs on issues of safety. The clubs were criticised for failing to provide adequate facilities to spectators and for spending large sums of money on player transfers and wages instead of upgrading their stadiums. The police were criticised for being too focused on the potential of a minority of fans to create disorder at the expense of guaranteeing the safety of the majority of well-behaved fans. The players were criticised for their on-field conduct and for inciting over-exuberant celebrations in the crowd. And the fans were criticised for a culture of turning up to games late and for often having taken too much drink. This last comment was tempered following Taylor LJ's visiting grounds in the UK and abroad and empathising with the fans wanting to spend as little time as possible in grounds that were outdated, unsafe and which provided few adequate facilities to improve the viewing experience.

The Final Report made it clear that very little that was being proposed was new as almost all of the proposals could be found in the reports of the previous enquiries. However it also made it clear that not all of the previous proposals were workable; in particular it was considered that the proposed Football Membership Scheme, recommended by Popplewell J and enacted in ss. 2–7 Football Spectators Act 1989, was unworkable within the then current technological boundaries (see further, 10.3.5.3). Finally the report stated clearly and unequivocally that if further disasters were to be avoided then its recommendations needed to be implemented and not ignored.

Perhaps the most controversial recommendation was that all designated football stadiums should provide only seated accommodation for spectators by the start of the 1999–2000 season. The Football Spectators (Seating) Order 1994/1666 imposed this recommendation as a condition of receiving a licence to host a football match at a designated stadium for all clubs in the Premier League and what is now the Football League Championship from the start of the 1994–95 season. Each season any club promoted to the Championship has added to its licence a condition that only seated accommodation be provided for or used by spectators at its home ground. The aim of this condition is to make spectators at football matches more comfortable, to remove the boisterousness of the terraces and to enable easier identification of troublemakers by using their seat number as an identifier.

The recommendations concerning the need to conduct more effective inspections as part of the licensing procedure reinforced those put forward three years earlier by Popplewell J. Taylor LJ provided further detail for the framework created by the FSA 1989 by, for example, recommending that an advisory group be established for each designated football stadium. This group, comprising representatives from the local authority, the police, fire and ambulance services and the club's safety officer, and all other aspects of safety at football grounds are now overseen by the FLA.

The remaining recommendations impacted more on matters of best practice; those that have become legally binding have usually done so as a result of being included as a condition of a licence being awarded. Detailed recommendations were made about how terracing should be made safer, about the counting of spectators and the filling and monitoring of pens, particularly that exact capacities should be set for each section. Further technical advice was given regarding fencing, gates and exits, ensuring that spectators could no longer be trapped in stadiums from which they needed to escape. Clubs were urged to improve their stadiums generally and specifically to provide better information to all users and better stewarding to ensure that all spectators could be safe.

Clubs and the FLA were directed to pay more attention to the Green Guide, which was also to be updated in the light of the findings of the inquiry. Finally specific training on most aspects of the policing of a football game was recommended, as was the need for a greater degree of coordination between the various emergency services and the clubs.

Although this summary provides only a brief overview of the recommendations made in the final report, it highlights that its aim was to ensure that a disaster such as occurred at Hillsborough could not happen again. Each group of recommendations, even if acted on individually, could feasibly have prevented the disaster from occurring as they would have prevented the overcrowding in pens three and four, allowed emergency access to the pitch, ensured that those in charge were competent to oversee the safety of the crowd and, if the disaster still occurred though in more limited circumstances, provided the victims with significantly more effective emergency medical treatment.

9.7.4 The legacy

After nine official reports and many hundreds of deaths and injuries, the combined impact of the disasters at Valley Parade and Hillsborough finally produced the changes in spectator safety, at least at football grounds, that had originally been envisaged in the Shortt Report. The legislative, policy and procedural changes that have been implemented have made British football stadiums amongst the safest in the world. The FLA has ensured that the recommendations in the *Green Guide*, though still not mandatory, are implemented unless there are exceptional reasons for them not to be. The threat of having a stadium, or part of it, closed to the public has been sufficient to ensure compliance with a licence's conditions and the major incident and evacuation plans ensure that the effects of any unfolding disaster should be minimised.

However there is no room for complacency. The full force of the current regulatory framework only applies to designated football grounds. Although local authorities do license all designated sports grounds there has not been the same degree of urgency in upgrading stadium quality outside of football. Discussions are ongoing within Parliament and the government about whether to extend the remit of the FLA to cover all sports grounds and to begin to introduce to them the standards of safety that are now found in football (below, Hot Topic).

Hot topic . . .

SHOULD THE FOOTBALL LICENSING AUTHORITY'S POWERS BE EXTENDED TO ALL SPORTS GROUNDS?

Each of the British sporting disasters of the twentieth century, at Wembley, Burnden Park, Ibrox, Valley Parade and Hillsborough, was precipitated by events at or surrounding a football match. However in each case the terms of reference of the five Committees of Enquiry required recommendations to be made regarding spectator safety at all sports events, not just at football matches. As the most popular spectator sport in the UK and the sport at which each of these disasters occurred, it is understandable that football was the focus of the majority of the Committees' time and recommendations. Following the Popplewell and Taylor Reports, this focus culminated in the creation of the Football Licensing Authority (FLA). It must be remembered however that Taylor LJ's Final Recommendation 6(b) specifically stated that the powers of the FLA as proposed by Popplewell J should be extended to cover all sports grounds that were designated under either the Safety of Sports Grounds Act 1975 or the Fire Safety and Safety of Places of Sport Act 1987.

The FLA has ensured that all football grounds in England and Wales are now designed and managed in accordance with the highest standards of spectator safety, rather than their safety being considered to be an optional add-on. The FLA's power to withhold or withdraw a football ground's licence has ensured complete compliance with the various conditions that both it and the Secretary of State for Culture, Media and Sport have required to be met. However this focus on football stadiums has left a gap in the regulatory framework through which many potentially dangerous sports grounds could fall.

The duty imposed on local authorities to inspect all designated sports grounds leaves them with a wide discretion to determine whether a safety certificate should be granted to an individual stadium. The rigorous standards set and procedures followed by the FLA are rarely used by local authorities unless they are inspecting a newly built stadium. This leaves many older and smaller grounds subject to a less exacting regulatory regime. Although Taylor LJ realised that leaving a loophole like this could create a situation where another Hillsborough or Valley Parade could occur, the government decided that there was no need to extend the new regulations to sports other than football. This was partly because of the cost to stadium operators of making their premises safe, partly because of the cost that would be incurred by local authorities conducting the inspections and partly because the lack of crowd disorder at other sports events meant that it was less dangerous to go and watch them in a dilapidated stadium. This last point demonstrates quite clearly the kind of complacency that led to the disasters of the last century.

The success of the Football Licensing Authority and the improvements to all aspects of safety and safety management that it has required to be implemented at football grounds has led to discussions about whether its remit should be extended to cover all sports grounds. The advantage with expanding the FLA's powers in this way would be that it could ensure that all sports venues were brought up to the same level of safety now found at football grounds. This would lead to improvements in the design and redevelopment of sports venues, their operation and major incident planning in the case of disasters.

The Sports Grounds Safety Authority Bill, which received its first reading in February 2009, seeks to reconstitute the FLA as the Sports Grounds Safety Authority (SGSA) and to extend its powers. However it will not extend the FLA's licensing functions or its powers to oversee the discharge by local authorities of their duties under the FSA 1989. Nor will the reconstituted body receive any further funding or personnel. Instead clauses 2–4 of the Bill enable the SGSA to provide advice and guidance on safety at sports grounds to any person or body and in particular to the government, local authorities and sports governing bodies. The SGSA will also be able to advise foreign governments and organisations responsible for sports safety outside of England and Wales, including for example the organising committee of the 2016 Olympic Games. Clause 5 enables the SGSA to charge a fee for this advice.

The disadvantage of this proposal appears to be that in the form in which it was laid before Parliament the purpose of the Sports Grounds Safety Authority Bill was to allow the FLA to provide advice to other sports bodies at a commercial rate rather than to require improved levels of safety at all sports grounds. A genuine extension of its remit coupled with the provision of sufficient funding to enable it to provide the same level of service to all sports grounds as it does to football grounds would be welcomed. However if its effect is to dilute the work of the FLA by requiring its officers to examine too many stadiums or to have them involved in commercial activities, then the creation of the SGSA runs the risk of undermining the safety developments that the FLA has overseen in football since the Hillsborough disaster.

The real purpose of this Bill is unclear. If its aim is to make all spectators at sports events safer then the FLA's licensing powers should be extended to cover all designated sports grounds. If there is concern that the owners of these grounds cannot afford to reach such exacting standards then it is also unlikely that they will be able to afford to pay for the SGSA's very detailed safety advice when it is providing its services at a commercial rate. This halfway house option looks more like an exercise in income-generation rather than being designed to create a safer viewing environment for all sports fans.

As a Private Members' Bill it is unlikely that the Sports Grounds Safety Authority Bill will become law. However discussions about the future role of the FLA have become more frequent in recent years and it is likely that an extension of its powers will come back before Parliament at some stage. It took nine official enquiries, hundreds of deaths and thousands of injuries before football grounds were forced to reach modern standards of safety. The potential for diluting the impact of the FLA inherent in the Sports Grounds Safety Authority Bill needs to be addressed if future disasters are to be prevented.

Summary

9.1 The early disasters were usually caused by the defective construction of the sports grounds. Despite the high-profile nature of these incidents and in particular the numbers of casualties and fatalities, the government took no steps to regulate the organisation and management of major sporting events.

9.2 The events at Wembley led to the first governmental Committee of Enquiry into safety at sports grounds. The wide ranging recommendations of the Shortt Report, if implemented, could have prevented the disasters that followed.

9.3 The Burnden Park disaster should have provided the government with sufficient evidence that some kind of formal regulation of sports grounds was required. For reasons of cost the licensing regime proposed in the Moelwyn Hughes Report was rejected by the government, leading directly to the disasters of the 1970s and 1980s.

9.4 The increase in football-related disorder in the 1960s changed the focus of discussions from spectator safety to crowd control. This in turn led to resources being diverted from providing safe accommodation for spectators to identifying and containing potential troublemakers.

9.5 The second Ibrox disaster, which was very clearly not caused by crowd disorder, finally forced the government to introduce a much-needed and long overdue licensing regime. However its lack of application to lower division grounds and its piecemeal application by local councils led directly to the disasters at Valley Parade and Hillsborough.

9.6 The three disasters of 1985 caused a confused response from the government. The fire at Valley Parade should have focused government attention on spectator safety and the need to update unsafe football grounds. However these events were overshadowed by the riots in Birmingham and at Heysel. The Popplewell Reports proposed a wide range of responses to the regulation of football stadiums and football crowds that unfortunately had not yet been implemented when Hillsborough occurred.

9.7 Hillsborough provided the final wake-up call for the government, the police and everyone connected to football. Although directly caused by police incompetence and mismanagement of the crowd on the day, the subsequent review of all aspects of stadium design and safety management has resulted in much safer accommodation being provided to football spectators.

Further reading

Guide to Safety at Sports Grounds (5th edn, 2006, HMSO)

Moelwyn Hughes J, *Enquiry into the Disaster at Bolton Wanderers' Football Ground on the 9th March 1946*, Cmnd 6846 (1946, HMSO)

Popplewell J, *Committee of Inquiry into Crowd Safety and Control at Sports Grounds (Interim Report)*, Cmnd 9585 (1985, HMSO)

Popplewell J, *Committee of Inquiry into Crowd Safety and Control at Sports Grounds (Final Report)*, Cmnd 9710 (1986, HMSO)

Shortt, *Report of the Departmental Committee on Crowds*, Cmnd 2088 (1924, HMSO)

Taylor LJ, *The Hillsborough Stadium Disaster (Interim Report)*, Cm 765 (1989, HMSO)

Taylor LJ, *The Hillsborough Stadium Disaster (Final Report)*, Cm 962 (1990, HMSO)

Wheatley, *Report on Crowd Safety at Sports Grounds*, Cmnd 4962 (1972, HMSO)

Darby, Johnes and Mellor (eds), *Soccer and Disaster* (2005, Routledge) chs 1–4

Further reading cont'd

Shiels, 'The Ibrox Disaster of 1902' [1997] *Juridical Review* 230

Shiels, 'The fatalities at the Ibrox Disaster of 1902' [1998] 18(2) *The Sports Historian* 148

The Hillsborough Disaster

Hartley, *Exploring Sport and Leisure Disasters: a socio-legal perspective* (2001, Cavendish Publishing) chs 6 and 8

Scraton, *Hillsborough – The Truth* (2nd edn, 2002, Mainstream Publishing)

Stuart-Smith LJ, *Scrutiny of Evidence Relating to the Hillsborough Football Stadium Disaster*, Cmmd 3878 (1998, HMSO)

Links to relevant websites can be found at www.palgrave.com/law/james

Chapter 10

Crowd disorder and football hooliganism

Key words

- **Council of Europe** – a transnational body whose primary aim is to create a common democratic and legal area throughout the whole of Europe, ensuring respect for its fundamental values: human rights, democracy and the rule of law.
- **Police spotters** – police officers assigned to identify potential troublemakers at specific football clubs, who often travel with fans and liaise with the UK Football Policing Unit.

10.1 Background and context

Crowd disorder has long been associated with sporting events and was one of the main reasons for the criminalisation of prize-fighting at the end of the nineteenth century (*R v Coney and others* (1881–82) 8 QBD 534) (see further, chapter 7.2.1.2). However it is the particularly violent form of disorder that occurs at football matches that has attracted the majority of academic, media, political and police attention. Commonly referred to as football hooliganism, this category of crowd disorder is perceived to be both more organised and more widespread than the spontaneous outbreaks of violence at for example Victorian prize-fights.

From the 1960s onwards football hooliganism and the means to control those engaged in it has been a particular focus of the government, the police and the football authorities. Throughout the 1970s and 1980s a peculiarly English version of football-related disorder evolved as supporters of the England national team, rather than supporters of domestic club sides, ran riot throughout continental Europe. Although not immune from club-based violence it was the disorder associated with the England team that created many of the headlines and drove the subsequent policy initiatives.

The first two government-sponsored Committees of Enquiry, which had reported on the disasters at Wembley Stadium and Burnden Park, focused on increasing spectator safety. Improving crowd behaviour was seen as a natural corollary of making the spectators safer. Thus the only substantive recommendation made by either the Shortt or Moelwyn Hughes Reports was that the police should be in overall control of law and order in and around football stadiums. The 1960s saw government inquiries held with a more specific focus on spectator disorder. Despite this change of focus, spectator safety and crowd control continued to be examined as though they were integral parts of the same phenomenon; in reality they are very different issues with very different causes. With hindsight, conflating them can now be said to have been one of the biggest mistakes made by the various governments that commissioned the inquiries as the focus on controlling the potential for crowd disorder at the expense of spectator safety led in part to the disasters at Valley Parade and Hillsborough. This chapter examines the effectiveness of the legal and governmental responses to football-related disorder.

10.2 Government inquiries into crowd disorder 1967–1984

The 1960s saw a dramatic increase in the incidence of football-related disorder. Where previous outbreaks of violence had apparently occurred spontaneously, these new incidents had an element of organisation about them. Away fans developed deliberate strategies to infiltrate and take over the favoured terraces of the home team's fans; home fans strategically ambushed away fans on their way to or from the stadium. The police also became aware that some of those involved had begun to carry weapons. The focus of the violence was in general the stadium and the streets around it, though disorder could also break out at motorway service areas and railway stations where groups of fans came into contact with each other. The growing concern over this increase in football hooliganism caused the government to commission three reports into crowd disorder in 1967, 1969 and 1984 and the Scottish Office to commission its own study in 1976.

10.2.1 The Harrington Report – 'Soccer Hooliganism: A Preliminary Report'

The Harrington Report was prepared for the Minister of Sport following the rise in football-related disorder that occurred in the early 1960s. It identified the growth in violent conduct, the use of weapons and obscene chanting as the most commonly occurring forms of disorder without examining in any detail their causes. The report made suggestions rather than legislative proposals about measures that could be taken to control football crowds more effectively. As its name suggests, as a preliminary report these suggestions paved the way for a more detailed examination of football-related disorder by the following year's Department of the Environment Working Party.

The Harrington Report made two main suggestions to improve effective crowd control. Firstly that ground facilities should be improved to a nationally approved minimum standard. By providing better accommodation for spectators, it was suggested, crowds would be easier to control and outbreaks of hooliganism thereby prevented. The report explained that this could only be achieved by imposing legislatively defined minimum standards of safety and amenity on stadium owners because without such coercion, clubs had preferred to spend their money on the purchase of players and on their wages rather than on the ground improvements that had been previously recommended in the Shortt and Moelwyn Hughes Reports.

Secondly the Harrington Report suggested that more responsibility should be placed on clubs for the behaviour of their own spectators both within the stadium and whilst travelling to and from games. Instead of abdicating responsibility for fans' conduct to the police, the report considered that the most effective solution to the problem of football-related disorder would be to punish clubs that failed to control their own fans' behaviour. The failure of English football clubs to accept this responsibility led instead to the police seeking and eventually being granted much greater powers over those involved in football-related disorder. Although no specific action was taken as a result of this report, it set the scene for the more detailed inquiry that reported in 1969.

10.2.2 The Lang Report – 'Crowd Behaviour at Football Marches: Report of the Working Party 1969'

The Lang Report drew on the experiences of the previous governmental inquiries and on its own new research. It identified that the causes of football-related disorder were complex and often due to a combination of social, physical and management factors. The report produced 23 recommendations that were aimed at improving the surveillance, control and punishment of football hooligans. However despite the perceived importance of football hooliganism as a social problem that needed to be addressed, none of the recommendations of the Lang Report were acted upon by the government or football authorities at the time.

To improve the surveillance of crowds and the quality of evidence gathered, it was recommended that CCTV cameras be installed and used as a means of identifying those who were involved in the disorder. This recommendation was finally taken up by clubs after the Popplewell Reports were published (below, 10.3.3) and, together with the filming of suspected hooligans, has become a standard means of collecting evidence against in cases of football-related disorder.

In order to control access to stadiums more effectively it was recommended that ticketing policies be made more robust by monitoring advance sales and segregating opposing fans. It was also recommended that spectators should be prevented from entering the playing area. Although it was noted that alcohol played a part in outbreaks of disorder by making spectators more quarrelsome and providing them with missiles in the form of empty bottles, no recommendations were made about how this problem could be addressed. Finally it was recommended that those convicted of football-related offences should be prevented from attending future games.

Most of these recommendations have now become law following the Wheatley, Popplewell and Taylor Reports. However the Lang Report's emphasis on the development of a more cooperative approach to crowd control, bringing together the football authorities, the clubs, the police and the fans, saw its recommendations become aspirations to best practice rather than legal requirements.

10.2.3 The McElhone Report – 'Report of the Working Group on Football Crowd Behaviour'

Crowd disorder was not only occurring in England; it was also becoming a significant feature of football matches in Scotland. The McElhone Report was commissioned by the Secretary of State for Scotland and focused specifically on football hooliganism at Scottish matches. The Report's 52 recommendations covered much of the same ground as had the previous inquiries, however it stands out as being the first that led directly to legislative intervention.

In common with previous reports, the McElhone Report recommended that ground improvements would make crowd control easier and would attract a greater cross-section of society to attend games. In particular the report considered that if more women and children were to attend matches held in better quality accommodation then the overall behaviour of the crowd would improve. It also repeated previous recommendations that more severe punishments should be handed down to hooligans as a deterrent to them and others who may be tempted to engage in football-related disorder.

In order to reduce the opportunity for clashes inside the stadium, the report recommended that rival fans be segregated from each other. Moreover to increase the effectiveness of this segregation it was recommended that fences be erected to a height of not less than 1.8m to prevent spectators from accessing the playing area and areas in which opposing fans were accommodated. In proposing ways of reducing crowd disorder the report was inadvertently creating the circumstances in which spectator safety could be compromised.

One innovative recommendation was that clubs should improve engagement with their local community by for example providing players to conduct coaching sessions at nearby schools and clubs. The aim of this recommendation, reflected in clubs' 'Football in the Community' programmes, was designed to promote a club's responsibility for its fans and the fans' responsibility for the maintenance of the club's reputation by forging stronger ties between the two. None of these recommendations, whether being made for the first time or being repeated and updated for, in some cases, the fifth time had sufficient impact on the government to result in legislative action.

10.2.3.1 *Criminal Justice (Scotland) Act 1980 ss.68–77 – control of alcohol at sporting events in Scotland*

The only Parliamentary response was to the McElhone Report's recommendations on alcohol. At the time Scottish football clubs did not have licenses to sell alcohol inside their stadiums, leading to a culture of spectators drinking before the game began and also bringing their own drink with them into the ground. This not only led to drunkenness amongst the spectators but to a ready supply of missiles that could be thrown at opposing fans or players. Part V Criminal Justice (Scotland) Act 1980, which was subsequently amended by the Sporting Events (Control of Alcohol) Act 1985 and has now been replaced by Part II Criminal Law (Consolidation) (Scotland) Act 1995, introduced a package of criminal offences to restrict the consumption of alcohol by football spectators in Scotland.

The Act criminalises the possession of alcohol on public transport or in private vehicles capable of carrying more than eight passengers on the way to a designated football game. The operator of a public service vehicle or driver of a private vehicle is guilty of an offence by allowing alcohol to be carried in their vehicles. It is also an offence to carry alcohol into a football stadium, to have a container capable of carrying liquids in one's possession inside the ground and to be drunk at, or whilst trying to gain entry to a football match. Similar provisions were not enacted for the rest of the UK and in 1984 were specifically rejected as unnecessary by a Department of the Environment Working Group (below, 10.2.4). Part V Criminal Justice (Scotland) Act 1980 did however form the template for the Sporting Events (Control of Alcohol) Act 1985, which was passed in the immediate aftermath of the fatalities at Birmingham and Heysel.

10.2.4　Department of the Environment Working Group – 'Football Spectator Violence'

Following high profile incidents of disorder at England matches, in particular those held in Luxembourg and France during the qualifying rounds for the 1984 UEFA European Nations Championships, the Department of the Environment commissioned a further report on spectator disorder. Its proposals sought to restrict the opportunities for disorder through the better organisation of the sport as a whole and through more effective planning and preparation for disorder at high risk games. In contrast to the McElhone Report it found that there was no evidential basis for the claims that there was a link between alcohol and disorder. The Working Group rejected the need for legislation comparable to the Criminal Justice (Scotland) Act 1980 on the further ground that it would cause unnecessary financial hardship to the majority of clubs where disorder was not a problem.

Thus despite the similarity of both the findings and recommendations made by the Harrington, Lang, McElhone and Department of the Environment Reports, the only legislative action taken to improve the effectiveness of crowd control in the UK was to regulate the possession and consumption of alcohol at and on the way to football matches in Scotland. None of the reports made their recommendations with the same degree of forcefulness that had led to the enactment of the Wheatley Report's recommendations in the Safety of Sports Grounds Act 1975 (see further, chapter 9.5). Although almost all of what were then considered to be the more politically or financially controversial recommendations have subsequently been enacted, none were considered to be appropriate for Parliamentary intervention at the time.

10.3 St Andrew's, Birmingham, Heysel Stadium, Brussels and The Popplewell Reports, 1985–6

In contrast to the fire at Valley Parade, Bradford, the two other football disasters of 1985 were caused primarily by spectator disorder, not just the state of the premises or the mismanagement of the event. The Popplewell Reports examined all three disasters and made recommendations concerning how both spectator safety and crowd control could be improved in the future. In this section the incidents at St Andrew's and Heysel will be examined and the recommendations concerning crowd control discussed.

10.3.1 St Andrew's, Birmingham, 1985

On the same day as the fire at Bradford, a 15-year-old boy was killed and 20 others injured when a wall collapsed at St Andrew's Stadium, Birmingham.

▶ **St Andrew's, 9 May 1985**

Serious disorder had begun in the centre of Birmingham on the morning of the match and continued throughout the game. The police had been continually bombarded with missiles, including pieces of concrete and bricks that had been dislodged from the fabric of the stadium. There had been a pitch invasion by both sets of fans at half-time and disorder continued throughout the match.

At the end of the game, as most spectators were leaving the stadium, others continued to fight and throw things at each other. A surge of spectators pushed against a wall that divided the back of the stadium from the car park, causing it to buckle and collapse, killing one person. There was no indication that the wall was structurally unsound or that it had collapsed for any other reason than excessive force being applied to it. The only explanation given for the surge of spectators against the wall was that it was part of the ongoing disorder between the two sets of fans, though those crushed by the wall were simply passersby who were not involved in any violent conduct.

10.3.2 Sporting Events (Control of Alcohol) Act 1985

Before the publication of the Popplewell Reports and in time for the start of the 1985–86 football season the government decided that it needed to take action against what it saw to be drink-fuelled hooliganism. Although the previous year's Department of the Environment Report had recommended that there was no need to restrict access to alcohol at football grounds in England and Wales, the government disagreed. The Sporting Events (Control of Alcohol) Act 1985 enacted a framework for the control of alcohol at designated football matches based on the Criminal Justice (Scotland) Act 1980. Thus possessing alcohol whilst travelling to a designated football match on public transport or in a private vehicle capable of carrying more than eight passengers became offences, as did permitting another person to possess alcohol in such vehicles under ss.1 and 1A.

Moreover attempting to gain entry to a designated football ground whilst drunk and being drunk or possessing alcohol or possessing a container capable of holding liquid whilst in a designated football ground were criminalised under s.2 of the Act. As with the Scottish legislation this latter provision was passed to prevent bottles and cans from being used as missiles. Section 2 also bans sales of alcohol in sight of the pitch to prevent spectators from staying in a bar and drinking whilst watching the game. Thus Parliament took the pro-active step of preventing entry to football matches for spectators who were drunk, though no definition of 'drunk' is provided, preventing entry into the ground when possessing alcohol and preventing the consumption of alcohol in sight of the game. However a complete prohibition on the consumption of alcohol inside the stadium was not considered appropriate on financial grounds despite its apparent potential to create serious disorder.

10.3.3 The Popplewell Interim Report – 'Interim Report of the Committee of Inquiry into Crowd Safety and Control at Sports Grounds'

The Interim Report's recommendations on crowd control were aimed at improving the police's ability to conduct effective surveillance of large and disorderly crowds and criminalising specific types of conduct most commonly associated with football hooliganism. To improve police surveillance it was recommended that closed-circuit television cameras (CCTV) should be installed at all major football grounds so that those who were engaging in violent conduct could be more easily identified and eventually prosecuted. The practical benefits to the police and the consequent reduction of disorder inside the ground that was observed where CCTV had been installed meant that this recommendation was implemented by clubs without the need for further legislative intervention.

The Interim Report also recommended that the introduction of a national membership system be investigated so that football spectators could be more easily identified, and later banned if they were involved in disorder. It was also hoped that away fans could be prevented from attending all matches. Under this proposal attendance at football matches would only be granted to members of the home club who had been vetted by it in advance. As an incentive to good behaviour, their membership could be revoked if they were convicted of an offence of football-related disorder. By preventing away fans from attending a game it was hoped that the opportunity for clashes between rival fans would be removed and that therefore football-related disorder would be eradicated. This proposal was developed further in the Final Report and eventually formed the first part of the Football Spectators Act 1989 (below, 10.3.5.3).

Finally the Interim Report recommended that throwing missiles and chanting obscene and racial abuse at sports grounds should be specifically criminalised. The Interim Report identified that many injuries were caused by the throwing of missiles at other spectators and the police and that such conduct was often the precursor to more serious disorder between rival groups of spectators. By making the throwing of a missile an offence, the need to prove intent to harm another person and/or their property is removed thereby making it easier to secure a conviction.

The aim of criminalising obscene and racial chanting was to reduce the amount of anti-social behaviour at football matches, to improve the overall conduct of the spectators and to remove the possibility of retaliatory disorder on the part of those who had been abused. Both of these proposals were examined further in the Final Report before being enacted in the Football Offences Act 1991 (below, 10.4.1).

10.3.4 Heysel Stadium, Brussels 1985

Just over two weeks after the Bradford fire and the collapse of the wall at St Andrew's, the events at the Heysel Stadium during the European Cup Final between Liverpool and Juventus changed the focus of attention from spectator safety in outdated sports grounds to the need for better and more effective control of disorderly and violent football crowds.

▶ **Heysel Stadium, 27 May 1985**

The build up to the final had seen sporadic outbreaks of violence both within and outside of the stadium. This grew worse as the opposing fans began by throwing missiles at each other and ended with a riot during which a large group of Liverpool fans attacked a group of Juventus fans in the neighbouring pen. The direct cause of the Heysel disaster was an aggressive charge by a group of Liverpool fans into an adjoining section of the ground that was populated predominantly by Juventus fans. As the Juventus fans tried to escape the threat of an imminent attack, they became cornered against a wall that separated the end of the terrace from one of the stadium's entrance corridors. As the pressure against the wall mounted it collapsed, causing many fans to fall and many more to pile on top of them; as a result 39 spectators were crushed to death and over 400 were injured.

Heysel occupies a controversial place in the history of stadium disasters involving British football clubs; the disaster was clearly and obviously caused by a riot involving a large group of people intent on committing violence. That the direct cause of the resulting deaths was not the physical state of the stadium nor the failure to manage the safety of the spectators inside the ground distinguishes it from the disasters discussed in Chapter 9. What is less frequently examined is that the scale of the Heysel disaster was exacerbated by a poor quality stadium, mismanagement of the crowd on the day and a lack of any appropriate licensing procedures.

Had Heysel been located in England it is unlikely that it would have satisfied the safety requirements of the Safety at Sports Grounds Act 1975. The concrete steps that formed the terracing were decaying and pieces were easily broken off and used as missiles; lengths of piping that had been left at the back of the terracing were also used as missiles and weapons when the violence broke out. Further, the pens dividing the terraces were separated only by insubstantial plastic coated wire which was easily torn down. Thus the physical condition of the ground was not safe enough to host a match of this size and importance and helped to create the circumstances in which the disorder could arise and then escalate.

Despite the best intentions of the organisers, segregation of the opposing fans was not maintained. Neutral zones of terracing were placed between the Liverpool and Juventus fans so that there would be some considerable distance between them, thereby minimising the opportunities for disorderly interaction between them. Tickets for these zones were supposed to be restricted to Belgian nationals purchasing them from the stadium's ticket office. In reality the majority of these tickets were purchased by Juventus fans, resulting in a complete breakdown in segregation at one end of the ground. This was compounded by a misunderstanding in the division of roles between the two police forces on duty at the match. The lack of one overall commander in charge of policing on the day left the local police on duty inside the ground whilst the more highly trained and better equipped gendarmes were largely based back at their barracks on standby in case disorder broke out. When rioting did break out they found it difficult to cross the city quickly because of the weight of traffic making its way to the stadium.

Finally neither the Belgian state authorities nor UEFA, which had chosen Heysel to host its showpiece final, had any criteria against which to judge the appropriateness of a stadium to stage a game of this magnitude. Heysel was chosen because it was a large stadium that hosted international football games; therefore it was assumed that it was also capable of hosting the European Cup Final.

The choice of stadium and mismanagement of the crowd by both the police and event organisers created the conditions in which a riot could occur. This is not to detract from the fact that the disaster was caused by violence and disorder carried out by a sizeable minority of spectators, some of whom were armed and some of whom had gained access to the ground illegally. What it highlights is that where organisational and operational protocols are either not in place or not adhered to then the conditions in which disorder may occur can be exploited by those intent on acting violently, all of which had been highlighted by the UK government's reports into spectator disorder.

10.3.5 The Popplewell Final Report – 'The Final Report of the Committee of Inquiry into Crowd Safety and Control at Sports Grounds'

The Popplewell Final Report examined the Heysel Stadium disaster in detail before analysing in more depth some of the issues that had been raised in the Interim Report. Of the 15 final recommendations, five related to crowd control. Despite a wide ranging review of the sociological, criminological, historical and legal literature on football hooliganism, the final report was unable to explain why people became involved with football-related disorder. Although the cause or causes of the disorder could not be definitively identified the final report does propose a series of preventive measures that should be taken to reduce the incidence of football-related disorder. The main proposals covered the need for the police to have extended powers to stop and search football spectators, the creation of new offences that covered specific forms of disorder and the creation of a national football membership scheme.

10.3.5.1 Criminal Justice and Public Order Act 1994 s.60 – police powers of stop and search

One of the main concerns of the Committee was that the police were unable to carry out effective searches of spectators before they entered a football ground. Under the s.1(3) Police and Criminal Evidence Act 1984 the police were only able to search a person or vehicle where there were reasonable grounds for suspecting that stolen property or offensive weapons would be found. The police knew that some spectators carried weapons but not which ones. As s.1(3) does not provide a general power to search unless there were reasonable grounds for suspecting that a specific individual was carrying a weapon, a search could not be carried out. The Final Report recommended that the police be given an unfettered power to stop and search anyone entering or trying to enter a football ground.

This general power was not at first considered appropriate by the government. However s.60 Criminal Justice and Public Order Act 1994 enacts the final report's recommendation but in an even wider form than that proposed, as it is not just applicable to football spectators. Section 60 enables the police to stop and search any person or any vehicle where a police officer of the rank of Inspector or above reasonably believes that incidents of serious violence may take place and that it is expedient to use this power to prevent them from occurring or where there are reasonable grounds for suspecting that dangerous instruments or offensive weapons are being carried without good reason. Authorisations under s.60 have become commonplace as a means of gathering intelligence about football spectators and preventing people from carrying weapons in and around football grounds.

10.3.5.2 Criminalising disorderly conduct at sports grounds

Both the Interim and Final Reports considered the need for specific offences to be enacted to control commonly occurring types of disorderly conduct at football matches. The final recommendation was that a generic offence of disorderly conduct at a sports ground should be created that would criminalise a range of anti-social behaviour. The specific concerns of the Committee were the throwing of missiles, obscene and racial chanting and pitch invasions.

Although it was acknowledged that the proposal involved criminalising a relatively low level of disorderly behaviour, it was considered that there were two grounds for targeting these particular forms of conduct. Firstly no existing legislation adequately covered these types of conduct. Where missiles are thrown it can be difficult to prove that the thrower has the requisite mens rea for a criminal assault unless there is clear evidence that the missile was thrown at someone. It would also be difficult to prove that these three types of disorder could constitute offences under ss.4, 4A and 5 Public Order Act 1986 (below, 10.5.1) because the prosecution would still need to prove that someone was caused harassment, alarm or distress by such conduct. Thus the proposed offence sought to close a genuine loophole in the law.

Secondly the Final Report highlighted that conduct of these kinds was often a precursor to more serious disorder. The throwing of missiles would often escalate through retaliatory missile throwing to a full scale riot; the verbal abuse of an opposing team's players or spectators could likewise lead to a violent reaction in those seeking to defend the person or people being abused, and running on to the pitch was often the final act before a confrontation between opposing sets of fans. If this kind of conduct could be stopped at as early a stage as possible, it was argued, then the incidence of serious disorder inside the stadium could be reduced significantly.

The Final Report acknowledges that the investigation and enforcement of crimes such as these would be difficult when large numbers of people may be committing the same offence at the same time. However it was also considered that the new offence could create a significant deterrent to engaging in disorderly conduct; the symbolic effect of the legislation and its use against a few offenders may be enough to stop others from joining in. Before being able to enact a criminal offence based on this recommendation the Taylor Report's more specific recommendations for enacting three separate offences of throwing missiles inside a stadium, engaging in indecent and/or racial chanting and encroaching on to the pitch without lawful excuse led to the passing of the Football (Offences) Act 1990 (below, 10.4.1).

10.3.5.3 Football Spectators Act 1989 ss.2–7 – the National Membership Scheme

The most controversial proposal of the two reports was that a compulsory football membership scheme should be created. The scheme would require anyone who wanted to watch a football match live at a stadium to become a member of the club that they supported. Only club members would be allowed to buy tickets to games and only home fans would be allowed entry to the stadium. The aim of the scheme was to ensure that anyone who participated in football-related disorder would have their club membership revoked and would not then be able to go to any designated football match. This scheme was to work in tandem with a court's newly created ability to impose Exclusion Orders under Part IV Public Order Act 1986 on people convicted of football-related offences. These Orders, the forerunners of the Football Banning Order (below, 10.6), would prevent anyone convicted of an offence of violence or disorder at a football match from attending future games.

The scheme had the support of the government, the Football Association, the Football League and many clubs. The final report argued that it would not impose too great a burden on clubs as many already operated similar such schemes or had other restrictions on the purchase of tickets to high profile or potentially disorderly games. Its impact would have been not only to reduce the ability of those convicted of football-related disorder to attend football matches but would also have seen the end of away fans and casual spectators; changing the face of football fandom in this way was considered to be a price worth paying to remove the hooligan element from the game.

The scheme was enacted in ss.2–7 Football Spectators Act 1989 but never brought into force because of the recommendations of the Taylor Reports into the Hillsborough disaster in 1989 (below, 10.4.3.1). The scheme was eventually repealed by sch.5 para.1 Violent Crime Reduction Act 2006.

10.3.6 European Convention on Spectator Violence

A further and less well-known legal instrument that was created as a direct response to the events at Heysel is the Council of Europe's 'European Convention on Spectator Violence'. The aims of the Convention mirror those of each of the governmental reports discussed here: to prevent and control spectator violence on the one hand and to ensure the safety of spectators at sports events on the other. The Convention was signed and ratified by the UK on 19 August 1985 and came into force on 1 November of that year, however its terms are not legally binding on the UK Parliament. Despite this there is a high degree of coincidence between the terms of the Convention and the statutes enacted and policies pursued by all UK governments since 1985.

To achieve its aims the Convention seeks to standardise the approaches of the governments of Europe towards the policing and control of potentially disorderly crowds, to improve cooperation and knowledge sharing between law enforcement agencies, to improve standards of stadium safety and to educate fans about the cultures and customs of their opponents. In respect of each of these issues the UK has been at the forefront of legal and policy developments.

Although most police forces now routinely exchange information on potential risk spectators, cross-border policing and judicial cooperation was at its highest profile during the 2006 FIFA World Cup in Germany where uniformed English police spotters patrolled with their German colleagues in the cities where England played. This enabled the English police to identify potential troublemakers, monitor their behaviour and take appropriate action to diffuse situations that could escalate into violence. Further, representatives of the Crown Prosecution Service travelled to Germany to ensure that anyone arrested for a football-related offence could have a Football Banning Order imposed on them on their return to the UK. Cooperation between the English and German authorities in these ways ensured that disorder was kept to a minimum and where it did happen it was punished in the same way that it would have been had it occurred at a game in England.

The licensing regime established by the Football Spectators Act 1989 and the creation of the Football Licensing Authority have ensured that football stadiums are safer and more comfortable places in which to watch football. This in turn has encouraged fans to take a more proactive approach to self-policing. In particular the creation of the Football Supporters Federation and the work that it has done through its fan embassies at international football tournaments has helped to change the reputation of those travelling abroad to watch football through education. By providing information and advice to fans travelling to games overseas, especially finals tournaments, spectators are more aware of what they should not do to antagonise local people in general and the local police in particular.

10.4 Hillsborough Stadium, Sheffield and The Taylor Reports 1989–90

As the main cause of the Hillsborough disaster was mismanagement of the crowd on the day (see further, chapter 9.5), the majority of the Taylor Reports' recommendations naturally concerned spectator safety. However the final report also proposed the creation of four new criminal offences and made suggestions concerning the efficacy of Parts I and II of the recently enacted Football Spectators Act 1989. The Popplewell Reports had identified three specific forms of anti-social behaviour that were often the precursor to more serious outbreaks of disorder: throwing missiles, chanting obscene and/or racialist abuse and going on to the field of play without a reasonable excuse. In his final report Popplewell J had recommended that a generic offence of disorderly conduct at a football match be enacted to cover each of these three types of conduct.

Taylor LJ reviewed this proposal and the operation of the Public Order Act 1986, which had come into force after the publication of the Popplewell Reports. He concluded that none of the existing offences or the generic crime proposed by Popplewell J adequately covered these three specific acts.

10.4.1 The Football (Offences) Act 1991

The Football (Offences) Act 1991 enacted these recommendations by creating three new football-specific offences rather than one of disorderly conduct at a sports ground. Under s.2 it is an offence to throw anything at or towards the playing area or any other area where spectators or other persons are without lawful excuse. Although obviously aimed at the throwing of objects such as coins, bottles and pieces of masonry, it is drafted widely enough to include any object.

Section 3 creates the offence of indecent or racialist chanting. There is no definition of 'indecent' however it is clear from the tone of the final report that any abusive and/or crude chanting was considered to be unwelcome at football matches. Racialist is defined as including threatening, abusive or insulting words aimed at a person's colour, race, nationality, ethnic or national origins. A specific person does not have to be the target of the chanting; the offence is committed if the chanting is in fact indecent or racialist. In *DPP v. Stoke-on-Trent Magistrates' Court* [2003] EWHC 1593 (Admin), the High Court held that a chant of, 'You're just a town full of Pakis', which was directed at Oldham Athletic FC fans by Port Vale FC fans was racially abusive despite a finding that there were no persons of Pakistani, Asian or black origin in the crowd or on the playing field. A loophole in the original Act, that this offence could only be committed if the chanting was engaged in by two or more persons was closed by a later amendment; the s.3 offence can now be committed by one or more people chanting indecent or racial words.

Finally s.4 makes it an offence to go on to the playing area or any area adjoining the playing area without lawful excuse. Thus running on to the pitch is a criminal offence unless for example it is to escape from a fire or to avoid being attacked by others engaged in disorder. The police have generally avoided prosecuting the occasional over-exuberant celebration but where threatening behaviour has been directed at players, match officials, club employees or other spectators, then a prosecution will usually follow (*R (on the application of White)* v. *Blackfriars Crown Court* [2008] EWHC 510 (Admin)) (below, 10.6.1).

Each of these three crimes can only be committed at a designated football match. This has been extended on two occasions since 1991 and now includes all matches where at least one of the teams involved is a member of the English Premier League, the Football League, the Football Conference, the League of Wales or represents a territory or country (Football (Offences)(Designation of Football Matches) Order 2004/2410). This leaves the rather strange situation that where for example a sports ground hosts both football and rugby games, the Act applies when a football match is being played, but not when a rugby match is played. Despite the cogent justification for the creation of these new offences they are only rarely used by the police to prosecute football-related disorder (below, 10.5).

10.4.2 Criminal Justice and Public Order Act 1994 ss.166 and 166A – regulating ticketing touting

The fourth offence recommended by the final report was that the unauthorised sale of tickets to a designated football match, or ticket touting, should be criminalised. The justification for this proposal was that ticket touting can create disorder in two specific ways. Firstly it can lead to the breakdown in segregation of the opposing fans as the tout is unlikely to pay much attention to the allegiance of their purchaser. If opposing fans are to be kept apart so that they cannot fight with each other inside a football ground then ticket touting could seriously undermine this basic crowd control tactic. Secondly the act of selling can create disorder amongst the prospective purchasers, either through creating a crowd of prospective purchasers or because of disputes over price.

Ticket touting was eventually made a criminal offence at designated football matches by s.166 Criminal Justice and Public Order Act 1994 (see further, chapter 13.2.4). In its current form s.166(a) defines a sale as being unauthorised where it is concluded without the written consent of the match organiser, ensuring that any sale not conducted by an authorised ticket agent is a crime (see further, chapter 13.2). Under s.166(2)(aa) 'selling' is given a particularly wide meaning to include offering to sell a ticket, exposing a ticket for sale, making a ticket available for sale by another, advertising that a ticket is available for purchase and giving a ticket to a person who pays or agrees to pay for some other goods or services or offering to do so. This wider meaning of selling was enacted in the light of activities undertaken by touts to avoid being caught simply selling or offering to sell tickets under the more basic original definition of the offence.

In 2007 in response to the growth in unauthorised ticket sales taking place online s.166A was added to the Criminal Justice and Public Order Act 1994 to impose criminal liability on internet service providers (ISPs) in certain limited circumstances. An ISP is not liable simply for hosting or enabling unauthorised sales to take place on its service; it will only be liable in one of two specific situations. Firstly when it is aware that the information supplied to it by a user contains material that contravenes s.166. Secondly that having become aware that information on its service contravenes s.166, it fails to remove it or disable access to it expeditiously. Thus only where an ISP has specific knowledge that a specific individual is selling tickets on its service without the authorisation of the primary rights holder will an offence be committed. From a practical perspective this means that unless a specific unauthorised sale is brought to the attention of the ISP, which is often done by the primary rights holder, and it takes no action to remove it from its service then no offence is committed.

10.4.3   Recommendations for amending the Football Spectators Act 1989

The final report also reviewed the Football Spectators Act 1989 which had enacted some of the key recommendations of the Popplewell Reports. Two aspects in particular were analysed in some depth: the National Membership Scheme and the means by which exclusion and restriction orders, the forerunners of Football Banning Orders (below, 10.6) could be made more effective.

10.4.3.1 The National Membership Scheme

The aim of the National Membership Scheme was to restrict entry to designated football grounds to people who held valid membership cards. The application for a membership card would enable a check to be carried out on the applicant to determine whether or not they were associated with football hooliganism and whether they were an appropriate person to be allowed to watch live football games. The card would contain information including the name, address, photograph, club and national allegiance of the member and would have to be presented when purchasing tickets and when attempting to gain entry to a stadium. The scheme was to be administered by the Football Membership Authority, which would hold a database of anyone who was ineligible to hold a members card including anyone who had been the subject of an Exclusion or Restriction Order. It was hoped that the restrictions on membership and the ability of the Authority to monitor and exclude members would break the connection between violent disorder and football.

Taylor LJ reviewed the scheme and how practically it would work and came to the conclusion that he could not support its introduction at that point in time. He identified three specific concerns with the scheme that he thought would make it unworkable and potentially create danger to those using it. Firstly he considered that checking the membership cards at the turnstiles would slow down entry into the stadium to such an extent that congestion and crushing outside of the ground would be exacerbated. The inadequate technology of the time was considered to pose greater problems than it would solve and for this reason alone should be abandoned. Secondly it was observed that since the introduction of CCTV cameras at designated football grounds, most violence and disorder took place outside of the stadiums. Therefore restricting access to the ground to known hooligans would not prevent disorder inside the stadium as this had already been reduced to a minimum. Thirdly the impact on police resources would be too great as each turnstile would require at least two officers to be on duty in case a banned person attempted to gain entry to the ground. Thus instead of recommending the implementation of the National Membership Scheme the Taylor Report recommended that further and more restrictive conditions should be added to the Exclusion Orders imposed on those convicted of football-related disorder.

10.4.3.2 Exclusion Orders

The second element of his review of the Football Spectators Act 1989 examined why Exclusion Orders appeared to be ineffective at deterring football hooligans from engaging with disorder at football matches. A court's ability to impose an Exclusion Order on a person convicted of a football-related offence had been introduced by s.30 Public Order Act 1986. Its aim was to prevent violence or disorder at or in connection with football matches. Where an Order was imposed its effect was to ban the person subject to it from entering every designated football ground in England and Wales for a minimum of three months.

Taylor LJ's concern was that these orders were not being imposed often enough on conviction and where they were, there was no effective means of enforcing them. He proposed that attendance centre orders should be attached to Exclusion Orders so that anyone subject to a ban would have to attend a specific place during the time that a football match involving the team supported by the subject was taking place. Alternatively it was recommended that the subject of the order should be electronically tagged so that their whereabouts on match days could be monitored remotely. Although these recommendations were not taken up, the development of the Football Banning Order and of the surveillance technology that enables its restrictions to be monitored and enforced effectively has ensured that being banned from a ground and specific areas around it is more easily policed than Taylor LJ might have imagined at the time (below, 10.6).

10.5 General legislation applicable to disorderly crowds

There is no legal definition of 'football hooliganism' and no crime of being a 'football hooligan' known to English law. Anyone who is accused of being involved in football-related disorder will be charged either with an offence under one of the football-specific pieces of legislation mentioned above or with one of a relatively small number of criminal offences. In sports other than football, only the general criminal offences discussed below will be available to the prosecutor.

Despite the wide range of offences with which a person involved with spectator disorder could be charged, the Home Office's statistics on football-related arrests and banning orders for the past ten years show that football fans are arrested for comparatively few crimes. In general around half of all arrests are for offences under the Public Order Act 1986, in particular the offences of public disorder under ss.4 and 5. A further third are for alcohol-related offences under the Sporting Events (Control of Alcohol) Act 1985. Only ten per cent of all arrests are for offences under the Football (Offences) Act 1991, with the remainder being for a range of crimes including ticket touting, breaching a Football Banning Order, assault and criminal damage.

The football-specific crimes and their evolution into their current forms have been discussed throughout this chapter. The rest of this section will focus on the more common offences with which those accused of creating disorder at sports fixtures are charged. Where these offences are committed 24 hours before kick-off or 24 hours after the end of a designated football match a Football Banning Order can be imposed on the defendant (below, 10.6).

10.5.1 Public Order Act 1986

The Public Order Act 1986 (POA 1986) consolidated and updated the law in accordance with the recommendations of the Law Commission's Working Paper, 'Offences Against Public Order.' Its Parliamentary progress was also influenced, albeit at the last minute, by concerns raised in the Popplewell Reports. The offences created by the POA 1986 cover almost all conduct that could be considered to be acts of hooliganism and is regularly relied on by the police and the CPS to secure convictions against those involved with disorder at all sports fixtures.

10.5.1.1 Public Order Act 1986 ss. 1–5 – riot, violent disorder, affray and public disorder

Sections 1–5 POA 1986 create a hierarchy of offences that vary in their seriousness depending on how many people are involved in the disorder and the nature of the conduct in which they are engaged. The most serious of these offences, riot, is defined in s.1 POA 1986. Riot occurs where 12 or more people who are present together use or threaten unlawful violence as part of a common purpose. If their conduct is such that it would hypothetically cause a person of reasonable firmness present at the scene to fear for their personal safety then each of the people using or threatening to use unlawful violence is guilty of riot. The persons involved in the riot do not have to threaten unlawful violence simultaneously nor does a person of reasonable firmness actually have to be present at the scene of the disorder for the offence to be committed. Although many instances of sports-related disorder could constitute riot, the offence is rarely used to prosecute suspected hooligans. The difficulties associated with proving that a minimum of 12 people each had the same common purpose, particularly where not all of them have been prosecuted, means that offenders are more likely to be charged with violent disorder or affray under ss.2 and 3 POA 1986 respectively.

Violent disorder is defined in almost exactly the same way as riot but requires only three people to be using or threatening to use unlawful violence. Affray can be committed in the same way as violent disorder but by one person acting alone. The only difference between these two offences and riot, apart from the minimum numbers required to be involved with the disorder, is that riot requires proof that the people involved were acting with a common purpose when using or threatening to use unlawful violence whereas violent disorder and affray do not. Thus to secure a conviction for riot it must be proved that for example 12 or more people were acting with a common purpose of attacking the supporters of the opposing team. However to secure convictions for violent disorder or affray the people involved may each be motivated by different reasons for acting with unlawful violence, for example one is involved in a fight with someone against whom he has a longstanding grudge, another in threatening violence towards opposing spectators and another is engaged in committing criminal damage. As long as their conduct taken as a whole would cause a person of reasonable firmness to fear for their personal safety then the offences are committed.

Although almost all incidents of sports-related disorder could constitute at least one of the offences under ss.1–3 POA 1986, it is more likely that anyone engaged in this type of conduct will be arrested and charged with an offence under ss.4, 4A or 5 POA 1986 because of the comparative ease of proving that one of these crimes has been committed. In particular the ability of the prosecution to rely on a police officer's evidence that they were put in fear, harassed, alarmed or distressed by the defendant's conduct makes these offences much easier to prove.

Each of these three offences is committed where a person uses threatening, abusive or insulting words or behaviour towards another or who displays to another person any writing or makes any sign to them which is threatening, abusive or insulting. The difference between them is in the intent of the defendant when using or displaying the words or signs and its impact on the other person. For an offence under s.4 POA 1986 the defendant must have had the intent to cause another person to believe that immediate unlawful violence would be used against them or against somebody else, or that their behaviour would provoke others to use immediate unlawful violence, or that it is likely that such violence would be used or provoked. Under s.4A the defendant must intend only that their conduct would cause another person harassment, alarm or distress, whilst under s.5 it is only necessary for the conduct to have taken place within the hearing or sight of someone likely to be caused harassment, alarm or distress.

Almost all disorderly conduct and much that is simply part of fan culture at football games could be caught by one of these three offences. As it is not necessary to show that the target of the threats or abuse was in fact threatened or caused harassment, alarm or distress, then it is possible for the police to claim that they were the ones who were put in fear that violence would be used or provoked, or that they were harassed, alarmed or distressed by the defendant's behaviour. This ability of the police to give evidence that they were the victims of the disorderly conduct, rather than opposing spectators or players, has made the offences under ss.4, 4A and 5 powerful tools with which to control spectators. Where football-related disorder is concerned it has also enabled Football Banning Orders to be applied for on conviction of what would otherwise be minor public order offences.

10.5.1.2 Public Order Act 1986 ss.17–19 – inciting racial hatred

The offences under ss.18 and 19 POA 1986 criminalise a range of racist behaviour and can be used to control racism at any sports fixture including football. These offences are drafted more widely than the offence of indecent or racialist chanting under s.3 Football (Offences) Act 1991 because they cover individual instances of racial abuse not just those that are repeated as is required for the s.3 offence, and are generally applicable rather than being restricted to regulating incidents that occur at designated football matches.

The s.18 offence is committed by a person who intends to stir up racial hatred by using words, or behaviour, or by displaying written material, which is abusive, threatening or insulting. The offence under s.19 is committed by publishing or distributing material of the same kind. The offences are also committed where, having regard to the surrounding circumstances, racial hatred is likely to be stirred up by the defendant's conduct. Racial hatred is defined in s.17 POA 1986 as being hatred against a group of persons defined by reference to colour, race, nationality, citizenship or ethnic or national origins. Thus the offences will cover abuse spoken or shouted by spectators, written signs or banners containing racist comments and leaflets, pamphlets or other printed material that incites racial hatred.

10.5.1.3 Public Order Act 1986 ss.30–37 – Exclusion Orders

The POA 1986 gave the courts the power to impose Exclusion Orders on persons convicted of offences connected to a football match. The aim of the Orders was to prevent football-related violence or disorder by banning their subjects from entering football grounds for a minimum of three months. An Exclusion Order could only be imposed on a person who was convicted of an alcohol-related offence or an offence of violence towards another person or property that was committed either in or around a football ground or on the way to or from a regulated football match. A further restriction was that the offence had to take place within two hours of the game's kick-off or one hour after it had ended.

The Taylor Final Report criticised the courts' lack of use of this provision and the inability of the police to enforce those that had been imposed on convicted hooligans. Since then the name, scope and conditions attached to Orders that ban those who have been convicted of, or who are suspected of having committed football-related disorder have changed on a number of occasions (below 10.6).

10.5.2 Other relevant legislation

Outside of the football specific legislation and the offences contained in the POA 1986, the majority of arrests at sports fixtures are for assault, aggravated trespass and criminal damage. The various assault offences with which a person could be charged have already been discussed (see further, chapter 6). The remaining offences are outlined below.

10.5.2.1 Criminal Justice and Public Order Act 1994 s.68 – aggravated trespass

Although originally introduced to prevent certain forms of industrial action that had been prevalent in the 1980s and to control the rave scene of the early 1990s, s.68 Criminal Justice and Public Order Act 1994 (CJPOA 1994) can also be used to prosecute pitch invasions in sports other than football (where s.4 Football (Offences) Act applies). The offence is committed by a trespasser who intimidates, obstructs or disrupts anyone who is carrying out or is about to carry out a lawful activity on the land or on adjoining land. A further offence is committed under s.69 CJPOA 1994 where a trespasser fails to leave the land having been required to do so by a police officer. Aggravated trespass is wide ranging enough to cover any situation where a spectator runs on to the playing area whilst a game is in progress, or where damage is caused to the playing area, or where ground-staff are prevented from preparing or maintaining any part of the stadium.

10.5.2.2 Criminal Damage Act 1971

The final category of crimes that are likely to be committed by those engaged in sports-related disorder is criminal damage. The basic offence of criminal damage is committed where the defendant intentionally or subjectively recklessly damages any property belonging to another person (s.1(1) Criminal Damage Act 1971 (CDA 1971)). The aggravated offence is committed where the defendant intentionally or recklessly endangers the life of another person by damaging or destroying property (s.1(2) CDA 1971). If either of these offences is committed by fire then the offence is charged under s.1(3) as arson. There are further offences of threatening to destroy or damage property under s.2 and possessing items with the intent to destroy or damage property under s.3 of the Act. Any harm caused to the fabric of the stadium, the playing area or even the clothing of another person present at a sports match can constitute criminal damage.

10.6 Football Banning Orders

Since the introduction of Exclusion Orders in the POA 1986, a comprehensive framework for banning people who have been involved in football-related disorder has been developed and is now contained in the Football Spectators Act 1989 (FSA 1989). This regime has been amended and revised on a number of occasions over the years, most significantly by the Football (Offences and Disorder) Act 1999 and the Football (Disorder) Act 2000, and is considered to be one of the most effective tools for controlling football hooliganism. Despite these claims, disorder still occurs and controversy continues to surround the use of Football Banning Orders (FBOs) as a means of controlling spectator behaviour; their legality is analysed in the Hot Topic section.

10.6.1 Football Spectators Act 1989 s.14A – Football Banning Orders on conviction

Where a person has been convicted of a relevant offence the court may impose an FBO on them in addition to any punishment handed down. According to sch.1 FSA 1989 a relevant offence is any crime of violence or disorder, or which is alcohol-related, that is committed at or in connection with or on the way to or from a regulated football match and which occurs within 24 hours of the game's kick-off or within 24 hours of its end. A regulated football match now has the same meaning as a designated football match and includes any game where one of the teams is a member of the Premier League, Football League, Football Conference, League of Wales or is a national or regional representative team or whose home ground is situated outside of England and Wales (Football Spectators (Prescription) (Amendment) Order 2006/761).

Where there are reasonable grounds for believing that the imposition of an FBO on the defendant will help to prevent violence or disorder at future regulated football matches the court *must* impose an order in addition to any sentence that it has handed down. If the defendant was sentenced to a period of imprisonment then the FBO must be in place for between six and ten years; where a non-custodial sentence is imposed it must be in place for between three and five years.

The Taylor Report criticised the lack of use of Exclusion Orders by courts in the late 1980s as being one of the main reasons for their lack of effectiveness in controlling football-related disorder. Now FBOs must be imposed by a court if it will help to prevent violence or disorder at future regulated football matches unless it can be justified in open court why an order would be inappropriate. The prosecution will ask for an FBO to be imposed as a matter of course where a relevant offence has been committed and in the vast majority of cases this will be granted.

▶ *R v. Hughes* [2005] EWCA Crim 2537

The Court of Appeal held that a three-year FBO could be imposed on a person without the need to show a propensity to violence or that there had been any repetition of the disorderly conduct. Hughes had thrown one punch at an opposing spectator and had been convicted of affray under s.3 POA 1986; he had no previous football-related convictions. Section 14A FSA 1989 requires only that a person has been convicted of a relevant offence, which Hughes had been, and that the court was satisfied that the imposition of the FBO would help to prevent disorder at future football matches, which it was. Therefore the FBO had been imposed correctly.

This approach has recently been supported and developed.

▶ *R (on the application of White)* v. *Blackfriars Crown Court* **[2008] EWHC 510 (Admin)**

A three-year FBO had been imposed on White after he had pleaded guilty to running on to a football pitch, contrary to s.4 Football (Offences) Act, and committing a common assault on the referee. In dismissing his appeal Richards LJ stated that although this was an isolated incident on the part of the defendant the court was entitled to take into account the general deterrent effect of imposing an FBO in circumstances such as these. In other words the FBO was a warning to other fans not to run on to the pitch and assault the referee and therefore was capable of helping to prevent violence or disorder at future regulated football matches.

10.6.2   Football Spectators Act 1989 s.14B – Football Banning Orders on complaint

Under s.14B FSA 1989 a Chief Officer of Police or the Director of Public Prosecutions can apply for an FBO to be imposed on a person without the need to secure a conviction for a relevant offence against them. Where it can be proved that a spectator has at any time caused or contributed to any violence or disorder, whether in the United Kingdom or elsewhere, and the court is satisfied that there are reasonable grounds for believing that making an FBO would help to prevent violence or disorder at or in connection with any regulated football matches, then the spectator *must* be made the subject of an order.

This means that an FBO can be imposed on a person who has not been proved to have been involved in any criminal activity but is only suspected of being a hooligan. Evidence of having caused or contributed to any violence or disorder can be provided by producing a person's previous football-related convictions, or any non-football-related convictions for violence or disorder, or even on the basis that the spectator has been seen with known hooligans but has not been convicted of any relevant offence themselves. Thus even though there is not sufficient evidence to secure a conviction against a spectator they can still be the subject of an FBO for a period of three to five years, following a successful application under s.14B.

▶ *Gough* v. *Chief Constable of Derbyshire* **[2002] EWCA Civ 351**

Where the subject of an FBO under s.14B appealed against its imposition on the basis that he had never been proved to have engaged in football-related disorder, the Court of Appeal justified the imposition of the order on the basis that FBOs are preventive, not punitive; there is therefore no need to prove that the conduct has occurred, just that the order will prevent it from occurring in the future. As this is a civil application under s.14B FSA 1989 hearings are not subject to the normal rules of evidence or procedural safeguards required of a criminal trial. Although it was stated that a court should be satisfied to a standard approaching the criminal standard of beyond reasonable doubt before imposing an FBO, much of the evidence submitted would not be of a sufficient quality to go before a criminal court. Thus spectators who have never been convicted of a football-related offence can be banned from attending football matches for a similar length of time to those who are guilty of a relevant offence.

10.6.3 The effect of being subject to a Football Banning Order

Around a thousand new FBOs are imposed under ss.14A and 14B each year. A series of relatively standard conditions are contained in each one in an attempt to prevent those to whom they apply from being involved in football-related disorder. Firstly each FBO will ban its subject from entering every designated football ground in England and Wales. This will include an exclusion zone around the banned person's home football ground on match days and may also involve a ban from going to specific pubs where fans congregate before a match.

Secondly it will ban the subject from travelling abroad when England and Wales are playing matches away from home. Thirdly it will ban the subject from travelling when either the FIFA World Cup Finals or UEFA European Nations Cup Finals are taking place. Fourthly a travel ban will be imposed on the subject if their team is playing away from home in an international club competition. Furthermore if any English club team is playing against a team or in a country that is considered to be high risk in terms of the potential for crowd disorder then everyone who is subject to an FBO will be banned from travelling regardless of their club allegiance.

Under s.14C FSA 1989 the various travel bans are in place from five days before the game until the end of the relevant match or, where an international finals tournament is taking place, from a minimum of five days before the date of the first game until the end of the final match. To ensure that the ban is enforceable the subject must surrender their passport to a named police station five days before the game or tournament begins.

Finally under s.14J FSA 1989 the breach of any of the conditions contained in a FBO is an offence. Where a person is found guilty of breaching the conditions of an FBO the offence is a relevant offence for the purposes of s.14A, enabling the court to impose a new FBO on them.

Hot topic . . .

ARE FOOTBALL BANNING ORDERS IMPOSED UNDER S.14B FOOTBALL SPECTATORS ACT 1989 LEGAL?

These are particular problems when FBOs are imposed following an application under s.14B, where there is no need to prove that the spectator has ever committed an offence connected to a designated football match.

Football Banning Orders are one of the cornerstones of the government's anti-hooligan strategy. The object of an FBO is to prevent a person from engaging in football-related disorder by keeping them away from the places where such disorder might break out and from other spectators who may be involved with it. Thus FBOs contain a variety of conditions that prevent their subjects from being in specific places for significant periods of time when relevant games are taking place. However they also represent a significant restriction on a banned person's liberty and movement.

Technically FBOs are civil orders imposed following an application to the relevant court. Applications under s.14B FSA 1989 are usually made by the Chief Officer of Police for the area where the spectator's club is based in an attempt to pre-empt the respondent's involvement with football-related disorder. The main concerns that have been raised with the s.14B procedure are that the standard of proof required for the imposition of an FBO is too low, that they are punishments imposed without the usual procedural safeguards of a criminal trial and that they are disproportionate in their effect.

The standard of proof usually required for a civil order of this nature is that its imposition is necessary on the balance of probabilities. In *Gough* however the Court of Appeal held that because of the serious nature of the allegations being made against the respondent and the impact upon them of an FBO a standard of proof approaching that required in a criminal trial should be used. Thus an FBO should only be imposed where the court is satisfied so that it is sure that it will prevent violence and disorder at football matches in the future. Such a finding contains an inherent contradiction; the evidence presented to the court has to be capable of proving beyond reasonable doubt that an FBO will prevent future football-related violence or disorder, yet it is not of sufficient quality to be used to prosecute and convict the respondent. In other words the respondent is banned because there is a proven suspicion that they are a football hooligan, but that same evidence is not sufficient to prove beyond reasonable doubt that they actually are a football hooligan.

In *Gough* the spectators who were the subject of FBOs also claimed that the procedure used was unlawful as it constituted the imposition of a punishment when it had not been proven that they had committed a crime, contrary to Art. 7 European Convention on Human Rights and Fundamental Freedoms. The Court of Appeal neatly sidestepped this argument by stating that FBOs are preventive, not punitive in their nature because their aim is to protect society from football-related disorder not to punish the subject of the order. The jurisprudence of the European Court of Human Rights has regularly stated that the effect of the order, not its form, is the key to determining whether or not it is a punishment. To ban a person from watching live football for between three and five years and to prevent them from travelling abroad for, in some years, up to three months of the year certainly has the appearance of a punishment and has yet to be explored fully by the appellate courts (*R v. Hughes*).

Following on from the previous argument is the claim that the impact of an FBO is disproportionate when compared to its aim. Although the aim of an FBO is to prevent violence and disorder there is no proof that it can have that effect where there is no proof that the respondent has ever been involved with football-related disorder. Furthermore all FBOs must contain a travel ban even where the respondent does not travel abroad to watch their club side or the England national team. The impression given is that FBOs are generic punishments imposed on suspected football hooligans rather than being specifically targeted at known troublemakers.

The s.14B procedure has the ability to subvert the normal criminal process. Instead of collecting evidence on suspected football hooligans with a view to prosecuting them the current tactic appears to be to collect only enough evidence to secure an FBO against them. The current justification of the legality of FBOs provided by the Court of Appeal is not sufficiently robust and will continue to be challenged until one can be provided.

Summary

10.1 Violence and disorder have been occurring at sports fixtures for many years. It is important to distinguish the causes of disorder from those affecting spectator safety, a distinction not clearly made by either the government or the football authorities.

10.2 Despite government concerns about the increasing number of violent incidents occurring at football matches, both in the UK and when some English fans travelled overseas, very few steps were taken to control spectator conduct. The four reports that were published between 1967 and 1984 did little more than identify that hooliganism had become a problem; the only legislative response was to control the consumption of alcohol at football matches in Scotland (ss.68–77 Criminal Justice (Scotland) Act 1980).

10.3 The fatalities at St Andrew's and Heysel resulted in a piecemeal rather than a coordinated legislative response to football-related disorder. The use of CCTV became a commonplace surveillance tool, the Sporting Events (Control of Alcohol) Act 1985 regulated the consumption of alcohol at football matches in England and Wales and the police were granted increased powers of stop and search by s.60 Criminal Justice and Public Order Act 1994. Further proposals made in the Popplewell Reports were amended, developed or dropped post-Hillsborough.

10.4 As part of its review of all aspects of crowd management the Taylor Reports recommended a number of new criminal offences. The Football (Offences) Act 1991 criminalises throwing missiles, indecent and racial chanting and running on to a football pitch without lawful authority; ticket touting was made an offence under s.166 Criminal Justice and Public Order Act 1994 and the comparatively ineffective Exclusion Orders were replaced by the much more stringent Football Banning Orders. The proposed National Membership Scheme was dropped as being technologically unworkable at the time and likely to cause more disorder than it would prevent.

Summary cont'd

10.5 The Public Order Act 1986 can be used to prosecute most disorderly conduct that occurs at sports fixtures. The police most frequently resort to charges under ss.4, 4A and 5 as it is relatively easy to identify someone who has been harassed, alarmed or distressed by the disorderly conduct. The Offences Against the Person Act 1861 and the Criminal Damage Act 1971 are used to control the more extreme cases of disorder.

10.6 Football Banning Orders, whether imposed on conviction under s.14A Football Spectators Act 1989 or on complaint under s.14B, are now a standard response to football-related disorder. They constitute severe restrictions on the subject's freedom of movement and in particular their ability to attend or be in the neighbourhood of designated football stadiums on match days. Despite claims of their effectiveness as a control mechanism, over a thousand new orders are issued each year demonstrating that the police are yet to reach the root of the problem.

Further reading

Greenfield and Osborn, *Regulating Football* (2001, Pluto Press)

Herring, *Criminal Law: text, cases and materials* (3rd edn, 2008, Oxford University Press) chs 6 and 11

Pollard, Parpworth and Hughes, *Constitutional and Administrative Law: text and materials* (4th edn, 2007, Oxford University Press) ch 11

Deards, 'Human rights for football hooligans' (2002) 27 (6) Ent L Rev 765

James and Pearson, 'Football Banning Orders: analysing their use in court' (2006) 70 (6) Journal of Criminal Law 509

Pearson, 'Qualifying for Europe? The Legitimacy of Football Banning Orders 'on complaint' under the principle of proportionality' (2005) 3(1) Entertainment and Sports Law Journal, online

Pearson, 'Contextualising the Football (Disorder) Act: proportionality under the hammer' in Greenfield and Osborn (eds.), *Readings in Law and Popular Culture* (2006, Routledge)

Pearson and James, 'The Legality and Effectiveness of Using Football Banning Orders in the Fight Against Racism and Violence at Sports Events' in Gardiner, Parrish and Siekmann (eds.), *EU, Sport, Law and Policy* (2009, TMC Asser Press)

Tsoukala, *Football Hooliganism in Europe: Security and Civil Liberties in the Balance* (2009, Palgrave Macmillan).

Government Reports

Chester, *Report of the Committee on Football* (1968, HMSO)

Department of Environment Working Group, *Football Spectator Violence* (1984, HMSO)

Harrington, *Soccer Hooliganism: A Preliminary Report* (1968, John Wright and Sons: Bristol)

Lang, *Crowd Behaviour at Football Matches* (1969, HMSO)

Law Commission Working Paper No.82, *Offences Against Public Order* (1982, HMSO)

McElhone, *Report of the Working Group on Football Crowd Behaviour* (1977, Scottish Education Department, HMSO)

Popplewell J, *Committee of Inquiry into Crowd Safety and Control at Sports Grounds (Interim Report)*, Cmnd 9585 (1985, HMSO)

Popplewell J, *Committee of Inquiry into Crowd Safety and Control at Sports Grounds (Final Report)*, Cmnd 9710 (1986, HMSO)

Part 4

The commercialisation of sport

Chapter 11

Regulating sporting relationships in English law

Key words

▶ **Direct discrimination** – conduct that treats a person less favourably on the grounds of their sex, race or disability.

▶ **Indirect discrimination** – conduct that appears to be objectively neutral but has a disproportionate and adverse impact on a person because of their sex, race or a disability.

▶ **Restraint of trade** – conduct that restrains a person from earning a living, is unreasonable as between the parties involved and is not in the public interest.

11.1 The changing nature of sporting relationships

Since the more formal organisation of sport began in earnest during the second half of the nineteenth century there has been a dramatic shift in the balance of power that exists between the players, the clubs and the governing bodies. The dominant position of the NGBs has been gradually eroded, first by the rising financial power of their more successful club members and more recently by the rise of 'player power'. The impact of challenges to the authority and practices of some NGBs has been seismic; for example when the Rugby Football Union refused to sanction payments to players so that they could be compensated for having to take Saturday mornings off work to play, a group of northern clubs considered themselves to be successful and powerful enough not only to challenge the authority of the RFU but to break away from it altogether to form what is now the Rugby Football League (see further, chapter 2.2.2).

Almost exactly a hundred years later professional sports participants in general and footballers in particular finally achieved something approaching the contractual freedom experienced by employees in other industries; they were allowed to move to alternative employment on the expiry of a fixed term contract without the need for their new employer to pay a fee to their previous employer (*Union Royale Belge des Societe de Football Association ASBL* v. *Bosman* (C-415/93) [1995] ECR I-4921) (see further, 12.2.1). The *Bosman* decision highlights how the changing nature of these sporting relationships has often resulted from specific legal challenges to a restrictive practice; however sometimes the mere threat of legal action has been sufficient to effect change. For example although the transfer system was not altered until it was declared to be incompatible with what is now Art.45 Treaty on the Functioning of the European Union (TFEU) by the European Court of Justice in *Bosman*, the maximum wage that players in the English football leagues could earn was abolished by the Football Association in 1963 following a campaign by the Professional Footballers' Association (PFA) that was accompanied by an underlying threat of legal action if this wage restriction was not removed. The PFA's successful challenge to the maximum wage, which was £20 per week at the time, was just one of many steps taken by sports participants against the restrictions placed on their earnings potential by clubs and governing bodies alike.

As sport has become more commercialised there has become a need to re-evaluate many of the relationships that exist within it. Litigation has been a key driver of the clarification, amendment or abolition of various practices that had become entrenched in sporting relationships. Practices that were considered to be normal within sport but would never be contemplated as lawful in other industries have been challenged, usually to the benefit of the players. Despite these changes the courts have always employed a degree of pragmatism in their approach to sports cases; just because the practice is unusual does not automatically mean that it will be declared unlawful. If a legally satisfying justification for the existence of the practice can be provided then the courts have shown a willingness to take into consideration that sport is different and have applied a more pragmatic and sports-friendly interpretation of the law (*Manchester City FC v. Royle* (below, 11.2.2) and *Eastham v. Newcastle United FC* (below, 11.4.2)). However without such a justification the courts have always been prepared to declare that the restrictive practices operated by NGBs, clubs, promoters and agents are unlawful.

11.2 Identifying and interpreting sports contracts

Sports contracts are nowadays almost always evidenced in writing. Not only will they exist physically but they will generally have to make use of a standard form or contain certain standard clauses that will have been negotiated between representatives of the players, the clubs and the NGB. This basic standard form contract will include terms that are applicable to all players of that sport and which provide a minimum level of protection for all parties. It will also invariably include terms that require the player to conform to the rules of the NGB and ISF, in particular the disciplinary and anti-doping procedures (see further, chapter 2.3.3). Any additional terms, for example those covering the commercial exploitation of the player's image rights, will usually be individually negotiated by the parties.

11.2.1 Identifying the existence of a contract

As the majority of the terms included in sports contracts are either imposed on the parties by the NGB or ISF or are negotiated by the parties or their representatives, there is little scope for examining the basics of contract law at this stage. The contract is formed by a series of offers and counter-offers that are eventually accepted by the parties and which are evidenced in a written contract that was clearly formed with the intention to create a legally binding relationship. In the past several high profile football managers have famously declared that they have never signed a contract and that they were simply working on the basis of a gentleman's agreement entered into between themselves and their chairman. Although they may never have signed a formal written agreement, a legally enforceable contract of employment would have been in place between themselves and their club. The existence of the contract would have been implied, had a dispute over its terms ever come before the courts, on the basis of the course of dealings that had occurred between the parties.

This level of informality is unlikely to be acceptable to either the NGB, who will often now require the contract of employment to be registered with it, or the players, coaches, managers or clubs seeking to protect themselves by entering into more formal contractual relationships. For example in football under s.Q(7) Premier League Handbook all Premier

League managers' contracts must now be evidenced in writing and registered with the League's Secretary. All such contracts must also include the series of standard terms and conditions that are set out in Appendix 8 of the Handbook. Furthermore where there is a history of contracts being evidenced in writing it will be almost impossible for a claimant to establish that a binding agreement has been entered into where there is no such physical evidence (*Sports Network Ltd* v. *Calzaghe* [2009] EWHC 480 (QB)). This growing level of formality can result in highly complex contractual arrangements in certain circumstances.

▶ *Leeds Rugby Ltd* v. *Harris and Bradford Bulls Holdings Ltd* [2005] EWHC 1591 (QBD)

The complexity of the contractual relationships entered into by a modern professional sportsperson can be seen in the multiple agreements entered into when Iestyn Harris moved from playing rugby league for Leeds Rhinos to rugby union for Cardiff Blues and Wales. To enable this move to take place, four interlocking agreements were entered into by Harris, Leeds, Cardiff and the Welsh Rugby Union (WRU). Firstly Leeds and Harris entered into an agreement that released him from his existing playing contract with Leeds. This contract also contained an option which would enable Leeds to re-employ Harris should he wish to return to playing rugby league in the future. Secondly Cardiff agreed to employ Harris as a professional rugby union player for four years. This contract contained a clause enabling Harris to unilaterally terminate the agreement after three years. Thirdly a tripartite agreement between the WRU, Cardiff and Leeds contained the terms of the transfer fee to be paid to Leeds. Fourthly a contract between the WRU and Harris contained the terms on which Harris would play for Wales if selected.

A dispute arose when, after three years of playing rugby union for Cardiff, Harris terminated his playing contract with them and entered into an agreement to play rugby league for Bradford Bulls. Leeds claimed that Harris was contractually bound to play for them for one season on his return to rugby league whilst Harris claimed that the terms of any such agreement were an unlawful restraint of trade. The court held that all four of the original contracts had been validly entered into and that their terms were sufficiently clear to be enforced. The court also held that although the contract between Harris and Leeds was a restraint on his ability to choose which club to play for, it was neither unreasonable nor an unlawful restraint of trade (below, 11.4.2). Therefore Harris was in breach of contract by entering into an agreement to play for Bradford and Leeds was compensated for their loss of Harris' services.

In *Harris* the initial problem was in identifying which contracts were enforceable between the various parties. The court stated that the entire contractual framework had to be examined, not just individual terms of individual contracts and in doing so was able to provide additional context to the agreements. Once the validity of the agreements was confirmed the next step was to interpret the effect of the applicable terms. In *Harris* this was a relatively straightforward matter as the terms were clearly drafted. In other cases a sports-friendly interpretation to contractual terms has been followed by the courts.

11.2.2   Interpreting the terms of the contract

Most issues of interpretation occur on breach or termination of the contract. Specific challenges made to contractual terms or the rules of an NGB that are claimed to be in restraint of trade or operating in a discriminatory manner are discussed separately (below, 11.4 and 11.5 respectively). Breach of contract is where one of the parties does not comply with the terms by which they have agreed to be bound. Where one party is in breach the other can treat the contract as at an end and sue for compensation that will put them into the same position that they would have been had the contract been successfully completed. In the sports cases the breach will usually be quite straightforward: either the club will have sacked one of its employees, or one of its employees will be seeking to leave to work for another club. The issues of interpretation will determine who breached the contract, at what time and how much compensation will need to be paid. The courts have allowed a degree of flexibility into their interpretation of sports contracts, enabling a certain amount of pragmatism and the customs and conventions of sports employment to contextualise the decision-making process.

▶ *Manchester City Football Club Plc v. Royle* **[2005] EWCA Civ 195**

The parties were in dispute over the amount of compensation to be paid after the club had sacked Royle from his role as first team manager. On 1 June 2000 the parties had entered into a four-year agreement for Royle to act as manager of Manchester City FC. The contract included a term such that if the club terminated the agreement before its end on 31 May 2004 it would pay Royle compensation amounting to 12 months' salary if it was in the Premier League at the time and six months' salary if it was in the First Division; the amounts would have been £750,000 and £150,000 respectively.

On 19 May 2001, following their last match of the season, Manchester City finished 18th in the Premier League and were relegated to the First Division. Following a meeting with the club's chairman on 21 May, Royle was sacked and his contract was terminated. Royle argued that he was entitled to compensation at the Premier League rate because as of the 21 May 2001 the club was still a shareholder-member of the Premier League. The club claimed that as it had been relegated on 19 May it was no longer a Premier League team and compensation was payable at the lower First Division rate.

The Court of Appeal held that the test to be applied when interpreting the contract was that of the reasonable person with knowledge of football. As the reasonable person with a knowledge of football would assume that a football club had been relegated to the league below at the end of the final game of the season, not on the transfer of its shareholding in the league of which it had previously been a member, then the compensation payable on termination of Royle's contract was the First Division rate.

The sports-friendly approach followed by the court is appropriate for two reasons. Firstly it takes account of the way that a football season actually operates: relegation takes place on the last day of the season after the final league standings have been calculated. As Manchester City had finished 18th, any reasonable person with knowledge of football would consider that they were relegated on 19 May, two days before Royle was sacked. Secondly the interpretation put forward by the defendant would have rewarded him for failure during the 2000–01 season; he had overseen the club's relegation to the First Division and should therefore be compensated at the lower level. The realities of modern sport and the litigation to which it gives rise have been taken into consideration not only in the cases coming before the national courts but also before the specialist tribunals such as CAS.

▶ *Mutu v. Chelsea Football Club Ltd* **CAS 2008/A/1644**

Following an appeal to determine the circumstances in which a club could terminate a player's contract of employment, CAS confirmed the findings of a series of hearings that had taken place before itself, FIFA's Dispute Resolution Chamber (DRC) and the Premier League's

Appeals Committee. Firstly it acknowledged that Mutu had breached his contract of employment with Chelsea by testing positive for cocaine following a targeted drugs test conducted by the Football Association. Secondly it acknowledged that under English Law Chelsea was entitled to accept Mutu's conduct as a repudiatory breach of contract and that it was entitled to treat the contract as terminated with immediate effect. Thirdly it found that the DRC had adopted the correct approach when calculating the amount of compensation due to Chelsea as a result of Mutu's breach of contract. This required the DRC to take into consideration the relevant principles of English law, Art.22 FIFA Regulations for the Status and Transfer of Players and the specificity of sport.

CAS explained that this approach was appropriate for this dispute because, according to the contract itself, English law was applicable to all disputes arising from it. Furthermore the Regulations for the Status and Transfer of Players were incorporated into that contract by a term that required all relevant rules of FIFA to be adhered to. Finally it was noted that the jurisprudence of both the DRC and CAS allowed the specific nature and needs of the sport to be taken into consideration. Thus when providing its reasons for the resolution of a dispute the interests of not only the parties involved but the whole football community had to be taken into account. By acknowledging the need to consider the specificity of sport, both the DRC and CAS were able to take account of the impact that the decision to award Chelsea in excess of €17m would have on football, the signs that it would send out to players and clubs alike about drug taking and the importance of following proper procedures when terminating a contract of employment.

Reliance on a sports-specific analysis of this kind is likely to occur more frequently in the future as parties try to convince the courts and specialist tribunals before which they are appearing that it is not just the applicable law that should be taken into consideration when determining the outcome of their dispute but also the customs and conventions of their sport.

11.3 Conduct interfering with the performance of a contract

Where a contract has been validly concluded it is unlawful for any other person to procure its breach or to interfere with its performance. Where sporting relationships are concerned this will usually occur where a third party who is unconnected with the contract seeks to lure one of the parties to move from one employer to another (below, 11.3.1) or in some other way actively prevent them from fulfilling the terms of their contract (below, 11.3.2). Further, a potential conflict of interest can arise in a contractual relationship where one of the parties acts in two or more roles that can influence how the contract is performed (below, 11.3.3). This kind of problem now occurs much more rarely than in the past and is only likely to occur where an NGB has inadequate regulatory safeguards in place.

11.3.1 Procuring a breach of contract

The tort of procuring a breach of contract occurs when a third party, A, intentionally induces one of the parties to a contract, B, to break any of the terms of their contract with the other party, C (*Lumley* v. *Gye* (1853) 118 ER 749). In order for C to be able to make a claim for damages against A, C must be able to prove that: B has breached their contract with C; A knew that their conduct was interfering with an existing contract between B and C in such a way as to cause its breach; and that A intended by their conduct to cause a breach of the contract between B and C (*OGB Ltd* v. *Allan* [2007] UKHL 21).

The most common situation where the procurement of a breach of contract may occur is when a professional football club, A, causes a player, B, to move from their existing club, C, following an unauthorised approach to the player by club A. Although there is very little litigation on this point, particularly as the rules governing unauthorised approaches to contracted players are now much more strictly defined and enforced by the football authorities, there is no reason why the tort would not be committed if it could be proved that player B had breached their contract of employment with club C in order to move to new employment with club A (*Middlesbrough Football and Athletic Co (1986) Ltd* v. *Liverpool Football and Athletic Grounds Plc* [2002] EWCA Civ 1929). Outside of football the expansion in the number of highly lucrative twenty20 cricket events may see this tort being used to challenge the International Cricket Council's eligibility rules for 'authorised' competitions.

▶ *Greig v. Insole; World Series Cricket Pty Ltd v. Insole* **[1978] 1 WLR 302**

In early 1977 World Series Cricket (WSC) entered into contracts with 34 of the world's leading cricketers. Its aim was to organise a series of private test matches and one day games that would be played primarily at venues in Australia but with the option to stage events in other countries should the opportunity arise. The contracts were not exclusive and were designed to run alongside each of the players' existing obligations, not to replace them.

On 26 July shortly after news of these privately organised matches had broken the International Cricket Council (ICC), the ISF for cricket, announced a change in its rules so that any player who took part in or made themselves available to take part in an unauthorised cricket match after 1 October 1977 would be disqualified from playing ICC sanctioned Test Matches. The ICC then passed a resolution declaring that all matches organised by WSC between 1 October 1977 and 31 March 1979 were unauthorised cricket matches. On 5 August the Test and County Cricket Board (TCCB), the NGB for cricket in the UK, announced that it intended to implement the decision of the ICC, dependent on the outcome of the challenges brought by the claimants. The TCCB also stated its intention to ban any player who had been disqualified in these circumstances by the ICC from playing county cricket for a period of two years following the last day of the unauthorised game in which they had played or made themselves available to play in. WSC challenged these rule changes on the basis that they acted as an inducement to the contracted players to breach their contracts with WSC by forcing them to play only in 'officially sanctioned' cricket matches. A group of the players also made challenges alleging that the rules acted as a restraint of trade (below, 11.4.2).

The High Court held that the ICC's rule change and the changes proposed by the TCCB were inducements to the players to breach their contracts with WSC. The finding was based on the defendants' knowledge of the existence of the contracts between the players and WSC, the timing of the introduction of the rule changes and their retrospective impact on the players. Taken as a whole the defendants' conduct was specifically designed to apply pressure to the contracted players to withdraw from their obligations to WSC. As they were unable to provide any justification for the rule changes, the defendants were inducing the players to breach their contracts.

The key issue here is not the rule changes themselves, but the timing of them. If such a rule had been in place before WSC had entered into agreements with the players then WSC would have been guilty of inducing a breach of contract, not the cricket authorities. Alternatively if the rule changes had been designed to come into force once the 34 players' obligations were fulfilled then that too would not have been inducing a breach of contract. The problem was that the rule changes were specifically designed to induce the players to breach their contracts not to promote the better organisation or administration of the sport. The current, legally defensible version of the rule ensures that players can only play in authorised competitions, such as the Indian Premier League, whilst those who play in unauthorised events, such as the Indian Cricket League, may find themselves with eligibility problems for some authorised events.

11.3.2 Unlawful interference with the performance of a contract

The tort of unlawful interference is committed where D deliberately interferes with the performance of a contract between E and F by unlawful means and with the intent to cause harm to the commercial interests of either E or F by such interference. The difficulty for any claimant trying to establish that this tort has been committed is the need to prove D's intention at two separate stages: the intent to act unlawfully and the intent to cause harm to the claimant by the unlawful act. These difficulties were highlighted in *Watson and Bradford City Association Football Club (1983) Ltd* v. *Gray and Huddersfield Town Association Football Club Ltd* [1998] The Times, 26 November (see further, chapter 4.4.3.2). Alongside the claim of negligence brought by Watson, Bradford City claimed that in injuring their player the defendants had unlawfully interfered with the performance of his playing contract. The basis of Bradford City's claim was that Gray had intentionally caused serious injury to Watson by fouling him. As both players were professionals Gray would have known that Watson was playing under a contract of employment with Bradford City. Therefore any injury intentionally caused to Watson by Gray must of necessity have been accompanied by an intention to interfere with Watson's ability to perform the obligations defined in his contract of employment with Bradford City. Although Bradford's claim was dismissed on the grounds that Gray had acted only negligently, it demonstrates that in the most exceptional of cases, where it can be proved that a player, D, deliberately injured an opponent, E, the tort may be capable of being established by E's employer, F. The benefits of succeeding in a claim of unlawful interference are potentially huge, including recouping the costs of paying and rehabilitating an injured player and recruiting a replacement for the period of their injury.

11.3.3 Conflicts of interest in the contractual relationship

The opportunity for conflicts of interest to arise is becoming increasingly rare as contractual arrangements become more formalised and NGBs' regulatory procedures become more stringent. The most important development has been to prevent one party to a contract from acting in two or more roles in relation to its performance. For example in *Watson* v. *Prager* [1991] 1 WLR 726, one of the arguments put forward by the claimant boxer for why their contract should be set aside was that the defendant was unable to represent him effectively as the defendant acted as both his manager and the promoter of his fights. In his role as manager the defendant was contractually obliged to use his best endeavours to negotiate terms and conditions that were as favourable as possible for the claimant. However when acting as the promoter of the claimant's fights the defendant would be trying to maximise his own personal profit from the event. As a conflict of interests of this nature was inherently unreasonable, despite the disputed terms being imposed on the parties by the British Boxing Board of Control, the contract was unenforceable.

In football an analogous situation developed where agents would act for both sides to a transaction, for example the player and the buying club. The conflict arises here because the agent will be attempting to negotiate the best possible deal for the client-player whilst at the same time trying to reduce the outlay of the client-club. Regulation C of the FA's Football Agents Regulations now specifically prevents dual representation of this kind.

11.3.4 Constructive dismissal

Where the conduct of an employer undermines the ability of an employee to carry out their job effectively, the employee may be able to claim that they have been constructively dismissed. The employee's claim will be successful if they can prove that the employer's behaviour amounted to a fundamental breach of contract such that they have in essence been sacked by being unable to carry out the job that they had originally agreed to carry out.

> ▶ *Keegan* v. *Newcastle United Football Club Ltd* **Premier League Manager's Arbitration Tribunal, 2 October 2009**
>
> During negotiations between the parties concerning the appointment of the claimant as the defendant's first team manager, the claimant understood that he was to have the final say on all matters relating to the transfer of players into and out of the club. On the basis of this understanding the claimant agreed to take up the post from 16 January 2008. On 31 August 2008, contrary to the express wishes of the claimant, the club signed Ignacio Gonzalez. Over the next few days the club made a series of public statements reaffirming that the final say on all transfers was Keegan's and that he was in charge of first team matters. On 4 September, after the parties had failed to resolve the matter of who was in charge of player transfers, the claimant resigned.
>
> In the course of evidence the club's witnesses admitted that the signing was made for 'commercial purposes' as a favour to two South American agents, not to improve the playing strength of the first team squad. Moreover they admitted that the public statements made at the beginning of September concerning Keegan having the final say on all transfers were part of a public relations exercise designed to reassure the fans, not a truthful statement that they intended to be bound by. The panel found that having the final say on transfers was a duty usually associated with football managers unless the parties agreed specifically to the contrary and that therefore signing a player against the claimant's express wishes was a fundamental breach of contract. The claimant was therefore entitled to treat himself as having been constructively dismissed and could accept the club's repudiation of the contract.

11.4 Restraint of trade

The purpose of the doctrine of restraint of trade is to ensure that a person or an organisation is not restricted in their ability to earn a living or make a profit. There are three stages to establishing that the doctrine has been infringed: firstly the claimant must be able to prove that they have as a matter of fact been restrained from earning money from their chosen profession; secondly the defendant must demonstrate that any restraint affecting the claimant's ability to work is reasonable and proportionate as between them; thirdly the claimant must then satisfy the court that the restraint is not in the public interest in the way that it operates (*Nordenfelt* v. *Maxim Nordenfelt Guns* [1894] AC 535).

Where sport is concerned, the provisions of any contract that affect the ability of for example a club to maximise its profits or a player to earn a living can be capable of being in restraint of trade, as can the rules and decisions of an NGB or ISF. However the mere fact that a restriction exists does not mean that a restraint of trade has occurred. Where the restraint of trade is necessary and proportionate for the proper administration of a sport and it is in the public interest, it can be held to be justifiable and therefore lawful.

11.4.1 Restraints affecting clubs

The restraints of trade that are capable of affecting sporting clubs are usually imposed on them by the NGB or ISF of the sport in question. As any such rules or decisions are usually incorporated into the club's contract of membership with the NGB, the action will have to be brought for breach of that contract (see further, chapter 2.3.3.1). Where no contractual relationship can be established the club may be able to invoke the court's supervisory jurisdiction to pursue a challenge (*Enderby Town FC* v. *Football Association* [1971] Ch 591) (see further, chapter 2.3.2). The club will usually be seeking an injunction to stop the NGB from operating a rule in a specific way, or a declaration that the rule should or should not be applied in a particular way, or compensation for the harm caused by the adverse effects of the rule restraining the club from maximising its profits. The courts have long held that where an NGB is exercising monopoly power in this manner, it is within their jurisdiction to see that it is not abused (*Nagle* v. *Feilden* [1966] 2 QB 633) (below, 11.5.1).

> ▶ *Newport Association Football Club Ltd* v. *Football Association of Wales Ltd* (unreported) High Court (ChD), 12 April 1995
>
> In 1992 the Football Association of Wales (FAW) took steps to establish a professional football league in Wales. Until that time the more successful of the Welsh professional and semi-professional football clubs had competed in the English league structure. Having failed in its attempts to encourage all professional teams based in Wales to join the new league, the FAW passed a resolution that prevented any Welsh club from playing games at its home ground if it chose to remain playing in the English leagues. The only clubs that were exempted from this ruling were those already playing in the Football League or Football Conference at the time: Cardiff City, Swansea City, Wrexham and Merthyr Tydfil.
>
> The effect of this resolution was that Newport County was forced to play its home games 50 miles away in Moreton-in-Marsh, Gloucestershire. The club challenged the resolution as being in restraint of trade because by forcing it to play 'home' games so far outside of its normal catchment area it was unable to attract enough supporters to make its continued existence viable. At trial the judge accepted that this reduction in income was in fact a restraint on the club's ability to maximise its takings from attendance at the game, in accordance with the first part of the test established in *Nordenfelt*. As the FAW was unable to prove that the restraint was a reasonable means of protecting its own legitimate interests when balanced against those of the club, a declaration was granted to the club that allowed it to continue playing in the English league structure and to play its home games in Newport.

Newport County and other similarly affected clubs wanted to remain in the English league structure because of the possibility of being promoted to the Football League with the higher financial rewards that are on offer there when compared to those which are available in what is now the Welsh Premier League. The FAW hoped that by forcing the more established Welsh clubs to play in the new league the standard of play and rewards on offer would improve significantly. However the resolution passed by the FAW was a disproportionate means of trying to create a truly national professional league. Therefore the interests of the club in trying to maximise its earnings potential was considered to be more in need of protection than the FAW's desire to create a new league. In order for such a claim to succeed the affected club must ensure that it challenges the rules by which it is playing in a timely and appropriate manner.

▶ *Stevenage Borough Football Club Ltd v. Football League Ltd* (1997) 9 Admin LR 109

Having won the Football Conference at the end of the 1995–96 football season, Stevenage Borough FC challenged the Football League's refusal to promote it to the Third Division. The club's argument was that the requirement that it must satisfy the League's criteria on stadium capacity by 31 December 1995, over four months before it knew whether or not it would finish top of the Football Conference, was an unreasonable restraint of trade. The basis for this claim was that the criteria required a small club of modest financial means to expend large amounts of money speculatively on ground improvements that would only be necessary should it win the Conference. As the required stadium improvements would in fact have been completed before the start of the 1996–97 Football League season the club argued that it should be promoted despite not having met the original deadline of 31 December 1995.

At trial the judge found that the Football League had failed to justify why the deadline for the completion of ground improvements should be set at so early a date in the season. However regardless of whether this criterion was an unlawful restraint of trade, the judge refused to grant the declaration on the grounds of delay, a decision which was upheld in the Court of Appeal. Both courts highlighted that the club was aware of the League's stadium criteria well before the start of the 1995–96 football season and that it had sought clarification on them on a number of occasions. As a result it could not challenge the rules by which the competition had been run after it had finished; any challenge to the lawfulness of the rules should have been made at the start of the season not after its completion.

Although the judgment of the Court of Appeal was reserved on whether the criteria were being operated in restraint of trade, and the trial judge's opinion is in reality obiter, it seems likely that Stevenage Borough were correct in their arguments as the League changed the date by which the criteria must be met for the following season to 30 April 1997. However neither court was prepared to allow the club to change the rules that had governed the competition retrospectively as this would undermine the proper administration of the League. A more timely challenge could have seen Stevenage Borough succeed in having the criteria changed and its being promoted.

11.4.2 Restraints affecting players

The same test to establish a restraint of trade applies to contracts, rules and decisions that affect players as it does to clubs, however the variety of ways in which a sportsperson's ability to earn a living can be restricted is significantly wider. The internationalisation of elite sport has led to fewer cases being decided on the basis of restraint of trade as many of the practices that operate as restrictions will have a European element and are therefore more likely to be challenged as infringements of the freedoms of movement protected by Arts.45 and 56 TFEU (ex Arts.39 and 49 ECT) or as anti-competitive practices under Arts.101 and 102 TFEU (ex Arts.81 and 82 ECT) (see further, chapters 12.2–4). Specific restrictions on a sportsperson's ability to compete that are based on sex, gender, race and disability discrimination are also examined separately (below, 11.5). Despite these developments the common law doctrine of restraint of trade has not only played an important role in the development of national sports law, it has the ability to continue to do so in the future.

11.4.2.1 Restraints imposed by contract

Where a player has specifically agreed to be bound by a restriction it is likely to be held to be reasonable in the way that it operates as between the parties. In *Leeds* v. *Harris* (above, 11.2.1) one of the interlocking agreements entered into by the parties to transfer Harris to Cardiff Blues provided Leeds with the option of requiring him to play for it for one year should the player decide to return to playing rugby league. Harris claimed that the agreement was void for being a restraint of trade, however the court held that this was a valid and enforceable contract that he had breached by signing a contract to play for Bradford Bulls. Although the option exercisable by Leeds was a restriction as it prevented Harris from playing for the club of his choice for a year, it was reasonable and proportionate in the circumstances because he had voluntarily entered into it on the basis of legal advice and was to be paid an appropriate salary.

This reasoning could potentially be used by analogy to justify the legality of a salary cap in a sport. In these circumstances the terms of the salary cap will have to be negotiated by representatives of the NGB, the employing clubs and the employee players; the players will usually be represented by their union. Although no legal challenges have been made to any of the salary caps currently in force in the UK, because for the most part they have helped to secure the financial viability of the clubs and sports involved, at common law they are likely to be objectively justifiable restraints of trade provided that the players have been involved in the negotiation process that establishes the level and impact of the cap.

11.4.2.2 Restraints imposed by a rule of the NGB

Many of the employment restrictions imposed on professional athletes are justifiable as being necessary for the proper administration of a sport by its NGB. For example, many team sports have a final date by which transfers of players between sides must be completed, or specific dates during which such transfers can be made. This is to protect the integrity of a competition by promoting contractual stability throughout the playing season.

However where the restriction has been implemented specifically to prevent a certain type of conduct then the timing of its introduction is all important. In *Greig* v. *Insole* (above, 11.3.1) the passing of a resolution that had retrospective effect was held to be an unlawful restraint of trade. Greig had entered into a contract to play in a series of cricket matches organised by World Series Cricket Pty Ltd (WSC). At the time that he did, there was nothing in the rules of either the International Cricket Council (ICC) or the Test and County Cricket Board (TCCB) to prevent him from playing for a potential rival like WSC, if only because the cricketing authorities had never contemplated that such an event could happen. Once the ICC and TCCB became aware of WSC's plans they passed rules that would mean that any player who was contracted with WSC would be banned from playing international and county cricket for two years following the date of the end of the last unauthorised game in which they had played or for which they had made themselves available.

This rewriting of the eligibility rules was held to be an unlawful restraint of trade because it had been deliberately designed to prevent the players from playing in 'unauthorised' forms of cricket. If the rule had been in place before Greig had entered into a contract to play for WSC, then he would have been aware of the impact of his choice and would have been aware that he would be banned for acting in the way that he had. However at the time that he signed with WSC, there were no such rules in place and there was no such thing as an 'unauthorised' cricket match. The ICC and TCCB could only change their rules by giving adequate notice to the players who had signed with WSC that the eligibility criteria would change at some point in the future. The retrospective effect of the ban is what caused the restraint to be unlawful.

Most NGBs and ISFs now include prohibitions in their rules that prevent players from playing for a rival organisation or in unauthorised competitions. This has again come to a head in cricket where the Indian Premier League twenty20 competition is authorised but the rival Indian Cricket League is not. Thus those players who have competed in the Indian Cricket League have found themselves ineligible to play in some authorised competitions.

11.4.2.3 Restraints imposed by suspension from competition

Perhaps the most high profile restriction on a person's ability to play and therefore earn a living from sport is when they are banned or suspended from being able to compete by their NGB or ISF. Suspensions are usually imposed on players following a breach of the NGB's rules and include bans for taking performance enhancing and/or recreational drugs, using violence, illegal techniques or equipment, financial misconduct and bringing the game into disrepute.

In *Gasser* v. *Stinson* (unreported) High Court (QBD), 15 June 1988, the claimant was an athlete who had been banned from competing for two years by the International Association of Athletics Federations (IAAF) following a positive test for a performance enhancing substance. She challenged the legality of the ban by claiming that it was an unlawful restraint of trade as it would prevent her from having the opportunity to compete for reward as a professional runner. The High Court acknowledged that as a matter of fact a ban of this nature could act as a restraint of trade, however it held that the two year suspension imposed on Gasser in this case was reasonable in order to protect the integrity of the sport from those choosing to cheat.

Thus where an NGB or ISF can provide a justification for the necessity of a restriction such as a ban or suspension, and it is proportionate in that it is no more than is necessary for the proper administration of the sport and the protection of its integrity, then there is no unlawful restraint of trade (see further, chapter 12.3.1 for the position in EU law). What would have been interesting, had it gone to trial, would have been the court's opinion of the reasonableness of the lifetime ruling of ineligibility imposed on Dwain Chambers by the British Olympic Association as a result of his having committed a serious doping offence when compared to the two year ban that had been imposed by the IAAF (*Chambers* v. *British Olympic Association* [2008] EWHC 2028 (QBD)) (see further, chapter 2 Hot Topic).

11.4.2.4 Restraints imposed by the operation of the transfer system

The transfer system, particularly as it has been operated in professional football, is a unique sporting arrangement. Instead of being able to resign and move to a new employer, many professional athletes must effectively ask their employer's permission to resign or wait to be sacked or sold on to a new club. There are no notice clauses in most sports contracts, though Art.15 of FIFA's Regulations on the Status and Transfer of Players allows a player to move for 'sporting just cause' where they have played in fewer than ten per cent of the club's matches for no good reason. Such a situation would be unthinkable in any other industry.

Although any restrictive practices emanating from the operation of the transfer system are now likely to engage EU law, especially after *Bosman* and its progeny (see further, 12.2.1), common law restraint of trade remains a live issue. The ongoing attempts of both FIFA and UEFA to reinforce the transfer system mean that it is important to understand how these organisations have reacted to being challenged in the past.

▶ *Eastham* v. *Newcastle United Football Club Ltd, the Football League Ltd and the Football Association* [1964] Ch 413

Prior to this case, professional football's transfer system operated in a markedly different way to how it does today. When a player came to the end of a fixed-term contract with their employing club, the club had four options: (1) offer the player a new contract; (2) place the player on the transfer list; (3) place the player on the retained list; (4) allow the player to leave on a free transfer. If option (2) was pursued the employing club let it be known that the player was no longer wanted and could move on payment of an appropriate fee to a new club. If option (3) was pursued the club had to pay the player a reasonable wage of at least the Football League minimum. The employing club did not have to pick the player to play for it nor did it have to sell him. In effect it could pay him to do nothing and prevent him from playing for any other professional club.

During the 1959–60 football season Eastham, a Newcastle United player, asked his club's permission to be transferred; Newcastle refused. For the 1960–61 he was retained for a further year on his previous salary but did not sign a new contract, choosing instead to work outside of football. From 1961 he was to be paid the Football League minimum wage and kept on the retained list by Newcastle, unable to play professional football for any other club. Eastham argued that taken together options (2) and (3) operated as an unlawful restraint of trade by preventing him from moving to a new employer of his choice after his fixed-term contract had come to an end.

The defendants argued that charging a transfer fee enabled clubs to recoup the money that they had expended on training and developing players during their time with them. Moreover that the fees helped to redistribute wealth within the game by trickling money down from the richer buying clubs to the poorer selling clubs. Finally it was argued that transfer fees helped to reinforce the competitive balance within the League by preventing clubs from hoarding the best players.

The court rejected these claims and held that the 'retain and transfer' system as operated was an unlawful restraint of trade. The 'retained' element was immediately declared void, enabling Eastham to complete his move to Arsenal for an undisclosed fee. However the judge thought that the transfer system on its own was justifiable because a player could appeal to the League's Management Committee against his club requiring an unreasonably high transfer fee and because it facilitated the circulation of both players and money throughout the game. He concluded that there was a restraint but not one that was either unlawful or as serious as that found in the combined 'retain and transfer' system.

It is important to note that this dispute took place after the expiry of the claimant's contract. He was not able to 'run down' his contract as players now do because the club was entitled to place him on the retained list and prevent him from playing elsewhere. Thus despite technically not being employed by Newcastle, the club was still able to influence where he could work next, including preventing him from working as a professional footballer altogether.

The transfer system which operated in Belgium that gave rise to the *Bosman* case was at least as restrictive as the pre-*Eastham* English system (see further, 12.2.1). The new rules put in place by the FA after *Eastham* meant that it was unlikely that a similar challenge would have been made in England; if a player was offered the same money or more than he had been on previously and he rejected it, he could only move clubs if a transfer fee was paid, however if he was offered less than he had been previously earning he could leave on a free transfer.

The football authorities put forward the same arguments in both *Eastham* and *Bosman* to justify the use of the transfer system; that transfer fees caused a 'trickle down' of money to less well-off clubs, that they facilitated a redistribution of wealth and helped to provide competitive balance to the league. In both cases these arguments were put forward with no evidence to back them up and in both cases the players won. The only way that the football authorities will be able to justify the restrictive practices that they seek to uphold and the new ones that they hope to introduce will be to provide evidence to a court of why these restraints are necessary and proportionate for the proper administration of the game.

11.5 Discriminatory behaviour

Sport is riddled with what would be considered to be discriminatory practices in almost any other context. The vast majority of sports practice a form of sex discrimination by preventing men and women from playing alongside of and competing against one another. Where quotas restrict the number of foreign nationals that can play in the same team, there is the possibility of race discrimination on the grounds of nationality. And in some circumstances equipment and medication that would enable disabled athletes to compete alongside those without disabilities are considered to be unfairly performance enhancing and are banned (*Pistorius* v. *International Association of Athletics Federations* CAS 2008/A/1480) (below, 11.5.4). Yet in sport such discrimination is often not only tolerated but is so culturally entrenched as to receive statutory backing.

Discrimination in sport can occur for any number of reasons. It can be blatant, such as the ban on allowing women to train racehorses prior to *Nagle* v. *Feilden* [1966] 2 QB 633 (below, 11.5.2.1); it can be misguided paternalism, as has been seen by the reluctance to allow women to box professionally (*Couch* v. *British Boxing Board of Control* (unreported) Employment Appeal Tribunal, 31 March 1988) (below, 11.5.2.2); it can be protectionist, as is seen in the rules governing nationality quotas (see further, chapter 12.2.1) and it can be culturally driven, as are many of the explanations for why men and women should not compete against each other. However in many cases discrimination has been justified as being both in the best interests of the sport and of those who play sport.

Conduct amounting to discrimination is unlawful when practised by employers against employees, by organisations such as NGBs that have the power to confer qualifications or authorisations on a person or to provide them with vocational training, and by providers of sports facilities and services. This section focuses on how the main anti-discrimination laws operate in the context of sport together with how and why some of the more obviously discriminatory practices have been justified by the legislature and the courts.

11.5.1   Direct and indirect discrimination

All forms of discrimination can be grouped into two main classes: direct and indirect discrimination. This distinction can be made regardless of the actual type of discrimination being practised against a person (s.1 Sex Discrimination Act 1975, s.1 Race Relations Act 1976 and ss.4, 13 and 20 Disability Discrimination Act 1995). Direct discrimination is where the criterion applied to a person is objectively the reason for their less favourable treatment. For example the complete ban on women acting as licensed racehorse trainers simply because they were women was direct sex discrimination (*Nagle* v. *Feilden*).

Indirect discrimination is where the criterion applied is objectively neutral but has a disproportionate and adverse impact on a member of a protected class. For example UEFA's 'home grown player' rule could be considered to be indirectly discriminatory as the applicable criteria are much more easily fulfilled by players born and raised in the same country as the employing club than those born and raised abroad. Despite the rule being drafted in such a way as to make it appear to be capable of being fulfilled by any person regardless of nationality, from a practical perspective it indirectly discriminates against players of a different nationality to that of where the club which employs them is based. Indirect discrimination can only be lawful where it can be objectively justified by the discriminator as appropriate in the circumstances.

11.5.2   Sex discrimination

The aim of the Sex Discrimination Act 1975 (SDA 1975) is to ensure that all people are treated equally regardless of their sex or gender. In particular it is supposed to outlaw generalisations about a person's competence to perform tasks that are based on sex or gender, though a special exemption from this aspect of the law is provided to sport in some circumstances.

11.5.2.1 *Discriminatory practices*

Although pre-dating the SDA 1975 *Nagle* v. *Feilden* is perhaps the clearest example of direct sex discrimination. The claimant was an experienced racehorse trainer who had applied to the Jockey Club for a trainer's licence on a number of occasions. The Club consistently refused to grant her a licence even though it had been prepared to license her male employees. The Court of Appeal held that the Club's policy of not granting a licence to a person on the grounds that the applicant was a woman was unlawful and should be amended. Discrimination of this kind would now be unlawful under s.13 SDA 1975 as the Jockey Club was a body that had the power to confer an authorisation on a person and had refused to do so solely on the grounds of the applicant's sex.

Under s.29 SDA 1975 it is unlawful to discriminate against groups of users of facilities and services. In *James* v. *Eastleigh Borough Council* [1990] ICR 554 the defendant charged retired people a lower amount to use its facilities than those who were not retired. At the time the retirement age for women was 60 but for men was 65. The differential charging policy was found to be discriminatory as between the ages of 60 and 65 men and women were charged different amounts solely on the basis of their sex.

11.5.2.2 Sex Discrimination Act 1975 s.44 – the sports exemption

Despite one of the aims of the SDA 1975 being to abolish discrimination on the basis of generalisations about the competence of one sex's ability to perform specific tasks, s.44 provides an exemption for sport that has precisely this effect.

> ▶ **Sex Discrimination Act 1975 s.44 – sports etc**
>
> (1) Nothing in Parts II to IV shall, in relation to any sport, game or other activity of a competitive nature where the physical strength, stamina or physique of the average woman puts her at a disadvantage to the average man, render unlawful any act related to the participation of a person as a competitor in events involving that activity which are confined to competitors of one sex.

The aim of s.44 is twofold: it is supposed to protect women from being injured by larger, stronger men and to preserve competitive balance within sport by shielding women from having to compete against men. The exemption means that for example in heavy contact sports like rugby, separate competitions for men and women can be organised so that the greater 'physical strength and physique' of the average man will not cause unnecessary injury to the average woman. Furthermore it enables separate competitions to be held in athletics, for example where the 'stronger and faster' average man will usually put them at a competitive advantage when competing against the average woman.

What is unusual about s.44 is that it introduces precisely the kind of generalisation about the attributes of men and women that the rest of the SDA 1975 is trying to make unlawful. Its effect is to legitimise stereotypical assumptions about men's and women's sporting attributes rather than base conclusions about eligibility to compete on merit; unusually for sport, in this situation it is not how good you are that counts. Whatever the rights and wrongs of s.44 the exemption has proved to be culturally expedient and at least for now it appears to reflect societal attitudes towards sports participation. For many disparate reasons, in general men and women appear to be happy to compete in separate events and in separate competitions.

To reflect the unusual position of s.44 SDA 1975 it has been interpreted narrowly by the courts in an attempt to limit its impact. Firstly the exemption only applies to the participants in a sporting competition. In *British Judo Association* v. *Petty* [1981] ICR 660, Petty had been denied the opportunity to referee national standard judo bouts between men despite being qualified to do so. The British Judo Association (BJA) justified its refusal on the grounds that women in general, rather than Petty in particular, did not have the necessary physical or vocal strength to be able to referee men's bouts. As the BJA did not provide any objective justification capable of demonstrating why a referee would need these attributes, it was held to have acted in a discriminatory manner contrary to s.13 SDA 1975. Further, the Employment Appeal Tribunal held that the BJA was unable to rely on s.44 as the exemption only applied to competitors in a sporting event not to the match officials, as this latter group should not need to become physically involved with the participants during the course of the bout.

Secondly the exemption only applies to prevent mixed-sex competitions, not those that only involve members of one sex. In *Couch* v. *British Boxing Board of Control*, the claimant challenged the BBBC's decision not to award her a licence to box professionally in the UK.

The BBBC claimed, amongst other things, that it was unsafe for women to box because their weight varies during the course of their menstrual cycle, making it impossible to determine which weight category they should fight in, and because women are accident prone and emotionally unstable when experiencing pre-menstrual syndrome. The BBBC also claimed that boxing was an unsuitable sport for women to compete in because of the lack of strength, stamina and physical stature of the average woman. The Tribunal held that as there was no evidence that Couch suffered from any of the medical conditions identified as problematic by the BBBC, there was no objective justification for denying her a licence to box professionally and therefore the Board of Control had acted contrary to s.13 SDA 1975. Furthermore the Tribunal also stated that s.44 only applies to prevent men and women from competing against one another. As Couch only sought a licence to fight other women, she was not at a competitive disadvantage within the meaning of s.44.

Finally there must be actual evidence of the participant being at a competitive disadvantage, not just an assumption that they are. In *Thompson v. Professional Pool Players' Organisation* (unreported) Employment Appeal Tribunal, 11 March 1992, the PPPO was found to have acted contrary to s.13 SDA 1975 by repeatedly refusing to grant Thompson professional status. An argument that she was at a competitive disadvantage when compared to male players was dismissed on the basis of her repeated victories in open competitions.

11.5.2.3 Gender Recognition Act 2004

Where a person has been issued with a gender recognition certificate, they must be treated for all purposes as being of their acquired gender (s.9 Gender Recognition Act 2004 (GRA 2004)). This would appear to mean that once a certificate has been issued the person should be able to participate in sport without their original gender being disclosed. However where a sport is gender-affected, a transgendered-person can be discriminated against where it is necessary for the purposes of securing fair competition and/or the safety of other competitors according to s.19 GRA 2004. Under s.19(4) a sport is gender-affected where the physical strength, stamina or physique of average persons of one gender would put them at a disadvantage to average persons of the other gender as competitors in events involving the sport.

The legislature appears to be concerned that male-to-female transgendered persons will be at a competitive advantage when compared to non-transgendered female participants and that the transgendered person will pose a risk of physical harm to the non-transgendered person. As with s.44 SDA 1975, the problem with s.19 GRA 2004 is with its general approach to legitimising discriminatory rules and conduct rather than requiring the individual circumstances of each participant to be addressed on a case-by-case basis. The lack of litigation on this point leaves open the question of whether or not this will cause problems for transgendered persons hoping to participate in competitive sports in the future.

11.5.3 Race discrimination

The Race Relations Act 1976 (RRA 1976) makes it unlawful to discriminate against a person on the grounds of their colour, race, nationality or ethnic or national origins (s.3 RRA 1976). As with other forms of discrimination, race discrimination can be committed either directly or indirectly. Direct discrimination in sport will often take the form of harassment of the affected person whilst indirect discrimination, which will be much more difficult to prove, may be found on the rules of the NGB.

11.5.3.1 Discriminatory practices

Race discrimination in sport has usually occurred by means of either victimisation or harassment. Under s.2 RRA 1976 victimisation has a specific meaning that encompasses discriminatory treatment arising out of making use of the Act to challenge the behaviour of the discriminator. For example in *Leeds Rhinos Rugby Club Ltd, Lance, Howes and Hetherington* v. *Stirling* EAT 267/01, the Tribunal found that Stirling had been victimised by his club because it had failed to investigate properly his claims that racism had been a factor in the coach's decision not to select him for the first team.

Under s.3A RRA 1976 a claim of harassment requires the affected person to establish that their dignity has been violated or that they have been subjected to an environment that is intimidating, hostile, degrading, humiliating or offensive. In *Hussaney* v. *Chester City Football Club and Ratcliffe* EAT 203/98 the Tribunal found that a football manager had called a young player a 'black cunt' whilst he was out of the room. This kind of abuse would now constitute harassment under s.3A RRA 1976. A further claim that Hussaney had been victimised by the club when it had failed to offer him a professional playing contract was not established on the facts; it was objectively justifiable on the evidence of the coaching staff that he was not good enough to play professional football.

11.5.3.2 Race Relations Act 1976 s.39 – the sports exemption

A specific, limited exemption has been granted to sport to enable the proper administration of representative fixtures to take place.

▶ **Race Relations Act 1976 s.39 – sports and competitions**

Nothing in Parts II to IV shall render unlawful any act whereby a person discriminates against another on the basis of that other's nationality or place of birth or the length of time for which he has been resident in a particular area or place, if the act is done –

(a) in selecting one or more persons to represent a country, place or area, or any related association, in any sport or game; or
(b) in pursuance of the rules of any competition so far as they relate to eligibility to compete in any sport or game.

The exemption granted by s.39 serves two specific and distinct purposes. Firstly it ensures that genuinely representative sports teams are not acting in a discriminatory fashion when applying their eligibility criteria. To insist that a person was born in a specific county, region or country is not race discrimination when the purpose is to pick a team to represent that county, region or country. Secondly it enables an NGB to organise competitions to establish who the best player from a particular area is in a particular sport. For example it is not race discrimination to insist that only British players take part in a British Championships where the purpose of the competition is to find the best British player. Outside of these two limited situations discrimination on the basis of race is unlawful.

11.5.4   Disability discrimination

The Disability Discrimination Act 1995 (DDA 1995) has a different structure to the previous three pieces of legislation, though its broad purpose remains the same in that it makes discrimination on the basis of disability unlawful. The DDA 1995 outlaws four categories of discrimination. Direct discrimination and victimisation operate in the same way as the corresponding provisions of the SDA 1975 and RRA 1976, however discrimination for a disability-related reason and failure to comply with a duty to make reasonable adjustments for a disabled person are disability-specific provisions defined in ss.3A and 20 DDA 1995 respectively. As there is no sports-related litigation on these issues, two high profile cases from other jurisdictions are used as examples of how the law is likely to operate in the UK. Discrimination for a disability-related reason would include any situation where a person is treated less favourably because they suffer from a disability and where there is no objective justification for such differential treatment.

> ▶ *Pistorius* v. *International Association of Athletics Federations* CAS 2008/A/1480
>
> The claimant, who was a double amputee, sought to overturn the IAAF's decision to ban him from using 'Cheetah Flex-Foot' prosthetic legs. One of his grounds of challenge was that it was discriminatory of the IAAF to prevent him from using these prosthetics as without them he could not compete against able bodied athletes. The IAAF argued that as the prosthetics gave the user a mechanical advantage over runners who were not using them, they provided him with unfair assistance. The IAAF produced scientific evidence in support of its case which provided the necessary objective justification for its decision to ban the use of these particular prosthetics. A blanket ban on the use of all prosthetic limbs, or a ban not supported by the necessary scientific evidence, would be likely to be found discriminatory before both the English courts and CAS.

A failure to comply with a duty to make reasonable adjustments for a disabled person can also result in a finding of discrimination under ss.4A and 21 DDA 1995. An NGB does not have to take all steps necessary to enable a disabled person to compete in their competitions but if reasonable adjustments can be made it is discriminatory not to make them. For example in *PGA Tour Inc* v. *Martin* 532 US 661 (2001) the Supreme Court of the United States held that it was reasonable to allow a disabled golfer to use a golf cart to enable him to play competitive golf at a professional level. The rules of the PGA Tour did not allow the use of golf carts as it considered that it was an integral part of the game of golf that the player be able to walk unaided around the course. Martin argued that as a result of his suffering from a degenerative circulatory disorder that obstructed the flow of blood from his right leg to his heart, he could only play golf at a professional standard if he was able to use a golf cart to transport him around the course. The Supreme Court agreed with Martin that as there was nothing in the Rules of Golf that required a player to walk the course as opposed to be transported around it in a cart, such a proposal was a reasonable adjustment that would enable him to compete as a professional golfer alongside able bodied players. Again a similar result would be likely under English law.

11.5.5 The potential impact of anti-discrimination challenges to sports rules

A successful challenge to some of the more overtly discriminatory practices that are inherent in sport could see a move towards more genuinely 'open' competitions. The CAS decision in *Pistorius* took this debate to a new level of sophistication on both sides and left open the possibility that the use of the next generation of artificial limbs could be found to be a reasonable adjustment that enables a disabled athlete to compete against their able-bodied contemporaries rather than artifical limbs being banned for being performance enhancing. The scientific evidence relied on by the IAAF to prevent Pistorius from using the 'Cheetah Flex-Foot' artificial limb also provides the manufacturers with the information that they need to develop a product that could fall within the IAAF's rules in future.

If such an application is successful and leads towards a greater degree of openness as far as eligibility criteria are concerned, a further development could be that gender restrictions are removed from some sports. Although at present there is no great clamour for all events in all sports to be completely open, there is no reason why a challenge could not be made by a successful female athlete to a restriction that prevented her from competing against men of a similar standard of skill and ability. Success in sport is rarely determined by an athlete's 'strength, stamina or physique' alone, leaving open the possibility of the claim that a female athlete should be allowed to test whether or not she is good enough to compete against men rather than being told unequivocally that she is not big enough or strong enough to do so.

Hot topic . . .
THE TEVEZ AFFAIR

The litigation that resulted from the transfer of professional footballer Carlos Tevez from Corinthians in Brazil to West Ham United FC in 2006 required each of the tribunals involved to examine in detail three interlocking relationships and their impact on Sheffield United FC. The first of these was the relationship between Tevez and West Ham and focused on the unusual nature of the contract by which the player was employed by the club. The second was between Sheffield United and the Football Association Premier League (FAPL) and required an investigation into whether Sheffield had sufficient standing to challenge a disciplinary decision that was directed at another club, in this case West Ham. The third relationship under analysis was that between Sheffield and West Ham and whether the latter should be liable to pay compensation to the former for the losses it suffered on relegation.

Although each of the hearings was before a tribunal or arbitral panel constituted according to the rules of the Premier League, they were conducted as they would have been had the same questions been heard before a national court. In particular when examining the first two of the relationships at the heart of these proceedings, the Arbitral Tribunal (AT) claimed to be exercising a supervisory jurisdiction over the conduct of the Disciplinary Commission (DC) by relying on *Bradley* v. *Jockey Club* [2005] EWCA Civ 1056 to determine the scope of its powers and the grounds on which Sheffield could base its challenge.

Partway through the 2006–07 Premier League football season, the unusual contractual relationship between Carlos Tevez and West Ham United came to light and an FAPL investigation was launched. At the first instance hearing on 27 April 2007 West Ham pleaded guilty to breaches of Rule B13 by failing to act with utmost good faith in not disclosing the full nature of Tevez's contractual arrangements and of Rule U18 on player

contracts. The breaches were caused by West Ham having entered into an agreement with a third party who would have the right to exercise control over decisions concerning the future transfer of Tevez and the termination of his contract with West Ham and West Ham's repeated failure to disclose the existence of this contract to the FAPL. The purpose of Rule U18 is to ensure that an outside party does not have the ability to influence team selection and potentially the outcome of a match; similar rules are in place regarding club ownership (see further, chapter 12.4.3.2).

The DC fined West Ham £5.5million but decided not to deduct any points from the club even though it had the power to have done so. Three reasons were given by the DC for only fining West Ham: the club was now under new ownership who had cooperated fully with the investigation; a deduction would at such a late stage of the season guarantee that the club would be relegated; and the adverse effect that relegation in this manner would have on West Ham's players and fans. Thus the final league standings were confirmed as:

15	West Ham United	41 points
16	Fulham	39
17	Wigan Athletic	38
18	Sheffield United	38
19	Charlton Athletic	34
20	Watford	28

This meant that Sheffield United, Charlton Athletic and Watford were relegated but West Ham remained in the Premier League.

Sheffield challenged the decision of the DC, claiming that the three justifications given for not deducting points from West Ham were unreasonable, that it had taken into consideration irrelevant factors and that it had failed to take account of other factors that were directly relevant. In particular Sheffield argued that regardless of the change of ownership, a serious breach of the rules had still occurred and that a failure to deduct points from West Ham would guarantee Sheffield's relegation when it had played the entire season according to the rules of the FAPL. If the DC had come to its decision lawfully and after proper consideration, it was argued that the only reasonable finding that it could have reached was to deduct points from West Ham that would have seen it relegated to the Championship instead of Sheffield.

The AT upheld all of the findings of the DC and declared that its final decision to fine West Ham was within the range of appropriate and reasonable responses that it could have reached. Although it expressed sympathy with Sheffield's case and stated that had it heard the case at first instance it would have deducted points from West Ham, the AT held that

the DC had reached its decision in accordance with the correct procedures. As the AT had no jurisdiction to amend the DC's decision, Sheffield was relegated.

Sheffield then instituted proceedings against West Ham to recover monies that it had failed to earn as a result of its being relegated. The amount claimed included lost income from the PL's broadcasting contracts and reduced earnings that it could make from sponsorship, merchandising and ticket sales, totalling around £50million. The cause of action was breach of contract based on West Ham's deliberate breach of the Rule U18 Premier League Rules. In the final arbitration hearing West Ham was found liable and later reached a settlement with Sheffield to pay it an undisclosed sum of compensation.

In a final twist to the saga West Ham attempted to appeal the finding of liability against it to CAS. Following an application by Sheffield the High Court granted an injunction preventing any such appeal on the basis that to do so was in breach of the final and binding arbitration agreement that the parties had entered into.

For Sheffield United this was probably the best result in the circumstances, although of course nothing could compensate the club, its players and fans for being relegated when a rival had been found guilty of deliberately breaking the rules of the game. In the aftermath of the hearings it was rumoured that the Sheffield players and coaching staff were also considering suing West Ham for their own lost earnings, as all would have seen a significant reduction in their income on relegation. Although these claims have not been taken any further they appear to be valid, though any attendant litigation would undoubtedly be complex.

The importance of the Tevez Affair is its demonstration of the growing jurisdiction and juridification of sports tribunals and arbitral panels. Litigation of this kind and complexity would normally be heard before the High Court. However both the DC and the AT considered themselves to be sufficiently experienced both legally and in football terms to be competent to hear the various claims. In particular the AT's use of *Bradley* to justify a supervisory jurisdiction over decisions of the DC and its decision to grant Sheffield's standing to challenge a decision of the DC to which it was not a party were groundbreaking. The eventual legacy of these hearings may be that it marks the true starting point for domestic sports law in the UK.

Case references:

Original disciplinary hearing against West Ham United:

Football Association Premier League Ltd v. *West Ham United Football Club plc* (unreported) FAPL Disciplinary Commission, 27 April 2007

Sheffield United's challenge to the Disciplinary Commission's decision:

Sheffield United Football Club Ltd v. *Football Association Premier League Ltd* [2007] 3 ISLR SLR 77

Sheffield United's claim for compensation from West Ham United:

Sheffield United Football Club Ltd v. *West Ham United Football Club Plc* [2009] 1 ISLR SLR 25

Sheffield United's application for an injunction to prevent West Ham United appealing to CAS:

Sheffield United Football Club Ltd v. *West Ham United Football Club Plc* [2008] EWHC 2855 (Comm)

Summary

11.1 During the course of the last century there has been a shift in the balance of power in professional sport from the NGBs to the clubs and players. This has to a large extent been driven by the increasing commercialisation of sport and the desire of players to earn their 'fair share' from the games in which they play. The changes that have occurred to practices that had long been accepted as normal within sport have often been driven by the outcome of specific legal disputes or occasionally by the threat of legal action.

Summary cont'd

11.2 Most contracts affecting professional sporting relationships are now clearly identifiable and a written copy of the document will often have to be lodged with the appropriate NGB. Although some contractual relationships have become extremely complex, the courts and the specialist tribunals hearing these cases have been prepared to provide sport-friendly interpretations to the disputed clauses to ensure that they operate appropriately in the sporting context which they inhabit.

11.3 Overt interference with the performance of a contract has become increasingly rare in sport as a result of the greater regulation of such conduct by NGBs and ISFs. Its most common occurrence is where one club seeks to entice a player to breach their current contract of employment in order to join it. The increased formality of contractual relationships which more clearly define both parties' obligations, and the better administration of these relationships by the governing bodies leaves fewer opportunities for unlawful approaches to be made.

11.4 Both clubs and players can be subjected to restraints of trade that prevent them from being able to maximise their income. Any such restraints are unlawful unless they can be justified as being necessary, reasonable, proportionate and in the public interest. Although historically this was an important cause of action for protecting clubs and players, most actions that are in restraint of trade are now likely to have a European aspect that will engage EU law.

11.5 Conduct that discriminates against a person on the grounds of their sex, race or disability is unlawful if practised by an employer, such as a club, or a body responsible for granting qualifications and authorisations, like an NGB. Some limited exemptions exist within the legislation to allow single-sex sports and representative teams to be lawful despite the inherent discrimination involved in their eligibility criteria.

Further reading

Beale (ed), *Chitty on Contracts* (30th edn, 2008, Sweet and Maxwell) ch 1–170–173

Dugdale, Jones and Simpson (eds), *Clerk & Lindsell on Torts* (19th edn, 2009, Sweet and Maxwell) ch 25

Furmston, *Cheshire, Fifoot and Furmston's Law of Contract* (15th edn, 2007, Oxford University Press) chs 6 and 18

Lewis and Taylor (eds), *Sport: Law and Practice* (2nd edn, 2008, Tottel) chs D1–3

Harding, *Living to Play* (2004, Robson Press)

Pannick, *Sex Discrimination in Sport* (1983, Equal Opportunities Commission)

McArdle, 'Can legislation stop me from playing? The distinction between sport competitors and sport workers under the United Kingdom's sex discrimination laws' (1999) 2(2) *Culture, Sport, Society* 44

McArdle, 'One hundred years of servitude: contractual conflict in English professional football before *Bosman*' [2000] 2 *Web Journal of Current Legal Issues*, online

McArdle, 'Just one of the challenges of 21st-Century life: Oscar Pistorius in the Court of Arbitration for Sport' (2008) 5(2) *Script-ed*, online

Wolbring, 'Oscar Pistorius and the future nature of Olympic, Paralympic and other sports' (2008) 5(1) *Script-ed*, online

Links to relevant websites can be found at www.palgrave.com/law/james

Chapter 12

Regulating sporting relationships in EU law

Key words

▶ **Direct effect** – where provisions of EU law are clear, precise and unconditional enough to be justiciable, they can be relied on by individuals as the basis of their cause of action before national courts.

▶ **Training compensation fee** – the fee payable by the new employing club to all those involved in training a young footballer each time that the player moves club before their 23rd birthday.

▶ **Transfer fee** – the fee payable by a new employer to facilitate the release of a player from their current contract of employment.

12.1 Engaging EU law through sporting relationships

Making use of the protections enshrined in the Treaty on the Functioning of the European Union (TFEU) to resolve sports disputes is a relatively new phenomenon. This is most easily explained by the fact that until comparatively recently most elite athletes would have played out their entire career in their home country. The internationalisation of sports employment and of the sports employment market has not only seen many athletes now expecting to spend at least part of their career playing abroad but has led employing clubs to consider that there are no geographical boundaries to the catchment area from which they can draw their players. Where once clubs would have recruited from the areas surrounding the towns and cities where they are based, they now draw talent not just from the whole of Europe but from all over the world. As a result the employment rights of many elite sports performers will engage EU law even if the specific relationship itself does not breach it.

EU law is engaged whenever the conduct of at least one of the parties to a dispute infringes the directly effective provisions that affect a person's protected rights. In particular this means that the fundamental freedoms of movement created to enable the operation of the single European market and the competition law provisions of the TFEU are applicable to sports disputes (see further, chapter 3.2). The recently acquired competence to act in respect of sport, as defined by Arts.6 and 165 TFEU (see further, chapter 1.5.3) creates an as yet unexplored potential for further increases in the scope of the engagement of EU law with sports disputes.

Most of these disputes have challenged the legality of an administrative rule or procedure, or a common practice operated by an ISF or other sports authority that is acting in a similar manner. The ISF will generally try to argue that its conduct is normal behaviour in the context of the running of its sport or that it is necessary for the proper administration and functioning of the sport under its control. Where a practice is particularly unusual the ISF will usually claim that the 'specificity of sport' provides sufficient justification for its conduct being held lawful despite any restrictive consequences that it might cause.

The potentially unlawful behaviour of a club will usually be evidenced by a restrictive contractual term that prevents a player from maximising their earnings or from moving to a new employer. The relevant ISF and/or NGB will usually be joined as a party to proceedings of this nature as the restrictive contractual term will often have been incorporated into the playing contract at the insistence of the governing body or as the result of a collective bargaining agreement. For example the compulsory player release clauses that enable international representative competitions to take place are incorporated into a player's contract through the agreements between their club and the NGB of which it is a member and then through the membership agreement between the NGB and its ISF (see further, chapter 3 Hot Topic).

Unlike under English law, where a claimant's cause of action is based on EU law there is no need to prove the existence of a contractual relationship between the parties although the existence of a valid contract will usually be central to many cases; nor is there a need to invoke a 'supervisory jurisdiction' of the ECJ. If the conduct of a club or sports authority affects an economic activity such as a person's employment, then EU law can be engaged and ultimately the case may fall under the jurisdiction of the ECJ. If the activity is not economic in nature or the restriction is of a kind that does not breach EU law then it is lawful and can continue to be practised (see further, chapter 3.2.2).

The TFEU has direct effect on collective regulatory bodies that have the power to regulate employment relationships, such as ISFs and NGBs, ensuring that they must design their rules and procedures in accordance with EU law (*Walrave and Koch* v. *Association Union Cycliste Internationale* (Case 36/74) [1974] ECR 1405) (see further, chapter 3.2.2). With the continuing internationalisation of the sports employment market, EU law will be engaged more frequently than it has been in the past and will encompass many of the disputes that would previously have relied on a domestic cause of action such as restraint of trade (see further, chapter 11.4). This chapter will examine in detail the provisions of the TFEU that have had the biggest impact on sport and those which are as yet underexplored but have the potential to effect major changes on the way that sport is administered, played and consumed.

12.2 Treaty on the Functioning of the European Union Art.45 (ex Art.39 ECT) – freedom of movement for workers

The freedom of movement for workers is secured by Art.45 TFEU. Its aim is to enable a worker to travel freely throughout the EU in order to work and to be treated as would be a national of the country in which their employment is based. It specifically outlaws discrimination based on the grounds of nationality and ensures that all citizens of the EU are treated in the same way regardless of the member state in which they are working.

> ▶ **Treaty on the Functioning of the European Union Art.45**
>
> '1 Freedom of movement for workers shall be secured within the Union.
> 2 Such freedom of movement shall entail the abolition of any discrimination based on nationality between workers of the Member States as regards employment, remuneration and other conditions of work and employment.
> 3 It shall entail the right, subject to limitations justified on grounds of public policy, public security or public health:
> (a) to accept offers of employment actually made;

(b) to move freely within the territory of Member States for this purpose;
(c) to stay in a Member State for the purpose of employment in accordance with the provisions governing the employment of nationals of that State laid down by law, regulation or administrative action;
(d) to remain in the territory of a Member State after having been employed in that State, subject to conditions which shall be embodied in implementing regulations to be drawn up by the Commission.'

Despite the clarity of the wording of Art.45 sports authorities appeared not to realise that EU law in general and the free movement provisions in particular could apply to sporting relationships. From the early 1970s a series of well-reported cases including *Walrave* had been heard before the ECJ, though the potential impact of EU law was largely ignored by the bodies at which these judgments were directed.

12.2.1 The *Bosman* decision

It was not until the decision of the ECJ in *Union Royale Belge des Sociétés de Football Association ASBL* v. *Bosman* (Case C-415/93) [1995] ECR I-4921 that ISFs finally realised that some of the practices that they considered to be integral to the organisation of their sports were unlawful according to EU law. It could be said that in terms of public perception and impact, it is *Bosman* that marks the true starting point of the development of European sports law as it was through this case that EU law finally came to the attention not just of EU lawyers but of everyone connected with sport, including administrators, clubs, the players and the fans.

From May 1988 to 30 June 1990 Bosman was employed as a professional footballer by RC Liège on a gross basic salary of BFr75,000 per month; with the addition of bonuses, his average monthly salary was BFr120,000. In April 1990 Liège offered Bosman a new one-year contract for the following season at the league's minimum salary of BFr30,000 per month. Bosman rejected this offer and was transfer listed at a fee of BFr11,743,000, referred to by the Belgian Football Association (URBSFA) as compensation for training a player, and which had been calculated in accordance with its transfer regulations on the basis of his previous season's salary.

As no club was prepared to pay such a high transfer fee for him, Bosman contacted a number of clubs with a view to moving to them in time for the start of the 1990–91 football season. In July 1990 US Dunkerque of the French second division agreed to pay him the equivalent of BFr90,000 per month and to pay Liège a training compensation fee of BFr1.2m in order to secure his services for the following season. At the end of this contract Dunkerque had the option to effect his permanent transfer by the payment of an additional BFr4.8m to Liège. Liège however had doubts about Dunkerque's solvency and failed to request the necessary international clearance certificate from the URBSFA, causing the contracts to lapse and Bosman to be left unemployed.

Bosman initially sued Liège and the URBSFA for BFr100,000 per month for the period of time until he was able to find suitable alternative employment to that which had been offered to him by Dunkerque. In the course of the protracted litigation, UEFA was also joined as a defendant. Bosman's case eventually focused on two specific claims. Firstly that the transfer system as operated in Belgium and sanctioned by UEFA was contrary to

Art.45 TFEU (ex Art.39 ECT) as it restricted him from being able to take up an offer of employment in another member state.

Secondly he argued that the '3+2' Rule operated by UEFA was also in contravention of Art.45. The '3+2' Rule, which had been introduced in July 1992 whilst the litigation was progressing through the courts, prevented a club from fielding more than three players who were eligible to play international football for a national association other than the one where their employing club was based. A further two foreign players could be fielded if they had played for five years continuously in the country in question, of which at least three years had to have been as a junior. Bosman argued that this rule limited the number of non-Belgian clubs that were able to employ him, as many would have already filled their foreign quota, and therefore it impeded his ability to work throughout the EU as a professional footballer.

The Belgian courts referred the following questions to the ECJ for a preliminary ruling: Is Art.45 TFEU to be interpreted as:

1 prohibiting a football club from requiring and receiving payment of a sum of money upon the engagement of one of its players who has come to the end of his contract by a new employing club;
2 prohibiting the national and international sporting associations or federations from including in their respective regulations provisions restricting access of foreign players from the EU to the competitions which they organise?

The ECJ was unequivocal in holding that the demanding of a transfer fee by a former employer after the conclusion of a fixed term employment contract was an obstacle to the freedom of movement for workers as it impeded and potentially prevented a professional footballer's ability to move to new employing club. Therefore the rules providing for such payments were unlawful unless it could be shown that they were necessary and proportionate for achieving a legitimate objective.

UEFA and URBSFA advanced two main justifications for the existence of the transfer system. Firstly they argued that it helped to maintain financial and sporting equilibrium between clubs. The ECJ accepted that this was a legitimate aim for a governing body's rules to achieve but rejected the claim that the transfer system was an appropriate means of securing such an outcome. The operation of this transfer system did not preclude the richest clubs from securing the services of the best players nor could it restrict their commercial activities to such an extent as to create a financial level playing field. Furthermore as potentially less restrictive mechanisms, such as collective wage agreements, solidarity payments and the pooling and sharing of income, had not been investigated, the continuation of the transfer system could not be justified on the basis that it was necessary to promote competitive balance. The ECJ required further proof based on cogent evidence for it to be able to justify why such a clear infringement of Art.45 should be lawful on this basis.

Secondly it was argued that transfer fees represented compensation for costs expended by a club on the training of a player. The ECJ again accepted that this was potentially a legitimate aim of the rules; however as there was no identifiable relationship between the compensation fees demanded and the actual costs involved with training a player, the transfer system was not necessary for the achievement of this aim. The ECJ specifically noted that the transfer system operated in Belgium calculated the fee payable on the basis of the salary previously paid to the player not on the costs associated with training him. Only if a reasonable sum representing the actual training costs incurred by the club could be calculated objectively could a transfer system be justified. Therefore question one was answered in the affirmative: a rule that requires the payment of a transfer, training or development fee to a previous employer to enable an out of contract player to move to a new employer is prohibited by Art.45 as being an obstacle to the freedom of movement of workers.

The ECJ was equally unequivocal that nationality quotas which restricted an EU citizen's opportunity to play for their employing club were obstacles to their ability to work unimpeded as professional footballers. Therefore the '3+2' Rule would also be unlawful unless it could be shown that it was a purely sporting rule falling outside of the scope of the treaty or that it was necessary and proportionate for achieving a legitimate objective.

The ECJ was not prepared to accept that a nationality quota of the kind being operated by UEFA was a purely sporting rule that was necessary for the proper functioning of the game. Whereas nationality restrictions were inherently necessary for the composition of international representative teams, as was the case in *Walrave*, the same arguments could not be used to explain the need for quotas at club level. In reaching this conclusion the ECJ began its move away from the concept of providing exemptions for purely sporting rules by requiring instead that UEFA objectively justify the need for imposing nationality restrictions through the '3+2' Rule.

UEFA argued that there were three justifications for the existence of the Rule: that it helped to maintain the traditional link between a club and the country in which it was based; that it ensured that there was a sufficient pool of nationally qualified players playing in a country's top league to feed its national team and that it maintained a competitive balance between clubs by preventing the richest clubs acquiring all the best players. The ECJ again dismissed each of these claims. Firstly it held that it is not necessary for the organisation of football that a club maintain a link with its home country, region or locality through the engagement of players from specific areas. Although it is justifiable to impose eligibility restrictions based on nationality for genuinely representative competitions, UEFA had not provided evidence of the need for a corresponding restriction at club level.

Secondly it held that as a player could be selected to play for his national team whilst registered with a club based anywhere in the world, the Rule did not of itself create a pool of players eligible to compete for a national team. If players could be based at clubs outside of the country for which they would compete nationally, they should be able to play for any club within the EU without restriction.

Thirdly the ECJ did not accept that the Rule was capable of maintaining a competitive balance between clubs. The richer clubs would still be able to recruit the best foreign players and would still have the ability to horde excess players by employing but not always playing them. They would also retain the ability to acquire the services of the best domestic players when their foreign quota was full. Therefore question two was also answered in the affirmative: a rule that imposes restrictions on the ability of an employer to recruit employees that is based on their nationality alone is prohibited by Art.45 as being an obstacle to the freedom of movement of workers.

The ECJ's ruling in *Bosman* came as a shock not just to the football authorities but to the ISFs of all professional team sports. Despite the case's striking similarity to *Eastham*

(11.4.2.4) and that *Walrave* had already served as a warning to ISFs that their rules could be subject to EU law, UEFA and its member associations still appeared to think that they could operate without interference from the courts on the basis that all of their rules would be covered by the sporting exception defence. *Bosman* demonstrates quite clearly that only the rules that are necessary for the organisation of sport are completely exempt from the operation of EU law; all other rules will require an objective justification to explain why they should be lawful, something that UEFA was unable to provide to the Court.

Looked at from a contractual perspective it seems absurd to think that it could be lawful for a club to demand compensation from the new employer of a former employee whose contract has ended. Like Eastham, Bosman was technically no longer employed by his previous club but was unable to work elsewhere until a fee had been paid to them. Treating players as tradable assets rather than employees occurred in professional team sport for almost the entire twentieth century until *Bosman* brought sports employment more into line with the employment practices operated in other sectors. As a result of the ECJ's ruling, transfer fees can no longer be charged for out of contract players, though training compensation of a significantly lower level must now be paid when a player under the age of 23 moves clubs (below, 12.2.2.1). Further, discriminatory nationality quotas should not be used to restrict the number of EU players that a club can field or employ, despite recent moves to the contrary, unless they are capable of being objectively justified (below, Hot Topic). Following *Deutscher Handballbund eV* v. *Kolpak* (Case C-438/00) [2003] ECR I-4135 and *Simutenkov* v. *Ministerio de Educacion y Cultura* (Case C-265/03) [2005] ECR I-2579, players from countries with which the EU has Association Agreements or Agreements on Partnership and Cooperation can also benefit from this non-discrimination principle for the purpose of any nationality quota imposed on a club's playing staff, provided that they were already employed within the EU at the time that they were seeking to invoke it.

The importance of the *Bosman* decision must not be underestimated. Not only was it a landmark ruling on the application of Art.45 but it marked a change in the relationship between sport and the EU. The ECJ made it clear that it would no longer tolerate such a flagrant disregard of EU law in such a high profile activity without a robust objective justification, something that UEFA was unable to provide. The case also marks the beginning of the European Commission's much more proactive examinations of sports regulation. After *Bosman* ISFs could be under no illusion but that they were subject to EU law and that some of the practices that they considered to be inherent in the proper organisation of their sports were in fact unlawful.

It also began a process of greater collaboration between ISFs when responding to EU initiatives and the juridification of the language of their interactions with EU institutions. For example in 2008 the European sports federations responsible for basketball, football, handball, rugby and volleyball (FIBA Europe, UEFA, EHF, FIRA-AER and CEV), together with the International Ice Hockey Federation presented a joint document, *Safeguarding the heritage and future of team sport in Europe*, to the European Council outlining measures that it felt should be protected from the unchecked operation of EU law (below, 12.4.4). The document discusses the definition of the specificity and autonomy of team sports, the protection and education of young players and the need for good governance, providing the platform from which perhaps the kind of justifications demanded of UEFA by the ECJ in *Bosman* may in the future be developed.

12.2.2   The impact of the *Bosman* decision

The *Bosman* decision is applicable to all professional sports, a point reflected by much of the subsequent case law heard before the ECJ. However it has had its biggest impact on football where a player 'doing a *Bosman*' is a frequent topic of conversation. Despite creeping into football's vernacular, FIFA and UEFA did not accept the judgment willingly and since it was handed down they have spent much of the intervening period attempting to find ways of limiting its impact.

12.2.2.1 Requiring a training compensation fee instead of a transfer fee

FIFA's Regulations on the Status and Transfer Players were introduced in 2001 following an agreement between the EU, FIFA, UEFA and FIFPRO, the International Federation of Professional Footballers' Associations, on how post-*Bosman* transfers should be administered. According to Art.20 FIFA Regulations, a 'training compensation fee' is payable to the club or clubs where a player was trained when they enter into their first professional playing contract and each subsequent occasion on which they are transferred until the end of the season during which they turn 23 years of age. This fee, which is calculated in accordance with Annexe 4 of the Regulations, is payable regardless of whether the transfer takes place during or at the end of the player's contract. By providing clubs with a means of calculating the fee payable, a more easily justifiable and considerably smaller sum is required to be paid in compensation to the training club for its work with the player. When read in conjunction with Art.21 FIFA Regulations concerning solidarity payments, which disperses a small amount of any future in-contract transfer fee to each club involved in the training of a player between the ages of 12 and 23, FIFA's aim is to ensure that the clubs responsible for finding, training and developing young players are compensated for their efforts where they are unable to reap the benefits of their work because the player has chosen to play elsewhere.

Art.20 reintroduces transfer fees for players under 23 years of age in the guise of a requirement that the new club pay compensation to the previous employer for having provided the player with training. As transfer, training and development fees were declared by the ECJ to be unlawful in *Bosman*, this restriction on a young player's freedom of movement as a worker needs to be capable of being justified objectively if it is avoid being found to infringe Art.45 TFEU. In *Olympique Lyonnais* v. *Bernard and Newcastle United FC* (Case C-325/08), Advocate General Sharpston, although refusing to comment on the legality of Art.20 FIFA Regulations as not being relevant to the case before her, gave her opinion on the legality of a French law that covers a similar situation. In line with *Bosman* she advised that a rule that requires the payment of a fee to the previous employer once the contract of employment is at an end is in principle prohibited by Art.45 TFEU. However she stated that it may be possible to justify such a law by the need to encourage the recruitment and training of young professional footballers. The Advocate General stated that where it is necessary to train n players in order to produce one who will be successful professionally, then the cost to the training club and therefore the amount that it could recover in compensation from the next employer would be the cost of training n young players. If the player rather than their new club was to be personally liable, the Advocate General considered that it was fair that only the individual cost of training him or her could be recovered. What she found unacceptable was that Olympique Lyonnais had calculated the amount of compensation due to them by reference to the salary that it had offered Bernard and not to the cost that it had incurred in training him.

The method of calculating the compensation due to a training club used by Advocate General Sharpston is strikingly similar to that used in Art.20 FIFA Regulations and supports the view of the football authorities that a club that has trained a player, but for whatever reason cannot convince them to stay and play for it, should be compensated for the effort that it has expended. Further, as Art.21 provides a mechanism for the redistribution of a part of any later in-contract transfer fee to the clubs responsible for training the player, FIFA appears to have demonstrated the importance of training young players and the cost involved in creating someone capable of playing sport professionally. Provided that the ECJ accepts her opinion when giving its final judgment Art.20 could well receive the Court's seal of approval as an objectively justifiable breach of Art.45 TFEU.

12.2.2.2 Receiving compensation for breach of contract instead of a transfer fee

Where a player breaches their contract without just cause in order to join a new club, Art.17 FIFA Regulations defines how the compensation payable to the original employing club should be calculated. In *FC Shaktar Donetsk* v. *Matuzalem Francelino da Silva, Real Zaragoza SAD and FIFA* CAS 2008/A/1519 and 1520 (see further, chapter 3.3.2.1) CAS stated that Art.17 did not give a player the right to unilaterally terminate their agreement but was instead the equivalent of a liquidated damages clause that defined the consequences of a player's breach of contract and the methodology to be followed when calculating the compensation payable. Thus the law of the country where the previous club was based, the specificity of sport, the value of the player's services to FC Shaktar Donetsk, the status of the player, his standing at the club, his behaviour and the timing of his departure were all to be taken into account when calculating the amount of compensation payable. On this basis, and taking into account the savings made in respect of the salary that Shaktar would not have to pay Matuzalem now he had moved to another club, the total amount payable was €11.9m. In the light of Advocate General Sharpston's opinion in *Olympique Lyonnais*, Art.17 also stands a good chance of being found lawful on the grounds of its being an objectively justifiable means of calculating the current value to a club of a player who has left it in breach of contract.

12.2.2.3 Buy-out and player release clauses instead of transfer fees

Mutually agreed in-contract transfers are in reality subject only to market forces. In some jurisdictions, clubs try to protect themselves to a certain extent by inserting player release clauses or buy-out clauses into the contract of employment, though these are not universally legal. Art.21 FIFA Regulations requires a maximum of five per cent of the fee to be paid through the solidarity mechanism to the training clubs, but apart from this redistributive element, the fee is that which is negotiated by the parties. Where a player is out of contract, they can now 'go on a *Bosman*'. In other words, once the contract is at an end, the player becomes an unattached free agent and is able to join any club that is prepared to employ them.

12.2.2.4 The juridification of football

It is possible, in the light of the creation of the FIFA Dispute Resolution Chamber and the ability of the parties to a football dispute to appeal to CAS, that cases such as *Matuzalem* may not be heard before national and European courts in the future. This formalisation and juridification of football's dispute resolution framework could be said to have been one of the most important developments to have been caused by the *Bosman* decision.

The case can also be said to have contributed significantly to the juridification of FIFA and UEFA's language and their approach to proposed developments within their sport. For example UEFA's 'home grown players' rule and FIFA's proposed '6+5' rule both reintroduce, or seek to reintroduce, nationality quotas that were ostensibly outlawed by *Bosman*. Their attempts to justify these restrictive practices are couched in EU law terms as being necessary and proportionate for the proper administration of football or are claimed to be purely sporting rules outside of the jurisdiction of EU law on the basis of the specificity and autonomy of sport (below, Hot Topic). Taken together with the newly established dispute resolution framework these developments indicate the lengths to which the football authorities have gone to in order to avoid the much-feared '*Bosman 2*' whilst at the same time highlighting the ways in which they continue to try to subvert the original decision.

12.2.3   Extending the reach of Art.45 TFEU

Since *Bosman* further challenges have been brought against what have long been accepted as common practices within the sports sector. For example in *Lehtonen v. Federation Royale Belge des Sociétés de Basket-ball ASBL* (Case C-176/96) [2000] ECR I-2681, the legality of the transfer deadlines operated in European professional basketball were called into question. On completion of the national championships in Finland, Lehtonen, a professional basketball player and Finnish national, moved to Castors Braine in order to compete for it in the play-offs of the Belgian championships. The Belgian Basketball Federation operated two separate transfer deadlines: 28 February for transfers from clubs based within Europe and 31 March for transfers from all other areas.

The ECJ held that transfer deadlines such as these are restrictions on the freedom of movement of workers because they create obstacles to a player's ability to take up employment elsewhere within the EU. However they are objectively justifiable as necessary to protect the integrity of a sporting competition. The basis of this justification was that late-season transfers have the potential to change the competitive strength of an individual team disproportionately, thereby calling into question the comparability of results between all participants over the course of a season-long championship. In other words it is a legitimate objective of a governing body to prevent a team from buying in better players at the last minute in order to distort the true picture of its performance over an entire season. Thus a single transfer deadline was lawful but further justification was required for the operation of two separate deadlines that were based on a player's residency in order for the rule to be compatible with Art.45 TFEU. The more recent practise of using transfer windows as a means of securing contractual stability as well as the integrity of a competition would therefore also appear to be objectively justifiable.

The use of salary caps in some sports could also give rise to claims that Art.45 has been infringed. Where a player is unable to play for a prospective employer who has reached the overall level of the cap, or has to accept a lower salary in order for the club to come within the cap's conditions, a clear obstacle to the player's right to free movement appears to have been raised. Using the 'specificity of sport' analysis introduced in *Meca-Medina and Majcen v. Commission* (Case 519/04) [2006] ECR I-6991 (see further, chapter 3.2.2), the more obvious the restriction, the more robust the justifications will have to be in order for the practice to be declared lawful. Where such salary restrictions are in place these could be justified on the basis of securing the financial stability of a sport, and therefore its future existence and the competitive balance of its competitions. Although the legality of any particular salary cap would depend on its definition and operation there is no reason why one that is appropriately drafted should not be found to be compatible with EU law.

12.3 Treaty on the Functioning of the European Union Art.56 (ex Art.49 ECT) – freedom to provide services

Where Art.45 TFEU is used to protect the freedom of movement of workers or employees, Art.56 provides similar protection for those who provide their services for remuneration or who are self-employed. This enables individual athletes, as opposed to those who are employed to play team sports, to ply their trade anywhere within the EU without being discriminated against on the grounds of nationality.

> ► **Treaty on the Functioning of the European Union Art.56**
>
> '[Restrictions] on freedom to provide services within the Union shall be prohibited in respect of nationals of Member States who are established in a member State other than that of the person for whom the services are intended.'

Art.56 prevents the creation of obstacles to a person who is ordinarily based in one member state from being able to provide their services elsewhere in the EU. Where individual athletes are concerned it ensures that they can compete anywhere in the EU provided that they have satisfied the necessary entry criteria for the tournament in question.

12.3.1 The *Deliège* decision

Despite the high profile and drawn out nature of the *Bosman* litigation, ISFs failed to appreciate that other provisions of the TFEU might also apply to sporting relationships. As most athletes are either employees and therefore workers or self-employed and therefore providers of services, the next natural extension of EU law to sport was that its rules and procedures could be subject to Art.56 TFEU.

> ► *Deliège* **v. Ligue Francophone de Judo et Disciplines Associées ASBL, Ligue Belge de Judo ASBL (LBJ) and Union Européenne de Judo (UEJ) (Joined Cases C-51/96 and C-191/97) [2000] ECR I-2549**
>
> Deliège was an elite level judoka who hoped to compete in the 1996 Atlanta Olympics. In order to achieve a high enough ranking to be invited to compete in Atlanta, she had to participate in a number of specific tournaments in the run up to the Games. The UEJ had stipulated that at all 'Category A' ranking tournaments, each national federation, in this case the LBJ, could enter only seven judoka of each sex. This would enable each NGB to enter one person into each of the seven weight categories open to each sex. Where there was nobody of sufficient standing to participate in a particular category, additional judokas could be entered into any of the other weight divisions at the discretion of the NGB.

Despite being one of the highest ranking judokas in her weight division Deliège was not selected to compete at several Category A tournaments. In an attempt to facilitate her participation in the Paris International Tournament she challenged the entry criteria of the UEJ and the selection criteria of the LBJ, claiming that their refusal to allow her to compete was an unlawful restriction on her freedom to provide her services as a judoka in another member state.

The ECJ began by stating that Art.56 TFEU (ex Art.49 ECT) was directly effective in the same way that Art.45 was and could therefore be invoked against non-state bodies such as ISFs and NGBs, where the rules of such bodies were regulating gainful employment. However, also in accordance with the rulings on Art.45, Art.56 would only be engaged where the athlete was involved with an economic activity. The UEJ and LBJ both argued that as judo was an amateur sport Deliège could not be engaged in an economic activity and that as a result there could be no breach of Art.56. The ECJ rejected this argument on the basis that Deliège had received grants from the state and had entered into personal sponsorship agreements with various corporations, both of which constituted the necessary remuneration to classify her activity as being economic in nature. Thus as the criteria operated by the UEJ and LBJ together prevented her from being able to provide her services as a judoka at international tournaments, the rules were potentially an unlawful restriction contrary to Art.56.

However the ECJ held that the selection and entry criteria operated by the defendants were inherently necessary for the proper administration of the sport and therefore fell outside of the scope of the treaty. The rules of the UEJ were inherent in the organisation of elite level judo tournaments as it could not be expected that each national federation would be allowed to enter an unlimited number of competitors to any and every tournament; a limit of one person per weight division per NGB was an appropriate means of regulating the maximum number of entrants able to compete at an event. Moreover unless the definition of the selection criteria used by the LBJ or their operation by it could be proved to have been in bad faith, which it could not, then decisions regarding how the members of a team should be selected were a matter for the appropriate national federation not the ECJ.

Following the updated reasoning used by the ECJ in *Meca-Medina* the same outcome would be arrived at: the rules of the UEJ and LBJ both had the potential to create obstructions to an athlete's ability to move freely about the EU to provide their services, however both sets of rules can be objectively justified as being necessary and proportionate for the proper administration of elite level judo tournaments. Thus whereas *Walrave* justified the use of restrictive practices on the grounds of nationality where the athletes were competing in international representative competitions, *Deliège* allowed restrictions to be imposed on the ability of individual athletes to compete in a tournament where to do so was necessary from an administrative point of view.

12.3.2   The impact of *Deliège* on English law

The leading English authority on Art.56 TFEU was *Edwards* v. *The British Athletic Federation and the International Amateur Athletic Federation* [1998] 2 CMLR 363; however in the light of both *Deliège* and *Meca-Medina*, *Edwards* now needs to be significantly revisited. Edwards had been banned from competing as an athlete for four years following the commission of a doping offence. The IAAF routinely allowed athletes to be reinstated after serving only two years of a ban if they were based in a country where a four year ban was considered to be disproportionate and therefore unlawful, on the grounds that exceptional circumstances existed that would justify it commuting the punishment. After serving two years of his ban Edwards applied to the IAAF for reinstatement, however his application was rejected on the basis that there were no exceptional circumstances relevant to his case as a four year ban was considered to be reasonable and therefore lawful in the UK.

Edwards applied to the High Court to have the decision of the IAAF ruled unlawful for being contrary to Art.56 TFEU. He argued that by allowing the ban to continue for a further two years he was being prevented from providing his services as a professional athlete to tournament organisers when other EU nationals would have been automatically reinstated. On a preliminary point, the Court did not pass judgment on whether Edwards' services were 'normally provided for remuneration' as to do so was not necessary for the disposal of the case. In the light of *Deliège*, however it would appear that any monies received by way of grants, prize money or sponsorship are sufficient to constitute the necessary earnings and therefore to engage Art.56.

The Court then went on to hold that the IAAF's anti-doping rules and the bans imposed on athletes who had breached them merely regulated sporting conduct not any economic activity. The basis of Lightman J's decision was that as the rules were designed to ban cheating by drug-taking, a practice which was banned to ensure that athletes competed on a level playing field, then this was a purely sporting rule that had only an incidental economic impact. After the ECJ's ruling in *Meca-Medina* this can no longer be considered to be the correct approach; the anti-doping regime designed by WADA and implemented by most ISFs does have an impact on economic activity but it is justifiable as necessary for the maintenance of the integrity of sporting competition and for the protection of athletes' health.

Further, Lightman J found that there was nothing unlawful in the IAAF imposing bans of different lengths on athletes from different countries. He states that if there was no such body as the IAAF or if the IAAF left the punishment of athletes to its constituent member NGBs then differential punishments that were in accordance with the law of the country in which an NGB was based would be the norm. However the judge's hypothetical reasoning misses the reality of the situation; the IAAF does in fact exist and was in fact sanctioning punishments of differing lengths on athletes who had committed the same doping infringement on the basis of their nationality. Therefore it is difficult to come to any other conclusion than that the IAAF was acting in a discriminatory fashion.

Finally it was accepted by the Court without any significant analysis that a four year ban for a doping offence was reasonable, justified and proportionate. In the light of the various revisions to the anti-doping rules operated by most ISFs and of their adopting the provisions of the World Anti-Doping Code, it is extremely unlikely that a ban of more than two years in length would now be considered to be a proportionate response to a first doping offence. Thus almost every aspect of the judgment is now open to question after the ECJ's decisions in *Deliège* and *Meca-Medina*.

12.4 Treaty on the Foundation of the European Union Arts.101 and 102 (ex Arts.81 and 82 ECT) – competition law

Fully developed claims that sports authorities have acted in breach of EU competition law have so far been comparatively rare. Although some of the most important sporting references to the ECJ have included assertions that a governing body has engaged in anti-competitive behaviour, including *Bosman*, *Lehtonen* and *Deliège*, few had provided a sufficiently detailed factual context on which the Court could base a preliminary ruling.

The competition law provisions have the potential to exert significant influence over the governance of sport. The purpose of Art.101 TFEU is to prevent an informal group of undertakings or a more formal association of undertakings from agreeing together to act in an anti-competitive manner. ISFs and NGBs are both undertakings capable of entering into anti-competitive agreements by themselves and are also associations of undertakings capable of acting anti-competitively. Following *Meca-Medina* they are undertakings by reason of being entities that are engaged in economic activity and they are associations of undertakings as their constituent members are undertakings in their own right; in the case of an ISF, its NGB members are undertakings and in the case of NGBs, the member clubs are also undertakings. Thus any rule or practice that interferes with the operation of the sports market, from anti-doping and transfer rules to nationality restrictions and eligibility criteria, has the potential to be anti-competitive and therefore unlawful.

▶ **Treaty on the Foundation of the European Union Art.101**

'1 The following shall be prohibited as incompatible with the internal market: all agreements between undertakings, decisions by associations of undertakings and concerted practices which may affect trade between Member States and which have as their object or effect the prevention, restriction or distortion of competition within the internal market and in particular those which:
(a) directly or indirectly fix purchase or selling prices or any other trading conditions;
(b) limit or control production, markets, technical development, or investment;
(c) share markets or sources of supply;
(d) apply dissimilar conditions to equivalent transactions with other trading parties, thereby placing them at a competitive disadvantage;
(e) make the conclusion of contracts subject to acceptance by the other parties of supplementary obligations which, by their nature or according to commercial usage, have no connection with the subject of such contracts.

2 Any agreements or decisions prohibited pursuant to this article shall be automatically void.

3 The provisions of paragraph 1 may, however, be declared inapplicable in the case of:
 – any agreement or category of agreements between undertakings,
 – any decision or category of decisions by associations of undertakings,
 – any concerted practice or category of concerted practices,
which contributes to improving the production or distribution of goods or to promoting technical or economic progress, while allowing consumers a fair share of the resulting benefit, and which does not:
(a) impose on the undertakings concerned restrictions which are not indispensable to the attainment of these objectives;
(b) afford such undertakings the possibility of eliminating competition in respect of a substantial part of the products in question.'

Art.102 TFEU was implemented to prevent the dominant undertaking in a particular market from abusing its position of power to exploit its own market dominance or exclude or restrict entry to the market of potential competitors, as was at issue in *Motosykletistiki Omospondia Ellados NPID (MOTOE)* v. *Eilliniko Dimosio* (Case C-49/07) [2008] ECR I-4863 (see further, chapter 3.2.6). The administrative framework of most sports creates a series of monopolies as an inherent by-product of their using the pyramidal structure or European model of sports governance. This leads to an NGB being dominant in the domestic or national market, the continental association being similarly dominant in the continental market and the ISF dominating the global market. Thus the rules or practices of many sports authorities have the potential to be abusers of their dominant position as those affected by such rules have no option other than to adhere to them or face punishment or expulsion.

> ▶ **Treaty on the Foundation of the European Union Art.102**
>
> 'Any abuse by one or more undertakings of a dominant position within the internal market or in a substantial part of it shall be prohibited as incompatible with the internal market in so far as it may affect trade between Member States.
>   Such abuse may, in particular, consist in:
>
> (a) directly or indirectly imposing unfair purchase or selling prices or other unfair trading conditions;
> (b) limiting production, markets or technical development to the prejudice of consumers;
> (c) applying dissimilar conditions to equivalent transactions with other trading parties, thereby placing them at a competitive disadvantage;
> (d) making the conclusion of contracts subject to acceptance by the other parties of supplementary obligations which, by their nature or according to commercial usage, have no connection with the subject of such contracts.'

Although the early sports litigation did not follow through on the competition law issues, recent case law has brought to the fore the potential scope of Arts.101 and 102 TFEU as ways of challenging the rules and decisions of sports authorities. At the same time as this potential extension has occurred however, the development of the claim that a rule is justified as being necessary because of the 'specificity of sport' has gone some significant way to ameliorate the difficulties that this could cause.

12.4.1 The 'dual role' of sports authorities

In order for an ISF or NGB to be subject to Arts.101 and 102 TFEU, it must first be found to be operating as an undertaking. This key issue saw diametrically opposed views be put forward by the parties to competition law disputes. On the one hand the sports authority would claim that it was a purely regulatory body that was not engaging in any economic activity and therefore could not be classified as an undertaking. On the other hand the claimants would argue that the rules, practices and decisions of the sports authority had such a significant impact on their ability to earn a living that its activities had to be considered to be economic in nature. In *MOTOE* (see further, chapter 3.2.6) the ECJ held that in reality ISFs and NGBs perform a 'dual role' when governing their sports; they act as purely regulatory bodies when administering the rules of their sports and the framework in which they are organised but as commercial entities when they enter into sponsorship, broadcasting and insurance contracts in respect of their own tournaments or where their rules and decisions have an impact on the economic activity of others.

In acknowledging the existence of this 'dual role' the ECJ accepted that it is possible for a sports body to be an undertaking when it performs these commercial functions but not when it acts purely as a regulatory body. However the dividing line between the commercial and regulatory functions of these bodies is often indistinct. Therefore the Court went on to add that where the combination of regulatory and commercial functions performed by a sports authority has the *potential* to lead to market abuse unless properly regulated, then the competition provisions are engaged. Thus it is the creation of the possibility of market abuse by the unregulated existence of the 'dual role', not the proof of actual anti-competitive behaviour, which appears to lead to the infringement of Arts.101 and 102 TFEU.

The effect of *MOTOE* and *Meca-Medina* is to subject the conduct of most ISFs and NGBs to the possibility of scrutiny by EU competition law, particularly where professional and elite sport is concerned, as so many of them perform this dual role. However where their rules can be justified as necessary for the proper administration of their sport or where there is an appropriate review or appeals process in place, there will be no actionable infringement of Arts.101 and 102 (below, 12.4.4). The development of the 'specificity of sport' argument will provide a significant degree of protection to the majority of activities engaged in by ISFs and NGBs. Provided that they can produce a sufficiently robust explanation for why their conduct should fall outside of the scope of the competition provisions it is unlikely that either the ECJ or the European Commission will find them to have been acting unlawfully.

12.4.2   The 'dual role' of sporting rules

A related difficulty arises with trying to determine whether the disputed rule, practice or decision of an ISF or NGB is one that has an impact on economic activity or whether it has been implemented for a purely sporting purpose. Such a distinction is somewhat artificial and can be misleading as much of the conduct of these bodies can fall into both categories at the same time, especially where professional and elite sport are concerned. *Meca-Medina* and *MOTOE* now require that the rules, practices and procedures of an ISF or NGB be examined in more detail in order to determine whether the sports authority has infringed Arts.101 or 102 ECT (see further, chapter 3.2.2).

In *Meca-Medina* the ECJ held that the mere fact that a rule appears to be purely sporting in nature does not automatically remove it from the scope of the treaty. In *MOTOE* the ECJ elaborated on this reasoning by stating that this could be because the rule was fulfilling a 'dual role'. The anti-doping rules operated by FINA were not purely sporting because they also had an impact on economic activity by banning from competition any athlete who had tested positive for a doping offence. Therefore the rules could only be lawful if they were inherent in the conduct and proper organisation of the sport. The anti-doping regime operated by FINA had been implemented to ensure equality between the participants, the uncertainty of results, competitive balance and the integrity of the competition. These objectives were held by the ECJ to be legitimate and therefore the rules adopted to achieve them were inherent in the proper organisation of international swimming championships. Moreover the anti-doping regime implemented by FINA was proportionate because the rules creating it were no more than was necessary to achieve its sporting objectives. Thus the anti-doping rules were held to fall outside of the scope of the treaty because they were not restrictions according to Art.101 TFEU. If an ISF is unable to prove that there is an inherent need for a rule, practice or decision, then it will instead have to claim that it is exempted under Art.101(3) TFEU.

Conduct protected from the scope of EU law

The judgments of the ECJ and the decisions of the European Commission have established that what would otherwise be anti-competitive conduct in most other contexts can be justified as being necessary because of the 'specificity of sport'. In particular where a rule has been implemented to protect the integrity of a sport it will generally be held to be lawful if it is proportionate. It is also likely, because of the similarity of the tests used under both the competition and free movement provisions, that conduct which has been found not to breach Arts.45 and 56, such as in *Walrave* and *Deliège*, will also be found not to have infringed Arts.101 and 102 (see further, chapter 3.2.2).

12.4.3.1 Anti-doping regimes and disciplinary bans

Following *Meca-Medina* it is unlikely that any anti-doping regime that is operated in accordance with the World Anti-Doping Code will be found to be unlawful. Although clearly having an economic impact and the potential to be anti-competitive by banning athletes and teams from participating in major competitions, the ECJ held that anti-doping rules are both necessary and proportionate for the proper administration of sport. In particular the ECJ considered that the protection of the integrity of sports competitions, the maintenance of competitive balance between the participants and the protection of the health of the athletes were sufficient justifications for the legality of anti-doping rules.

The ECJ also held that banning those athletes who were found to have breached anti-doping provisions was necessary as a means of ensuring that the rules were complied with by the athletes at whom they were aimed. Provided that the bans are proportionate to the gravity of the particular doping infringement committed and the length of an athlete's career, it is lawful to prevent a person or team from competing in a sport for a specified period of time. Similar reasoning could be used to justify the legality of bans imposed for violent conduct and other forms of cheating.

In *Chambers* v. *British Olympic Association (BOA)* [2008] EWHC 2028 (QBD) (see further, chapter 2 Hot Topic) a claim of anti-competitive behaviour contrary to Arts.101 and 102 TFEU (ex Arts.81 and 82 ECT) was pleaded but not pursued in respect of the BOA's refusal to invite Chambers to compete in any future edition of the Olympic Games following his commission of a doping offence. As Chambers had already served a two year ban imposed by the relevant ISF, the IAAF, had his competition law claim been pursued at trial the BOA would have been forced to justify why its rules were more punitive than those recommended by the World Anti-Doping Code. There is no doubt that a participation ban is lawful as long as it is proportionate. The question left open for future cases by *Chambers* is whether the Olympic Games are so different from other elite level competitions that a lifetime ban can be justified as proportionate following the commission of a first doping offence.

12.4.3.2 Preventing multiple ownership of clubs in the same competition

In *ENIC plc/UEFA* IP/02/942 27 June 2002 the European Commission adopted a decision that upheld the legality of a UEFA rule that was designed to protect the independence of clubs from undue influence by one another when competing in the same competition and which is now found in rule A3 of the Regulations of the UEFA Champions League and Europa League competitions. The rule in question prevented: a club from owning or being involved in the management, administration or sporting performance of another club; a person from being involved in the management, administration or sporting performance of more than one club at a time; and two or more clubs from being under common control. For the purposes of the rule, common control was established where an individual or other legal entity held or could exercise a majority of the shareholders' voting rights or had the right to appoint or remove a majority of the members of the administrative, management or supervisory body of two or more clubs at the same time.

ENIC was an investment company that owned stakes of various sizes in six professional football clubs. When two of the clubs in which it had a major shareholding were drawn to play against each other in the UEFA Cup, UEFA stated that the lower ranked of the two according to its seeding system would have to withdraw from the competition in accordance with its rules on the independence of clubs. ENIC complained to the Commission that this rule was anti-competitive as it restricted its ability to invest freely in European football clubs.

The Commission concluded that although the rule was a decision taken by an association of undertakings and could in principle engage Art.101, it was inherent in the organisation and proper conduct of sport because it was necessary for the protection of the integrity of its competitions. UEFA's concern was that where two or more clubs were controlled by the same person or body, that person or body could influence the outcome of the game between the two sides and as a result undermine the competitive balance of the particular game in question and the integrity of the results of the competition as a whole. In other words it was concerned about the possibility of match-fixing and this rule was a means of reducing the possibility of this practice occurring.

The rule was not only necessary, it was also a proportionate means of achieving this legitimate goal. Investors were not completely banned from owning stakes in more than one club; they were only banned from owning controlling interests in two or more clubs at the same time. As the UEFA rule did no more than was necessary to protect the uncertainty of the results in the competitions that it organised, it was a proportionate response to a legitimate concern and therefore was not a restriction on trade for the purposes of EU competition law.

12.4.3.3 Rules of a purely sporting nature

The Commission has also upheld the validity of requiring ties to be played on a 'home and away' basis (see further, chapter 3.2.5). In *Royal Excelsior Mouscron* IP/99/965 9 December 1999 the owners of a football stadium in Lille, France complained that the UEFA decision to refuse the request of the Belgian football club Excelsior Mouscron to play its 'home' games in Lille was anti-competitive. The request had come about because Mouscron's home stadium was small and it wanted to maximise the profits it could make from a forthcoming UEFA Cup tie with the French first division side FC Metz. As the closest major stadium to Mouscron was in Lille it sought permission to play its 'home' game there.

The Commission upheld the legality of the UEFA rule on the basis that this was an isolated situation that was unlikely to reoccur and that there was therefore an insufficiently serious interference with trade between member states to engage EU competition law. Thus although the owners of the stadium in Lille had lost the opportunity to hire out their facility for a major European game the UEFA rule was considered to be of too small an impact on the operation of the internal market to infringe EU law.

A further reading of the decision has been that it was legitimate from a sporting perspective to require a club to play its 'home' fixtures at its own stadium unless there were compelling reasons for it not to do so. If the club is able to demonstrate that its request falls into one of the exceptions to the rule, then it is also legitimate for UEFA to require that its 'home' fixtures are played at a stadium within the territory of its NGB because football in Europe is organised along national lines according to the European model of sport. Thus to require a Belgian club to play its home games at its own stadium, or where appropriate at an alternative stadium within Belgium, was a legitimate sporting requirement that was needed to ensure equality between clubs.

12.4.4 Future developments

Despite the concerns of the European ISFs, the ECJ and the Commission have been prepared to accept that sport is different and is deserving of some degree of protection from the unfettered application of EU law. Provided that the ISFs can demonstrate that their restrictive practices are necessary and proportionate for the proper organisation of sporting competitions, that they are there to ensure equality and competitive balance between participants, preserve the uncertainty of outcome and, overall, operate in a way that guarantees the integrity of sporting competition then their conduct will be lawful. However both institutions are more concerned when the ISFs seek similar treatment for more overtly commercial practices.

In its 2008 document, *Safeguarding the heritage and future of team sports in Europe*, the European Team Sports Federations identified 15 matters whose legal position it considered to be in need of further clarification. Each of these 15 issues falls into one of three broad groups. Four could be said to concern issues of a purely sporting nature: in-game rules and the structure of championships; rules relating to the organisation of sport according to the European or pyramidal model; solidarity mechanisms; and the use of alternative dispute resolution mechanisms. A further eight are rules that have the potential to restrict trade between member states but are capable of objective justification in certain circumstances: rules concerning player transfers and contractual stability; rules that protect and encourage attendance at and participation in amateur sport; rules concerning the composition of national teams and player release clauses; anti-doping and disciplinary rules; rules to promote the use of club licensing systems; rules preventing the common control of clubs in the same competition; rules promoting youth development and the recruitment of local players; and rules concerning financial stability. The final group appear to be issues that are much more commercial in nature but which have a significant impact on the organisation of sport: the regulation of agents; the sale of commercial rights; and the protection of the integrity of results from the threat of match-fixing.

Of these issues the Federations identified the training and education of young players, the need to introduce a licensing framework and associated monitoring body to ensure good governance amongst clubs and the regulation of agents as the matters requiring the most urgent attention. These three matters are likely to have been flagged as urgent in an attempt to prevent further litigation in these areas. Following *Meca-Medina* and *MOTOE* rules concerning each of these three issues can in principle infringe Arts.101 and 102 TFEU by preventing players, clubs and agents from acting in ways that would allow them to maximise their earnings by forcing them to satisfy a range of non-sporting criteria before they can act in a certain capacity or are allowed to compete in certain tournaments. To be lawful the Federations will have to provide objective justifications for the need to make rules that regulate these activities. By appealing to the European Council to request the Commission to work with them, the Federations are hoping to avoid the costly litigation of the past and to influence proactively the development of European sports law in the future.

Hot topic . . .

CAN NATIONALITY RESTRICTIONS EVER BE LEGAL?

After the ECJ's judgment in *Bosman* and its extension in *Kolpak* and *Simutenkov*, restrictions on the number of non-domestic (EU and associated nation) players that a club could field in any game were held to be unlawful. Since then UEFA has reintroduced nationality quotas in the club competitions that it organises (the Champions League and the Europa League) in the form of the 'home-grown players' rule, whilst FIFA has proposed a similar system that it wants to be applied throughout professional football with its '6+5' rule.

Art.18 of the Regulations of both the UEFA Champions League and UEFA Europa League require that a club submit a squad list of 25 players from whom the team to play in these competitions will be selected. Of these 25, eight must be 'locally trained players' and of these eight, a minimum of four must be 'club-trained players' and a maximum of four must be 'association-trained players'. Club-trained players must have been registered for at least three years with the club for which they are now playing between the ages of 15 and 21, whilst association-trained players must have been registered for at least three years with a club or clubs affiliated to the same national association as their current club, again between the ages of 15 and 21.

FIFA's proposal is that the starting 11 players of any professional football team must include a minimum of six players who are qualified to play for the national association to which their current club is affiliated, with the remaining five being able to come from anywhere else in the world. Substitutes can also come from

any country meaning that under current rules, it would be possible for a maximum of eight of the 14 players who could play for a team in any game to be 'foreign' players.

Both FIFA and UEFA claim that their rules are of a 'purely sporting interest' only and therefore are not capable of engaging EU law on the basis that they affect nothing more than the composition of a team. However the reality is that these are 'dual role' rules that, although having a clear sporting objective, also have an impact on economic activity, which is sufficient to engage Art.45 TFEU as was the case in *Bosman*. Following *Meca-Medina*, as both rules are decisions of an association of undertakings that have an impact on the operation of the employment market for professional footballers, Art.101 TFEU is in principle also engaged. Therefore further investigation of their legality is required.

Art.45 as interpreted by *Bosman* prohibits restrictions on the freedom of movement for workers on the grounds of nationality. The FIFA rule requires direct discrimination against all players who are not eligible to play for the national association of which their current club is a member. This creates a situation where clubs will have to discriminate against non-nationals of the country in which they are based in order to fill the six places in the team reserved for domestic nationals. As sport does not fall within any of the derogations to Art.45 and as direct discrimination cannot otherwise be justified in EU law, the rule appears to be unlawful in its current form.

The UEFA rule requires only that a player is 'locally trained' and applies irrespective of their nationality. It is therefore not directly discriminatory. However as the condition is much more easily fulfilled by nationals of the country where a club is based, it is indirectly discriminatory. The rule may appear to be neutral but its effect is to discriminate against the group of people who find it more difficult to comply with, in this case the young foreign players who were trained abroad and who later want to move to a club established elsewhere in the EU. An indirectly discriminatory rule is lawful only if it can be objectively justified.

It is likely that, after *Meca-Medina* and *MOTOE*, infringements of both Arts.45 and 101 will be capable of being justified on broadly similar grounds. As both provisions are in principle infringed by the 'home-grown player' rule, the quality of the justifications put forward by UEFA must also be interrogated; for the sake of completeness FIFA's arguments will also be examined even though they cannot be used to justify the direct discrimination that the '6+5' rule appears to promote. Both FIFA and UEFA claim that their rules promote competitive balance by spreading the available talent across a greater number of clubs and that they encourage the proper training and protection of young players. FIFA also argues that its rule promotes the link between a club and the country in which it is based and increases the pool of talent available to be chosen to play international football.

The ECJ has long held that it is a legitimate objective of the rules of an ISF to seek to maintain a competitive balance between the participants in a championship and to ensure the uncertainty of results. The problem faced by both FIFA and UEFA however is that there is no proof that these rules can achieve these aims. In either case there is nothing to stop the richest clubs buying the best players in accordance with the quotas and nothing to stop them from hoarding excess players in order to stop them from playing for a rival, thereby perpetuating the imbalance that the two Associations are seeking to eradicate. The UEFA rule can be further undermined by a club deciding simply not to fill any of the eight places constituting its 'locally trained' quota. For example a club could choose to name 17 world-class 'foreign' players on its squad list and still be able to compete in either of UEFA's tournaments. Thus the rules appear from the outset to be neither necessary nor inherent in achieving competitive balance or securing the uncertainty of results.

It is also a legitimate objective of an ISF to have rules that both encourage and protect the development of young players. Again however there is no proof that either of these rules can actually achieve this aim. Under FIFA's rule a rich club could simply buy in six nationally qualified players without the need to have trained any of them in its youth team or academy structure, potentially creating an additional problem of undermining its goal of securing contractual stability, a key theme of its Regulations on the Status and Transfer of Players.

There are more varied problems faced by the UEFA rule. Firstly it can be undermined by a club simply choosing not to name any players in the club-trained category, while allowing it to buy in four association-trained players and 17 foreign players. As with the FIFA rule, there is nothing in the way that the UEFA rule is drafted that forces a club to develop new players if it chooses not to. Secondly it can be subverted by naming four academy players who have no realistic prospect of making it on to the

field of play except in the most extreme of circumstances; if the players are not going to be exposed to playing at the highest level, it cannot be said to be developing their career by their sitting on the substitutes' bench. Thirdly the rule might actually create the conditions in which the trafficking of young players can occur as clubs seek to bring in players at as young an age as possible to ensure that they can qualify as club-trained despite being qualified to play for a foreign international representative team. Fourthly, and perhaps rather strangely, on a strict reading of Art.18 of UEFA's Regulations for its two main club competitions, a player who is under the age of 18 cannot be counted as a club-trained player even if they have only ever been with that one club because they will not yet have been registered with it for the necessary three years. For example when Jack Wilshire made his first Champions League appearance for Arsenal aged 16 years and 329 days, he was neither club-trained nor association-trained as he had only been registered with Arsenal for one year and 329 days since his 15th birthday.

If young players need not be exposed to the highest levels of play as a result of these rules then there appears to be no justification for implementing them in the first place. Therefore it is neither necessary nor inherent in either rule that young players will be developed by professional clubs as the rules cannot guarantee that a club's own youth system will be used as a supply of players for their first team or for selection in UEFA competitions.

Finally FIFA has not been able to explain why a link needs to be created between a club and the country in which it is based nor how its rule can create a pool of players available to play in international representative fixtures. Although historically many players did play for their local team, it has never been a requirement that a club's playing staff

reflects the demographics of the area in which it is based. Nor has there ever been a requirement that the players chosen for international representative matches play for a club in that country. Further, a counter-argument from many smaller nations might be that their players need to play abroad in order to fulfil their potential when playing for their national team. Thus without a considerably stronger evidence base on which to found its arguments FIFA appears not to be pursuing legitimate objectives on these two grounds.

The rules put forward by FIFA and UEFA appear to be on uncertain legal ground. FIFA's '6+5' rule in particular appears to be little more than an attempt to reintroduce the kind of directly discriminatory measure that was specifically declared unlawful in *Bosman* and in its current form is unlikely to withstand the scrutiny of either the European Commission or the ECJ. UEFA's 'home-grown players' rule appears to pay greater regard to the requirements of EU law but there remain problems with whether it is a necessary and proportionate means of achieving what would otherwise be legitimate and protectable goals.

A solution may present itself to both bodies should they decide to focus more on the training, education and protection of young players and on rewarding clubs for the operation of successful academies and their work in the community, rather than on trying to reintroduce nationality quotas. If the restrictions based on nationality are challenged it is possible that they will be found to infringe EU law. However a justification for such quotas that can be based on the improvement of the all round education of young athletes and the prevention their exploitation in the labour market is likely to meet with the explicit approval of the institutions of the EU, provided that the rules are appropriately drafted.

Summary

12.1 Since *Walrave* it has been held that sporting rules and relationships are capable of engaging EU law when they have an impact on an economic activity. In particular where the rules and decisions of an ISF or NGB affect an athlete's ability to engage in gainful employment, it must be ensured that they do not infringe EU law. As the provisions of the TFEU have direct effect on sports bodies, an athlete is able to rely on a breach of its provisions as their cause of action before the national courts of the EU.

12.2 Art.45 TFEU guarantees the freedom of movement for workers to travel throughout the EU for employment purposes. *Bosman* interpreted Art.45 to mean that no restrictions can be placed on this fundamental freedom by requiring the payment of a fee to enable an athlete to join a new club after the expiry of their previous contract of employment or through the imposition of nationality quotas. An exemption has been granted to genuinely representative sporting competitions to enable regional and international tournaments to continue on the basis that they are not economic activities. Following *Meca-Medina*, it may be better to describe the restrictions created by the rules governing international sport as inherent in the proper organisation of such competitions rather than as an exemption. In order to determine whether a rule, decision or practice of a sports authority breaches the free movement provisions of the Treaty, the Court must address four issues. Firstly is the conduct in question a restriction on a worker's freedom of movement under Art.45 TFEU? Secondly if the rule is a restriction, is its use capable of being justified objectively? Thirdly is the rule effective in promoting the objectives pursued? Fourthly is the rule a proportionate means of achieving the objectives?

12.3 Art.56 guarantees a person established in one member state the freedom to provide their services in any other member state of the EU. It has the effect of extending the same protections to self-employed individual athletes as are guaranteed to athletes employed by clubs under Art.45. *Deliège* made it clear that there are no restrictions on a person's right to provide their services where they are necessary and proportionate for achieving a legitimate goal. The selection criteria operated by NGBs when picking national teams and the entry criteria operated by the organisers of elite level championships are both lawful because they enable international sport to be administered effectively. In order to determine whether a sports authority's rules, decisions or practices breach Art.56, the ECJ will follow the same four steps that it would when considering a breach of Art.45.

12.4 Arts.101 and 102 TFEU apply to the conduct of sports bodies where they are engaged in economic activity. As most ISFs and NGBs have 'dual roles' in respect of the governance of their sport, meaning that they perform both regulatory and commercial functions, their conduct will usually engage EU competition law at least in principle. As ISFs and NGBs are undertakings in their own right, and are associations of undertakings taking decisions that have an impact on the market in which they operate, many of their rules and decisions have the potential to infringe Art.101. As the pyramidal structure or European model of sport has the effect of creating jurisdictional monopolies, it is also possible for their decisions to constitute an abuse of a dominant position. Whether or not a rule conforms with EU competition law can be determined by asking four questions. Firstly is the collective regulatory body that is seeking to rely on the potentially restrictive rule an undertaking or an association of undertakings? Secondly is the rule a restriction of competition contrary to Art.101(1) TFEU or an abuse of a dominant position under Art.102 TFEU? Thirdly if the rule is a restriction, does it affect trade between member states? Fourthly if it does affect trade within the internal market, can it be justified under Art.101(3) TFEU on the basis that its beneficial effects outweigh the restrictions that it imposes? Where the rules in dispute are necessary and inherent to the proper administration of sport, protect its competitive balance and the uncertainty of its results then no breach of competition law will be established.

Further reading

Craig and De Burca, *EU Law* (4th edn, 2008, Oxford University Press) chs 21, 22, 25, 26

Lewis and Taylor (eds), *Sport: Law and Practice* (2nd edn, 2008, Tottel) chs B2 and 3

Parrish and Miettinen, *The sporting exception in European Union Law* (2008, TMC Asser Press)

Majani, 'An excavation into the legal deficiencies of the FIFA '6+5 Rule' and the UEFA 'Home-grown Players Rule' in the eyes of European Union Law' [2009] 1/2 *International Sports Law Journal* 19

Manville, 'The UEFA 'Home-grown Player Rule' and the Meca-Medina judgment of the European Court of Justice' [2009] 1/2 *International Sports Law Journal* 25

Miettinen, 'Policing the boundaries between regulation and commercial exploitation: lessons from the MOTOE case' [2008] 3/4 *International Sports Law Journal* 13

Szyszczak, 'Competition and sport' (2007) 32(1) *European Law Review* 95

Van Rompey, 'Fair access to exclusive sports rights still a long shot in UK pay TV market' (2009) 14(4) *Communications Law* 118

Weatherill, 'Anti-doping revisited – the demise of the rule of 'purely sporting interest'? (2006) 27(12) *European Competition Law Review* 645

Weatherill, 'Article 82 EC and sporting 'conflict of interest': the judgment in MOTOE' [2009] 1/2 *International Sports Law Journal* 3

Links to relevant websites can be found at www.palgrave.com/law/james

Chapter 13

The fan as consumer and the commercial exploitation of sport

Key words

> ▶ **Commodification** – the repackaging and rebranding of an event or competition that creates a commodity that can be more easily marketed to the public.
> ▶ **Primary rights holder** – the owner of the commercial rights vested in an event, competition or product.
> ▶ **Ambush marketing** – the unofficial or unauthorised association of a product or service with an event in an attempt to undermine the marketing strategy of one or more of the event's official sponsors.

13.1 The commercialisation and commodification of sport

The commercialisation of sport has affected not only athletes, clubs and administrators but has also had a significant impact on the ways in which sport is now consumed by the fans. The quest for success both on and off the field of play has led in recent years to an unprecedented growth in sports sponsorship, merchandising sales and the value of broadcasting rights. Whilst providing some elite athletes, clubs and competition organisers with access to additional income streams that dwarf what they could previously have expected to earn, it has been the fans who have bankrolled these commercial developments.

The commercialisation of sport is not just about replica kits and scarves; many clubs now sell a range of sportswear, leisurewear, gifts and even financial services. Nor is it just about the main television deals; some professional clubs now run their own TV channels and stream live games and highlights packages online and to mobile communications devices. Nor is it just about corporate hospitality and executive boxes; ordinary ticket prices have increased dramatically over the past 20 years, particularly in professional football and also since the introduction of all-seater stadiums, a development that is very much contrary to the predictions of Lord Justice Taylor in the aftermath of the Hillsborough disaster. The commercialisation seen in modern sport is about the creation of new income streams and the development of new markets in which to sell these products and services.

An integral aspect of this commercialisation has been the commodification of sport. This marketing phenomenon is where a valuable asset is repackaged and rebranded, turned into a more attractive commodity and sold back to the consumer as something new. Perhaps the most well-known example of this in British sport is the creation of the Premier League in 1992. A national professional football league had existed in England since 1888. After receiving a marketing and administrative makeover, the top division of English football was sold back to the public as the Premier League as though the previous era had not happened. One of the main differences to the fan-consumer is that what was once available for free on terrestrial television is now only available on subscription services.

The money involved with some of the more commercialised sports and events is huge: the sale of broadcast rights to the Beijing Olympics in 2008 is estimated to have brought in over $1.7bn for the Organising Committee and the IOC; in April 2009 the Forbes valuation of the world's major football teams estimated that the five leading clubs were each worth over $1bn; meanwhile from 2010 Formula 1 racing teams have agreed to restrict their budgets to around £100m per season in an attempt to curb the free spending that had seen some teams rumoured to have spent almost three times that amount in the 2008 season. Either directly or indirectly this spending is funded by the fans; it is the fan, now often referred to as simply a loyal consumer, who buys ever more varied merchandising, who subscribes to the various broadcast platforms and who buys the products of the corporate sponsors who aim at developing a relationship with them by associating themselves with their team, their sport or the event that they are attending.

This chapter analyses from a legal perspective the impact of the commercialisation of sport on the fan-consumer. As tickets to some events have become more difficult to acquire, a sophisticated secondary market in unofficial sales has developed; a similar market has evolved for cheaper unlicensed copies of unofficial merchandise and counterfeited products. Where subscription-based broadcasting of events is concerned, a range of methods have been tried by fan-consumers to find cheaper alternatives to paying the necessary fee to the official broadcaster, even if it means watching an event with a foreign commentary. The legality of these alternative markets has become increasingly contested as clubs and competition organisers seek to maximise their profits and protect their investments, whilst fans try to put some limit on the exploitation of their limited financial resources.

13.2 Ticket touting and the regulation of secondary ticket sales

Ticket touting involves the unauthorised resale of tickets to a sporting event. It is a practice that has long been associated with UK sport in general and football in particular. Touting refers to any unauthorised resale of a ticket, regardless of how many tickets a tout is selling, whether the sale is made in public or online and whether or not the tout makes or intends to make a profit on those sales. The person who sells a genuinely spare ticket intending only to recoup their initial outlay can be considered to be a tout in just the same way as is the person who makes their living from selling tickets on the secondary market.

All unauthorised re-sales are breaches of the original contract between the initial purchaser and the primary rights holder. The initial purchaser of a ticket does not have the right to trade it; all that the ticket represents is a licence granted by the primary rights holder to the purchaser to attend the venue for the purpose of watching the event. However pursuing each individual breach of contract would be too costly and too time-consuming for the primary rights holder, especially as it is difficult to prove that they have suffered a loss when an event is sold out; they have still sold a ticket at face value as they wanted to, it is just that someone else has sold it on, perhaps for a higher sum. Thus the activities of most touts are ignored by the law unless they are acting overtly criminally in some way (below, 13.2.2–3).

Not only does touting exist in this grey area between the civil and criminal law but fans' attitudes towards it are equally confused. Primary rights holders claim to be acting on behalf of fans when they call for all ticket touting to be made criminal, however there is little call for a generally applicable anti-touting offence from fans who not only see touts as a means of getting hold of tickets to popular events but also expect to be able to sell their own unused tickets on the secondary market, and at a profit, should the need or opportunity arise. It is against this backdrop that the regulation of the secondary market needs to be examined.

13.2.1   The evolution of the secondary market

The conditions necessary for the creation of a secondary market are near perfect where the unauthorised resale of tickets to sports events is concerned. For many popular events the face value of the ticket is below, and occasionally very far below, its value on the open market. The comparatively low price charged for tickets can be for a variety of reasons: the primary rights holder may be trying to enable the widest possible cross-section of people to attend its event by charging variable ticket prices; it may be trying to guarantee that the event is sold out to ensure the best possible atmosphere is generated; it may be trying to inculcate a culture of attendance and support at the live event; or it may be rewarding fans for their attendance at previous events. In each of these cases the actual ticket price is less than some people are willing to pay to attend the event in question.

Moreover the very nature of sports competitions means that the primary rights holder cannot provide an appropriate alternative to attendance live at the event. Fans do not want to go and watch a different team or different sport when tickets to a specific event are sold out and it is not within the power of the event organiser to stage extra performances for those who were unable to buy tickets from official sources. Each game is unique and incapable of substitution for an alternative; matches cannot be played multiple times just because demand outstrips supply.

This situation is exacerbated by the ease with which a ticket holder or potential tout and those seeking to purchase tickets can now engage with the secondary market. Online sales and auction sites have enabled anyone with access to the internet to buy and sell tickets whilst indifference amongst consumers to the ethics and legality of ticket touting ensures that few question the operation of the secondary market provided that their tickets arrive in time for them to attend the event. Thus wherever demand outstrips supply, there is the potential for the emergence of a secondary market in tickets to a sports event.

The difficulty for the law in this situation is to determine the basis on which it should regulate this secondary market. The standard terms of most sports event tickets include a prohibition on their resale without the specific authorisation of the primary rights holder, who will also retain property in the ticket itself (*R v. Marshall* [1998] 2 Cr App R 282). The only exemption to this general prohibition is where a profit is neither made nor intended to be made by the resale, enabling the purchaser to sell tickets at or below face value to other members of the group with whom they will be attending the event. Despite this specific prohibition, the need to commence multiple actions for breach of contract and the bad publicity generated by excluding those who have bought touted tickets to 'must-see' events make the enforcement of these terms before the courts financially inefficient and practically ineffective as a means of protecting the primary rights holder.

Where touts have provided inadequate, inaccurate or false information about specific qualities of the ticket or fail to provide any ticket at all, they can be prosecuted for fraud or for breaching consumer protection legislation (below, 13.2.2–3). A further justification for legal intervention can be provided where public order may be compromised by causing a breakdown in the segregation of rival fans at designated football matches (below, 13.2.4). However outside of these situations it is difficult to identify who has been harmed by ticket touting and who is in need of protection from whom when both parties engage in a process of negotiation and are in possession of all of the facts necessary to enable them to enter into a transaction.

13.2.2 Regulation by generally applicable criminal law provisions

Any person acting as a ticket tout for any sporting event runs the risk of being found guilty of a criminal offence either during the course of negotiating the sale or at the point at which the sale is concluded. Of particular importance in these circumstances are the Fraud Act 2006, the Consumer Protection from Unfair Trading Regulations 2008/1277 and the Consumer Protection (Distance Selling) Regulations 2000/2334.

13.2.2.1 Fraud Act 2006 ss.2 and 3

The new offences of fraud that are defined in ss.2 and 3 Fraud Act 2006 are so widely drafted as to be capable of criminalising almost any ticket touting transaction where the tout has failed to provide the purchaser with all relevant information about the ticket or where they deliberately fail to provide the ticket that has been paid for.

> ▶ **Fraud Act 2006 s.2 – fraud by false representation**

'(1) A person is in breach of this section if he –
  (a) dishonestly makes a false representation, and
  (b) intends, by making the representation –
    (i) to make a gain for himself or another, or
    (ii) to cause loss to another or to expose another to a risk of loss.
(2) A representation is false if –
  (a) it is untrue or misleading, and
  (b) the person making it knows that it is, or might be, untrue or misleading.
(3) "Representation" means any representation as to fact or law, including a representation as to the state of mind of –
  (a) the person making the representation, or
  (b) any other person.
(4) A representation may be express or implied.
(5) For the purposes of this section a representation may be regarded as made if it (or anything implying it) is submitted in any form to any system or device designed to receive, convey or respond to communications (with or without human intervention).

Fraud Act 2006 s.3 – fraud by failing to disclose information
A person is in breach of this section if he –
  (a) dishonestly fails to disclose to another person information which he is under a legal duty to disclose, and
  (b) intends, by failing to disclose the information –
    (i) to make a gain for himself or another, or
    (ii) to cause loss to another or to expose another to a risk of loss.'

Under s.2 fraud is committed where the tout makes a false representation about any quality of the ticket, for example advertising it as being for a front row seat when it actually has a restricted view or is at the back of the stadium. Alternatively where the tout fails to disclose that, for example they are not an authorised seller of the ticket, then the offence under s.3 could be committed. It is important to note that no sale actually has to take place; the offences are complete where the tout intends to make a profit for themselves or another, for example by charging the purchaser a higher amount on the basis of incorrect information about the quality of the ticket, or where they intend to cause a loss to the purchaser, for example by not providing them with any ticket at all, or by exposing them to the risk of loss, for example by failing to inform the purchaser that the ticket is void for having been bought from a tout.

These two sections of the Fraud Act 2006 have the potential to apply to almost all touting transactions and in respect of any sports event. In particular they can be used to prosecute the more serious forms of ticket touting where the tout is deliberately misleading the purchaser or where the tout has no intention of supplying the purchaser with any tickets. However this more obviously criminal conduct represents a minority of secondary market transactions and therefore other means of regulation must also be considered.

13.2.2.2 Consumer Protection Regulations

The Consumer Protection from Unfair Trading Regulations 2008/1277 (CPUTR) and the Consumer Protection (Distance Selling) Regulations 2000/2334 (CPDSR) provide further protections to purchasers buying tickets from professional touts who are selling tickets in the course of business or as traders. Although a 'trader' is not defined in the Regulations, it can be assumed that it will require the seller to be engaging with the secondary market with multiple ticket sales on a regular as opposed to an ad hoc basis.

The CPUTR make it a criminal offence for a trader to mislead a consumer in any way and in particular about a specific quality of the ticket being sold such that it materially distorts the purchaser's economic behaviour. Regs.5, 6 and 7 and Sch.1 contain comprehensive but non-exhaustive lists of what can amount to unfair commercial practices. Where ticket touting is concerned this would include providing untruthful or misleading information about the existence or provenance of a ticket, about its material characteristics, for example its original face value or position in the venue, or about restrictions contained in its terms, such as if becoming invalid when resold by an unauthorised vendor. All of this information must be transmitted to the purchaser before the transaction is completed. Thus where the average consumer's ability to make an informed decision is impaired by the conduct of the vendor and causes them to purchase a ticket that they would not otherwise have done, an offence is committed.

The CPDSR apply to suppliers who are acting in a commercial or professional capacity when selling tickets otherwise than in a face-to-face transaction, including online and telephone sales. Reg.7 again requires the supplier to provide the purchaser with the material characteristics of the ticket prior to the conclusion of the contract. Where the purchaser discovers that this has not occurred, Reg.11 provides them with the right to cancel the contract and to have their money refunded. However as it will often be the case that inaccurate information about the material characteristics of the ticket will only become known upon its receipt, the purchaser is usually left with a choice of either attending the event with the sub-standard ticket that they have purchased or not attending it at all. Further, as only the price of the ticket and not related expenditure such as travel and accommodation can be recovered, the CPDSR provide only limited protection to consumers.

The protections provided by both sets of Regulations suffer from one significant flaw: they only apply to sales by traders acting in the course of a business or in a professional capacity. As very few touts are able to trade officially in sports event tickets because they are acting in breach of contract by selling the tickets in their possession without the specific authorisation of the primary rights holder, it appears that few secondary market transactions are protected by these Regulations. However what is left open by both sets of Regulations is whether a seller can be proved to be a 'trader' by reason of the regularity with which they engage with the secondary market or on the basis of the volume of sales that they make. If the concept of a trader is fluid enough to cover sales by such unofficial sellers then the protection provided to fan-consumers would be greatly enhanced.

13.2.3 Regulation of specific instances of ticket touting

At present there are only three situations where there is an absolute prohibition of the unauthorised resale of tickets to a sporting event. This means that it will always be a criminal offence to sell tickets to a designated football match, whilst the majority of unauthorised sales to events at the London Olympic and Paralympic Games and the Glasgow Commonwealth Games will also be a crime.

13.2.3.1 Touting at designated football matches – Criminal Justice and Public Order Act 1994 s.166

Ticket touting at designated football matches was made illegal by s.166 Criminal Justice and Public Order Act 1994. The sole reason for criminalising this specific form of touting was to prevent outbreaks of public disorder caused by a breakdown in the segregation of rival groups of fans at football matches (see further, chapter 10.4.2). Thus the harm being prevented was harm to society as a whole rather than the protection of the purchaser's financial position or the primary rights holder's commercial interests.

> ▶ **Criminal Justice and Public Order Act 1994 s.166 – sale of tickets by unauthorised persons**
>
> '(1) It is an offence for an unauthorised person to –
>   (a) sell a ticket for a designated football match, or
>   (b) otherwise to dispose of such a ticket to another person.
> (2) For this purpose –
>   (a) a person is 'unauthorised' unless he is authorised in writing to sell or otherwise dispose of tickets for the match by the organisers of the match;
>   (aa) a reference to selling a ticket includes a reference to –
>   (i)   offering to sell a ticket;
>   (ii) exposing a ticket for sale;
>   (iii) making a ticket available for sale by another;
>   (iv) advertising that a ticket is available for purchase; and
>   (v)   giving a ticket to a person who pays or agrees to pay for some other goods or services or offering to do so.'

Designated football matches are those where at least one of the teams involved is a member of the English Premier League, the Football League, the Football Conference, the League of Wales or represents a territory or country (Football (Offences) (Designation of Football Matches) Order 2004/2410). It is updated every year to take account of promotion and relegation to and from the Football Conference and ensures that all major professional and semi-professional games in England and Wales are covered by the legislation.

Under s.166 all unauthorised sales are prohibited regardless of whether or not the seller is a trader or intends to make a profit. The extended definition given to 'selling' in s.166(2)(aa) was introduced to enable the police to prevent unauthorised sales at the earliest possible opportunity, the offer to sell, and to counteract the initiative of ticket touts who were for example selling vastly overpriced merchandise whilst giving away a free match ticket with every purchase.

In response to the growing number of unauthorised sales taking place online, s.166A clarifies the position of Internet Service Providers (ISP) whose services are being used by touts. An ISP is guilty of a criminal offence where it is aware that information supplied to it by a user of its services contains material that contravenes s.166 and that having become aware that information on its service contravened s.166 it failed to remove it or disable access to it expeditiously. ISPs will usually become aware that they are hosting information that enables sales that breach s.166 to take place when they are informed of the problem by the primary rights holder. In such a case they must ensure that the information cannot be accessed as soon as is reasonably practicable.

Although the criminalisation of unauthorised ticket sales to some professional football matches is undoubtedly justifiable on public order grounds, the need for an absolute ban on sales to all designated games is not borne out by Home Office arrest statistics. For the seasons 2002–03 to 2007–08, the police made 489 arrests for ticket touting, of which over 95 per cent were at Premier League, UEFA Champions League or International representative fixtures. During the same period over 33 million spectators attended designated football matches in England and Wales. This would seem to suggest that touting is not one of the police's priorities on match days or that the move to online sales has made it more difficult to regulate the activities of touts.

13.2.3.2 Touting at the London Olympics 2012 – London Olympic and Paralympic Games Act 2006 s.31

The unauthorised sale of tickets to any event at the London Olympic and Paralympic Games is an offence under s.31 London Olympic and Paralympic Games Act 2006. Whereas the criminalisation of ticket touting at designated football matches was justified on the grounds of preventing public disorder, no corresponding justification has been put forward for the need to criminalise touting at London 2012 events (see further, 14.4.3).

▶ **London Olympic and Paralympic Games Act 2006 s.31 – sale of tickets**

'(1) A person commits an offence if he sells an Olympic ticket –
  (a) in a public place or in the course of a business, and
  (b) otherwise than in accordance with a written authorisation issued by the London Organising Committee.
(2) For the purposes of subsection (1) –
  (a) "Olympic ticket" means anything which is or purports to be a ticket for one or more London Olympic events,
  (b) a reference to selling a ticket includes a reference to –
    (i)   offering to sell a ticket,
    (ii) exposing a ticket for sale,
    (iii) advertising that a ticket is available for purchase, and
    (iv) giving, or offering to give, a ticket to a person who pays or agrees to pay for some other goods or services, and

> (c) a person shall (without prejudice to the generality of subsection (1)(a)) be treated as acting in the course of a business if he does anything as a result of which he makes a profit or aims to make a profit.'

The offence under s.31 is broadly the same as that found in s.166 Criminal Justice and Public Order Act 1994. The one subtle difference appears to be that if a London 2012 ticket is not sold in public and no profit is made or intended to be made on the sale then no offence is committed. Thus if a London 2012 ticket is sold online or on private premises for face value or less, no offence is committed whereas any sale howsoever made and whether or not for profit of a ticket to a designated football match is a criminal offence. This enables a single purchaser to buy tickets for a group of spectators and to recoup their initial outlay from them without committing a crime.

No formal explanation has been provided by either the government or the London Organising Committee of the Olympic Games for why it was considered necessary to enact s.31. It appears from their various pronouncements that it is a requirement of the IOC's bidding process that such a provision is in place. Further, it appears that all parties are concerned that 'real fans' are not exploited by unscrupulous touts charging excessive prices for popular events. However if this was the case then existing criminal and consumer protection legislation could have been tightened to provide the necessary safeguards for purchasers of tickets to all popular sports events. Instead s.31 provides the kind of specific protection to the Olympics and Paralympics that has been consistently denied to other major events that take place in the UK. Without a convincing justification for this position the primary rights holders of other major events are likely to continue to seek similar legislative protection (below, Hot Topic).

13.2.3.3 Touting at the Glasgow Commonwealth Games 2014 – Glasgow Commonwealth Games Act 2008 s.17

A similar provision to that found in s.31 London Olympic and Paralympic Games Act 2006 will criminalise most unauthorised sales of tickets to the Glasgow Commonwealth Games.

> ▶ **Glasgow Commonwealth Games Act 2008 s.17 – ban on ticket touting**
>
> '(1) It is an offence to tout a Games ticket ("the touting offence").
> (2) A person touts a Games ticket if the person does any act falling within subsection (3) –
>   (a) in a public place,
>   (b) in relation to the sale, or proposed sale, of a Games ticket for an amount exceeding the ticket's face value, or
>   (c) with a view to making a profit.
> (3) Acts which fall within this subsection are –
>   (a) selling a Games ticket,
>   (b) offering to sell a Games ticket,
>   (c) exposing a Games ticket for sale,
>   (d) advertising that a Games ticket is available for purchase,
>   (e) making a Games ticket available for sale by another person, and
>   (f) giving away (or offering to give away) a Games ticket on condition that the person given the ticket pays a booking fee or other charge or acquires some other goods or services.'

This provision has many similarities with the touting offences at designated football matches and London 2012. As with the Olympic offence an online or private sale where the seller either does not charge in excess of the ticket's face value or does not make or intend to make a profit on the transaction appears to be lawful, distinguishing it from the absolute prohibition on ticket sales to designated football matches. The success or otherwise of the Olympic offence and the development of further technological advancements in the years preceding the Glasgow Commonwealth Games in 2014 are likely to have an impact on the final form of s.17.

13.2.4 Future developments

The difficulty with any discussion about the regulation of ticket touting and the operation of the secondary ticket market is that it involves a complex combination of social, legal, economic and ethical interests. Whilst claiming to act for the benefit of the fan-consumer, the legislation passed to date seems to be aimed at preventing touts from making a profit and/or protecting the commercial interests of primary rights holders. Parliament generally only criminalises conduct where to do so would prevent a specific and identifiable harm from occurring. To date it is unclear who is being harmed by ticket touting, particularly where full disclosure of the material characteristics of the ticket is made by the seller. In May 2009 the Department for Culture, Media and Sport launched a consultation to determine the future direction that anti-touting law and policy should take. The final report of its findings when published may help to determine an appropriate means of regulating the secondary market in tickets to sporting events.

13.3 The exploitation of merchandising rights

The sale of goods and services associated with a particular team, event or sport has become an important income stream for many sports bodies. It is through the sale of an ever-growing range of merchandise that many sports clubs in particular are able to meet the wage demands of their star players. However as the primary rights holders have sought to exploit this new income stream ever more creatively, various secondary markets have evolved to provide fan-consumers with alternatives to officially branded products. This section explores the situations in which the law has engaged with various practices to ensure that an appropriate balance is maintained between protecting the commercial rights of clubs and event organisers and ensuring that the fan-consumers are not unlawfully exploited.

13.3.1 Replica kits

The last 20 years have seen an unprecedented growth in sales of replica sports kits. Most major professional sports clubs in the UK generally now use at least one home kit and one differently coloured away kit in any playing season; replica versions or reproductions of these kits, including shirts, shorts, socks and training outfits, are then made available for sale to fans. Each of these designs usually has a life of two seasons, enabling the clubs to bring out a new version of one or other of their kits every year. Some clubs have begun to register a third kit in yet another colour scheme whilst others use modified versions of one or more of these kits when participating in specific competitions such as the UEFA

Champions League and the Heineken European Rugby Cup. Within this market, the sale of replica shirts has become a cornerstone of many clubs' merchandising strategies.

In the late 1990s the Office of Fair Trading (OFT) began an investigation into the replica football kit market because all kits available for purchase in the UK appeared to be sold at the same price regardless of the team, manufacturer or retailer concerned. Its investigation into price-fixing and related concerted practices came to a head in the Umbro litigation.

▶ *JJB Sports plc* v. *OFT; Allsports Ltd* v. *OFT* [2004] CAT 17 and *JJB Sports plc* v. *OFT* [2006] EWCA Civ 1318

JJB Sports (JJB), a national sportswear retailer, had become concerned about the pricing strategy of a rival store, Sports Soccer (SS), which was aggressively discounting replica football shirts with a view to securing for itself a larger share of the market. JJB was concerned about SS's reduction in the price of some of the most popular replica kits and in particular those of Manchester United FC, Celtic FC and the England national team. Each of these kits was produced by the same manufacturer, Umbro Holdings plc. In the course of its dealings with Umbro, JJB provided Umbro with information that led it to apply commercial pressure on SS in an attempt to persuade it not to reduce the price at which it sold replica football shirts below £40.

Following an extensive investigation by the OFT it was found that JJB, Allsports and a number of other high street stores, together with Umbro and Manchester United were guilty of price fixing and/or other concerted practices that distorted the market in replica football kits to the detriment of consumers contrary to s.2 Competition Act 1998. It was found that prices were being maintained at an artificially high level throughout the sector and that competition between rival stores was stifled as a result. JJB and Allsports appealed against this finding to the Competition Appeal Tribunal, however their appeals were rejected. JJB made a further unsuccessful appeal to the Court of Appeal.

The motives behind why the various companies involved in this litigation engaged in such an obviously illegal activity as price-fixing were varied. The six retailers were concerned about losing market share and profits in the event that one company, in this case Sports Soccer, decided to discount its prices significantly. Manchester United and the FA appear to have been attempting to maintain their status as 'premium brands' that were sold in proper sports shops, not by discount retailers or in supermarkets. As Umbro would also hope that sales of its replica kits would encourage consumers to buy its performance wear, it too appears to have wanted to its goods to be sold at premium prices in reputable sports shops.

Although each of these concerns is legitimate from a purely commercial perspective, anti-competitive behaviour of this kind is unlawful and is severely punished. A brand can be protected from damage but it cannot be isolated from legitimate competition in the market. The four companies who were fined the largest amounts all appealed against the punishments imposed on them ([2005] CAT 22). JJB Sports plc, Umbro Holdings Ltd and Manchester United plc eventually had their fines reduced to £6.7m, £5.3m and £1.5m respectively whilst Allsports Ltd had theirs increased to £1.42m.

The OFT investigation into the replica kits market unearthed the lengths to which the parties involved were prepared to go in order to exploit this new revenue stream and to protect their own commercial interests. The result was an initial reduction in the price of shirts, followed by a degree of variation in the amount charged by different retailers for the kits of different clubs. Appendix 1 of the Premier League Rules now specifically prohibits manufacturers of replica kits from imposing minimum sale prices on retailers. Although fan-consumers have received a degree of protection by the OFT requiring a greater degree of freedom to retailers to charge a genuinely competitive amount for replicas, the proliferation in the number of kits produced by some teams ensures that this income stream will continue to be a lucrative one for the foreseeable future.

13.3.2   Protecting other merchandising rights

Whereas the market for replica kits is relatively new, the market for products incorporating other symbols of allegiance are of much greater longevity. The wearing of hats and scarves in a particular team's colours or sporting its badge or crest has long been associated with fan culture. These items were seen as a means by which fans could express their support for their club rather than being products sold by it as part of an integrated merchandising strategy. As a result the market was originally supplied by unofficial and unlicensed manufacturers and retailers; when clubs began to appreciate the true value of these markets they began to take action to enforce their intellectual property rights in the symbols and signs that were most commonly associated with them.

The problem for many clubs was that these symbols were often unprotected. Most were not registered as trade marks, enabling unlicensed products to use them comparatively freely; those clubs which had gone through the registration process had rarely if ever adequately asserted their rights over their trade mark, effectively allowing the protection to lapse under ss.42 or 46 Trade Marks Act 1994. Further, actions for breach of copyright are difficult to sustain because of the difficulties associated with identifying the original author or current owner of the symbol. Where the oldest and most traditional symbols are at issue, copyright lapses 70 years after the end of the year in which its author died (s.12(2) Copyright, Designs and Patents Act 1988); where the author is unknown, copyright lapses 70 years after the end of the year in which the symbol was first made available to the public (s.12(3)). Thus clubs have been forced to resort to a variety of strategies to protect these valuable commercial rights from exploitation by unofficial competitors.

13.3.2.1 Passing off

The tort of passing off was originally developed to prevent one business from unfairly exploiting the goodwill and reputation of another (*Warnik* v. *Townend* [1979] AC 731). First it must be established that the claimant owns goodwill in relation to its business, goods or services. Secondly the defendant must have in the course of its trade made a misrepresentation that the goods or services that it supplies in a common field of activity are connected in some way to the claimant. Thirdly there must be a real likelihood of confusion in the mind of the public that there is or might be a material connection between the defendant's goods and services and those of the claimant. Finally there must be harm to the claimant's goodwill as a result of the defendant's conduct.

Now sometimes referred to as unfair trading or unlawful competition, the tort is more widely defined and encompasses not only passing off, but also the situation where the unrestricted use by others of a company's goodwill or reputation so dilutes it as to render the original worthless or meaningless (*Vine Products Ltd* v. *Mackenzie and Co Ltd* [1969] RPC 1). On the face of it the tort enables clubs to prevent the sale of any unofficial merchandise where it can be proved that the manufacturer or retailer was either expressly or impliedly representing that their produce was in some way connected to the club by the use of words or symbols commonly associated with it.

There are two difficulties facing a primary rights holder seeking to bring an action for passing off. First it must prove that there has been an actual misrepresentation by the defendant, as opposed to a simple misuse of their trade marks or other related symbols. Only where the impression is given that the products in question are official will the claimant be able to prove this element of the tort. Secondly it may be difficult for a claimant to prove that potential consumers were confused about the provenance of the products as they will usually be able to distinguish between what is and what is not officially licensed merchandise. Although the more modern form of the tort might be of some help if unfair trading practices could be established on the part of the defendant, a much more effective means of protecting the goodwill and reputation of a club and the use of its symbols and insignia will be by registering them as trade marks.

13.3.2.2 Trade marks

The Trade Marks Act 1994 enacted the Trade Marks Directive 89/104/EEC and created a new framework of protection for signs designating the trade origin of a product. Under s.1(1), a trade mark is defined as being any sign capable of being represented graphically and which is capable of distinguishing the goods or services of one undertaking from those of other undertakings. The registration of a trade mark provides the proprietor with an enforceable property right relating to its improper use under s.2(1). Thus any infringement of the trade mark allows the proprietor to claim damages from the infringer, to request an injunction prohibiting them from further infringements and under s.16 delivery up of any infringing goods in the possession of any person acting in the course of business.

▶ **Trade Marks Act 1994 s.10 – infringement of registered trade mark**

'(1) A person infringes a registered trade mark if he uses in the course of trade a sign which is identical with the trade mark in relation to goods or services which are identical with those for which it is registered.
(2) A person infringes a registered trade mark if he uses in the course of trade a sign where because –
  (a) the sign is identical with the trade mark and is used in relation to goods or services similar to those for which the trade mark is registered, or
  (b) the sign is similar to the trade mark and is used in relation to goods or services identical with or similar to those for which the trade mark is registered,
  there exists a likelihood of confusion on the part of the public, which includes the likelihood of association with the trade mark.
(3) A person infringes a registered trade mark if he uses in the course of trade in relation to goods or services, a sign which –
  (a) is identical with or similar to the trade mark, where the trade mark has a reputation in the United Kingdom and the use of the sign, being without due cause, takes unfair advantage of, or is detrimental to, the distinctive character or the repute of the trade mark.
(4) For the purposes of this section a person uses a sign if, in particular, he –
  (a) affixes it to goods or the packaging thereof;
  (b) offers or exposes goods for sale, puts them on the market or stocks them for those purposes under the sign, or offers or supplies services under the sign;

(6) Nothing in the preceding provisions of this section shall be construed as preventing the use of a registered trade mark by any person for the purpose of identifying goods or services as those of the proprietor or a licensee.

But any such use otherwise than in accordance with honest practices in industrial or commercial matters shall be treated as infringing the registered trade mark if the use without due cause takes unfair advantage of, or is detrimental to, the distinctive character or repute of the trade mark.'

The object of a trade mark is to designate the origin of a product, without any possibility of confusion, as being produced or supplied by a specific undertaking. Its use on a product provides a consumer with a guarantee of its quality, provenance and originality and prevents others from exploiting the reputation of the proprietor by using the trade mark without the proprietor's consent. The Act provides two specific forms of protection to the proprietors of registered trade marks. Section 10(1) prohibits unauthorised copies of the trade mark proprietor's products from being produced and marketed with the protected symbol on them whereas under s.10(2), attempts to confuse consumers by the use of a symbol similar to that which has been registered or by using the trade mark itself on goods similar to those currently being produced by the proprietor is prohibited.

Where clubs, governing bodies and event organisers have registered as a trade mark a crest, badge, logo or other symbol commonly associated with them, they can prevent anyone from using it to promote the marketing of similar products. Although this form of protection was rarely considered before the late 1980s boom in sports merchandising, it is now commonplace for a range of symbols and words to be registered in an ever increasing range of categories of products and services and for infringements to be vigorously pursued. The one exception to this trend is the Olympic Games, whose symbol, motto and associated words are specifically protected by the Olympic Symbol (Protection) Act 1995 (see further, chapter 14.3).

13.3.2.3 Scarves, badges and retro kits

A number of these issues finally came to a head in respect of a tradesman's sale of Arsenal scarves in the vicinity of their previous home ground, Highbury.

▶ *Arsenal Football Club Plc v. Reed (No.2)* [2003] EWCA Civ 96

Arsenal had registered as trade marks specific symbols related to the club for use with various categories of clothing. Its official merchandise was sold bearing these marks through approved retailers. Reed was a stallholder who had since 1970 sold both licensed and unlicensed goods from a pitch nearby Arsenal's home ground. Both classes of goods bore the symbols that Arsenal had registered as trademarks and Reed accepted that he had used the protected marks without Arsenal's consent on the unlicensed products that he was selling. In an attempt to distinguish between the two categories of products, Reed ensured that the licensed products had swing tickets and labels indicating that they were official Arsenal merchandise, whilst the unlicensed products were sold from behind a sign that drew to the attention of potential purchasers that these items had no commercial connection with Arsenal.

Arsenal claimed that by selling unlicensed scarves that bore its registered trade marks alongside officially licensed versions of the same product Reed was in breach of s.10(1) Trade Marks Act 1994. As its registered trade marks were a designation of the origin of the goods, Arsenal argued that only its officially licensed products were legally entitled to carry the protected symbols so that consumers would be able to distinguish its products from those which were unlicensed. The club also claimed that by using their trade marks in the way that he had, Reed was passing off his unlicensed products as being official Arsenal merchandise.

Reed responded by claiming that there was no breach of s.10(1) because he was not using the registered trade marks in the course of trade. Instead he was using the symbols as a means of enabling fans to express their support, loyalty and affiliation to Arsenal FC; as he was not in any way trying to assert that the products were official, a claim corroborated by the sign on his stall, he claimed that he could not have infringed Arsenal's registered trade marks. Furthermore he argued that as he had made it clear to all prospective purchasers which goods were licensed and which were not he was not misrepresenting the origin of the merchandise but was simply enabling fans to express their support for Arsenal and was not therefore passing off the unlicensed scarves as official club products.

At trial Laddie J held that Reed's use of the trademarked symbols as a badge of allegiance, rather than as designation of their origin, was not an infringement of Arsenal's rights. Furthermore as Reed had made no claim that the unlicensed products were anything other than unlicensed, he could not be said to have been passing them off as official Arsenal merchandise.

When the case eventually reached the Court of Appeal, via a reference to the ECJ, the trial court's decision regarding the Trade Marks Act 1994 was reversed; there was no appeal in respect of the finding on passing off. The Court held that the relevant consideration in cases of this nature was to determine whether the use of the trade mark complained of by the proprietor was likely to affect or jeopardise the guarantee of origin, which was the primary function of the protected symbol, not whether it was being used as a trade mark by the infringer. As the unauthorised and unrestricted use of a registered trade mark by another damages this primary function by affecting its ability to act as a guarantee of the origin of the product, an infringement of Arsenal's rights was established.

Each of the courts involved in this litigation appears at various stages to have overcomplicated their analyses of infringement by discussing whether or not there was a need for confusion on the part of potential purchasers of the products. What *Arsenal* v. *Reed* holds is that where the actual trade mark is used on the same products as those on which the proprietor uses the mark then there is an infringement of s.10(1) Trade Marks Act 1994, even where the infringer is only using the protected symbol as a means of enabling the purchaser to demonstrate their support, loyalty, affiliation or allegiance to the proprietor of the mark; in this case, Arsenal. However in the course of the reasoning of the ECJ and the Court of Appeal it was also stated that by using the registered marks in the way that he did, Reed had created a material link between his unlicensed products and Arsenal. This was because anyone who had not seen the sign on his stall would be likely to assume that scarves bearing the Arsenal trade marks would be official Arsenal merchandise. Thus if he used the registered trade mark on products similar to those officially licensed by Arsenal or had used a symbol similar in design to the registered trade mark on products actually sold by the club then he would also have committed an infringement of Arsenal's registered trade marks contrary to s.10(2) Trade Marks Act 1994.

The practical effect of *Arsenal* v. *Reed* was that all major sports clubs, governing bodies and competition and event organisers that had not already done so redesigned the crests, badges and symbols that they used on their merchandise and registered them as trade marks. The degree of change varies dramatically between the many trade mark proprietors in the sports sector, as does the range of products for which protection is sought. However the growth in the importance of merchandising means that all sports proprietors will now pursue any infringement of their trade marks to ensure that they are able to protect what has become one of their most important income streams.

This leaves traders in the position of Reed able to sell unlicensed products in the club's colours and to use old, unprotected symbols where it is clear that the product on which it is sold is not an official one and where to do so does not create a material link between the merchandise and the club as undertaking. Expressions of loyalty and allegiance however are not a justification for infringing the club's trade marks.

The recent growth in the market for old-fashioned/retro replica shirts has given rise to similar legal problems. Whether it is a preference for heavy duty cotton tops, nostalgia for the kits from the fans' youth or for replicas free from sponsorship logos, the demand for replica kits other than those currently produced officially and under licence continues to expand. As the manufacturers of these shirts seek to produce as authentic a facsimile of the original as is possible, questions have been raised about the legality of the badges and insignia used on these kits.

▶ *Score Draw Ltd v. Finch* **[2007] EWHC 462 (Ch)**

The respondent had registered as a trade mark the official emblem of the former Brazilian Football Federation which had been used as an identifying badge on the football shirts of the Brazilian national football team between 1914 and 1971 (the CBD badge). The respondent had then licensed the use of this mark to TOFFS, a manufacturer and retailer of historical football shirts. The applicant, which was also a manufacturer and retailer of historical football shirts, had used the CBD badge for over ten years prior to the respondent's application to register the CBD badge as a trade mark and wished to continue to do so. The importance of the CBD badge to the parties was that both wanted to use it on replica versions of the football shirts used by the Brazilian World Cup winning teams of 1958, 1962 and 1970, which are amongst the most popular of this kind of merchandise. The applicant appealed against the finding of the hearing officer that the CBD badge was sufficiently distinct to be registered as a trade mark.

In the High Court Mann J found in favour of the applicant and held that under s.3(1)(b) Trade Marks Act 1994, the symbol under consideration was not sufficiently distinct to be registered as a trade mark. Although it is possible for a trade mark to be both a designation of origin and a badge of affiliation, as with the officially licensed merchandise in *Arsenal* v. *Reed*, that was not the case here. The CBD badge was used by TOFFS and others as a means of maximising the authenticity of the replica shirts that they were producing; the mark was not used by TOFFS in a way that would make consumers automatically assume that on seeing it on an item of historical sportswear, the product could only have been produced by TOFFS and no other undertaking. Thus the CBD badge was not being used as a designation of origin to denote that the garment had been produced by TOFFS and was not capable of being registered as a trade mark. Further, its use by both parties and others over at least the previous ten years had robbed the mark of its distinctive characteristics as a trade mark and therefore under s.3(1)(b) it was not sufficiently distinct to be used as a trade mark by the proprietor. As the CBD badge was so closely associated with the Brazilian national football team in the minds of the consumers most likely to buy the replica shirts, it could not be used as a designation of origin by any undertaking.

Although technically obiter as the decision of the court turned on the issue under s.3(1)(b), Mann J also held that the CBD badge was, according to s.3(1)(d), descriptive of a characteristic of the clothing which bears it in the sense that it connotes that the clothing has an association with the historic Brazilian national football team. Thus the judge was reinforcing that the CBD badge was an essential requirement for an authentic replica of the relevant shirts, not a mark that identified a particular manufacturer or producer with the garment.

Only marks or symbols that denote the trade origin of a product can be protected under the Trade Marks Act 1994. If the symbol is used only as a means of producing historical authenticity or accuracy, or has been used by so many undertakings that it has become generic, it will be found to be either descriptive or not sufficiently distinctive to be capable of registration.

In the light of *R* v. *Boulter* [2008] EWCA Crim 2375 it is also worth noting that it is no defence for a person accused of infringing a registered trade mark to claim that the reproduction of the mark was of such poor quality that no confusion as to the provenance of the product could have arisen in the minds of potential consumers. The Court of Appeal was not prepared to allow counterfeiters to use this ingenious line of reasoning to undermine the purpose of s.10 Trade Marks Act 1994. A copy of the mark, no matter how poor the quality, is capable of infringing s.10(1) and if applied to the same category of goods that are produced by the proprietor will be considered to be capable of confusing a consumer as required by s.10(2).

13.3.3 Ambush marketing

Ambush or parasitic marketing is the unofficial or unauthorised association of a product or service with an event. The undertaking conducts the ambush by strategically attaching itself to the goodwill or high profile of a team, event or competition and in doing so undermines the rights of an official sponsor of a similar product or service, who will usually have paid a substantial sum to be associated exclusively with the primary rights holder. The interpretation and ambit of ambush marketing is far from clear with many ambushers claiming that their own marketing practices are being unfairly curtailed by anti-ambushing laws. In the UK at present only the Olympic Games is specifically protected from some of the more obvious ambushing techniques under s.19 London Olympic and Paralympic Games Act 2006 (see further, chapter 14.4.2).

The potential impact on fans of anti-ambush marketing strategies is usually only recognised when an event organiser takes particularly unusual action in order to protect the commercial rights of an official sponsor. For example at the FIFA World Cup 2006 in Germany male Dutch fans were forced to remove orange lederhosen-style shorts that were emblazoned with the name and logo of the brewer 'Bavaria' before being allowed into the stadium to watch a game. The justification provided by FIFA for requiring the stewards to take this action was that the shorts constituted advertising that conflicted with that of the official beer of the tournament, Budweiser. In protecting the commercial interests of its official partners FIFA saw nothing wrong with forcing some fans to watch the match in their underwear. Whether or not spectators at the London Olympics will be subjected to similar restrictions is as yet unclear.

13.4 Regulating access to televised sport

Since BSkyB first acquired the exclusive right to broadcast live Premier League football matches in 1992 the pay TV market for sports events has grown from strength to strength.

With sport often being used as a driver for recruiting new subscribers, many events and competitions that were once freely available on terrestrial television are now only available via subscription satellite, cable or internet services. Although this has often been to the financial benefit of NGBs, event organisers, sports clubs and professional athletes, the impact of collective and exclusive selling practices has been borne predominantly by the fan-consumer.

The creation of this new market in sports broadcasting rights has given rise to a number of specific legal issues. In particular it has led many people to try and receive subscription services without paying for them, or paying for them at a reduced rate, and it has required the government to update the list of events that cannot be transmitted exclusively by subscription broadcasters. This in turn has led to a distortion of the market in favour of terrestrial broadcasters in respect of a limited number of sporting events.

13.4.1 Collective sales and exclusive deals

Two models for the sale of sports broadcasting rights have emerged over the past 20 years. Collective selling is where all teams in a competition join together and sell their rights through one communal body, usually the competition organiser or NGB. In contrast individual selling is where each participant sells the rights to its home games and is in competition with every other participant when trying to secure broadcasting deals. In the UK collective selling has become the norm though this is not the case in other European countries such as Spain.

Both models require exclusive access to the product in order to maximise profits for the primary rights holder; this is where one broadcaster alone has the right to screen the event to the exclusion of all others. Exclusivity ensures rarity in the supply chain allowing the primary rights holder to charge a premium to the broadcaster and to maximise its earnings from the rights sale. However this in turn requires the broadcaster to charge as high a subscription rate as the market will bear in order to recoup its initial outlay and if possible make a profit.

The sale of the broadcast rights for English football's Premier League in England was first investigated by the OFT in 1999. The OFT was concerned that the collective and exclusive elements of the agreements entered into by the Premier League, BSkyB and the BBC were distorting competition to the detriment of rival broadcasters and fan-consumers. In *Re Televising Premier League Football Matches* [2000] EMLR 78 the OFT outlined its main concerns with the agreements as being that they stifled competition between broadcasters by making it too difficult for rivals to acquire the rights to show live Premier League matches, that they forced an artificially high sale price of the rights and that too few games were made available live to fan-consumers.

The Restrictive Practices Court disagreed with the OFT and held that the benefits to the consumer of the collective and exclusive selling arrangements outweighed any potentially anti-competitive disadvantages. Four benefits were specifically highlighted by the Court. Firstly that the combination of collective and exclusive selling of the rights enabled a package of games that was representative of the entire championship to be sold, which was what the public wanted access to. Secondly that this strategy provided financial benefits to the clubs by enabling them to maximise their income as a group, which in turn improved their solvency, allowed them to develop their stadiums and to purchase better quality players, thereby producing a better quality product for fan-consumers. Thirdly the agreements provided a model for the distribution of the income generated by the rights sale that most effectively provided a financial level playing field between clubs in the same competition and fourthly they allowed the Premier League to keep a greater degree of control over the timing of fixtures than would a series of individual deals.

Despite these findings concerns about the legality of collective and exclusive broadcasting agreements persisted, particularly under EU competition law. In an attempt to avoid investigation by the European Commission in respect of the sale of the rights to the Champions League UEFA applied for an exemption from the application of EU competition law to the broadcasting agreements it had entered into under Art.101(3) TFEU (ex Art.81(3) ECT). By the Commission Decision of 23 July 2003, Comp/C-2/37.398 Joint Selling of the Commercial Rights to the UEFA Champions League, the new arrangements devised by UEFA were granted an exemption from Art.101 TFEU (ex Art.81 ECT). UEFA had ensured that there was a variety of rights packages available to both free-to-air and subscription broadcasters and that after the two premium packages per jurisdiction had chosen the two matches each that they wished to show, all remaining matches were available for broadcast on subscription or pay-per-view channels. If any matches were left unsold the home club would have the non-exclusive right together with UEFA to sell the rights to individual games. Additional packages were available for internet, 3G, audio and delayed broadcast rights. Each of the rights deals was to last for a maximum of three years.

The Commission approved these arrangements on the basis that they improved the production and distribution of a quality branded product through a single point of sale. Further, consumers would benefit by being able to access a variety Champions League packages and that the overall quality of the broadcasting of the product would be likely to improve as a result of these arrangements. Finally as the restrictions were indispensible for the achievement of these benefits the exemption was granted.

This Commission Decision had an impact of each new sale of the Premier League's broadcast rights, with both the bidding rules and the packages of rights that it offered to broadcasters being amended gradually in an attempt to avoid further investigation by UK and EU competition authorities. As a result of increased cooperation between the Premier League and the Commission a similar approval was granted to the Premier League's arrangements by Commission Decision of 22 March 2006, Comp/C-2/38.173 Joint Selling of the Media Rights to the FA Premier League. The most controversial element of these arrangements was that no single broadcaster was allowed to buy all six of the live TV rights packages, effectively ending the exclusivity that had been enjoyed by BSkyB since 1992. Furthermore the six available packages had to be more evenly balanced in terms of their content, ensuring that each was genuinely representative of a Premier League season. As with the Champions League Decision, these arrangements were considered to strike an appropriate balance between the needs of the League, the broadcasters and consumers and to be of benefit to each of the affected parties.

Although these collective and exclusive selling practices appear to benefit both the primary rights holders and the broadcasters by enabling them to maximise their incomes, the benefits to the fan-consumer are less easy to indentify especially in the absence of specific complaints made by the public about either deal. The ability to buy a package that represents an entire championship or tournament from one broadcaster, rather than having to buy individual games or bundles of games from a number of rights holders is a clear benefit. However where Premier League games are concerned the viewer now needs to purchase subscriptions from both Sky and ESPN instead of the one subscription from Sky that was previously the case, in order to watch the live games featured in all six packages. This leaves the slightly strange outcome of the Commission's intervention being that where Premier League football is concerned, and as is so often the case this is likely to act as the template for similar deals in other sports, consumers are left paying more for their sport than they were previously.

13.4.2   Live sport in pubs

The increased cost to sports fans of subscription services and the increasing number of events that have migrated to them has led to the watching of live sport in pubs and bars becoming increasingly popular. However some licensees have found that the higher rate of subscription that they are charged by broadcasters has become prohibitive in recent years. Rather than not show games at all some have resorted to showing games via satellite feeds from other countries from both within and outside of the EU. In order to do this licensees have purchased satellite dishes, decoders and decoder cards from an overseas broadcaster and paid for a subscription that enables them to watch foreign versions of popular British sports events.

The FA Premier League has been particularly vigilant in pursuing what it considers to be the unauthorised screening of football matches in which it owns the copyright. In *Murphy* v. *Media Protection Services Ltd* [2007] EWHC 3091 (Admin) and [2008] EWHC 1666 (Admin), a pub licensee was prosecuted for breach of copyright under s.297(1) Copyright, Designs and Patents Act 1998 for showing live Premier League football matches on a Greek subscription channel. In *Football Association Premier League Ltd* v. *QC Leisure* [2008] EWHC 1411 (Ch), the League brought civil actions for copyright infringement and the possession of unauthorised decoders against the suppliers of the satellite equipment that enabled the viewing of the foreign feeds of its games and the licensees who had used the equipment to screen live Premier League football matches. References including 18 questions have now been made under Art.267 TFEU (exArt.234 ECT) to the European Court of Justice to determine the legality of the behaviour of each of the defendants.

These two cases have highlighted the extreme tension that exists between current copyright and broadcasting law on the one hand and the free movement of goods and services and EU competition law as regulated by Arts.49, 56 and 101 TFEU (ex Arts.43, 49 and 81 ECT) on the other. Where copyright law generally prohibits the unauthorised screening of copyrighted programmes in the way that the licensees in these cases have done, Art.56 would generally allow a person living in England to buy a Greek product, for example the decoder and decoder card, and would allow the same person to contract for Greek services, for example the provision of the Greek version of a live football match. Further, copyright and broadcasting law is usually enforced along national lines that compliment the licensing framework according to which primary rights holders, such as the Premier League, allow media organisations to broadcast their games. This can again be contrasted with one of the fundamental principles of the TFEU which is to break down national barriers to trade and create one single market for products and services throughout the EU. Thus it is now in the hands of the ECJ to determine the compatibility of the current regime for protecting copyright in broadcasts with the TFEU and the legality of screening events such as live football matches without the necessary authority of the copyright holder.

13.4.3 Protected events of national importance

The advent of subscription TV channels and their voracious appetite for live sport has forced Parliament to revisit whether some sports events could be said to be of such cultural importance to the British public that they should only be available on free-to-air channels. By protecting some competitions or the finals of some competitions in this manner, it ensures that almost the entire country can watch events that are considered to be of national importance, should they wish to do so. However it also means that the market for selling the rights to these events is significantly restricted as only a limited number of broadcasters are able to screen these events.

The framework for the protection of sports events is provided by ss.97–105 Broadcasting Act 1996 with supplementary provisions including the relevant powers of Ofcom being found in the Television Broadcasting Regulations 2000/54 and the Communications Act 2003. A sports event can be 'listed' where the Secretary of State for Culture, Media and Sport considers that the event or competition has 'national resonance' in that it unites the nation or is a shared date on the national calendar. An event is not protected simply because it is popular; something more than that is needed. Perhaps the best of example of an event of this nature is the Grand National where many people with no interest in horse racing or gambling will talk about the race, run sweepstakes, bet on the race and eventually watch it for no other reason than it being the Grand National.

Listed events are currently divided into two groups (see box below). If an event or competition does not appear in either group then any broadcaster is free to purchase the rights to transmit it. Exclusive live coverage of Group A events must be made available in the first instance to 'qualifying broadcasters'; if no qualifying broadcaster purchases the rights to a Group A event, then it can be covered by a non-qualifying broadcaster. Exclusive live coverage of Group B events is allowed by non-qualifying broadcasters provided that adequate arrangements are made for highlights or delayed coverage to be shown by a qualifying broadcaster. At present, only BBC 1, BBC 2, ITV 1, Channel 4 and Channel 5 meet the necessary conditions of being freely available and accessible by at least 95% of the population of the UK to be categorised as qualifying broadcasters. Thus the rights to Group A events must be offered to these channels in the first instance and highlights or delayed coverage packages must be made available to them if they have not secured the exclusive live rights to Group B events.

▶ **Ofcom Code on Sports and Other Listed and Designated Events, Appendix 1 UK Listed Sporting Events**

Group A
The Olympic Games
The FIFA World Cup Finals Tournament
The FA Cup Final
The Scottish FA Cup Final (in Scotland)
The Grand National
The Derby
The Wimbledon Tennis Finals
The European Football Championship Finals Tournament
The Rugby League Challenge Cup Final
The Rugby World Cup Final

Group B
Cricket Test Matches played in England
Non-Finals play in the Wimbledon Tournament
All Other Matches in the Rugby World Cup Finals Tournament
Six Nations Rugby Tournament Matches Involving Home Countries
The Commonwealth Games
The World Athletics Championship
The Cricket World Cup – the Final, Semi-finals and Matches Involving Home Nations' Teams
The Ryder Cup
The Open Golf Championship

The need for and impact of listing sports events in this manner is highly controversial. Some primary rights holders want to have their events delisted so they can charge full market value for their broadcast rights, whilst many fan-consumers want the list to be expanded so they can see more events for free. Following the exclusive live broadcast of the England football team's World Cup qualifying match away to Ukraine on the internet site Kentaro on 10 October 2009, the first time that a competitive England match had not been broadcast on either terrestrial or satellite television, this debate was brought to a head once again. Before determining whether further events should be listed or delisted the Secretary of State must conduct an extensive consultation with broadcasters, primary rights holders, regulators and the public. A DCMS consultation on the future of listed events and the criteria for determining listing reported its findings in the *Review of free-to-air listed events – report by the independent advisory panel to the Secretary of State for Culture, Media and Sport* on 13 November 2009. Its proposal to expand the number of 'Group A' events and the controversy that this has generated demonstrates once again the tension that exists between the desire for free access to sports events amongst spectators and the need for profit maximisation for the primary rights holders.

Hot topic . . .

IS THERE A NEED FOR A GENERAL OFFENCE OF TICKET TOUTING?

The desire of a number of the major British NGBs to see the enactment of a general offence of ticket touting, or at least one that extends to major events that take place in the UK, resulted in four high profile meetings between a number of the major players in the secondary ticket market, the primary rights holders and DCMS. This in turn led to the launch of a DCMS consultation on ticketing and ticket touting which took place between 19 February and 15 May 2009.

The government's current preference is not to extend the current legislation or to create a new offence of ticket touting but to promote good practice in the resale of tickets by means of a code of conduct. This strategy appears to miss the point of the clamour for the increased regulation of ticket touting in two ways. Firstly it is not the major players in the secondary market, the more organised of whom are represented by the Association of Secondary Ticket Agents, who cause many of the problems experienced by purchasers but those who engage with the secondary market on a more informal or ad hoc basis. The production of a code

of conduct will not prevent unscrupulous people from taking advantage of fans who are desperate to attend a sold out event.

Secondly it does not address the undermining of the primary rights holders' ticketing strategies that occurs when any unauthorised resale takes place. Many event organisers do not sanction any secondary selling of tickets to their events, regardless of whether or not the sale takes place in accordance with a government or OFT-endorsed code of conduct. They have policies for the distribution and sale of tickets in place and do not want these rendered worthless by the operation of the secondary market.

These problems have been compounded by the government's

unquestioning acceptance of the need for a ticket touting offence to be introduced for the unauthorised resale of tickets to Olympic and Paralympic events at the London 2012 Games. By failing to provide any theoretically grounded explanation for the enactment of the s.31 offence and instead relying on the IOC's demand that such legislation be in place as a condition of hosting the Games, the government has left itself open to demands from many other event organisers that their ticketing arrangements should be similarly protected.

This differential treatment of similar events can be illustrated by comparing the legal position of ticket touting at the Olympic tennis tournament and the Open Championships at Wimbledon. Tickets to the Olympic tournament are publically available on a first-come first-served basis and their unauthorised resale is a criminal offence. The majority of tickets to Wimbledon are distributed through a public ballot and their unauthorised resale is a breach of contract but not a crime. There is little doubt that in the eyes of players, spectators and the general public that Wimbledon is the more important and more culturally significant event, yet its tickets do not receive the same degree of protection as those for the Olympic tournament. Furthermore the unauthorised resale of Wimbledon tickets undermines its entire ticketing strategy,

that everyone who applies has an equal chance of getting tickets through the ballot, by allowing those with sufficient money to jump the queue and buy their way in to the event.

The simplest legislative response would be to create a new crime of ticket touting based on the three existing offences but which is applicable to all sports events. A perhaps more subtle approach to the problem would be to target only those people who make a living from touting or who sell sufficient numbers of tickets to be found to be acting in the course of trade. If the professional tout, or even the enthusiastic amateur, fell within the definition of a 'trader' as is required to engage the consumer protection regulations, then almost all unauthorised sales of sports tickets on the secondary market would be criminal.

Whichever approach is taken, including the non-interventionist options of leaving the situation as it is currently or allowing the secondary market to regulate itself, there needs to be a more intellectually satisfying justification for the criminalisation of what has become such a culturally entrenched activity. The DCMS consultation may lead to a more coherent approach to the regulation of ticket touting in the future if it can establish who needs protecting from what and how the law can provide that protection. Where criminalising the touting of

football tickets is justified on the grounds of public order considerations, the corresponding Olympic offence appears to have been introduced on the grounds of commercial imperatives and the need to protect commercial interests. Before introducing further legislation the government needs to identify the harm caused by ticket touting and the interests that need to be protected. Its concerns appear to be twofold.

Firstly that some purchasers are sold tickets on the basis of false information regarding the quality or even the existence of the tickets. Such conduct is already covered by the general criminal law and in many cases will also fall foul of consumer protection legislation. Secondly it is concerned by the profiteering that takes place when sums many times a ticket's face value are charged for popular events. This is a much trickier issue for the government to address as many fan-consumers enter into these transactions in full knowledge of what they are doing and how much they are paying so it is much more difficult to identify who or what has been harmed in this situation. The combination of legal, ethical, social, political and economic factors at play in this area ensure that whatever the outcome of the DCMS consultation, it is unlikely that all of the affected parties will be happy with the outcome.

Summary

13.1 The rapid commercialisation of sport in recent years has had a significant impact on the ways in which fans now interact with the sports that interest them and the teams that they follow. As sports clubs in particular have sought new income streams to exploit in order to fuel stadium redevelopments and players' wages, the fan has come to be treated as a consumer of the goods and services that it supplies.

13.2 The unauthorised resale of sports tickets has become a controversial sporting, legal, ethical and political issue. Whereas the criminalising of ticket touting in respect of football matches could initially be justified on public order grounds, no similar justification has been proffered for the corresponding offences relating to tickets for events at London 2012 and Glasgow 2014. Although touting at other events is regulated to some extent by the general criminal law and various consumer protection regulations, discussions are ongoing about whether all instances of ticket touting should be criminalised or whether this should remain a civil matter for the primary rights holders to pursue.

Summary cont'd

13.3 The increase in sales of sports merchandise has led many clubs and event organisers to reassess the importance of officially licensed products as a source of income. Sports clubs and sportswear manufacturers in particular have sought to regulate the use of specific symbols, badges, insignia and crests that were traditionally associated with a club in order to exploit this market with greater efficiency than had previously been the case. The use of registered trade marks has been particularly effective in preventing the sale of unlicensed merchandise and the growth in anti-ambush marketing laws has ensured that these valuable rights are protected from novel means of infringing them.

13.4 Since 1992 the growth in the value of sports broadcasting rights has been unprecedented. As sport has been used as a driver for new subscriptions to pay TV services, the high price paid by broadcasters for these rights has inevitably been passed on to sports fans. Collectively negotiated exclusive deals have become the norm in the UK and provided certain safeguards are in place are considered capable of being in the public interest despite their anti-competitive appearance and their ability to inflate the value of the rights being sold. Innovative attempts to circumvent payment for subscription services have been found to be criminal, though the compatibility of the current framework of copyright in broadcasts with the TFEU remains uncertain. Further restrictions on the ability of some primary rights holders to sell their rights to the highest bidder are found in the listed events procedure under the Broadcasting Act 1996.

Further reading

Touting

House of Commons Culture, Media and Sport Committee, 'Ticket Touting' (HC 202, 2008)

Secretary of State for Culture, Media and Sport, 'Government Response to the Culture, Media and Sport Select Committee Report on Ticket Touting' (Cm 7346, 2008)

Campbell Keegan Limited, 'The Secondary Market for Tickets (Music and Sport) Qualitative Research Report' (prepared for DCMS, 2007), available at http://www.culture.gov.uk/images/research/secondarymkt_tickets_qrr.pdf

James and Osborn, 'Tickets, policy and social inclusion: can the 'European White Paper on Sport' deliver?' [2009] 1/2 *International Sports Law Journal* 61

Intellectual Property

Lewis and Taylor (eds), *Sport: Law and Practice* (2nd edn, 2008, Tottel) ch G1

Dugdale, Jones and Simpson (eds), *Clerk & Lindsell on Torts* (19th edn, 2009, Sweet and Maxwell) ch 27

Burton and Chadwick, 'Ambush marketing in sport: an assessment of implications and management strategies' (2008) Centre for the International Business of Sport Working Paper Series, No.3

Fields, 'Too poor to be afforded protections as a trade mark?' (2009) 20(4) *Entertainment Law Review* 157

Johnson, 'Look out! It's an ambush!' [2008] 2/3 *International Sports Law Review* 24

Yap, 'Making sense of trade mark use' (2007) 29(10) *European Intellectual Property Review* 420

Broadcasting

Geey, 'The legality of football broadcasts in the UK and the lack of choice for publicans in the Premier League broadcasting market' (2007) 5(1) *Entertainment and Sports Law Journal*, online

Further reading cont'd

Geey and James, 'The Premier League-European Commission broadcasting negotiations' (2006) 4(1) *Entertainment and Sports Law Review*, online

Lefever and Rompuy, 'Ensuring access to sports content: 10 years of EU intervention. Time to celebrate?' [2009] 2 *Journal of Media Law* 243

Massey, 'Referee! Illicit device and copyright issues in football broadcasting referred to the European Court of Justice' (2008) 19(8) *Entertainment Law Review* 174

Massey, 'The Karen Murphy reference' (2009) 20(1) *Entertainment Law Review* 34

McAuley, 'Exclusively for all and collectively for none: refereeing broadcasting rights between the Premier League, European Commission and BSkyB' (2004) 25(6) *European Competition Law Review* 370

Parrish and Miettinen, *The sporting exception in European Union Law* (2008, TMC Asser Press) ch 6

Stothers, 'Copyright and the EC Treaty: music, films and football' (2009) 31(5) *European Intellectual Property Review* 272

Links to relevant websites can be found at www.palgrave.com/law/james

Chapter 14

The law and the Olympic Games

Key words

▶ **Olympic Movement** – the collective body of sports organisations and individuals who have agreed to be bound by the Olympic Charter; its three main constituents are the International Olympic Committee, recognised International Sports Federations and National Olympic Committees.

▶ **International Olympic Committee** – the body responsible for implementing the fundamental principles of Olympism and of running the Olympic Movement on a day-to-day basis.

▶ **Olympism** – the fundamental principles of the Olympic Movement, which include fair play, respect for the rules and other competitors and anti-discrimination; the aim of Olympism is to build a peaceful and better world through sport.

▶ **National Olympic Committee** – the body responsible for representing the IOC in each nation state; in the UK this is the British Olympic Association.

14.1 The modern Olympic Movement

The modern Olympic Movement can trace its roots back to the creation of the original set of Olympic principles at the International Athletic Congress held in Paris in 1894. The International Olympic Committee (IOC), which was created at the same time, has since then become the most powerful multi-sports body in the world and is charged with promoting Olympism and leading the Olympic Movement at a global level. Over time the original principles have evolved into the Olympic Charter, which now acts as the basic legal document of the Olympic Movement.

By far the most well-known, most visible and most easily identifiable manifestation of Olympism is the Olympic Games. These are held in the first year of each four year Olympiad, beginning with the Athens Olympics in 1896, and have grown into the largest sporting and cultural event in the world. The Winter Olympics, which were first held in Chamonix, France in 1924, have been held in the third year of each Olympiad since 1994 rather than the same year as the summer version, to ensure that each instalment of the Games has a distinct identity and can exploit the commercial rights associated with the Olympics more efficiently.

The aim of the Olympic Movement is much more than to deliver successful instalments of the Olympic Games; it aims to build a better, fairer and more peaceful world through sport. In order to achieve this it focuses its work in six specific areas: education; development; environmental awareness; the promotion of women's participation in all aspects of sport; the encouragement of grassroots sport and the promotion of peace, particularly during the Games themselves when all participating nations are encouraged to respect the Olympic Truce. Furthermore one of the IOC's specialist Commissions, Olympic Solidarity, provides funding to emergent and less financially secure National Olympic Committees to enable them to develop their own sport and education programmes so that they can develop their leading athletes to a standard where they will eventually be able to participate at the Olympic Games.

The Olympic Movement has also been actively involved with the creation of two of the most important administrative developments in modern elite level sport. In 1984 the IOC established the Court of Arbitration for Sport (CAS). Although since 1994 this has been a completely independent institution to ensure that there is a formal separation of powers between the IOC as executive body and CAS in its judicial role, the IOC has helped to establish CAS's credibility by using it as the sole dispute resolution chamber for Olympic matters (see further, chapter 1.3 and 3.3). In response to the need for an expedited procedure for use at the Olympic Games CAS created an Ad Hoc Division that is able to provide a rapid resolution to disputes and which is now used at a number of major international championships.

The IOC has also been instrumental in ensuring the almost universal acceptance of the authority of the World Anti-Doping Agency (WADA) and the World Anti-Doping Code as the standard by which all doping cases are judged. By requiring all ISFs whose sports are included on the Olympic programme and also all those which want to be included to have incorporated the World Anti-Doping Code into their rules, the IOC has ensured its general implementation throughout the sporting world. Moreover as Arts.13.1.1 and 13.2.1 of the Code require all appeals in doping cases that involve WADA or international level athletes to be heard exclusively by CAS, the IOC has contributed further to the acceptance of CAS as the leading sports law tribunal for international disputes. Thus the Olympic Movement and its ideals encompass much more than the biennial sporting extravaganza that is broadcast on television and includes the development and promotion of structures through which sport can be made fairer, more accessible and be more fairly governed.

14.1.1   The structure of the Olympic Movement

Membership of the Olympic Movement requires recognition of a body or individual by the IOC and that it adheres to the Olympic Charter. Rule 1(2) Olympic Charter states that the three main constituents of the Olympic Movement are the IOC, the recognised ISFs and the NOCs. Rule 1(3) acknowledges that the NGBs, clubs and individuals that make up an ISF are automatically considered to be part of the Olympic Movement, as are the Organising Committees of each edition of the Olympic Games for the period of their existence.

The IOC currently recognises 28 sports and their ISFs for inclusion in the summer edition of the Olympics and a further seven for inclusion on the winter programme. Any ISF can apply to be recognised by the IOC even though its sports are not included on the Olympic programmes. An ISF may seek recognition in order to be considered for inclusion at future Games or, in some countries, may need to be recognised in order to qualify for public funding. Recognition at this lesser level can be secured by an ISF where it organises a sport or group of related sports at the global level, its membership consists of NGBs, it has incorporated the World Anti-Doping Code into its rules and provided that it conforms with the Olympic Charter. 33 ISFs are currently recognised in this way including several sports that have in the past been included on the main Olympic programme or which have been demonstration sports.

14.1.2   The Olympic Charter

The Olympic Charter acts as the constitutional instrument for the Olympic Movement as a whole and also serves as the governing statutes of the IOC. It begins with a statement of the Fundamental Principles of Olympism and is then divided into five chapters dealing with the Olympic Movement as a whole, including an explanation of the ownership of all relevant commercial rights associated with it, the establishment and role of the IOC, the recognition process and role of the ISFs, the mission and role of the NOCs and the organisation of and eligibility for the Olympic Games.

▶ **Olympic Charter, Fundamental Principles of Olympism**

1 Olympism is a philosophy of life, exalting and combining in a balanced whole the qualities of body, will and mind. Blending sport with culture and education, Olympism seeks to create a way of life based on the joy of effort, the educational value of good example and respect for universal fundamental ethical principles.
2 The goal of Olympism is to place sport at the service of the harmonious development of man, with a view to promoting a peaceful society concerned with the preservation of human dignity.
3 The Olympic Movement is the concerted, organised, universal and permanent action, carried out under the supreme authority of the IOC, of all individuals and entities who are inspired by the values of Olympism. It covers the five continents. It reaches its peak with the bringing together of the world's athletes at the great sports festival, the Olympic Games. Its symbol is five interlaced rings.
4 The practice of sport is a human right. Every individual must have the possibility of practising sport, without discrimination of any kind and in the Olympic spirit, which requires mutual understanding with a spirit of friendship, solidarity and fair play. The organisation, administration and management of sport must be controlled by independent sports organisations.
5 Any form of discrimination with regard to a country or a person on grounds of race, religion, politics, gender or otherwise is incompatible with belonging to the Olympic Movement.
6 Belonging to the Olympic Movement requires compliance with the Olympic Charter and recognition by the IOC.

The most recent version of the Charter was published in 2007 and is updated on a regular basis to reflect sporting, ethical and legal developments. For example in June 2008 the IOC Executive Board announced one significant amendment to Rule 45 which governs athletes' eligibility to compete in the Olympic Games. In response to the controversy generated by Dwain Chambers' attempts to force the British Olympic Association to invite him to compete in the 100 metres athletic event at the Beijing Olympics in the summer of 2008 (see further, Chapter 2 Hot Topic and below 14.2.1), the IOC added an eligibility restriction on athletes who have been found guilty of a serious doping offence.

▶ **Olympic Charter Rule 45 (amendment)**

Any person who has been sanctioned with a suspension of more than six months by any anti-doping organization for any violation of any anti-doping regulations may not participate in any capacity in the next edition of the Games of the Olympiad and of the Olympic Winter Games following the date of expiry of such suspension.

The amendment ensures that a person who has been banned, whether as an athlete or in any other role such as a coach, cannot be invited to the next two editions of the Games.

By restricting eligibility in this way a banned person who retires from competition to become a coach cannot attend the Games with the athletes whom they are training nor can they change sports to one that is included in the programme of the Winter Olympics in order to circumvent the suspension.

14.1.3 The International Olympic Committee

In the context of upholding the fundamental principles of Olympism, by the far the most important member of the Olympic Movement is the IOC. In many ways the IOC has the same basic structure as that which is used by ISFs to govern individual sports; the IOC is the global body to which five continental associations are affiliated and whose membership consists of the 205 NOCs representing the individual nation states that are eligible to send athletes to the Olympic Games. Each of these relationships is governed by the Olympic Charter.

According to Rule 1 Olympic Charter the IOC is a non-governmental not-for-profit organisation that is recognised under Swiss Law as an association with a distinct legal personality. The IOC is comprised of a maximum of 115 members, of which a majority but not more than 70 must be wholly independent of any other function or office that they hold. The remainder, of which there cannot be more than 15 members in any one category, comprise active athletes, senior office holders in an ISF or other IOC-recognised organisation and senior office holders in an NOC. At present there are 114 active members, of whom three are British: HRH the Princess Royal, Sir Philip Craven and Sir Craig Reeide. Members are expected to be politically and nationally independent; their role is to represent the IOC in their respective countries not to represent their country at the IOC. Each member is now elected for an eight year term of office at the end of which they can seek re-election.

The IOC holds an annual general meeting, the Session, at which major issues and policies are debated and developed. The implementation of these policies and the day-to-day administration of the IOC are carried out by its Executive Board, which comprises the President, four Vice-Presidents and ten IOC members. The role of the IOC through the Board is to uphold the Olympic Charter. In order to carry out its functions more effectively the Session and Executive Board are advised by seven specific Commissions representing the issues that are of the greatest importance to Olympism: the Athletes' Commission, which considers issues relating to competitors at the Olympic Games; the Ethics Commission, which updates the Code of Ethics and informs developments of the World Anti-Doping Code; the Nominations Commission, which oversees the election of IOC members; the Olympic Solidarity Commission, which provides development funding to poorer and emergent NOCs; the Evaluation Commission for Candidate Cities, which determines the application criteria for potential hosts of the Games; the Olympic Games Coordination Commission, which collects information from past host cities and disseminates it to the prospective and eventual hosts to in order to make the bidding procedures fairer and more open and the Medical Commission, which advises on anti-doping procedures and athlete healthcare issues.

Since its creation in 1894 the IOC has acquired for itself a sporting, cultural and political position unlike any other organisation. It is almost universally and often unquestioningly accepted as the most important sports body in the world. Despite its being self-appointed to this role and to its position as the guardian of the spirit of sport and of sporting good conduct there have been few serious challenges to its status. The revamped system of governance and the changes made to the procedures for electing its members following the corruption scandals of the 1990s have seen the IOC begin to reclaim its lead on sports ethics, particularly in the development of more robust anti-doping procedures. In 2009 the IOC applied for observer status at the United Nations because of its involvement with peace-keeping missions and its health and education programmes around the world. If as seems likely this application is accepted, its leading role in sport will be formalised in a way that even Baron de Coubertin could not have foreseen.

14.1.4 Law and the Olympics

Staging the Olympic Games, particularly the main summer edition, has always been seen as one of the most prestigious events that can be hosted by a city. However it has only been since the Los Angeles Games in 1984 that organisers have broken even or made a profit with any degree of regularity. The Montreal Games in 1976 saddled the city with decades of debt whilst the losses generated by other host cities have often been absorbed by regional and national governments. It is the development of the commercial side of the Olympics and of the Olympic brand, particularly the protections granted to the IOC in respect of its intellectual property and the association rights that it grants to its main sponsors, which have attracted the interest of lawyers and law makers.

By Rule 7 Olympic Charter, all rights in the Olympic Games and the 'Olympic Properties' lie with the IOC which has the exclusive right to exploit them. Rule 7(2) specifically states that the Olympic Properties include the interlocking five-ring Olympic Symbol, the flag, the motto (*citius, altius, fortius*) and any translations of it, the official anthem, depictions of the Olympic flame and the Olympic torches used to transport the flame from Olympia to the host city, any identifications, designations or emblems associated with the Olympic Movement and the phrases 'Olympic Games' and 'Games of the Olympiad'. The protection of the rights associated with these symbols and words falls to the NOC in each jurisdiction.

The level of protection afforded to the Olympic Properties varies significantly between jurisdictions. Since 1981, 44 nations have ratified the Nairobi Treaty on the Protection of the Olympic Symbol which provides the IOC with specific protection for the Olympic Symbol (below, 14.3). In other jurisdictions such as the UK specific legislation has been introduced to protect the Olympic Symbol and specific words and phrases for the benefit of the appropriate NOC (below, 14.3 and 14.4). In other countries the relevant protection is enforced by a mixture of copyright and trade mark law. The variety of means of protecting the Olympic Properties has led to the IOC requiring legislation to be implemented by the national government of the city where the Olympic Games is to be staged as a condition of the Host City Contract. The focus of legal discussions in the remainder of this chapter is on UK law and in particular the protections that have been developed in respect of the London Olympics.

14.2 British Olympic representatives

There are three ways in which the Olympic Movement can be represented in a country. Firstly any nation state recognised as independent by the international community can establish a National Olympic Committee and apply to have it recognised by the IOC. In the UK this role is fulfilled by the British Olympic Association (BOA). Secondly it may have one or more nationals who hold membership of the IOC; the UK currently has three active members of the IOC, with Sir Craig Reedie sitting on the Executive Board. Thirdly the city responsible for hosting an Olympic Games must establish an officially recognised organising committee; the London Organising Committee of the Olympic Games (LOCOG) has the task of delivering the Games of the 30th Olympiad.

14.2.1 The British Olympic Association

The BOA was established in 1905 and like many British sports bodies is a private company limited by guarantee. Its role is to represent the Olympic Movement in the UK, the Channel Islands, the Isle of Man and any British Overseas Territories that do not have their own NOC and to promote the fundamental principles of Olympism. The BOA is a wholly independent body which, unlike many other NOCs, receives no public money to support its activities. This independence enabled the BOA to send a British team to the Moscow Olympics in 1980 against the wishes of the government who wanted to join a US-lead boycott of the Games in protest at the USSR's invasion of Afghanistan. The BOA instead registered its disapproval by competing under the Olympic flag and having the Olympic anthem played at medal ceremonies.

The BOA's activities are entirely self-funded. Its main sources of income are the licensing of its Olympic marks and sponsorship agreements that help to fund Team GB's appearance at each edition of the Olympic Games and the various sporting and educational events that the BOA organises. This funding framework operates in a similar manner to and is complementary with those used by the IOC. The BOA is also the owner of the IOC's intellectual property rights in the UK though is only able to exploit them in accordance with instructions from the IOC to ensure that their respective sponsorship and partnership agreements are not in conflict with each other (Bye-law 1 to Rules 7–14 Olympic Charter).

Despite the obvious importance of its commercial activities, the two occasions when the BOA is most visible are when it puts forward to the IOC the nomination of a UK city hoping to host an edition of the Olympic Games and when it invites athletes to compete on its behalf as members of Team GB. Only an NOC can nominate a city to be a candidate for hosting the Olympic Games, thus where there are multiple prospective candidates it may have to run its own domestic competition to determine which city is finally put forward for consideration by the IOC. Once a single candidate is identified the NOC promotes the bid alongside a team from the prospective host city. If the bid is successful, as was the case with London 2012, the Games is organised by a separate committee such as LOCOG (London Organising Committee for the Olympic Games), not the NOC.

The BOA is also responsible for inviting athletes to compete on its behalf at each edition of the Olympic Games. The BOA does not technically pick the members of Team GB; the NGBs in charge of the sports on the Olympic programme nominate those athletes and teams who they consider to have reached the relevant qualifying standards. The BOA then invites those athletes who they consider to have fulfilled the eligibility criteria found in Rules 41–45 Olympic Charter to compete at the Games. Rule 45(2) Olympic Charter states that nobody has a right to compete at the Olympics even if they have reached the necessary standard. This enables limits to be placed on the total number of athletes who can be invited to each edition of the Olympic Games and the number of representatives of each NOC who can appear in any particular event. For example the IOC currently limits the total number of athletes to 10,500 by Bye-law 14 to Rule 45 Olympic Charter and the maximum number of athletes from a single NOC in any event to three according to Bye-law 11 to Rule 45.

The issue of eligibility to compete at the Olympics was the focus of Dwain Chambers' litigation with the BOA in the spring of 2008 (*Chambers* v. *British Olympic Association* [2008] EWHC 2028 (QBD)) (see further, chapter 2 Hot Topic). BOA Bye-law 25 states that any athlete who has been banned for a serious doping offence will not be invited to compete in the Olympics even where they have served their suspension and are free to compete in all other competitions by their ISF without further restriction. The BOA makes exceptions for minor infringements where it considers that the athlete was not at fault, such as in the case of Christine Ohuruogu, or for minor infringements that are punished by a suspension from competition of six months or less, but effectively bans for life anyone who has been found guilty of doping.

The BOA is one of only a handful of NOCs that take this hard line against doping, justifying it on the grounds that deliberate cheating of this kind is so contrary to the fundamental principles of Olympism that the athlete involved can no longer be considered to be an appropriate person to compete at the Games. As the case did not go to trial it is still uncertain whether the courts will accept this line of argument as a sufficient ground for acting in restraint of trade or contrary to the free movement provisions of the TFEU. However the controversy created by the case alerted the IOC to what it saw as the merits of the BOA's case. As a result the IOC amended Rule 45 Olympic Charter to ensure that anyone who has served a suspension of six months or longer for a doping offence will be ineligible to be invited to the two instalments of the Games following the completion of their ban (above, 14.1.2).

14.2.2   IOC representatives

There are currently three British members of the IOC, each of whom has substantial experience in sports administration and elite level competition. Their role is to represent the IOC not to act as delegates for national, international or sporting interest groups at the IOC and is therefore more of an ambassadorial than a representative role. Thus they could act as IOC representatives in the UK, the EU, throughout the Commonwealth and in the sports with which they have a connection. In Sir Philip Craven's case this would also extend to Paralympic Sports through his position as President of the International Paralympic Committee.

14.2.3   The London Organising Committee for the Olympic Games

The Olympic Movement's third manifestation in the UK is LOCOG. LOCOG was created in 2005 by the BOA, the Mayor of London and the Secretary of State for Culture, Media and Sport. The government's role in the organisation of the Games is now overseen by the Minister for the Olympics. LOCOG will continue in existence until 31 December 2012.

LOCOG is a private company limited by guarantee which has the task of organising the Olympic Games in 2012 and is a member of the Olympic Movement for the period of its existence. It reports through the Olympic Games Coordination Commission to the IOC on all matters relating to the organisation of the London Olympics. At the conclusion of the Games it is expected to pass on its knowledge and experience to the Coordination Commission whilst the intellectual property and commercial rights in all specifically commissioned works become vested in the IOC. According to Bye-law 4 of Rule 51 Olympic Charter this includes for example the mascots, songs, logos, posters and medals designed for use at a Games. This enables the IOC to exploit the historic rights associated with each edition of the Olympic Games and to continue to generate income for its various sporting and education programmes.

As a private body LOCOG has to be self-funding. Its main income-generating streams are ticket sales, the sale of sponsorship and merchandising rights together with a share of the IOC's official partnership and broadcasting deals. Public and lottery funding has been channelled thought the Olympic Delivery Authority (ODA), which was established by the London Olympic Games and Paralympic Games Act 2006. The ODA is responsible for creating the sporting and transport infrastructure for the Games and is a statutory corporation subject to public law. The ODA will also be partially responsible for the enforcement of the offences created by the London Olympic Games and Paralympic Games Act 2006 (below, 14.4).

14.3   Olympic Symbols etc (Protection) Act 1995

As the IOC began to exploit its commercial rights more effectively in order to generate sufficient funding for the host cities of the Olympics it sought a greater degree of protection for its intellectual property. In 1981 under the auspices of the World Intellectual Property Organization, the Nairobi Treaty on the Protection of the Olympic Symbol came into effect; 44 nations are currently signatories to its provisions. According to Art.1 any party to the treaty is obliged to refuse or to declare as invalid any attempt to register the Olympic symbol consisting of the five interlocking rings unless the use of the symbol is with the consent of the IOC. The only exceptions to this cover situations where the symbol had already been registered and used by an undertaking prior to the date on which the treaty came into force in the signatory nation.

The UK government of the time did not ratify the Nairobi Treaty, however similar protection was subsequently provided by the Olympic Symbols etc (Protection) Act 1995 (OPSA 1995) in respect of the generic intellectual property rights of the Olympic Movement. Two possible explanations can be given for the decision to afford statutory protection to a private body's commercial rights. Firstly it enables the BOA, as opposed to the IOC as is the case under the Nairobi Treaty, to exploit the right to be associated with the Olympic symbols more effectively and to raise sufficient funds for it to remain financially independent from the state. Secondly as British cities began to bid to host the Olympic Games in the 1980s and 1990s it became apparent that such protection would enhance the prospects of their candidature.

Under s.2 OPSA specific protection is provided for the Olympic symbol, the Olympic motto and associated protected words by the creation of the Olympics Association Right (OAR). The protected words are defined in s.18(2)(a) as: Olympiad; Olympiads; Olympian; Olympians; Olympic and Olympics. Further, s.3(1)(b) states that any representations or any words that are so similar to those which have been protected and the use of which is likely to create in the public mind an association with the Olympic Games or the Olympic Movement are also prohibited.

This protection has been updated by Sch.3 London Olympic Games and Paralympic Games Act 2006 (LOGA 2006) and extended by Sch.4 in the light of London's hosting of the 2012 Games (below, 14.4.1). A similar right, the Paralympics Association Right, is created by s.5A OPSA 1995 in respect of the commercial rights associated with the Paralympic Games which are owned by the International Paralympic Committee (IPC). The Paralympics Association Right protects the IPC's symbol and the words Paralympiad, Paralympian, Paralympic and their respective plurals. The OAR grants to the proprietor of the protected symbols the exclusive right to use them. Originally the BOA was appointed as the sole proprietor of the OAR, however for the period of its existence LOCOG is joint proprietor in order to facilitate its funding of the 2012 Games, Olympics and Paralympics Association Rights (Appointment of Proprietors) Order 2006/1119.

Under s.3 OPSA 1995 the OAR is infringed where a person uses the protected symbols and/or words in the course of trade or uses a representation of something so similar to them that it is likely to create in the public mind an association with them or with the Olympic Games or the Olympic Movement. It is drafted widely enough to ensure that any person connected with the manufacture, packaging, supply or sale of an unauthorised or unlicensed product infringes the OAR. Thus the Act provides the symbols with a statutory version of the protections afforded in other circumstances by trade marks (see further, chapter 13.3.2).

The OAR is not infringed in the limited number of circumstances defined in s.4 OPSA 1995. Two of the exceptions, ss.4(1) and (3) are of particular note. Firstly there is no infringement where the use of the protected symbols and words is for the purpose of reporting on specific Olympic events or about the Olympic Games in general. This enables the media to report freely on the Games and to advertise the material that they intend to publish or broadcast. Secondly there is no infringement where the use of the protected symbols and words does not suggest an official contractual, commercial, structural or financial association with either the Olympic Games or the Olympic Movement. The circumstances in which this exception could operate are likely to be extremely limited and when used in conjunction with the anti-ambush marketing provisions (below, 14.4.2) will only very rarely allow any infringement of the OAR.

Any infringement of the OAR is actionable by its proprietors, the BOA and LOCOG, under s.6 OPSA 1995. It enables them to claim damages for any losses caused and an injunction to stop further infringement of the OAR. Under s.7 the proprietors can request erasure of an infringing sign, delivery up or disposal of infringing goods and the forfeiture of counterfeited items. Furthermore under s.8 anyone involved in the production, packaging, supply or sale of anything that infringes the OAR with a view to making a gain for themselves or another, or with intent to cause loss to another, and doing so without the consent of the proprietor commits a criminal offence.

A further level of protection has been afforded to the words, 'The Olympics' and 'The Games of the Olympiad' and 'Olympic Games' and 'Olympiad' when used in combination with a representation of the Olympic Symbol by their having been registered by the IOC as Community Trade Marks E2827632, E8471369, E876383 and E1118165 respectively. The combination of statutory provisions and trade marking affords an almost unparalleled degree of protection to the Olympic Properties. The protections for the generic intellectual property of the Olympic Movement have been significantly reinforced by the protection afforded to the commercial rights associated with the London Olympics.

14.4 London Olympic Games and Paralympic Games Act 2006

LOGA 2006 provides the legislative basis on which the 2012 Olympic Games will be organised and gives effect to the commitments made by the government to the IOC during the bid procedure. The first part of the Act, together with Sch.1, establishes the Olympic Delivery Authority (ODA) and defines its powers to coordinate the planning and transport developments in order to provide the infrastructure necessary to host the London Olympics. Most of the remainder of the Act provides the framework of controls that will be applied to ambush marketing and the exploitation of the commercial rights associated with the Games. In particular it regulates advertising and street trading in and around Olympic venues, establishes a London Olympics Association Right and creates an offence of touting tickets to Olympic events.

14.4.1 The London Olympics Association Right

In addition to the amendments to the OAR contained in Sch.3 LOGA 2006 (above, 14.3), s.33 and Sch.4 create a specific London Olympics Association Right (LOAR) over which LOCOG has sole proprietorship. The framework used to protect the intellectual property rights in the London Olympics runs in parallel to the generic protection provided for the Olympic symbols by OPSA 1995. Thus by Sch.4 para.1, the creation of the LOAR prohibits a person acting in the course of their trade from making any representation of any kind without the consent of LOCOG that suggests to the public that they have an association with the London Olympics. Association is defined in the same way as it is for the OAR as meaning a contractual, commercial, structural or financial link with the London Olympics. When attempting to establish this link however there is no limit on the type of representation that can be used as evidence that an association has been suggested. Use of any of the many trade marks registered by LOCOG would undoubtedly be considered to be suggesting an association, as would the use of specific words and phrases though the wording of the provision appears to be wide enough to include any conduct that might suggest to the public that an association exists.

▶ **London Olympic Games and Paralympic Games Act 2006 Sch.4 para.3 – infringement: specific expressions**

'(1) For the purpose of considering whether a person has infringed the London Olympics association right a court may, in particular, take account of his use of a combination of expressions of a kind specified in sub-paragraph (2).

(2) The combinations referred to in sub-paragraph (1) are combinations of –
  (a) any of the expressions in the first group, with
  (b) any of the expressions in the second group or any of the other expressions in the first group.

(3) The following expressions form the first group for the purposes of sub-paragraph (2) –
  (a) "games",
  (b) "Two Thousand and Twelve",
  (c) "2012", and
  (d) "twenty twelve".

(4) The following expressions form the second group for the purposes of sub-paragraph (2) –
  (a) gold,
  (b) silver,
  (c) bronze,

(d) London,
(e) medals,
(f) sponsor, and
(g) summer.
(5) It is immaterial for the purposes of this paragraph whether or not a word is written wholly or partly in capital letters.'

This is a non-exhaustive list that can be added to by statutory instrument should it be thought necessary to do so. Taken together with the words protected by OPSA 1995 and the wide range of trade marks that have been registered by LOCOG to be used as symbols and logos for the promotion of the Games and on related merchandising, it is almost impossible for a person acting in the course of trade or business to use any word, group of words, phrase or symbol that suggests a link with the London Olympics unless they are an official partner of either the IOC, the BOA or LOCOG. Unlike with a claim for passing off or an action under s.10(2) Trade Marks Act 1994, there is no need for confusion to be created in the minds of the public or specific groups of consumers; a much lower standard of suggesting an association with the London Olympics is all that is required. A breach of the LOAR is actionable in the same way as a breach of the OAR under ss.6 and 7 OPSA 1995, however it is not currently a crime to breach the LOAR.

14.4.2 Preventing ambush marketing at the London 2012 Games

Whereas the creation of the OAR and LOAR can be seen as highly specialised forms of trade mark protection, the framework of regulations that will be in place for protecting the commercial rights in the London Olympics from ambushing marketing breaks entirely new legal ground in the UK. The aim of these provisions is twofold: to provide 'clean' venues for Olympic events and to prevent ambush marketing inside and in the vicinity of Olympic venues. The former is important to the IOC as it does not allow any advertising inside Olympic venues; it does not want undertakings providing spectators with items that will provide ambushers with free advertising that is not available to its official partners. The latter is important to both the IOC and LOCOG as they require protection from marketing strategies that undermine the value of the exclusive rights that have been sold to the various categories of official partners. Any diminution in the value of these rights could seriously affect a city's ability to host the Games successfully.

Ambush marketing is the unofficial or unauthorised association of a product or service with an event (13.3.3). In many cases it is also an attempt to undermine the marketing strategy of one or more of the event's official sponsors by making it seem as though the ambusher is the undertaking with the formal association with the event. In either case the ambusher is taking advantage of the goodwill associated with an event and is hoping to receive a tangible benefit from creating an apparent association with it for which it has not paid.

14.4.2.1 Regulating advertising in the vicinity of Olympic venues

Because of the difficulties associated with protecting marketing rights through traditional legal means, such as passing off, specific provision has been made to prevent the occurrence of specific types of ambush marketing at the London Olympics. Ambush marketing in the form of unlawful advertising is governed by s.19 LOGA 2006, an enabling provision under which further and more detailed regulations will be published at a time closer to the date of the beginning of the Games. Despite the lack of specific detail in the Act it is important to note at this stage the breadth of the protections provided to LOCOG in respect of the control of advertising of all kinds. Under s.19 advertising in the vicinity of all Olympic venues is to be regulated in the run up to, during and in the immediate aftermath of the London Olympics. Advertising is defined incredibly widely and in ss.19(4) and (5) includes advertising of a non-commercial nature, announcements of any kind and the distribution of documents and articles. Further, s.19(7) requires all advertising in the vicinity of an Olympic venue to have been authorised by a responsible body, a role that in all likelihood will eventually be fulfilled by LOCOG or the ODA.

The width of this provision appears to suggest that almost any public display that creates any kind of link to the London Olympics could be caught by s.19 LOGA 2006, particularly where LOCOG considers that it impacts negatively on the marketing rights that it owns or which it has officially licensed to its commercial partners. To ensure compliance with this provision the police and the ODA, as a designated enforcement agency for offences defined by LOGA 2006, have been granted the power under s.22 to enter premises that they reasonably suspect are being used for unlawful advertising or where they suspect advertising that is in breach of s.19 is being created, produced or stored. Any infringing article found on the premises can be removed, destroyed, concealed or erased. If further action is required the ODA can institute criminal proceedings against the infringer, in a similar way to Trading Standards Officers being able to bring actions under consumer protection legislation. Where a conviction under s.19 or its subordinate regulations is secured the Crown Court can impose an unlimited fine or, where the case is heard in the Magistrates' Court, a fine of up to £20,000 can be imposed (s.21(3) LOGA 2006).

14.4.2.2 Regulating street trading in the vicinity of Olympic venues

In addition to the regulation of advertising s.25 LOGA 2006 provides the enabling provision for a similar framework of controls over street trading. These further controls appear to have been introduced to ensure the quality of goods being sold to the public near Olympic venues, to prevent the sale of unofficial, unlicensed or counterfeited products and to restrict the outlets through which goods that are capable of ambushing official merchandise can be sold. The framework for the regulation of street trading mirrors that for the control of advertising: s.28 creates similar powers of enforcement by allowing entry to premises to remove infringing articles, s.29 enables the ODA to institute criminal proceedings against anyone who has committed the offence of unlawful street trading and s.27 imposes the same levels of punishment on those found guilty as are found in s.21.

The provisions of LOGA 2006 only apply to trading that occurs in a place to which the public has access, the highway and car parks but not to shops (s.25(4)); again further regulations will be published closer to the start of the London Olympics that will provide the missing details. In particular these will provide definitions of what is meant by trading and the nature of trading as well as providing the temporal and geographical limits within which the Act will apply. The regulations will ensure that only a trader who has been granted official authorisation by the ODA or its delegates will be able to trade in the vicinity of an Olympic venue during the time around the London Olympics. The need for this specific ODA-sanctioned authorisation takes priority over any pre-existing license that a trader may have. The ODA can, according to s.26, amend or disapply existing laws and licenses and require anyone to seek authorisation or re-authorisation to trade during the period of the Games. Once again the commercial interests of the IOC and LOCOG are provided with a very high degree of protection from the possibility of ambushing of almost any kind.

14.4.2.3 The impact of the anti-ambush marketing regime

Comparatively few concerns have been raised about the framework of protections created for the commercial rights associated with the London Olympics. The various provisions in LOGA 2006 are extremely widely drafted and seem to be able to catch almost any association made with the Olympics that has not been made by one of the official partners or in the course of legitimate reporting on its constituent events. Although more detail will eventually be provided, what is clear already is that LOGA 2006 provides unprecedented levels of protection for the commercial interests of a major international undertaking.

The nature of the protections granted goes far beyond that which would be available in any other circumstance. For example there is no need to prove that the public or specific groups of consumers have been confused as to the existence of an association between the ambusher and the London Olympics as would be required for an action in passing off; it is simply an offence to advertise a product without the authorisation of LOCOG. Thus the ability to advertise in the vicinity of an Olympic venue could be restricted to the official partners of the IOC and LOCOG or to the suppliers of goods and services that are not in competition with them.

The enforcement regime in respect of these provisions also gives rise to some concern. The symbiotic relationship between LOCOG and the ODA effectively means that these two ostensibly separate and distinct bodies are in reality joined to the common purpose of making the London Olympics a success. In respect of the provisions regulating advertising LOCOG will be able to control access to prime sites and regulate who can and who cannot advertise in the vicinity of venues whilst the ODA will be able to investigate and prosecute breaches of s.19 LOGA 2006. Where street trading is concerned the ODA will be able to authorise, investigate and prosecute breaches of s.25 LOGA 2006 whilst having to work with LOCOG to ensure that the terms of the Host City Contract are complied with. This means that the enforcement of the Act will be carried out by the two bodies with a vested interest in its most rigorous application.

Further concerns can be raised about the breadth of the definition of advertising, particularly the inclusion of 'non-commercial' advertising. This appears to be directed at political comment on or protest about the London Olympics which is made in public. This could mean that displaying a poster that complains about the financial or environmental cost of hosting the Games, or that your business or allotment had been compulsorily purchased in order to build the Olympic Park is a criminal offence under s.19 LOGA 2006, as is the designing, producing or storing of posters or leaflets making a similar complaint. Presumably should a group of protesters gather together in the vicinity of an Olympic venue each of them would also be guilty of the same offence.

If this is the correct interpretation of these provisions then LOGA 2006 appears to be in conflict with both Arts.10 and 11 European Convention on Human Rights and Fundamental Freedoms. The protesters' right to free speech guaranteed by Art.10 could be curtailed by preventing them from using certain words and phrases that constitute non-commercial advertising; if these same words and phrases are displayed by a group of protesters then their freedom of association and assembly under Art.11 could be infringed. Generally these fundamental rights can only be restricted by the state in the interests of national security, public safety, to prevent crime and disorder or for the protection of public health and morals; the protection of commercial rights should be protected by other means. How the police and the ODA through its enforcement officers choose to exercise their powers to enforce ss.19 and 25 LOGA could prove to be one of the more sensitive public order decisions that they have to take in connection with the London Olympics.

14.4.3   Ticket touting at Olympic events

LOCOG is also keen to keep a strict control over the sale and distribution of tickets to all Olympic events. The terms and conditions of each ticket are likely to include standard prohibitions on their unauthorised resale and on their use in commercial promotions; any breach of these terms and conditions will invalidate the ticket and, technically at least, enable LOCOG to prevent the invalid ticket-holder's entry to the venue. The first of these two prohibitions is the civil or contractual means of preventing ticket touting. The second is an attempt to reduce even further the opportunities available to undertakings to ambush the marketing strategies of the official sponsors and partners by preventing them from offering Olympic tickets as prizes in competitions. In addition the unauthorised resale of all Olympic tickets will almost always be a criminal offence under s.31 LOGA 2006 (see further, chapter 13.2.3.2 and chapter 13 Hot Topic).

▶ **London Olympic and Paralympic Games Act 2006 s.31 – sale of tickets**

'(1) A person commits an offence if he sells an Olympic ticket –
    (a) in a public place or in the course of a business, and
    (b) otherwise than in accordance with a written authorisation issued by the London Organising Committee.
(2) For the purposes of subsection (1) –
    (a) "Olympic ticket" means anything which is or purports to be a ticket for one or more London Olympic events,
    (b) a reference to selling a ticket includes a reference to –
       (i) offering to sell a ticket,
       (ii) exposing a ticket for sale,
       (iii) advertising that a ticket is available for purchase, and
       (iv) giving, or offering to give, a ticket to a person who pays or agrees to pay for some other goods or services, and
    (c) a person shall (without prejudice to the generality of subsection (1)(a)) be treated as acting in the course of a business if he does anything as a result of which he makes a profit or aims to make a profit.'

The s.31 offence provides the most comprehensive protection for any sporting or cultural event in the UK. The 'traditional' tout selling tickets on the approach to the venue acts unlawfully in respect of all sales whilst anyone intending to make a profit from the unauthorised resale of an Olympic ticket acts in an equally criminal manner. The only re-sales that are exempted from the operation of s.31 are private sales at face value or below.

This enables a purchaser of multiple tickets to sell them on to friends and family (and others, provided no profit is intended to be made) and allows a person who finds themselves with a genuinely spare ticket to recoup their initial outlay. Further s.166 Criminal Justice and Public Order Act 1994 will apply to criminalise all unauthorised ticket sales for the Olympic football tournament as the games involve representative sides and are therefore designated football matches (see further, chapter 13.2.3.1).

Little justification has been provided by the government for the need for such comprehensive anti-touting provisions. In response to a Freedom of Information Act request, CMS case number 106119, the IOC in assisting DCMS' explanation of why these provisions were necessary stated that:

> 'Olympic Games events are very popular and must be protected from individuals seeking to profit by selling on tickets above face value. Laws should both forbid: such sales; people from advertising and executing such sales. [Touting] of tickets is detrimental to the image of the Olympic Games particularly at Games-time. Local law enforcement should be able to take appropriate action against [touts] selling Olympic Games tickets.'

In other words the IOC is concerned solely with the protection of its and LOCOG's commercial rights and requires legislation to be implemented that prevents anyone from benefitting unofficially from the goodwill connected to the Olympic Games and the Olympic Movement. Although this aim is one that is pursued by all bodies that have created a commercially successful product, service or event, it is one that is usually protected by commercial means, such as trade marking, or by legal actions such as passing off, not by a statute imposing criminal liability on those who are in breach of its provisions.

14.5   The impact of 'Olympic law'

At each edition of the Olympic Games new lessons are learned about the most effective means of enforcing the commercial rights owned by the IOC and the local organising committee and how best to regulate the exploitation of those rights. This in turn leads the IOC to require as a condition of the Host City Contract increasingly sophisticated legal protections to be created by the national government of the country where the host city is based. The success of the Olympic legislation leads organisers of other major events to require similar protections for the commercial rights associated with their championships. In his article, 'Look out! It's an ambush!', Johnson has referred to these two phenomena as horizontal and vertical creep.

Horizontal creep is where the protection afforded to one edition of an event is used to justify protection of at least the same level at its next edition. Since the Sydney Olympics in 2000, which represented a step change in the degree of protection afforded to an Organising Committee of the Olympic Games, 'Olympic law' has evolved and extended into the protections which are found in LOGA 2006 and its subordinate regulatory frameworks. Vertical creep is where the protection afforded to the Olympics is then granted to a less prestigious or single sport event. For example the Glasgow Commonwealth Games Act 2008 provides an almost identical regulatory framework for advertising, street trading and ticket touting as does LOGA 2006 and a Glasgow Commonwealth Games Association Right that mirrors the LOAR is created by Glasgow Commonwealth Games Act 2008 (Games Association Right) Order 2009/1969.

The result of this creep is that all major event organisers, or the ISFs in charge of determining where a championships should be held, are slowly beginning to expect that such protections should be offered to them as a matter of course or demand that their event should be granted those protections as a condition of allowing a city to act as host. For example in response to the prospect of demands of this nature and in order to improve its chances of hosting major events in the future, New Zealand has passed the Major Events Management Act 2007 to provide such protections to all significant international sporting events. In order to qualify as a major event under s.7 the organisers must have taken all practicable measures to protect their commercial rights under existing law and hosting the event must offer substantial sporting, cultural, social and/or economic or other similar benefits to New Zealand or New Zealanders, thereby extending the range of championships and tournaments which can receive state protection dramatically. With ISFs and their chosen hosts needing to exploit their commercial rights in order to provide the necessary funding to stage an event, specific legislation such as OPSA 1995 and LOGA 2006 and generic legislation such as that now in force in New Zealand are likely to become commonplace at many major sporting events.

Hot topic . . .

WHY ARE THE OLYMPIC GAMES SPECIAL?

Since their reintroduction in 1896 the Olympic Games have become the largest and most important sporting event in the world. The summer edition of the Games is unique in terms of its size, its scale, the range of events included on its programme, the audience that watches it and the money that it generates. The introduction of the Winter Olympic Games in 1924 and since 1988 the hosting of the Paralympic Games in the same city as the Olympics has entrenched in the minds of the public the importance of the championships that are encompassed by the Olympic Movement. Only the FIFA World Cup Finals can come close in terms of the popular interest and money generated by the Olympics.

Yet despite its commercial success and that fully professional athletes are allowed to compete in many of its constituent sports, the Olympic Games continue to be seen by many people as the embodiment of values that are more often associated with amateur sport, including the fundamental principles of Olympism, fair play and respect for others. Olympic success is still seen by many

athletes in many disciplines as being the pinnacle of achievement in their sport. Even where there are discipline-specific world championships, such as in athletics, or highly lucrative professional tournaments, such as in tennis or basketball, Olympic success of and for itself remains one of the most sought after sporting distinctions.

However the tension that has been created between its sporting and commercial aims has seen much criticism directed at the Olympic Movement. Its self-appointed role as the guardian of sporting conduct and ethical play does not always sit well with its need to generate income and protect its commercial rights. Its promotion of the World Anti-Doping Code by requiring all sports included on the Olympic programme to have implemented its provisions has been seen as a major step forward in the regulation of doping and the harmonisation of anti-doping regimes. The promotion and protection of sports ethics and athletes' health is very clearly in accordance with the fundamental principles of Olympism and is the kind of

issue that the IOC could be expected to take a lead on.

In contrast concern has been raised about the rationale for the decision of the IOC Congress in 2009 to include golf on the Olympic programme from 2016 on the grounds that it is too costly to be sufficiently accessible to the majority of people throughout the world to satisfy the requirements of being an Olympic sport. The critics of golf's inclusion claim that this is a commercial decision that will increase the value of broadcasting and sponsorship rights not a sporting decision based on Olympic values. As the cost of staging the games increases, so does the need to guarantee sufficient income to host them, a commercial necessity not always in accordance with the spirit of Olympism.

There is no doubt that the Olympic Games are special, but are they special enough for the treatment that they receive, particularly in respect of the protections afforded to its commercial rights? In a wider form this is a question that has been asked of the courts for many years: why is sport so special that it should be treated differently by the law? The ECJ has begun to develop the most effective analytical framework for addressing these questions by directing courts to examine whether the 'specificity of sport' requires that the law should treat certain rules, procedures or conduct differently. Where it can be shown that the conduct of a sporting body is no more than is necessary and proportionate for the proper administration of a sport, to promote sporting competition or protect sports ethics, then it will be acting lawfully.

In order to justify its actions the IOC needs to be able to provide a legally robust explanation for what it is doing. At present its conduct is often accepted as appropriate without further question as prospective host cities and their governments accede to the IOC's requests in order to stand the best chance of securing the right to stage the Olympic Games. If it is to continue unchallenged in its current role then the IOC will need to develop a sporting explanation for why its increasingly commercial activities should be treated differently to those of other businesses and other sports organisations. Simply claiming to be unique may not always be enough; a legally defensible definition of the 'specificity of the Olympic Games' could provide the explanation that the law requires.

Summary

14.1 Since its creation in 1894 the Olympic Movement has grown into being one of the most high profile and powerful sporting bodies in the world. The members of the Olympic Movement, particularly the IOC, the ISFs and the NOCs are bound by the principles and rules defined in the Olympic Charter and are responsible for implementing them throughout the world and within their particular sports. The Olympic Games are the most visible celebration of these ideals and as the cost of hosting them has increased the IOC and the individual organising committees of each edition of the Games have sought ever greater and more sophisticated means of protecting their commercial rights in order to generate sufficient income to enable them to take place.

14.2 The Olympic Movement is currently represented by three groups of people in the UK. The UK's NOC, the British Olympic Association, represents the IOC on a day-to-day basis in the UK, the Isle of Man, the Channel Islands and Overseas Dependent Territories that do not have their own NOC. It is responsible for promoting host cities' bids to stage the Olympic Games and for inviting athletes to represent Team GB at each edition of them. The UK also provides three members of the IOC, each of whom has substantial competitive and administrative experience, including one who sits on the IOC's Executive Board. Finally a private company, the London Organising Committee of the Olympic Games, has been established for the purposes of staging the London Olympics in 2012. LOCOG will be a member of the Olympic Movement until its dissolution on 31 December 2012.

14.3 The Olympic Symbols etc (Protection) Act 1995 was introduced to provide protection for the generic intellectual property associated with the Olympic Movement. The Olympic Association Right was created for the benefit of the BOA to ensure that it could generate sufficient funds to remain independent of the state. During the period running up to the London Olympics, LOCOG is also a beneficiary of these trade mark-like protections.

14.4 The London Olympic Games and Paralympic Games Act 2006 creates the legislative framework within which the London 2012 Games can be organised. It creates the Olympic Delivery Authority, a public body responsible for building the infrastructure for the Games and for enforcing the offences created by the Act. The Act also provides specific protections for the commercial rights owned and managed by LOCOG and the BOA. In particular it creates a London Olympics Association Right which protects the words and symbols associated with the London Olympics, restricts advertising and street trading in the vicinity of Olympic venues and prohibits the unauthorised resale of Olympic tickets in the course of trade or with the intent to make a profit.

Summary cont'd

14.5 The protections afforded to the organisers of the London Olympics are the latest incarnation of 'Olympic law'. The 2006 Act demonstrates how, with each edition of the Olympic Games, the IOC requires the host nation to pass ever more protective legislation in favour of the local NOC and OCOG. This 'horizontal creep' ensures that the previous legislation is used as the basis for extending the law at each subsequent edition of the Games. The impact of the Olympic protections has also begun to produce 'vertical creep' where smaller and single sport championships insist on receiving the same protection that has been afforded previously to the Olympics.

Further reading

Lewis and Taylor (eds), *Sport: Law and Practice* (2nd edn, 2008, Tottel) chs H1 and 2

Maestre, *Law and the Olympics* (2010, Cambridge University Press)

Johnson, 'Look out! It's an ambush!' [2008] 2/3 *International Sports Law Review* 24

Michalos, 'Five golden rings: development of the protection of the Olympic insignia' [2006] 3 *International Sports Law Review* 64

Links to relevant websites can be found at www.palgrave.com/law/james

Index